PUBLIC-SECTOR BARGAINING

PUBLIC-SECTOR BARGAINING

INDUSTRIAL RELATIONS RESEARCH ASSOCIATION SERIES

Editorial Board

Benjamin Aaron

Joseph R. Grodin

James L. Stern

The Bureau of National Affairs, Inc., Washington, D.C.

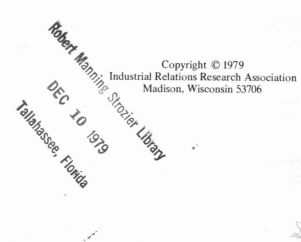

Copyright © 1979
Industrial Relations Research Association
Madison, Wisconsin 53706

Library of Congress Cataloging in Publication Data
Main entry under title:

Public-sector bargaining.

   (Industrial Relations Research Association
series)
   Includes index.
   1. Collective bargaining—Government employees—
United States—Addresses, essays, lectures.
2. Collective bargaining—Government employees—
Canada—Addresses, essays, lectures. I. Aaron,
Benjamin. II. Grodin, Joseph R. III. Stern,
James L. IV. Bureau of National Affairs,
Washington, D.C. V. Series: Industrial
Relations Research Association. Industrial Relations
Research Association series.
HD8005.6.U5P8   331.89'041'353   78-25655
ISBN 0-87179-291-5

Printed in the United States of America
International Standard Book Number: 0-87179-291-5

PREFACE

Public-sector bargaining, despite its relative infancy, has evidenced a precocious growth, and so has the amount of research devoted to it. In 1977 the IRRA Executive Board concluded that it was time to take stock: to review what we know about some key issues in this area, to analyze previous developments, and to project, to the extent possible, the direction of future trends.

The present volume in the IRRA Research Series is devoted to these purposes. Accordingly, the several authors have concerned themselves primarily with the organization, interpretation, and evolution of the data in hand, rather than with the undertaking of new research. This process has permitted them, however, with considerable success, to cast new light on the developments of the past 18 years.

We are pleased that the IRRA Executive Board requested The Bureau of National Affairs, Inc. to publish this volume and that BNA decided to do so, in order to make the book more available than it otherwise might be to students, practitioners, and others interested in this field. We wish to thank our fellow authors for a job well done, and to acknowledge the invaluable assistance of IRRA Editor, Barbara D. Dennis.

The Editors

CONTENTS

CHAPTER 1

THE EXTENT OF COLLECTIVE BARGAINING IN THE PUBLIC SECTOR*

JOHN F. BURTON, JR.†

Collective bargaining and membership in organizations that bargain have increased rapidly in the public sector since 1960. The increases are particularly impressive because they contrast sharply with the sluggish growth of private-sector unions in recent decades. The public-sector developments were largely unanticipated and cannot adequately be explained even on a retrospective basis. The developments were in part due to changes in workers' attitudes about the propriety of bargaining, to a more aggressive stance by many organizations representing public-sector workers, and to public-policy changes that facilitated bargaining. However, some of the favorable legislation was as much a result as a cause of the increased strength of public-sector bargaining organizations. This chapter reviews these developments and concludes that the post-1960 growth rates of public-sector bargaining and membership in bargaining organizations are unlikely to be sustained in the next decade.

*Support for this research was provided by the Center for the Management of Public and Nonprofit Enterprise of the Graduate School of Business, University of Chicago. I appreciate the comments on an earlier draft received from editors of this volume; from Cornell University colleagues Donald Cullen, Thomas Kochan, Hirschel Kasper, Robert Doherty, Ronald Donovan, and Ronald Ehrenberg; from University of Chicago colleagues Melvin Reder, Wesley Wildman, and Bernard Meltzer; and from Harry Cohany, Ronald Leahy, Charles Rehmus, Paul Gerhart, Charles Krider, John Pencavel, Arvid Anderson, James Begin, Alan Stevens, and Joseph Garbarino. Research assistance was provided by William Ryan. All are hereby absolved for remaining errors.

Portions of this chapter will be incorporated into the Studies of Unionism in Government, which are being conducted by The Brookings Institution with financial support from The Ford Foundation. The views in this chapter are mine and not those of the officers, trustees, or staff members of The Brookings Institution or of The Ford Foundation.

†University of Chicago and Cornell University.

Note: Throughout this chapter, reference will be made to one or another of the 40 books and articles listed by number in the Bibliography (pp. 41–43). In both the text and footnotes, a specific reference is noted by the number in brackets following the name of the author or authors.

An Overview of Developments

This section begins with a review of the changes since 1956 in membership in bargaining organizations in the private and public sectors,[1] followed by some general explanations of developments in each sector. Components of the public sector, such as the federal government, are examined in subsequent sections.

Membership Changes

Union membership as a percentage of all employees in the public and private sectors has dropped sharply in the past 20 years. In 1956, one in three of the employees in nonagricultural establishments was unionized; by 1976, only one in four was a union member (Table 1, panel A). This economy-wide record tells an incomplete story, however. More revealing is the union-organizing record by industrial sector. In manufacturing, long the union stronghold, unions have lost more than 350,000 members in the 20-year period and have seen the percentage of employees organized slip from 51.3 to 44.6 percent. In the balance of the private sector, unions have added almost 1.2 million employees since 1956, but because the number of new jobs in that sector has increased by more than 17 million, the percentage of the nonmanufacturing employees unionized has slipped from 29.9 to 20.9 percent. In sharp contrast is the union record in the government sector, where unions have increased their membership by more than 2 million since 1956, and the percentage organized has increased from 12.6 to 20.1.

The public-sector success story is even more compelling if membership data include bargaining associations as well as unions. Use of the terms *unions* and *bargaining associations* raises a general problem of measuring the extent of collective bargaining and the number of workers in organizations that engage in bargaining.[2] The issue of what constitutes an organization that engages in collective bargaining requires attention here because

---

[1]Although the chapter is nominally concerned with the extent of collective bargaining, much of the data and most of the reviewed studies pertain to the extent of membership in organizations that bargain since these data and studies are more common. For a discussion of the various aspects of bargaining and membership that can be examined, see Burton [11].

[2]A number of measurement issues are examined in Burton [11] and are only briefly discussed in this chapter.

Table 1
Membership for Total Economy and by Industrial Sector, 1956–1976
(Employment and Members in Thousands)

Year	All Nonagricultural Establishments			Manufacturing			Nonmanufacturing (Private Sector)			Government		
	Employees	Members[a]	Percent Organized	Employees	Members[b]	Percent Organized	Employees	Members[c]	Percent Organized	Employees	Members[b]	Percent Organized
Panel A: Membership in Unions												
1956	52,408	17,490	33.4	17,243	8,839	51.3	27,888	8,350	29.9	7,277	915	12.6
1960	54,234	17,049	31.4	16,796	8,591	51.1	29,085	8,375	28.8	8,353	1,070	12.8
1964	58,331	16,841	28.9	17,274	8,342	48.3	31,461	8,125	25.8	9,596	1,453	15.1
1968	67,951	18,916	27.8	19,781	9,218	46.6	36,325	8,837	24.3	11,845	2,155	18.2
1970	70,920	19,381	27.3	19,349	9,173	47.4	39,010	9,198	23.6	12,561	2,318	18.5
1972	73,714	19,435	26.4	19,090	8,920	46.7	41,284	9,458	22.9	13,340	2,460	18.4
1974	78,413	20,199	25.8	20,046	9,144	45.6	44,190	9,520	21.5	14,177	2,920	20.5
1976[P]	79,443	19,432	24.5	18,956	8,463	44.6	45,539	9,533	20.9	14,948	3,009	20.1
Panel B: Membership in Bargaining Organizations[d]												
1968	67,951	20,721	30.5	19,781	9,218	46.6	36,325	8,940	24.6	11,845	3,857	32.6
1970	70,920	21,248	30.0	19,349	9,173	47.4	39,010	9,305	23.9	12,561	4,080	32.5
1972	73,714	21,657	29.4	19,090	8,920	46.7	41,284	9,619	23.3	13,340	4,520	33.9
1974	78,413	22,809	29.1	20,046	9,144	45.6	44,190	9,705	22.0	14,177	5,345	37.7
1976[P]	79,443	22,463	28.3	18,956	8,463	44.6	45,539	9,721	21.3	14,948	5,853	39.2

Sources: Data for all nonagricultural establishments from U.S. Department of Labor, Bureau of Labor Statistics publications: (1) 1956 data from Handbook of Labor Statistics 1975, Table 158; (2) 1960–1974 data from Directory of National Unions and Employee Associations 1975 (Bull. 1937, 1977), Table 6; (3) 1976 data from *Labor Union and Employee Association Membership—1976*, news release, September 1977.
Data for industrial sectors: (1) 1956–1974 membership data from 1975 Directory, Table 15; (2) 1976 membership data from September 1977 news release; (3) employment data from 100 Monthly Lab. Rev. 87 (December 1977), Table 8.
Note: P = preliminary.
[a] Membership includes total reported membership excluding Canada. Also included are members of directly affiliated local unions. Members of single-firm unions are excluded.
[b] Membership includes members outside the United States.
[c] The nonmanufacturing employment figures exclude agricultural employees.
[d] Bargaining organizations include unions and bargaining associations, as those terms are defined in the text. The equivalent BLS terms are unions and employee associations.

of its particular significance for the public sector. A comparison of the government data in panels A and B of Table 1 indicates that while only 20.1 percent of the employees are in unions, some 39.2 percent of the employees are members of bargaining organizations.

Three types of organizations can be distinguished, although the classification system is best viewed as establishing a spectrum along which organizations can be roughly placed, rather than a taxonomic system with three well-defined categories. *Unions* stand at one end of the spectrum, and are characterized by primary reliance on collective bargaining to establish rules for working conditions, by assistance to individual employees when disputes arise concerning application of the rules, and by endorsement of the strike. Most unions also exclude supervisors from membership and are affiliated with the AFL-CIO, although there are important exceptions to these generalizations. At the other end of the spectrum are *nonbargaining organizations,* which include professional (or occupational) associations such as the American Bar Association (ABA). These organizations do not represent their employees as a group in dealing with individual employers in an effort to establish rules for working conditions. They are also characterized by concern with only a limited set of working conditions (jurisdictional definitions and qualifications for practitioners, but not wages or hours), by application of the rules to individual members rather than protection of individual members from application of the rules by employers, by rejection of the strike, by inclusion of members of the profession who are supervisors, and by nonaffiliation with the AFL-CIO.

Somewhere on the spectrum, between unions and nonbargaining organizations, are *bargaining associations,* which like unions rely on collective bargaining to achieve an agreement with an employer concerning working conditions. However, bargaining associations are more likely than unions to emphasize political action and professional sanctions (such as blacklisting employers) to gain influence over working conditions and to include supervisors as members. Also, bargaining associations are less likely to assist individual employees in resolving disputes concerning application of work rules (sometimes in the public sector because the civil service system already provides protection), are less likely to endorse strikes, are generally unwilling to be called unions, and are not affiliated with the AFL-

CIO.[3] The National Education Association (NEA) is an example of a bargaining association.[4]

This chapter is concerned with unions and bargaining associations, which collectively will be termed *bargaining organizations*.[5] In general, the distinction between unions and bargaining associations has probably narrowed over time, and for some of the analysis here the difference can be ignored. In particular, the union-bargaining association distinction should not obscure the most compelling implications of the data in Table 1, namely, the explosive growth of bargaining organizations in the public sector since 1960.

Private-Sector and Economy-wide Developments

The extent of unionization in the private sector and in the entire economy has varied through time, including a significant increase since the 1930s in the percentage of nonagricultural employees organized (13.2 percent in 1935) to a high point in the mid-1950s (34.7 percent in 1954), followed by the substantial decline in recent decades because of the lack of success in the private sector. Some of the explanations for these private-sector and economy-wide developments are briefly reviewed in order to glean ideas relevant for explaining the growth of public-sector bargaining organizations.[6]

Severe disruptions of the economy by catastrophes such as war or depression are alleged by some to cause abrupt changes in union strength, but there is no obvious catastrophe that ex-

---

[3]My term *bargaining association* is similar to Weber's *unionoid* [40, p. 6], although he apparently intends his term to be derogatory, which is not my intention. *Bargaining association* is also similar to the term *employee association* used by the Bureau of Labor Statistics (BLS) (see Table 1). I find their usage troublesome because it fails to distinguish adequately between associations that bargain (such as the NEA) and associations that do not (such as the ABA).

[4]The NEA provides an illustration of the difficulties of classifying organizations. In 1956, the NEA was a nonbargaining organization. In 1976, the NEA was classified as a bargaining association by the BLS and, with 1.9 million members, accounts for most of the difference between the union and bargaining-organization figures in Table 1. One problem is that it is impossible to decide exactly when in the 20-year period the NEA crossed over the line between a nonbargaining organization and a bargaining association. The BLS data on bargaining associations begin as of 1968, but that date is only a rough guide as to when the NEA became predominately a bargaining association. Another problem is that as of 1976, the NEA nationally may best be classified as a bargaining association, but its state and local affiliates range across the whole spectrum from units acting as unions to units shunning bargaining. (The NEA is discussed in more detail *infra* in the section on State and Local Education Employees.)

[5]Some data sources and analyses use the term *union* is a broad sense that is roughly equivalent to *bargaining organization* as that term has just been defined.

[6]More detailed reviews can be found in Ginsburg [20] and Bain and Elsheikh [3].

plains the post-1960 public-sector developments. Nor can the developments be explained by theories that relate union strength to macroeconomic fluctuations. Although variations in private-sector and economy-wide union membership appear to be associated with business-cycle developments, the magnitude and timing of bargaining-organization growth in the public sector since 1960 cannot easily be related to business-cycle developments.

Changes in the occupational and industrial composition of the labor force help explain union-membership developments. The declining share of total employment in manufacturing helps explain the decline in the economy-wide unionization rate, as does the rapid growth of white-collar workers, who continue to show an aversion to unionization.[7] Again, these factors provide little help in identifying the sources of bargaining-organization growth in the public sector, and if anything suggest that the growth is atypical since much has occurred among white-collar workers.

Factors controllable by unions and managements are also offered as explanations for membership developments. These factors include organizing strategy (e.g., shall workers be organized on a craft or industrial basis?), bargaining strategy (e.g., should strikes and lockouts be used?), and political strategy (e.g., what type of legislation is desirable?). Some argue that the overall decline in union strength in recent decades can at least partially be explained by the loss of missionary zeal by unions and by the increasingly intense resistance by employers. These controllable factors do appear to provide some help in understanding public-sector developments, since the post-1960 period included significant changes in factors such as the willingness of bargaining organizations to engage in strikes.

Another factor that arguably is an important determinant of union growth is the legal framework within which unions operate. Important aspects of public policy are whether the right to organize is protected and encouraged, whether the employer has the duty to bargain, and whether unions have the right to strike. Some writers stress the importance of public policy and cite the enactment of the National Labor Relations Act in 1935,

---

[7]White-collar union membership as a percentage of white-collar workers (except managers and administrators) was 10.9 percent in 1958, 11.4 percent in 1968, and 11.2 percent in 1976. Membership data are from sources cited in Table 1; employment data are from the *Employment and Training Report of the President* (1977), Table A-15.

the subsequent NLRA amendments, and the changes through time in the interpretations of the act as determinants of subsequent union developments. Others conclude that at least some aspects of public policy do not have a major impact on union strength. In particular, the influence of state right-to-work laws (which outlaw certain types of union-security agreements) is suspect because of recent studies showing little or no effect of such laws on the proportion of a state's labor force that is organized. Thus, the viewpoints of the different authors leave considerable uncertainty about the extent of the influence of public policy on union strength in the private sector.

Several "lessons" from this brief review of private-sector and economy-wide developments seem most relevant for the public sector. First, despite a literature dealing with private-sector and economy-wide union developments that is relatively extensive compared to the public-sector literature, the accomplishments are limited. Many assertions are of an ad hoc nature, and many predictions went astray. Probably the best-known and most impressive recent study, by Ashenfelter and Pencavel [1], does well in explaining American trade-union growth over the entire 1900–1960 period. However, Pencavel has indicated that its predictive ability for the post-1960 period may be limited (as some have argued) because the study "was not meant to be the estimation of a 'theory' of movements in union membership," but rather a "description of historical growth in trade union membership."[8] While the Pencavel distinction may be appropriate, it is not inconsistent with my judgment that studies of union growth in the private sector and the entire economy are inadequate in terms of theory and statistical evidence. I believe this judgment is important, because it helps place in proper perspective the examination of the public-sector literature that constitutes the balance of this chapter.

A second lesson of the review is that many of the central findings concerning private-sector and economy-wide developments are not useful in explaining public-sector developments. The aversion to unions of white-collar workers in the private sector has already been offered as an example of a finding of doubtful validity in the public sector. Another example, again drawn from the Ashenfelter and Pencavel study—done not to

---

[8]John Pencavel 1978: personal communication.

denigrate their work, but to emphasize a point by demonstrating that the best of the literature has limitations for the purpose of this review—is that one of their key variables that explains aggregate union-membership developments was the change in employment in four unionized sectors. Perforce this variable is irrelevant for explaining the key question for the public sector, namely, why did the sector transform itself from an unorganized to a relatively organized status after 1960?

The third lesson, previously drawn but worth emphasizing, is that examinations of the literature leave unclear the influence of public policy on union strength. Fundamental changes in the legal environment, such as enactment and effective implementation of the NLRA, undoubtedly have some impact on union strength, but more modest variations, such as a state's enacting a right-to-work law, have problematical influence. With these lessons as background, the section now examines the factors offered by various authors to explain the developments in the public sector.

Factors Inhibiting Organization in the Public Sector

Various writers have offered explanations of the lack of organization of government workers before the 1960s. Gitlow [21, p. 768] considered labor market conditions a detriment to organization because the stability of public-sector employment gave workers a sense of security. According to Moskow [32, p. 14], labor force developments were also detrimental because the public sector had increasing proportions of women, blacks, and white-collar workers, all traditionally difficult to organize. Several authors pointed to the unfavorable political environment, as well as adverse labor force developments. Gitlow [21, p. 760] argued that the public's attitude toward public-sector unions was negative partially because of an adherence to the sovereignty doctrine, which considers collective bargaining an illegal delegation of power. The political plight of unions was aggravated because of the rural domination of state legislatures, according to Stieber [39, p. 826]. Analysts also stressed that the unfavorable legal environment was a major obstacle to organization. There were prohibitions on strikes, which provide unions with much of their bargaining power, and there generally were no statutory requirements that public-sector employers recognize or bargain with unions. Some statutes even forbade collective bargaining (Gitlow [21, p. 769]). In addition, civil service laws provided a method of determining working conditions that was a rival for collective bargaining (Cohany and Dewey [15, p. 15]), which meant that unions were largely confined to lobbying and representing employees in grievances. Some aspects of union strategy also limited their success. For example, the American Federation of State, County, and Municipal Employees (AFSCME) originally tried to strengthen the civil service system, but lost members when it succeeded. Not until 1954 did AFSCME make a general commitment to collective bargaining (Kramer [25]).

This catalog of factors that inhibited organization of the public sector prior to the 1960s is reasonably persuasive. Indeed, the explanations seem so reasonable that it is easy to understand why analysts of the early 1960s would have dismissed the prospect of an impending surge in public-sector bargaining as a delusion.

Factors Facilitating Organization in the Public Sector

Three kinds of factors have been offered to explain the rapid growth of membership in bargaining organizations since 1960: those inherent or well-entrenched in government employment that make organization feasible; those that changed in the pre-1960 period, thus increasing the potential for organization; and those post-1960 factors that triggered or accelerated the growth of unions and associations. The distinctions among these three categories are somewhat arbitrary.

Inherent Factors. Factors inherent in government employment that make organization feasible include the characteristics of the employment relationship. Bakke [4] argued that several aspects of public employment encourage collective bargaining, including the absence of individual bargaining power because employees have few unique qualities, and the use of common standards for working conditions rather than individual employment agreements. Also, since the results of government employment are social products rather than goods or services produced by one worker, evaluation of employees as a group is necessary. In addition, in professions such as teaching there is a community of interest because of common skills and training, and a dependence of individual status on group status. This community of interest increases the interest in collective representation.

According to Stieber [37, p. 69], other factors of long

standing that facilitated organization of government workers were the traditional interest of professionals in participating in policy-making and the tradition in many jurisdictions of low wages and fringe benefits for public-sector workers. Still another facilitating factor was that many employees in the public sector were already in associations (mainly professional) prior to union organizing drives. These organizations could be co-opted by unions or transformed into bargaining associations. Or, if nothing else, they at least preconditioned workers to the notion of belonging to an organization (Moskow [32, p. 287]).

Pre-1960 Developments. Several factors changed between the 1930s and the postwar period that increased the potential for organization. Cohany and Dewey [15, p. 18] argued that the generally low unemployment rates meant the security of government jobs was no longer so valuable as workers became less willing to overlook undesirable aspects of the job in exchange for job security. They also asserted that as inflation became more of a problem, workers became concerned about the methods used to provide wage increases, since the procedures were considered sluggish. Moreover, improvements in private-sector personnel practices since the 1930s were not matched in the public sector (Stieber [37, p. 69]).

The rapid increase in public-sector employment in the 1940s and 1950s expanded the potential for subsequent organization. Also, as public workers became an increasingly important group of voters, they attracted the attention of politicians. Barrett [5] noted that the increasing public-sector labor force included more young workers, who generally distrusted employers, and minority workers, who did not trust the white-dominated management structure, and he argued that these workers were more inclined to support unions. However, this view is at least partially inconsistent with Moskow's explanation, previously discussed, about why unions did *not* emerge before 1960.

The political environment also changed prior to the 1960s in ways that encouraged organization of public employees, according to some writers. There was a general deterioration in the respect for law (Gitlow [21, pp. 772–73]) and an increasing public acceptance of militancy (Cohany and Dewey [15, p. 18]), which made union extra-legal techniques in the public sector tolerable.

Post-1960 Developments. There are, finally, a number of developments since 1960 that arguably triggered or accelerated the growth of public-sector bargaining organizations after that date. The economy's performance during the 1960s does not appear to provide an adequate explanation of the growth in bargaining organizations. Although the economy began a long period of sustained growth in 1961, this macroeconomic development cannot explain the disparate organizing records of unions in the public and private sectors. A more disaggregated economic theory was offered by Weber [40, p. 4], who argued that "the growth of public employee unionism was coincidental with the great expansion, if not explosion, of public services . . . [that] took place during the 1960's." However, he offers no data to buttress this theory, and casual empiricism provides contrary evidence. For example, the share of gross national product accounted for by the government sector increased from 12.1 percent in 1950 to 12.9 percent in 1960, and then dropped to 12.6 percent in 1970. Also, government employees represented 13.3 percent of all nonagricultural employees in 1950, 15.4 percent in 1960, and 17.7 percent in 1970. Perhaps there was an explosion of public services in the 1960s that can be identified by a more refined analysis, but there appears at best to have been a modest acceleration from the 1950s to the 1960s in the growth of employment accounted for by the public sector.[9]

A more likely explanation of the growth in bargaining organizations is that public employees' attitudes toward them changed significantly after 1960. It is hard to fathom what initiated the change; it might be explained in part by the fact that the public sector continued to attract younger workers and members of minority groups who were supporters of more militant action. In many cities the civil rights and public-sector-unionization movements became intertwined. As Weber [40, pp. 4–5] has argued, public-sector unions became the vehicle for groups such as women and blacks to elbow their way into the power system. Once the attitudes of pub-

---

[9]The data on gross national product and employment cited in the text are from the *Economic Report of the President* (1978), Tables B-10 and B-34. Disaggregation of the government sector into federal and state and local components does not particularly alter the text discussion. There was some acceleration of growth in the share of employment accounted for by state and local government during the 1960s, but no other evidence of a great expansion of public services.

lic-sector workers toward bargaining began to change, the
trend continued through most of the post-1960 period. One
reason was that bargaining triumphs and dramatic stoppages
added impetus to the movement; an outstanding example
was the 1961 breakthrough of New York City teachers
(Stieber [37, p. 68]). Although the initiating or sustaining
causes of the changing attitudes are not entirely evident, the
result is: during the 1960s many public-sector workers began
to "think the unthinkable" (Bornstein [8]).

As workers changed their attitudes, so also did employee organizations change their policies in order to attract or retain
members. The labor movement in general began to pay more
attention to the public sector. The Industrial Union Department
of the AFL-CIO placed considerable emphasis on organizing
public-sector workers beginning in the early 1960s, and several
predominantly private-sector unions provided direct assistance
to public-sector organizations, including the United Auto Workers' support of the American Federation of Teachers. Within the
public sector, unions became more militant and willing to use
tactics such as strikes. Professional associations often either lost
members to unions or transformed themselves into bargaining
associations. The considerable rivalry among AFL-CIO affiliates, independent unions, bargaining associations, and others
probably led to a larger number of public-sector workers being
organized than if interorganizational conflict had been avoided
(see Stieber [39, p. 830]).

Public-sector employers also made changes after 1960 that
encouraged or accommodated collective bargaining. The civil
service model broke down or was abandoned in many jurisdictions (Goldberg [22, pp. 59–60]). Management structure was
also adapted to collective bargaining, which in turn facilitated
further unionization (see Burton [9]).

One factor that encouraged the spread of bargaining was the
lack of resistance to union demands by many public-sector employers, which was related to the relative unsophistication on
industrial relations matters of many of the employers, as well as
the general lack of resistance to settlements among government
employers and the public (Weber [40, p. 5]). Not until the mid-
1970s did managers and the public stiffen their resistance to
collective bargaining demands because of the adverse publicity
resulting from events such as the New York City financial crisis,

which was associated by many with the impact of public-sector bargaining.[10]

Throughout the post-1960 period, public-sector bargaining organizations appeared to improve working conditions, which in turn attracted more members. In fact, however, the effect of public-sector bargaining on working conditions is unclear. The Lewin survey [28] indicates that the union influence on relative wages is less in the public sector than in the private sector, a result confirmed by Smith [35, pp. 120–29]. This finding suggests that public-sector employees have less to gain from joining a union than their private-sector counterparts, which if comprehended by workers presumably should mute their ardor for organization.[11] Still, there is probably a general presumption that public-sector bargaining has a large impact on wages, because the relative earnings of public-sector workers appear to have increased rapidly since 1960 while membership in bargaining organizations was growing, and the belief that the two phenomena were causally related made recruiting easier.

Several authors stress the importance of changes in public policy as a source of the growth in public-sector bargaining. The public-policy changes were caused in part by the 1962 and 1964 reapportionment decisions that transformed many state legislatures (Stieber [37, p. 68]), the aggressive lobbying by unions (Stieber [39, p. 827]), and the support of bargaining by all Presidents since Kennedy. The results at the federal level include Executive Orders 10988 and 11491, which were perhaps less significant for their content than as a symbol of presidential support for collective bargaining. Executive Order 10988 was

---

[10]A recent story illustrates the changing mood toward public-sector unions (New York Times, March 5, 1978, p. 1): "Complaints that New York City's employees are overpaid or have too many fringe benefits are believed to be a major reason that the city has a hard time winning help from Washington. But . . . New York is no special case. There seems to be widespread resentment of public employees that increases as their pay and fringe benefits increase. 'We've seen a growing animosity toward public employees over the last two years, and it continues to grow,' said William Luncy, secretary-treasurer of the American Federation of State, County, and Municipal Employees."

[11]Public-sector unions may use their political influence to increase wages for all public employees, rather than using bargaining to increase wages just for those public employees they represent. Likewise, a spillover effect may be operating whereby union wage gains in one jurisdiction (or for one occupation) are matched by employers of nonunion workers (see Ehrenberg and Goldstein [16]). If either of these phenomena is occurring, the union-nonunion wage differential within the public sector would understate the influence of public-sector unions on wages. Nonetheless, individual workers and even groups of workers may perceive little advantage to joining a union under these circumstances when they are likely to benefit from the union activities whether or not they are members.

also important because it encouraged changes at the state level
(Stieber [37, p. 68]). Favorable state legislation for collective
bargaining began with the 1959 enactment in Wisconsin; by the
end of the next decade, most industrialized states had followed.
Although these laws generally do not go as far as the NLRA in
encouraging unions and collective bargaining, in some instances—such as those statutes that mandate the agency shop—
there is an assist to organization greater than that provided in
the private sector (Stieber [39, p. 832]).

Although a number of authors assert that changes in public
policy were an important cause of the growth of public-sector
bargaining, skepticism about the assertion is warranted. There
is a dearth of statistical analysis of the role of public policy in
fostering growth in public-sector bargaining organizations,[12]
and thus drawing conclusions on this topic is particularly difficult. As a background, the earlier conclusions pertaining to the
private sector are useful: Fundamental changes in the legal environment have an impact on union strength, but the influence of
more modest variations is problematical. Also useful as a background for establishing the limits to the influence of public
policy is the conclusion of a study that examined the relationship
between the number of strikes by public employees and state
statutes that encouraged or discouraged collective bargaining,
provided for mediation or fact-finding, and prohibited or penal-
ized strikes. Burton and Krider [12, p. 171] concluded that these
elements of "public policy seem to have little impact on strikes."
Based on this background and a review of the studies and data
encompassed by this study, I believe that several conclusions
about the influence of public policy are appropriate.

Massive changes in public policy undoubtedly can have an

---

[12]Apparently the only econometric study of membership in the entire public sector
is by Moore [30], who found that the percentage of each state's government employees
unionized in 1968 was higher if (1) the state was urbanized, (2) a higher proportion of
government employees were women (an unexpected result), (3) a low percentage of
government employees were nonwhite (which contradicts earlier Moore findings for
private-sector unionization), and (4) the state had a comprehensive collective bargaining
law. The Moore study can be challenged, however, because the dependent variable is
the Cohany and Dewey [15] data that measure *federal*, state, and local government
employment and membership by state (over 60 percent of the union membership was
among federal employees), while the independent variables appear to be primarily
relevant for state and local government employees, especially the variables measuring
the status of state collective bargaining laws. The serious mismatch of dependent and
independent variables is unnecessary since data by state on union membership in state
and local governments are available (see the section, *infra*, on State and Local Noneducation Employees).

impact on the prevalence of bargaining and the extent of membership in bargaining organizations. Thus a swing from a policy outlawing collective bargaining to a policy requiring employers to bargain in good faith and allowing unions to strike or invoke arbitration would very likely lead to a substantial increase in membership. However, the actual shifts in policy that have occurred in the public sector have generally not been as dramatic as the example just given. At the federal level and in most states, the policy toward public-sector bargaining has evolved since 1960 from supine neglect to encouragement less avid than the national policy toward private-sector bargaining. This relatively limited shift in public policy seems incapable of explaining the magnitude of the growth in public-sector bargaining. Moreover, the lack of congruity between policy changes and membership growth in bargaining organizations is affirmed by the experience in several states—notably Ohio and Illinois—where the lack of major changes in policy has not precluded organization of a significant proportion of public-sector workers.[13] Furthermore, in some instances the enactment of favorable legislation was as much a result of membership growth as a cause of it. To be sure, there are undoubtedly some workers—those with inherently limited bargaining power (such as librarians and social workers) and those with marginal interest in bargaining (such as college professors)—for whom a favorable public policy is virtually a necessary precondition for organization; but, for the bulk of public-sector workers, the public-policy changes of the past 20 years have been no more important in explaining their organization than several other factors, including the changed attitude of these workers toward the propriety and usefulness of bargaining.

Conclusions on the Public Sector

One theme in the literature is that the growth of public-sector membership in bargaining organizations was surprisingly great (see, e.g., Stieber [39, p. 827] and Cohany and Dewey [15, p. 15]). Another theme is that the causes of the growth were multiple. Cohany and Dewey [15, p. 18] contrast this multiplicity of causes in the public sector with the experience in the private

---

[13]In 1976, 47.0 percent of Illinois public employees, 48.1 percent of Ohio public employees, and 49.8 percent of state and local employees nationally were organized. See Table 4 for data source.

sector where, they argue, a single factor (the depression) suffices to explain membership developments in mass production indus-tries. Although this assessment of the private sector seems too simple, nonetheless the causes of the surge of public-sector membership growth do seem more complex. Finally, while there are a number of ex post attempts to explain the post-1960 growth in public-sector bargaining, in general the phenomenon is still inadequately explained. In short, the public-sector bar-gaining surge that began after 1960 was unanticipated then and is inextricable now.

Federal Employees

One source of information for this analysis of the federal sector is the BLS data on membership in national unions and associations, which were used in Table 1 and which are disag-gregated to show federal government data in Table 2. Also, the Civil Service Commission (CSC) publishes data on any union, employee organization, or association granted exclusive recog-nition under Executive Order 11491 (or its predecessor), as shown in Table 3.[14] The main difference is that the BLS data are confined to members, while the CSC data include all em-ployees in exclusive bargaining units or under collective bargaining agreements.[15] The data indicate that many federal employees in bargaining units or covered by contract are not members.[16]

Table 2 shows that union membership in the federal sector increased rapidly from 1964 (the earliest year with available data) until 1968, and since then has been fairly stable, with the percent organized fluctuating in the 47–51 range. Mem-bership in bargaining associations is not significant in the federal sector, adding only about 1 percent to the union

---

[14]In 1976, in addition to the 1.198 million employees in the executive branch and 579,000 employees in the post office who were in exclusive units (Table 3), there were 64,000 employees in nonappropriated-fund activities (e.g., Army exchanges) and 76,000 employees in other jurisdictions (e.g., TVA) who were in exclusive units. See Burton [11] for data sources.

[15]The two types of CSC data are shown in Table 3. In 1977, for example, bargaining organizations had exclusive bargaining rights for 1.198 million workers in the executive branch, but had negotiated agreements for only 1.063 million of these workers.

[16]An important example is the American Federation of Government Employees (AFGE), which in 1976 represented 678,410 workers in 1774 exclusive units, but re-ported only 261,623 members. The data are from 71:209 GERR RF 144 (June 20, 1977) and 676 GERR A-11 (September 27, 1976).

Table 2
Percentage of Government Employees Organized
(Employment and Members in Thousands)

Year	Total Government			Federal Government			State and Local Government		
	Employment	Members[a]	Percent Organized	Employment	Members[a]	Percent Organized	Employment	Members[a]	Percent Organized
Panel A: Membership in Unions									
1956	7,277	915	12.6	2,209	—	—	5,069	—	—
1960	8,353	1,070	12.8	2,270	—	—	6,083	—	7.7
1964	9,596	1,453	15.1	2,348	897	38.2	7,248	556	7.8
1966	10,792	1,717	15.9	2,564	1,073	41.8	8,227	644	8.8
1968	11,845	2,155	18.2	2,737	1,351	49.4	9,109	804	9.6
1970	12,561	2,318	18.5	2,731	1,370	50.1	9,830	947	10.4
1972	13,340	2,460	18.4	2,684	1,355	50.5	10,656	1,105	13.4
1974	14,177	2,920	20.6	2,724	1,391	51.1	11,453	1,529	14.0
1976[P]	14,948	3,009	20.1	2,733	1,300	47.6	12,215	1,710	
Panel B: Membership in Bargaining Organizations[b]									
1968	11,845	3,857	32.6	2,737	1,391	50.8	9,109	2,466	27.1
1970	12,561	4,080	32.5	2,731	1,412	51.7	9,830	2,668	27.1
1972	13,340	4,520	33.9	2,684	1,383	51.5	10,656	3,137	29.4
1974	14,177	5,345	37.7	2,724	1,433	52.6	11,453	3,911	34.1
1976[P]	14,948	5,853	39.2	2,733	1,332	48.7	12,215	4,521	37.0

Sources: Employment: 100 Monthly Lab. Rev. 89 (October 1977), Table 8. Membership: 1968–1976 from U.S. Department of Labor, Bureau of Labor Statistics, *Labor Union and Employee Association Membership—1976,* news release, September 1977; 1956–1966 from U.S. Department of Labor, Bureau of Labor Statistics, *Directory of National and International Labor Unions in the United States,* 1965 (and 1967), Table 7.
Note: P = preliminary.
[a] Membership includes members outside the United States.
[b] Bargaining organizations include unions and bargaining associations, as those terms are defined in the text. The equivalent BLS terms are unions and employee associations.

Table 3
Federal Employees in Exclusive Units and Covered by Agreement, 1963–1977
(Employees in Thousands)

Year	Executive Branch Total Employment	Employees in Exclusive Units Number	Employees in Exclusive Units Percent of Total Employment	Employees Under Agreement Number	Employees Under Agreement Percent of Employees in Units	Total Employment	Post Office Employees in Exclusive Units Number	Post Office Employees in Exclusive Units Percent of Total Employment
1963		180					490	
1964		231	(12)	111	48.1		499	
1965		320	(16)	242	75.6		515	
1966		435	(21)	292	67.1		619	
1967		630	(29)	423	67.1		609	(86)
1968		798	(40)	557	69.8		619	(87)
1969		843	(42)	559	66.3		634	(87)
1970	1,928	916	47.5	602	65.7		626	(87)
1971	1,951	1,038	53.2	707	68.1		623	
1972	1,957	1,083	55.3	753	69.5	669	605	90.4
1973	1,941	1,086	56.0	837	77.1		615	
1974	2,015	1,142	56.7	985	86.2	698	607	87.0
1975	2,039	1,200	58.9	1,083	90.2	692	599	86.6
1976	2,054	1,190	57.9	1,060	89.1	661	579	87.6
1977		1,198	(58)	1,063	88.7	652	573	87.9

Source: Various volumes of U.S. Civil Service Commission's Union Recognition in the Federal Government, including the summaries in 71 GERR RF. Data for 1977 are from 754 GERR 7, 52–53 (April 10, 1978). Percentages calculated by the author except those in parentheses, which are from CSC publications. TVA employees (29,408 represented in 1976) were included in Executive Branch figures until 1976. All employees in Post Office in exclusive units were under agreement.

figures.[17] Executive branch employees in exclusive units increased from 12 percent in 1964 to 58 percent in 1977,
while the percentage of employees in exclusive units who
were also under agreement went from about 50 percent to
almost 90 percent during that 12-year span. Post office employees have been highly organized (86–90 percent) at least
since 1968, although as the number of postal workers has declined recently, so has the number of represented workers.
The BLS data indicate the percentage of organized federal
employees dropped about 4 percent between 1974 and 1976
(Table 2), but the CSC data show no corresponding decline
during those years (Table 3).

Explanatory Factors

This review concentrates on some unusual aspects of the federal sector and some recent developments. One distinctive feature is that federal civilian employment has grown slowly since
1956 and has shown no growth since 1968 (Table 2). However,
wages (and total compensation) for federal employees have
grown rapidly since 1962, and several recent studies argue that
federal employees earn considerably more than comparable private-sector workers (see, e.g., Smith [35]). Of interest, however,
is that the union-nonunion wage differential is smaller in the
federal sector than in the private sector (Smith [35]). The high
wages for federal employees may result from the success of
unions in increasing the wages for all federal employees, not just
wages for members.[18] Alternatively, the high wages for all federal workers may be due to factors other than unionization. In
either case, the economic advantages of joining a union in the
federal sector appear limited, thus complicating the unions' recruiting task.[19]

The relationship between public policy and the growth of
bargaining organizations in the federal sector is particularly
difficult to disentangle. The federal sector was a pioneer in

---

[17] Although most bargaining organizations in the federal sector are classified as
unions by the BLS, some have one or more of the characteristics of bargaining associations, such as inclusion of supervisors, aversion to strikes, emphasis on political action,
and nonaffiliation with the AFL-CIO.
[18] This result is not surprising since in general unions in the federal sector are precluded from negotiating over wages and can affect wages only indirectly by increasing
the entire wage scale.
[19] See note 11 for further discussion of this point.

adopting a public policy that supported unions and collective bargaining, beginning with President Kennedy's 1962 Executive Order 10988. However, even though extended by several executive orders, the policy for federal employees is not as favorable as that for the private sector or as the policy in a number of states for nonfederal public employees. In particular, the scope of bargaining is constricted by federal policy since "direct money items are generally nonnegotiable," as is union security (Howlett [23, p. 119]). In contrast, most state laws define the mandatory scope of negotiations as broadly as the NLRA and thus *inter alia* require bargaining on wages (Clark [13, p. 87]). Also, the federal civil service system has retained significant responsibility for matters such as recruitment, promotion, and discipline, contrary to the experience in many state and local governments where collective bargaining has largely displaced civil service from these functions (see Burton [9]). Another limitation of the federal policy is that it is embodied in an executive order and not in a statute, as in most states.

These aspects of the public policy for collective bargaining limit the benefits for federal workers if they join a bargaining organization, which raises an obvious question: Why have so many joined? Probably part of the answer is that the costs of joining are also limited. Workers can join without facing the prospect of going on strike. There are a few exceptions, such as postal workers, but the prevalence of strikes among federal employees is much less than among private-sector or even state and local government employees. Also, public policy requires federal agencies and departments to adopt a position of neutrality during union organizing drives. In contrast, private-sector employers may make noncoercive arguments in order to persuade their workers not to join a union.[20] In essence, membership in federal unions has not required a very deep commitment by workers. This analysis of the benefits and costs of bargaining suggests that the allegiance of federal workers to unions may be broad but shallow.

Legislation to provide more meaningful collective bargaining rights for federal employees has been introduced but never

---

[20]Section 8(c) of the National Labor Relations Act allows private-sector employers to express views, arguments, or opinions as long as such expressions contain no threat of reprisal or force or promise of benefit. The difference between private-sector policy and the policy for federal employees is discussed in *Old Dominion Branch No. 46, National Assn. of Letter Carriers* v. *Austin*, 94 S.Ct. 2770, 86 LRRM 2740 (1974).

enacted. One reason for the lack of enactment was a division within the union movement about the type of bill desired, although the extent of disagreement has declined recently.[21] The lack of progress is also due to increasing public hostility toward federal workers. The apparently high wages for federal employees, their relative immunity from unemployment during adverse labor market experience in the 1970s, and the alleged inability to sack incompetents have turned many persons against federal employees. Indeed, the perceived increase in public resentment of federal employees was described as the top development in federal labor relations during 1977.[22]

There is some chance that the legal environment for federal bargaining may change because of several 1978 developments. The Carter Administration has proposed an overhaul of the civil service system and has indicated its willingness to incorporate Executive Order 11491 (which now governs labor relations policy for federal employees) into the civil service reform bill. The federal employee unions have split over the proposal. The American Federation of Government Employees (AFGE), the largest of the federal unions, and other representatives of the AFL-CIO provided qualified approval of the civil service reorganization plan and indicated an initial willingness to study the proposal to write Executive Order 11491 into law.[23] In contrast, a coalition of federal unions not affiliated with the AFL-CIO rejected the Administration's proposal in favor of another bill (H.R. 9094) that would provide a broader scope of bargaining and a mandatory agency shop.[24] However, even one of the cosponsors of H.R. 9094, Congressman Ford, has indicated the chances for enactment are "very poor,"[25] which means that the Administration's proposal is about all that federal employee unions can hope for in the near future. Since that proposal does little more than codify the current policy (the Administration, for example, is unwilling to legalize the strike or to broaden the scope of bargaining to include wages, fringes, or union- or agency-shop provisions),[26] the immediate prospects seem dim

---

[21]See 726 GERR 7–10 (September 19, 1977).
[22]740 GERR 9 (January 2, 1978).
[23]757 GERR 6–7 (May 1, 1978).
[24]757 GERR 6 (May 1, 1978).
[25]749 GERR 10 (March 6, 1978).
[26]756 GERR 8 (April 24, 1978).

for a significant change in the legal environment for federal bargaining.[27]

Special Cases

One special case is the post office. Postal workers have a long history of organization and are now more highly organized than most other categories of federal employees (Table 3). The employees also have special legislative treatment (under the 1970 Postal Reorganization Act) that gives the National Labor Relations Board authority to determine bargaining units, conduct elections, and consider unfair-labor-practice charges, and that establishes mediation, fact-finding, and arbitration procedures to resolve collective bargaining disputes. Burton [10, p. 223] argued that postal workers received favorable consideration from Congress because, unlike most federal employees, their wide geographical dispersion gives them effective political leverage. The 1970 strike by postal workers also helped their quest for special treatment.

Another special case is the military, which is currently unorganized but the number of potential members is large. Although the AFGE leadership proposed and explored the idea of opening the union to the military in 1976, the membership defeated the proposal by a 4 to 1 margin in 1977. The reaction of both the military brass and the Congress to the AFGE exploration was intense.[28]

Conclusions

The seeds for federal workers' discontent with unions are sown. The unions' appeal is reduced by their inability to negotiate for many subjects (including wages) under the current executive order, and the political situation suggests that unions will have difficulty achieving public-policy changes that will enable them to increase their scope of influence. If my previous characterization is correct—that the allegiance of federal workers to unions may be broad but shallow—and if workers decide that unions are ineffectual, membership losses may occur. A modi-

---

[27]Another reason why a change in public policy for most federal workers is unlikely is that the special treatment accorded postal workers under the 1970 Postal Reorganization Act has diluted the interest of the postal unions in comprehensive reform.

[28]More detailed analysis of this issue can be found in Staudohar [36].

cum of evidence suggests that workers are concluding that federal unions are feckless. Manley [29] found that, between 1974
and 1976, federal scientists and engineers reported a drop in job
satisfaction and more negative attitudes toward management
and personnel practices, as well as a more negative view of
unions, apparently "expressing frustration with perceived impo-
tency of unions" (p. 33). A scintilla of evidence to support the
hypothesis that the disaffection may lead to membership losses
is provided by the 1974–1976 data in Table 2.[29] It would be
foolish to make too much of such fragmentary evidence, but
unwise to ignore possible portents.

State and Local Noneducation Employees

Data and analyses in this section are relevant primarily for
noneducation employees in the state and local sector. Information sources are the BLS membership data in Table 2 for state
and local government employees (which, however, cannot be
disaggregated into education and noneducation components)
and the Bureau of the Census–Department of Labor (BCDL)
data, shown in Tables 4 and 5. A few caveats are in order.

The BCDL data by themselves are confusing because some
pertain to full-time employees and some to all employees, full-
and part-time. Thus, the Table 4 data indicate that about half
of all full-time state and local employees are organized, while
Table 5 data show that only about one-third of all state and local
employees (full- and part-time) are in recognized bargaining
units, and only about one-quarter are covered by written contracts. That more employees are members than are in bargaining units or covered by agreements is a result that contrasts with
the experience in the federal sector.[30]

Even more perplexing are the large discrepancies between the
BLS and BCDL data in the number and percentage of state and
local government employees organized. For example, the BLS
data (Table 2, panel B) show 4.5 million members in 1976,
which is 37.0 percent of the total state and local employment of

---

[29]Federal-worker unions are particularly vulnerable to membership losses because
Executive Order 11491 prohibits all types of union-security agreements, including
maintenance-of-membership clauses.

[30]In a study of collective bargaining in cities, Nelson [33, p. 46] found that many cities
promulgate the results of bargaining in personnel regulations or executive orders rather
than written agreements.

Table 4
State and Local Government Employees Organized in 1972–1976
(Employees in Thousands)

Level of Government and Function	Total Full-Time Employment			Number of Full-Time Employees Organized			Percent of Full-Time Employees Organized		
	1972	1974	1976	1972	1974	1976	1972	1974	1976
State and local	8,578	9,177	9,514	4,293	4,724	4,737	50.0	51.5	49.8
State total	2,312	2,470	2,596	942	970	992	40.7	39.3	38.2
Education-teachers	266	271	282	82	92	97	30.9	33.9	34.3
Education-others	473	525	548	115	129	140	24.3	24.6	25.6
Highways	283	274	257	163	158	138	57.6	57.6	53.5
Public welfare	112	140	156	52	59	61	46.2	42.0	39.3
Hospitals	437	456	482	228	218	230	52.2	47.9	47.7
Police protection	62	68	68	34	34	35	54.2	48.6	51.8
All other	679	737	803	268	281	290	39.4	38.1	36.2
Local total	6,266	6,707	6,919	3,351	3,754	3,745	53.5	56.0	54.1
Education-teachers	2,454	2,646	2,721	1,807	2,017	1,963	73.7	76.3	72.1
Education-others	921	993	976	323	418	437	35.1	42.1	44.8
Highways	268	276	285	90	94	103	33.5	34.0	36.0
Public welfare	171	169	178	78	80	77	45.5	47.4	43.0
Hospitals	419	432	428	129	136	130	30.7	31.6	30.3
Police protection	411	448	463	229	251	253	55.8	56.1	54.7
Fire protection	194	205	210	149	152	151	76.5	74.4	71.6
Sanitation	117	121	119	59	60	59	50.1	49.7	49.2
All others	1,310	1,417	1,539	488	545	574	37.2	38.4	37.3

Sources: 1972 data from U.S. Bureau of the Census, Labor-Management Relations in State and Local Governments: 1974, Series GSS No. 75 (1976), Table 3, p. 18; 1974 data from U.S. Bureau of the Census, Labor-Management Relations in State and Local Government: 1975, Series GSS No. 81 (1977), Table 3, p. 18; 1976 data from U.S. Bureau of the Census, Labor-Management Relations in State and Local Government: 1976, Series GSS No. 88 (1978), Table 3, p. 18.

Table 5
State and Local Government Employees
Formally Represented in 1976
(Employees in Thousands)

	Total Employees (Full-Time and Part-Time)	Employees in Bargaining Units	Employees Covered by Contractual Agreement
State			
Number	3,343	752	546
Percent of total employees	—	22.5	16.0
Local			
Number	8,826	3,602	2,824
Percent of total employees	—	40.8	32.0
State and local			
Number	12,169	4,354	3,370
Percent of total employees	—	35.8	27.7

Source: U.S. Bureau of the Census, Labor-Management Relations in State and Local Governments: 1976, Series GSS No. 88 (1978), Table 1, pp. 9–10.

12.2 million. In contrast, the BCDL data (Table 4), although confined to 9.5 million full-time employees, show 4.7 million members, which is 49.8 percent of employment. A 12.8 percent differential is hard to ignore. The differential is partially explained by BLS undercounting (for example, municipal public-employee associations are excluded). A more significant explanatory factor is that the BCDL data include organizations that do not meet our definitions of unions and bargaining associations. After examining these and other factors that may explain the BLS-BCDL differences (Burton [11]), I concluded that the estimates cannot be entirely reconciled and that the BLS data are more appropriate for determining the extent of bargaining in the public sector.

The BLS data on state and local government employees show a rapid increase in bargaining-organization membership since the early 1960s, with a majority of the membership in bargaining associations (Table 2). The BCDL data indicate that local government workers are more highly organized than state government workers, and that the organized proportion varies substantially by function (Table 4).

The major story of the sector since 1960 is the association-union confrontation and convergence. In the early 1960s, the prevalent organization (especially at the state level) was the independent public-employee association. These usually were not "bargaining associations," but "other organizations" as those terms were defined earlier. Krislov [26] found that they were characterized by low dues ($27 per year the maximum), a limited range of services, avoidance of collective bargaining and strikes, reliance on "informal recognition," and concentration on legislative representation in order to gain influence. The nexus of the state associations was a concern for the civil service system, and they typically admitted all employees, including supervisors (Lelchook [27]).

Stieber [38, pp. 221–23] found a convergence of unions and associations between 1968 and 1972, with the association attitudes on collective bargaining and strikes becoming much more like union attitudes. Nonetheless, he stressed that many organizations at the state and local level that engage in collective bargaining are not unions because bargaining is not their primary purpose.

The current status of the former associations is varied. Some were defeated by unions and disappeared, others merged with unions, and a number now engage in collective bargaining. An interesting case study is the New York Civil Service Association, which had endorsed bargaining so avidly by the mid-1970s that it could be considered an independent union.[31] In 1978, the CSEA, after losing 45,000 members to an AFT-SEIU coalition, announced an affiliation agreement with AFSCME. The addition of 260,000 members claimed by the CSEA will make AFSCME the largest affiliate of the AFL-CIO.[32] Despite the general conversion of associations to the collective bargaining approach, there are some that still resist collective bargaining. In 1974, the Association of Government Employees (a national organization of state associations), which claimed to represent 700,000 workers, testified before Congress about proposed legislation to regulate state and local bargaining, and indicated its concern about the possible exclusion of supervisors (who belong to many associations) and the threat to the merit system.[33]

The factors that explain the substantial membership growth nationally in bargaining organizations for noneducation employees in the state and local sector have already been discussed. Several authors have attempted to explain the variations in or-

---

[31]Another interesting example is the Massachusetts State Employee Association, which merged with the National Association of Government Employees (NAGE), an independent union, in 1977. NAGE is now contesting for members with an AFSCME-SEIU alliance (728 GERR 16, October 3, 1977).

[32]757 GERR 14 (May 1, 1978).

[33]543 GERR B8 (February 25, 1974).

ganizational strength among jurisdictions.[34] According to Nelson [33, p. 43] and Stieber [38, pp. 225–32], relevant factors are the support of private-sector unions, with local governments more highly organized in regions with high proportions of private-sector workers organized, and city size, with employees more highly organized in large cities. Organizing success probably is also a function of the bargaining organizations' success in increasing wages for members. Most studies show a smaller union-nonunion differential in the state and local sector than in the private sector (Lewin [28]), which on average should provide a damper on organizing activities.[35] However, the ability of unions to influence wages probably varies considerably among jurisdictions. Wages and total compensation for state and local employees vary considerably by locality and sex. Most females in the sector receive wages equal to or greater than their private-sector counterparts, while males have wages that match, exceed, or fall short of private-sector wages, depending on their location (Smith [35]). Evidence that the union effect on wages also varies across jurisdictions is sparse, but such a variable influence seems reasonable and could help explain the differential organizing success across jurisdictions.

Another obvious candidate for explaining variations in organizational strength among jurisdictions is public policy. For example, state statutes vary in their stance toward collective bargaining, ranging from prohibition to imposing an obligation on both parties to bargain in good faith. However, as Stieber notes [38, p. 231], states with high percentages of representation are likely to enact favorable legislation, which "suggests an interaction between state laws and extent of public employee organization rather than a one-way relationship." This conclusion is consistent with my views expressed earlier about the role of public policy.

---

[34]Only one econometric study of noneducation membership was found, and that was cursory. Burton and Krider [12, p. 166] found that most of the variation among states in the percentage of local-government noneducation employees organized as of 1969 could be explained by four variables, all statistically significant. The percentage organized was higher (1) the higher the percentage of employees in cities over 50,000, (2) the greater the extent of private-sector unionization, (3) if a law were present permitting or encouraging collective bargaining, where the law was three or more years old, and (4) if the state did not have a law making bargaining illegal. The apparent impact of public policy must be used with some caution since the regression was ordinary least squares, and if public policy is endogenous, the coefficients on the policy variable may be biased.

[35]See note 11 for further discussion of this point.

I do not want to denigrate completely the role of public policy in determining the extent of bargaining and membership in bargaining organizations. Of some importance, for example, was the 1977 Supreme Court decision in *Abood* v. *Detroit Board of Education*, which held that state laws authorizing the agency shop do not violate the U.S. Constitution.[36] In New York State, the decision was followed by the enactment of a law that made the agency shop mandatory for state employees and a mandatory bargaining subject for local government negotiations. Unions have made gains as a result of the law, including an equivalent of 20,000 new members for AFSCME in New York City alone.[37] While the *Abood* case indicates that agency-shop agreements do not contravene the federal Constitution, state law may, of course, bar such agreements. As examples, in late 1977 the Maine Supreme Court held the agency shop coercive and illegal,[38] and in 1978 the Michigan State Tenure Commission ruled that a teacher who refused to remit payment under an agency-shop agreement could not be discharged because of the protection afforded by state tenure law.[39] These decisions demonstrate that public policy can affect the ability of majority-status unions to require all bargaining-unit employees to join or support unions.

State and Local Education Employees

Data and analyses in this section are relevant primarily for education employees in the state and local sector. Information sources are the BCDL data showing organized workers by function and level of government (Table 4), the BLS data on membership in bargaining organizations (Table 6), and the Garbarino data on faculty representation in higher education (Table 7). The Garbarino data pertain to both public and private institutions, but are used for this survey since over 90 percent of organized faculty members are in the public sector.[40]

---

[36] 97 S.Ct. 1782, 431 U.S. 209, 95 LRRM 2411 (1977). The paragraph in the text dealing with the *Abood* case has implications for both the education and noneducation components of state and local government.

[37] The 20,000-membership estimate was made by the Office of Municipal Labor Relations (New York City) as reported in The Chief (a civil employees' weekly published in New York City), April 7, 1977.

[38] 740 GERR 12 (January 2, 1978).

[39] 749 GERR 13 (March 6, 1978). This decision is being appealed.

[40] Data for 1977 from Joseph Garbarino 1978: personal communication.

Table 6
Membership in Major Organizations in Education, 1962-1976
(Employees in Thousands)

Year	American Federation of Teachers (AFT)	American Association of University Professors (AAUP)	National Education Association (NEA)	Total Membership in Bargaining Organizations
1962	71			71
1964	100			100
1966	125			125
1968	165		1,062	1,227
1970	205	90	1,100	1,395
1972	249	86	1,166	1,501
1974	444	72	1,470	1,986
1976	446	73	1,887	2,406

Sources: AFT 1962–1974 and NEA 1968–1974 from U.S. Department of Labor, Bureau of Labor Statistics, Directory of National Unions and Employee Associations, 1975 (Bull. No. 1937, 1977), App. D; AAUP 1970–1974 from U.S. Department of Labor, Bureau of Labor Statistics, Directory of National Unions and Employee Associations, 1971 (1973, 1975). All 1976 data were provided by or confirmed in personal correspondence from Harry P. Cohany, Chief of the BLS Division of Industrial Relations.
Note: The table makes the assumption that the transformation from professional association to bargaining association took place in 1968 for the NEA and in 1970 for the AAUP; these are the earliest years for which membership data for these organizations are available from the BLS directories. Workers who have dual membership (e.g., NEA and AFT) apparently are counted twice in these data.

Table 7
Faculty Representation in Higher Education, 1966-1978

Year	Total		Four-Year Schools		Four-Year as Percent of Total	
	Institutions	Faculty	Institutions	Faculty	Institutions	Faculty
1966	23	5,200	1	200	4.3	3.8
1967	37	7,000	2	300	5.4	4.3
1968	70	14,300	10	3,300	14.3	23.1
1969	138	36,100	26	16,100	18.9	44.6
1970	177	47,300	40	23,400	22.6	49.5
1971	245	72,400	84	45,400	34.3	62.7
1972	285	84,300	102	54,600	35.8	64.8
1973	310	87,700	121	57,400	39.0	65.5
1974	337	92,800	131	60,700	38.9	65.4
1975	398	102,300	162	67,300	40.7	65.8
1976	450	117,000	189	78,970	42.0	67.5
1977	476	134,000	196	81,600	41.2	60.9
1978 (6/30)	499	139,326	214	85,234	42.9	61.2

Sources: 1966–1974 from Joseph W. Garbarino, *Faculty Union Activity in Higher Education —1975,* 14 Ind. Rels. 110–11 (1975); 1975–1976 from Joseph W. Garbarino and John Lawler, *Faculty Union Activity in Higher Education—1976,* 16 Ind. Rels. 105–106 (1977); and 1977 and 1978 from John Lawler (1978: personal correspondence).

Although the data in Tables 4, 6, and 7 are not entirely
comparable (as discussed in Burton [11]), the basic message is
clear: the increase in membership in bargaining organizations
among education employees has been stupendous during
the past 15 years. In 1962, the AFT had 71,000 members,
and the NEA and AAUP were not bargaining. By 1976, the
AFT had 446,000 members (and had recorded the highest
percentage increase in the preceding decade of any union),
while the NEA and (to a lesser extent) the AAUP had been
transformed into bargaining associations; the total membership in bargaining organizations exceeded 2.4 million by 1976
(Table 6). The only blemish on the growth record of the bargaining organizations is the recently reported losses, with
the AFT down about 30,000 between 1975 and 1976,
and the NEA down about 200,000 from 1976 to 1977.[41]

At the local government level, about three-quarters of all
full-time teachers were organized in 1976, making teachers and
fire fighters the most highly organized functions at that level.
About 45 percent of nonteaching personnel in education were
also organized (Table 4). In higher education, the number of
faculty represented had grown rapidly, from 5,000 to 139,000
between 1966 and 1978 (Table 7). The organizing through
1968 was primarily in two-year institutions, but by the mid-
1970s about 40 percent of the organized institutions and 60–65
percent of the represented faculty were in four-year institutions.

Factors Explaining Elementary-Secondary Education Developments

The transformation of the NEA from a professional association to a bargaining association is the most important development in public-sector bargaining since 1960, because the NEA
is the largest bargaining organization operating primarily in the
public sector. The key to the conversion of the NEA to a bargaining association probably is the organizing success of the
AFT,[42] which began to grow rapidly in the early 1960s largely

---

[41]The data are from 41 GERR RF 101 (November 21, 1977). The large NEA loss
apparently resulted from the 1976 decision of the merged NEA-AFT New York State
United Teachers to disaffiliate from the NEA and remain in the AFT.

[42]A recent article by Moore and Marshall [31] provided a model and nonstatistical
analysis of AFT growth. The secular growth of the AFT was partially explained by the
increasing proportions of male, secondary-school, well-educated, and more experienced
teachers, all types with a high propensity to join unions. The M&M model also used four

at the expense of the NEA. The AFT was obviously taking advantage of a latent interest among teachers in aggressive representation, an interest not generally anticipated and still hard to explain. A partial explanation of the increasing interest by teachers in collective bargaining is provided by the factors reviewed at the beginning of this chapter. Perry and Wildman [34, pp. 13–15] provide additional reasons especially relevant for teachers, including the increasing percentage of males in the teaching force and the defensive reaction to the widespread criticisms of teachers ("justified or not") following the Russian launching of Sputnik I. As teachers' attitudes changed, the NEA—to its credit —showed strong survival instincts, and by 1970 had largely completed its transformation into a bargaining association,[43] with endorsement of collective bargaining and strikes (although euphemisms were often used for these concepts) (Cohany [14]).

As the NEA was transformed into a bargaining association, the differences in goals and methods between the NEA and AFT narrowed. What many felt would be a logical result—a national AFT-NEA merger—became more of a possibility in 1969 when the Flint, Michigan, affiliates merged. By 1973, a New York State merger occurred and explorations were under way for a national merger. But in 1974, NEA-AFT merger plans were called off, primarily at the initiative of the NEA. The main reasons were the NEA's unwillingness to have the merged organization affiliate with the AFL-CIO and its concern over an AFT internal struggle

---

categories of factors to explain the periods of AFT growth from 1916 to 1970. The factors that encouraged growth were a decline in teachers' real income, favorable government policy, increases in union membership in the total economy, and social forces. In general, the model is unsatisfactory. Most of the factors have empirical counterparts, and if statistical tests had been used, the model would have been much more persuasive or, more likely, shown to be of no predictive ability. Beyond the reliance on ad hoc explanations of exceptions to the general relationships between AFT growth and the four categories of factors, the model's serious deficiency is the focus on AFT growth. There was no attempt to explain the main development of the 1960s, namely, the conversion of the NEA into a bargaining association.

[43]The transformation of the NEA into a bargaining association is reflected in data on written agreements. In 1963–1964, a comprehensive national survey by Perry and Wildman [34, p. 12] found "only 419 documents of any kind relating to negotiations and a mere 17 substantive, signed contracts containing detailed provisions on salaries, hours, or other conditions of employment." By 1966–1967, the NEA reported 1531 procedural or negotiation agreements (in which, at a minimum, a teachers' organization was recognized); of these 1531 agreements, only 389 (or 25.4 percent) were classified as comprehensive contracts (in which salaries, hours, or other conditions of employment were included). By 1972–1973, the NEA reported 3958 negotiation agreements, of which 2556 (or 64.6 percent) were comprehensive contracts. The data pertain to the NEA, AFT, and other organizations, but over 90 percent of the agreements involved the NEA. The data are from the National Education Association, Negotiation Research Digest, June 1973, p. 14, and January 1974, pp. 15–16.

that saw Albert Shanker replace Dave Seldon as president. By 1976, the New York State United Teachers disaffiliated from the NEA and aligned itself with the AFT; in response, the NEA began an aggressive recruiting drive in New York. By 1977, the NEA and AFT were in sharp competition nationally, even though AFT President Shanker said it was the "height of insanity" not to be negotiating a merger.[44] In New York State and in most larger cities the AFT was dominant, while the NEA was ahead in most states, including California.

While the NEA-AFT courtship was unfolding, the labor market for teachers was deteriorating. During the 1960s, employment of teachers grew rapidly, but the growth has slowed in recent years and is even declining in some areas. Given the high percentage of employees organized, declines in employment are likely to translate into reductions in membership. The AFT, for example, reported in 1977 that most of its 30,000 drop in membership was due to layoffs and other attrition.[45]

As growth slowed in 1977, the AFT voted to organize "other institutions now providing education services," and President Shanker mentioned civil service employees and workers in libraries and the health field as examples.[46] This expanded AFT jurisdiction would overlap with other AFL-CIO unions, notably AFSCME. In contrast, the NEA voted in 1977 not to organize paraprofessionals and teacher aides, and several state NEA affiliates have signed agreements with AFSCME that limit competition for members.[47] Moreover, the NEA and AFSCME are members of CAPE (Coalition of American Public Employees), which the AFT has declined to join. Thus, paradoxically, the NEA has better working relations with AFSCME than does the AFT, although the latter two are both AFL-CIO affiliates.

The degree to which the NEA has transformed itself may now be a factor that limits its further growth. The "conservative, independent" National Association of Professional Educators is being touted in the South as an alternative to the NEA, and in Georgia, the NEA affiliate lost 8,000 teachers to NAPE in 1976.[48] Thus, while the transformation of the NEA has made it possible to cope with the threat of the AFT, it has occurred too

---

[44]723 GERR 17 (August 29, 1977).
[45]723 GERR 18 (August 29, 1977).
[46]Ibid.
[47]716 GERR 17 (July 11, 1977). In Michigan, however, the Education Association and AFSCME are competing for nonteaching personnel in education.
[48]GERR RF 152 (November 21, 1977).

fast for some NEA members. Whether the NEA can continue effectively to fight a two-front war is unclear; the loss of 200,000 members in 1976–1977 probably partially reflects a failure in this campaign.

Significant additional membership growth in secondary and elementary education is unlikely, primarily because the number of jobs will probably stabilize or decline, and because high proportions of teachers are already organized. There is some potential for additional members among nonteaching personnel, but significant gains there and among remaining unorganized teachers probably depend on significant changes in public policy.[49] Prospects for such changes at the federal or state level in the short run are dim, and in light of adverse employment prospects, organized membership is likely at best to maintain current levels.

Factors Explaining Higher Education Developments

Collective bargaining in higher education is one of the more controversial developments in public-sector bargaining. Indeed, a leading scholar (Garbarino [17, p. 1]) has referred to the development as "a lousy idea whose time has come."

Distinctions among the types of higher education institutions are important. As already noted, private institutions are largely unorganized; 90 percent of the organized faculty are in the public sector. Within the public sector, "established universities" are least interested in bargaining, while state colleges, "emerging universities" (often former teachers' colleges with an expanded mission), and junior colleges are more prone to organization. Aussieker and Garbarino [2, p. 124] argue that "unionism has been concentrated in relatively low-quality institutions." Collective bargaining became the way for some of these types of institutions to improve their economic position relative to established institutions. Begin, Settle, and Alexander [7, pp. 26–27], however, are skeptical of the asserted relationship between institutional quality and propensity to unionize, and argue that more important are factors such as whether the institution is included in a statewide higher education system, which encourages bargaining.

Through the 1960s, employment in higher education was

---

[49]The role of public policy in fostering membership growth has been discussed in earlier sections; see especially note 36 and the accompanying text.

growing rapidly and salaries were improving relative to those in other fields. By the mid-1970s, however, growth had slowed, openings for new faculty were scarce, new scholars were abundant, and in general earnings were declining in real terms. However, Garbarino [18, p. 79] argued that low salaries were not a direct inducement to unionization and that the most important single cause of unionization is a credible threat to tenure (p. 157). He also concluded that concerns over staff reductions are important. In contrast, a recent survey of college administrators found evidence that low salaries are more important than tenure and retrenchment as sources of union support.[50]

Several studies indicate that institutional transformation encouraged faculty unionization. The increasing size of many institutions sometimes caused informal decision-making by colleagues to be replaced with a more centralized bureaucracy, and the faculty turned to unions as a way to increase their participatory role. Also, as some institutions (most notably "emerging universities," nee teachers' colleges) changed their mission, older faculty members sometimes turned to unions for protection against younger colleagues of superior quality, while the new faculty sometimes used unions as a way to wrest control from administrators. Although, as Garbarino [18, p. 79] notes, the degree of faculty participation in governance is not related to unionization in a simple way, one basic explanation of interest in unionization is a desire to influence governance.[51]

The AAUP, exclusively a professional association a decade ago, has by now been partially transformed into a bargaining association. It will engage in collective bargaining and, if suitably goaded, even strike.[52] Nonetheless, since the transformation the AAUP has been in serious decline (Table 6), and while it has 1365 chapters, only 35 have bargaining rights.[53] The NEA and the AFT are the dominant bargaining organizations in higher education, with 40,000 and 54,000 higher education members, respectively, not all of whom have bargaining rights.[54] Despite its declining fortunes, the AAUP rejected a 1976 proposal from the NEA to form an al-

---

[50]650 GERR Supp. 3 (March 29, 1976).
[51]See Kemerer [24] and 650 GERR Supp.
[52]650 GERR Supp. (March 29, 1976).
[53]*Id.*, at 5.
[54]*Ibid.*

liance and divide functions, with the AAUP concentrating on academic standards and practices.[55]

The importance of public policy in determining the growth of faculty unionism is repeatedly stressed in the literature. For example, the slowdown of organization in 1973–1974 was attributed to the extensive organization of states with enabling legislation (Begin [6]). The 1975 Rodda Act in California spurred an organizing drive in California junior colleges that affected the 1975–1977 results, but the 1977 low level of organizing activity was attributed by Garbarino and Lawler [19] to the saturation of the market for unionization in states with supportive laws. Higher education thus appears to be one portion of the public sector where public policy is a crucial element for organizing success, probably reflecting the ambivalent attitude of most professors toward bargaining.

The prospects for additional gains are somewhat more favorable in higher education than at the secondary-elementary level, because of the relatively smaller proportion of higher education faculty already organized and an unbroken string of membership gains in recent years (Table 7), in contrast to the AFT and NEA membership declines at the precollege level. Nonetheless, significant gains are likely only if public policy is changed in a number of jurisdictions to encourage bargaining by college faculty, and prospects for wholesale enactment of such legislation appear unlikely.

Conclusions and Prognostications

Gossamer Conclusions

This study's conclusions about the extent and determinants of collective bargaining and membership in bargaining organizations are gossamer. The tenuous nature of our understanding is emphasized by reviewing briefly and then synthesizing some of the findings.

The BLS data on membership in bargaining organizations (used in Tables 1, 2, and 6) provide the most useful index of public-sector bargaining developments. The primary advantages of the BLS data are their availability since 1966 for both

---

[55]691 GERR 17 (January 17, 1977).

the federal and the state and local government sectors and their limitation to bargaining organizations as opposed to nonbargaining organizations.[56] The chief rival to the BLS data is the BCDL data (Tables 4 and 5), which can be disaggregated by state and by governmental function. However, the BCDL data are available only since 1972, and only for the state and local government sector, and—of most concern—they encompass some nonbargaining organizations and thus overstate membership in bargaining organizations.

The BLS data demonstrate the tremendous growth of public-sector bargaining organizations, especially in comparison to the private sector. For example, between 1968 and 1976, while bargaining organizations lost 755,000 members in manufacturing and gained 781,000 in the balance of the private sector, membership in the government sector was up 1.996 million (Table 1, panel B).

The reasons for these membership developments are unclear. The literature purporting to explain the developments in the entire economy or the private sector is generally unsatisfactory, although there are a few impressive studies. However, very little of the literature dealing with economy-wide or private-sector developments provides assistance in understanding the sudden surge in public-sector membership since 1960. Nor is the literature that attempts to explain the public-sector developments satisfactory: the recurrent themes are that the recent growth was unexpectedly large and the causes were unusually complex and inscrutable.

The most tantalizing question about the growth of public-sector bargaining is the role played by public policy. My thesis —elaborated at the beginning of this chapter—is that for most public-sector workers, the policy changes of the past 20 years that encouraged bargaining were no more important than several other factors in explaining the workers' decisions to join

----

[56]The BLS data also have the advantage of distinguishing between unions and bargaining associations. That the bargaining-association data date from only 1968 is not a serious problem since the transformation of professional associations into bargaining associations only became significant about then. One limitation of the BLS data is that no estimates are available for representation, as opposed to membership. Some members are not represented, and some represented workers are not members. It is not clear which phenomenon dominates in the public sector since the data presented earlier indicate that federal experience is contrary to state and local experience. Another limitation of the BLS (and other) data is that not all members or represented workers are covered by a written agreement, and the extent of the difference is not entirely clear. See, generally, Burton [11].

bargaining organizations.[57] Only for certain functions, such as higher education, was public policy the dominant influence in the growth of bargaining. This thesis is not without its detractors, who argue that public-policy developments were, in general, a significant cause of the membership growth.[58]

Research and Data Needs

Many of the basic questions about the growth of public-sector bargaining, including the role of public policy, are at best only partially answered by the literature. There is now a need to move beyond analysis by egregious example and casual empiricism if the industrial relations research in this area is to be improved.

A first step is the development of a theoretical model of the determinants of the extent of bargaining and of membership in bargaining organizations, followed by empirical examinations based on the model. The modeling and empirical testing have begun for the private sector and for the entire economy (see Bain and Elshiekh [3] for a survey), but similar studies of the public sector are virtually nonexistent, which is especially distressing in light of the relative abundance of disaggregated data.

This is not the place to develop and test such a model, but several elements of the task are worth mentioning. One is that the model must be specifically adapted to the public sector,

---

[57]While the changes of the last 20 years in the legal environment of the public sector tended to encourage bargaining, throughout the period the private-sector policy was generally more supportive of bargaining. It is even possible that the restructured policy in the public sector helped unions and bargaining associations to attract members. Since, with few exceptions, workers could not legally strike, the potential costs of belonging to an organization were reduced. Needless to say, some organizations in the public sector are every bit as militant as their private-sector counterparts, but many public-sector members, especially at the federal level, do not face the imminent prospect of striking. Further, some public-sector strikes are almost costless to participants, such as teachers' strikes that result in school-year extensions. Had the entire NLRA been applicable to the public sector, membership in bargaining organizations might have grown less rapidly after 1960 because some workers would have been reluctant to accept the risks associated with striking. One implication of this argument is that public-sector bargaining organizations may attract more members if impasses are resolved by fact-finding or arbitration rather than by strikes.

[58]For example, Ronald Donovan (1978: personal correspondence) argues "that the experience in the public sector offers strong evidence for the general proposition that once a substantial proportion of employees in any political jurisdiction . . . organize for collective bargaining under the protection of a collective bargaining statute, all other eligible employees of that same public employer will soon follow suit in order to protect their proportionate share of public expenditures." This interesting hypothesis could be partially tested using BCDL data on state-government employees. I suspect that if defensive organization is important, it is found in all jurisdictions regardless of their public policies.

where the bargaining outcome often is reflected in ordinances, laws, or documents other than written contracts, and where the bargaining process uses influence methods such as lobbying as a partial or total substitute for strikes. The set of explanatory variables for the outcome of bargaining and workers' decisions to join a bargaining organization should include economic factors (e.g., macroeconomic variables such as price changes and microeconomic variables such as a state's tax rate), political factors (e.g., the public's attitude toward bargaining), worker characteristics (e.g., age and job experience), and public policy (e.g., the legality of collective bargaining and strikes).

Although much of the data needed to test such a model are available, several changes in current data-gathering efforts would help. The distinction between bargaining organizations and other organizations needs to be clarified and used; the value of the BCDL data is reduced because of an overinclusive definition. Additional data are needed on workers represented by bargaining organizations and workers covered by agreements; the BLS data are confined to members. Above all, coordination among the data sets is needed. The BLS data on the entire public sector and its major components (Table 2) are not entirely compatible with the CSC data on federal government workers (Table 3) and the BCDL data on state and local government workers (Tables 4 and 5); unfortunately, the degree of incompatibility is unclear (see Burton [11]).

Prognostications

What is likely to happen to the extent of public-sector bargaining in the next several years? Such a prediction would be easier if the modeling and empirical examinations just described had already been performed for the 1960–1978 developments. Nonetheless, the past provides only a murky guide to the future, and at best the predictions for the next decade would be treacherous.

The hazards of prediction are illustrated by the record of Stieber, who predicted [38, p. 212] that the pace of organization in state and local governments would "probably decrease by the mid-1970s as a hard core of states refuses to enact legislation." The data do not provide much support for the thesis at least through 1976 (Table 2). Nor does his prediction (p. 213) seem likely to be fulfilled that, because of increasing support for a federal law, "by the end of the 1970s all state and local government employees probably will be protected in their right to organize and bargain collectively." Stieber could not have been expected to anticipate the legal obstacles to federal action thrown up by the Supreme Court in *National League of Cities* v. *Usery*[59] and the political obstacles thrown up by the New York City financial debacle, which, accurately or not, is associated with public-sector unions.

The failure of earlier pundits and the interposition of the *League of Cities* case did not deter Weber [40, pp. 7–8] from predicting the enactment within five years of federal law with basic standards for state public-sector bargaining laws and "a continued expansion of unionization in the public sector to the point where it becomes preponderant, if not nearly universal."

I probably should leave the predictions to Stieber and Weber and allow them the kudos or reproofs of time. But since my views differ from theirs, at least in some important particulars, I will make a few prognostications. I condition my predictions on the assumption that there will be no major disruptions of society, like a depression.

The prospects for major changes in public policy in the next five years seem limited. There may be some changes at the federal level for federal employees, such as the translation of the current bargaining rights from an executive order to a statute, but federal legislation establishing bargaining rights for state and local employees seems highly unlikely given the prospective constitutional and political limitations. Some states will probably change their laws dealing with public-sector bargaining, but most industrialized states already have relatively favorable legislation and additional converts will come slowly.

Membership in public-sector organizations that engage in collective bargaining grew from 915,000 (or 12.6 percent of employment) in 1956 to 5,853,000 (or 39.2 percent of employment) in 1976 (Table 2). The prospects of continuing this pace of growth (about 13 percent per decade) seem slim without widespread adoption of significantly more favorable legislation (which is unlikely). Some losses in absolute numbers of members seem almost inevitable for elementary and secondary education, given the high percentage of teachers already organized and the impending decline in teaching positions. The nonedu-

---

[59]96 S.Ct. 2465, 426 U.S. 833 (1976).

cation components of the government sector provide more potential for membership gains, but bargaining organizations have
a difficult recruiting task because the benefits from membership
appear to be limited. As discussed in previous sections, public-
sector bargaining organizations do not appear to have made
gains in wages comparable to the union wage gains in the private
sector. The problem of lack of benefits from membership is
particularly acute at the federal level (except for post office
workers) and in states without comprehensive bargaining laws,
where the scope of bargaining issues is constricted compared to
the private sector. Not only do these factors mean that further
membership gains will be difficult, when they are coupled with
the lack of worker commitment required to join a bargaining
organization in some jurisdictions (especially the federal sector), they suggest that for many currently organized workers
both the perceived benefits and perceived costs of membership
are relatively low. In essence, the allegiance to bargaining organizations among public-sector workers may be widespread
but not deep-felt. Because the prospects for changes in public
policy that would allow unions and associations more influence
are not promising, and because the changing attitude by the
public and government officials may result in stiffer resistance
to collective bargaining demands, the benefits to membership
may decline and the costs increase in the next five years.[60] If this
analysis is correct, there is even a remote possibility that mass
defections from public-sector bargaining organizations could
occur: the 19th-century experience of the Knights of Labor indicates that substantial membership losses as well as gains can be
mercurial.

A substantial decline in membership in public-sector bargaining organizations in the next five years seems highly unlikely, as
does a substantial increase in membership "to a point where it
becomes preponderant, if not nearly universal." The most likely
prospect is for a modest deceleration in the growth rate of the
percentage of government employees organized; rather than
growing at a 13-percent per decade rate, the increase will probably average less than 1 percent a year.

---

[60]If in the next few years the public and government officials become increasingly
hostile to all public employees—not just those in bargaining organizations—then the
workers may turn in significant numbers to these organizations for whatever degree of
protection they can provide.

Bibliography

1. Orley Ashenfelter and John H. Pencavel. "American Trade Union Growth, 1900–1960." *Quarterly Journal of Economics* 83 (1968): 434–48.
2. Bill Aussieker and Joseph W. Garbarino. "Measuring Faculty Unionism: Quantity and Quality." *Industrial Relations* 12 (1973): 117–24.
3. George Sayers Bain and Farouk Elsheikh. *Union Growth and the Business Cycle, an Econometric Analysis.* Oxford: Basil Blackwell, 1976.
4. E. Wight Bakke. "Reflections on the Future of Bargaining in the Public Sector." *Monthly Labor Review* 93(7) (1970): 21–25.
5. T. Barrett. "Prospects for Growth and Bargaining in the Public Sector." *Government Employee Relations Report* 534 (1973): F1–F4.
6. James P. Begin. "Faculty Bargaining in 1973: A Loss of Momentum?" *The Journal of the College and University Personnel Association* 25(2) (1974): 74–80.
7. James P. Begin, Theodore Settle, and Paula Alexander. *Academic Bargaining: Origins and Growth.* New Brunswick, N.J.: Institute of Management and Labor Relations, Rutgers University, 1977.
8. Tim Bornstein. "Public Sector Explosion to Continue." *Government Employee Relations Report* 426 (1971): B8–B11.
9. John F. Burton, Jr. "Local Government Bargaining and Management Structure." *Industrial Relations* 11 (1972): 123–40.
10. ———. "Federal or State Responsibility for Workers' Compensation?" In *Proceedings of the 29th Annual Meeting, Industrial Relations Research Association.* Madison, Wis.: IRRA, 1977. Pp. 219–27.
11. ———. *Public Sector Bargaining: A Critical Review of the Data.* Ithaca, N.Y.: Cornell University, 1978. Mimeo.
12. John F. Burton, Jr., and Charles Krider. "The Incidence of Strikes in Public Employment." In *Labor in the Public and Nonprofit Sectors,* ed. Daniel S. Hamermesh. Princeton, N.J.: Princeton University, 1975.
13. Theodore R. Clark, Jr. "The Scope of the Duty to Bargain in Public Employment." In *Labor Relations Law in the Public*

Sector, ed. Andria S. Knapp. Chicago: American Bar Association, 1977.

14. Harry P. Cohany. "The NEA Prepares for the 1970's." *Monthly Labor Review* 93(9) (1970): 30–31.
15. Harry P. Cohany and Lucretia M. Dewey. "Union Membership Among Government Employees." *Monthly Labor Review* 93(7) (1970): 15–20.
16. Ronald C. Ehrenberg and Gerald S. Goldstein. "A Model of Public Sector Wage Determination." *Journal of Urban Economics* 2 (1975): 223–45.
17. Joseph W. Garbarino. "Faculty Unionism in the West." *Industrial Relations* 13 (1974): 1–4.
18. _____. *Faculty Bargaining.* New York: McGraw-Hill Book Co., 1975.
19. Joseph W. Garbarino and John Lawler. "Faculty Union Activity in Higher Education—1977." *Industrial Relations* 17(1) (1978): 117–18.
20. Woodrow Ginsburg. "Review of Literature on Union Growth, Government and Structure—1955–1969." In *A Review of Industrial Relations Research,* vol. I. Madison, Wis.: Industrial Relations Research Association, 1970. Pp. 207–60.
21. Abraham L. Gitlow. "Public Employee Unionism in the United States: Growth and Outlook." *Labor Law Journal* 21 (1970): 766–78.
22. Joseph P. Goldberg. "Public Employee Developments in 1971." *Monthly Labor Review* 95(1) (1972): 56–66.
23. Robert G. Howlett. "The Duty to Bargain in the Federal Government." In *Labor Relations Law in the Public Sector,* ed. Andria S. Knapp. Chicago: American Bar Association, 1977.
24. Frank S. Kemerer and Victor J. Baldridge. *Unions on Campus.* San Francisco: Jossey Bass, Inc., 1975.
25. Leo Kramer. *Labor's Paradox.* New York: John Wiley & Sons, Inc., 1962.
26. Joseph Krislov. "The Independent Public Employee Association: Characteristics and Functions." *Industrial and Labor Relations Review* 15 (1962): 510–20.
27. Jerry Lelchook. *State Civil Service Employee Associations.* U.S. Department of Labor, Labor-Management Services Administration publication. Washington: U.S. Government Printing Office, 1973.
28. David Lewin. "Public Sector Labor Relations: A Review Essay." *Labor History* 18 (1977): 133–44.

29. T. Roger Manley and Charles W. McNichols. "Communications." *Monthly Labor Review* 100(1) (1977): 32–33.
30. William J. Moore. "Factors Affecting Growth in Public and Private Sector Unions." *Journal of Collective Negotiations* 6 (1977): 37–43.
31. William J. Moore and Ray Marshall. "Growth of Teachers Organizations: A Conceptual Framework." *Journal of Collective Negotiations* 2 (1973): 271–97.
32. Michael H. Moskow, J. Joseph Loewenberg, and Edward Clifford Koziara. *Collective Bargaining in Public Employment.* New York: Random House, 1970.
33. Richard R. Nelson and James L. Doster. "City Employee Representation and Bargaining Policies." *Monthly Labor Review* 95(11) (1972): 43–50.
34. Charles R. Perry and Wesley A. Wildman. *The Impact of Negotiations in Public Education: The Evidence from the Schools.* Worthington, Ohio: Charles A. Jones Publishing Co., 1970.
35. Sharon P. Smith. *Equal Pay in the Public Sector: Fact or Fantasy?* Princeton, N.J.: Industrial Relations Section, Princeton University, 1977.
36. Paul D. Staudohar. "An Assessment of Unionization in the Armed Forces." *Journal of Collective Negotiations* 6 (1977): 3–9.
37. Jack Stieber. "Collective Bargaining in the Public Sector." In *Challenges to Collective Bargaining,* ed. Lloyd Ulman. Englewood Cliffs, N.J.: Prentice-Hall, Inc., 1967. Pp. 65–88.
38. _____. *Public Employee Unionism: Structure, Growth, Policy.* Washington: The Brookings Institution, 1973.
39. _____. "The Future of Public Employee Unionism in the United States." *Industrial Relations/Relations Industrielles* 29 (1974): 825–37.
40. Arnold R. Weber. "Prospects for the Future." In *Labor Relations Law in the Public Sector,* ed. Andria S. Knapp. Chicago: American Bar Association, 1977.

Chapter 2

UNIONISM IN THE PUBLIC SECTOR

James L. Stern*

The dramatic increase in public-sector union membership associated with the spread of collective bargaining from the private to the public sector has been cited frequently as one of the more significant, if not the most significant, developments on the labor front in the past 15 years.[1] In this chapter, the characteristics of the major public-sector unions are examined.

At the outset it should be noted that with the exception of the federal sector, public-sector union decision-making is made primarily at the local and state levels. This is contrary to the pattern found in manufacturing, for example, and gives rise to a situation in which the role of the national union president of the public-sector union is relatively less important than that of his private-sector counterpart. Analysis of unions that are active at the municipal and state levels is complicated therefore by virtue of the decentralized decision-making structure and the various patterns of public-sector unionism that have emerged in different cities and different states.

Just the fact that the labor relations legislation may be unique to one group of employees provides sufficient grounds for differences in the way the union conducts itself in a particular locality. Clearly, where unions have not secured legal bargaining rights, they will act somewhat differently than in localities where this goal has been achieved. And the union structure, even its finances, and the role of the union leader will be affected.

Another problem complicating the analysis of public-sector unions is the entrance into this field of what Jack Stieber identified as the "mixed unions"[2]—those primarily private-sector

---

*University of Wisconsin.
[1]A review of the Proceedings of the Industrial Relations Research Association shows that many sessions have been devoted to various aspects of public-sector bargaining.
[2]Jack Stieber, Public Employee Unionism (Washington: The Brookings Institution, 1973).

unions which are now organizing public-sector employees. Several of these unions, such as the Teamsters, the Laborers, and the Service Employees (SEIU), have become important public-sector unions in some localities but represent no public-sector employees in others. The reader is warned therefore that generalizations about public-sector unions are advanced with more than the usual reservations about exceptions to general practices.

The format adopted in this chapter is to examine unions by level of government and governmental structure and function. In the first of the subsequent sections, the postal unions are discussed. This is followed by examinations of the unions covered by the federal executive order, then the unions active in the education field, including higher education, and finally the unions active at the local and state levels. The term *union* is used throughout this chapter to mean employee organization and includes groups which are popularly identified as associations (California State Employees Association), professional societies (AAUP), and fraternal orders (FOP). The concluding section of the chapter is addressed to membership trends of public-sector unions and speculation about their future.

The Postal Unions

The major postal unions, the National Association of Letter Carriers (NALC) and the American Postal Workers Union (APWU), date back to the turn of the century and are among the older American trade unions. The APWU is a 1971 amalgamation of the postal clerks union, three smaller craft unions, and one breakaway industrial union of clerks and carriers. The structure, policies, and problems of these and several smaller unions in the postal service are easier to explain and understand if one first examines the institutional framework within which they pursued their goals. Also, the examination of the institutional framework provides essential background information for understanding the subsequent review of activities of federal-sector unions outside of the postal service.

The Legal Framework for Lobbying and Bargaining

Postal unions are among the most experienced and effective congressional lobbyists. President Theodore Roosevelt attempted to restrict their lobbying efforts by announcing his 1906 "gag" rule forbidding such efforts. It was to no avail, however, as the postal unions obtained passage of the 1912 Lloyd-La Follette bill protecting the rights of federal employees to petition Congress for improvements in their wages and working conditions. It is interesting to note that the 1912 act is still the only congressional legislation protecting the right of non-postal federal employees to engage in efforts to improve their wages and working conditions.

From 1912 to 1961, postal unions, aided in later years by unions representing federal employees in other government departments, lobbied individual congressmen, pressed for favorable appropriations, and supported relevant legislation. Their power under both Democratic and Republican administrations was considerable. For example, one of the few Eisenhower vetoes which was overridden was a postal bill—an action which is generally attributed to the lobbying skill and power of the postal unions.

Despite their success through lobbying, postal union leaders mounted campaigns to replace what they characterized as "collective begging" by collective bargaining. During the 1960 presidential campaign, they were successful in extracting a pledge from John Kennedy that, if elected, he would support bargaining by postal and other federal employees. Lack of congressional support for fulfillment of this commitment led Kennedy to issue Executive Order 10988 in January 1962, establishing a labor-management relations program for federal executive-branch employees.

The initial executive order provided for only a limited scope of bargaining and did not create a central administrative agency, thereby leaving the final determination of such sensitive questions as unit determination and unfair labor practices to each cabinet-level department head. As a first step, however, Executive Order 10988 was regarded by postal unions and other federal employee unions as their "magna carta."

By the end of the decade, dissatisfaction with the framework for bargaining led to the issuance of Executive Order

11491.[3] The new order did not broaden the scope of bargaining, but it did establish a centralized administrative structure. Although it was the political clout of the postal unions which was primarily responsible for the creation of the revised bargaining system and although the new system was seen as a substantial improvement by nonpostal federal unions, it was a case of too little, too late, so far as postal unions were concerned. Led by the industrial union which represented postal workers in New York City, but which had not gained exclusive recognition at the national level under the bargaining structure created under 10988 and 11491, postal employees struck successfully for improved economic benefits and a new bargaining structure similar to the private-sector's.

The 1970 Postal Reorganization Act established the postal corporation and placed its labor relations activities under the private-sector Labor Management Relations Act. For purposes of representation, unfair labor practices, and other such matters, postal unions, like private-sector unions, could turn to the NLRB. Scope of bargaining was broadened greatly to include the wages, hours, and conditions-of-employment concept found in the private sector with specific exemptions for pensions, which were still set by Congress, and for some personnel actions maintained within the Civil Service jurisdiction. Also, compulsory union membership was prohibited and, in place of the right to strike, unions were given the right to take "interest" disputes to arbitration.

Postal Unions and the Old and New Bargaining Structures

Under the format that had been followed under Executive Order 10988, national agreements were negotiated by the Post Office Department with the seven craft unions holding national exclusive representation rights. These unions were (1) the NALC, the AFL-CIO union representing most city letter carriers; (2) the National Association of Post Office and General Services Maintenance Employees, a union of maintenance employees which at that time was an independent

---

[3]Executive Order 11491 was issued in October 1969. It has been clarified and revised slightly by subsequent amendments that are not relevant to this discussion of federal-employee unions. For example, employees of TVA and the State Department have been excluded from the scope of 11491 as amended. Since space limitations prevent a discussion of these unions, there is no need to explore the frameworks governing their labor relations activities.

union; (3) the National Association of Special Delivery Messengers, AFL-CIO; (4) the National Federation of Post Office Motor Vehicle Employees, AFL-CIO; (5) the National Rural Letter Carriers' Association, a union which was then and is still in 1978 an independent union; (6) the United Federation of Postal Clerks, AFL-CIO; and (7) the National Association of Post Office Mail Handlers, Watchmen, Messengers and Group Leaders, AFL-CIO, a craft union which has become the Mail Handlers Division of the Laborers' International Union, AFL-CIO. The two large unions represented letter carriers and clerks, while the other five unions represented the five smaller occupational groups.

Two important postal unions had not gained exclusive national bargaining rights under E.O. 10988, although they had formal recognition at the national level (in effect, consultation rights at that level) and exclusive bargaining rights in many localities. One of these unions was the National Postal Union (NPU), an industrial union with exclusive bargaining rights in New York City, Philadelphia, and St. Paul and a membership of over 80,000 in 1970, making it the third largest postal union. It was composed primarily of workers who had broken away from the clerks union in 1958. The other outside union in much the same position was the National Alliance of Postal and Federal Employees, a union claiming to have about 45,000 members, most of whom were black. The Alliance was the fourth largest postal union, holding exclusive bargaining rights in Washington, D.C., and other cities in the South and formal recognition at the national level.

When Congress passed the 1970 Postal Reorganization Act and restructured the labor relations framework, it gave the NLRB the authority to do away with the concept of minority-union representation, formal recognition, and dual recognition at two levels. This situation stimulated the amalgamation of the three small craft unions with the clerks union and the return to the fold of the breakaway NPU group. In 1971, the United Federation of Postal Clerks, the NPU, and the three small craft unions representing maintenance employees, motor vehicle employees, and special delivery messengers joined together to form the APWU, the largest postal union.

The Alliance lost its local exclusive bargaining rights under the new bargaining structure and its membership declined. It continues to exist primarily as a civil rights, labor, and fraternal organization for black postal workers and was reported to have about 22,000 members in 1976.[4] In an effort to maintain itself, the Alliance was seeking passage of a bill (H.R. 5023) that would permit it to represent its members in grievance proceedings even though it was no longer a recognized union.

Both the APWU and NALC are AFL-CIO unions, and their membership in 1975 was approximately 280,000 and 230,000, respectively. Since they are the major unions representing postal employees, each is discussed separately below. The only non-AFL-CIO union holding national exclusive bargaining rights today is the Rural Letter Carriers' union, with about 20,000 members. Although it cooperates with the AFL-CIO in national negotiations about basic economic matters, it negotiates its own national craft agreement, as does each of the six crafts within the AFL-CIO union structure.

The major concerns of postal unions today are similar to those of private-sector unions, but in addition these unions are faced with some problems unique to their industry as well as some that are faced by other unions representing federal employees. An example of a unique problem is the attempt by postal management to time-study carrier routes and use the results to revise routes. This procedure, known as the "Kokomo Plan" (because it was tried experimentally in Kokomo, Indiana), apparently has been blocked by an arbitration award favorable to the NALC.[5] An example of a concern shared by postal and other unions of federal employees is the attempt to amend the Hatch Act in order to permit greater freedom of political action by both postal and other federal employees.

Attempts to improve job security and to maintain union jurisdiction are illustrative of postal union efforts to solve problems similar to those faced in the private sector. For example, in the 1975 negotiations, the National Rural Letter Carriers' Association (NRLCA) reached an agreement that permitted substitute rural carriers to get vacant rural-carrier positions at the expense of postal employees represented by other unions. Negotiations are conducted both at the "main table" by a council of all seven unions and at seven separate "craft tables" dealing with problems of interest to each craft.

[4]672 GERR A14 (August 30, 1976).
[5]670 GERR A4, E1 (August 16, 1976).

The gain made by the non-AFL-CIO unions, the NRLCA, at its craft table was subsequently challenged through arbitration under the national agreement. The arbitrator ruled in favor of the NRLCA and thereby prevented encroachment of the territory of the independent union by members of the AFL-CIO craft unions.[6] Since postal employment is not increasing and cost problems are raising the threat of actual employment decreases—because of possible changes such as the abolition of Saturday mail delivery—interunion conflict about jurisdiction is likely to continue and to increase. In turn, this adds continuing pressure to consolidate negotiations further and to integrate activities of the different unions, and it increases internal political friction within each union. Some notion of the political stability and problems of postal unions can be gleaned from the brief review of APWU and NALC leadership changes and internal political developments.

The APWU in 1978

When the United Federation of Postal Clerks, the NPU, and the three smaller craft unions amalgamated in 1971 to form the APWU, each union preserved its craft rights by the perpetuation of the two-tier bargaining system and preserved its bureaucratic structure by maintaining the union positions that existed prior to the amalgamation. Although it was recognized that such a condition was necessary at the outset to get agreement on the amalgamation, it had been assumed that a smaller and more efficient top-leadership structure could be created as incumbents retired and the new union acquired a sense of identity.

Six years after merger, however, the structure was even more top heavy than it had been originally. The president of the APWU from its formation in 1971 until his death in 1977, Francis S. Filbey (who had been president of the NFPC prior to the merger), described the 1977, 54-member governing body of the union as unwieldy and overloaded, and said it

> was understandable, as the price of bringing five unions together in 1971, that you would need to retain a cast of characters bigger

---

[6]684 GERR A2 (November 22, 1976).

... than you would find in *War and Peace*, it went without saying that such topheavy totals were a temporary aberration. Everyone supposed that the profile would be slimmed down by attrition ... at least 20 national office holders have retired or died since merger [but] not a single office has been abolished. So much for attrition.[7]

These remarks were made about six months after the 1976 APWU convention delegates had refused to increase the per capita tax until five elected regional co-ordinators were added to the 49-member national executive board which had been created at the time of the merger. Although Filbey argued that regional co-ordinators should be appointed by and should be responsible to nationally elected officers, his views did not prevail. Perhaps, the popularity of direct election is attributable to the idea of giving the rank-and-file leader a greater say in the running of the union, or perhaps it is attributable to the idea of creating positions to which secondary union leaders can aspire. In any event, however, Filbey had continued a campaign of "useful discussion" in 1977 in order to persuade members that the number of paid APWU officials should be reduced from 112 to 63 and that the national executive board should be reduced from 54 to 20 members.

Upon Filbey's death, the national executive board selected Emmet Andrews, its director of industrial relations, to complete his unexpired term of office. There were five candidates for the office and the decision, requiring a two-thirds majority, took five ballots. Andrews, as a new president, faces national negotiations in 1978, a convention at which he will face the problem of streamlining the organization, and a national referendum at which he and others will contest for leadership positions in the APWU.

These immediate problems will place a severe strain on the APWU in the short run, but they are not new problems for Andrews and other top leaders of the APWU. It should be noted that the succession to the presidency of the APWU and its major predecessor union, the NFPC, has been an orderly one under which officials with long service at the local and national levels have taken office following the death of the incumbent. E. C. Hallbeck (long-time president of the old National Federation of Post Office Clerks, which became the UFPC) died at the end of

---

[7]691 GERR 5 (January 17, 1977).

1968 and was succeeded by Filbey, who had been a local union officer, a national vice president, and the national administrative aide before assuming the presidency of the UFPC in 1969. Andrews, in turn, had been a local union officer and a full-time vice president before being elected the director of industrial relations—the position he held at the time he was selected for the presidency.

Quite possibly, this orderly turnover which moves individuals with long years of service into the top spot will continue for some time, but it should be noted that approximately one third of the postal clerks are women and that in many large cities many of the clerks are black. Integration of these groups into the leadership of the union may pose problems in the future. A second and continuing problem faced by the union is whether it should increase its reliance on collective bargaining further or whether it should maintain its strong traditional interest in political action. And finally, there is what may be the most important problem, the reform of union structure, not only within the APWU but also in relationship to the NALC and two remaining small unions—the Mail Handlers and the Alliance. It is conceivable that there will be rapid movement toward one big postal union, but if the experience of the APWU in the past seven years is an indicator of the rate of social change, the emergence of one big postal union will occur only after many more years of discussion and planning.

The Letter Carriers

The NALC is similar in many respects to the old clerks union which now forms the core of the APWU. Leadership in the NALC flowed from Edward Gainor (1915–1941) to William Doherty (1941–1962) to Jerome Keating (1962–1968) to James Rademacher (1968–1976) and to Joseph Vacca (1977–). The usual road to the presidency was from local-union office to national office and eventually to the top spot. Until the 1977 election of Vacca, most elections had not been close, and the heir-apparent assumed office without strong opposition. The 1977 election illustrated, however, the increasing importance of collective bargaining and the spread of a militant caucus from a New York-based group to one with support across the country.

Vincent Sombrotto, president of the large New York City local, had run against Rademacher in 1974 but had been defeated by a large margin. In 1976, however, Sombrotto, running against J. Joseph Vacca, the executive vice president of the NALC and candidate of the outgoing administration, was defeated by only about 5,000 votes out of approximately 120,000 votes cast by 55 percent of the members in a national referendum.[8] The Vacca slate took most of the 27 offices by margins in excess of the margin at the top of the slate, although the Sombrotto slate won two national offices and three national business-agent positions. Sombrotto's campaign relied in part on membership dissatisfaction with the results of the 1975 negotiations and his claim that Vacca had not pressed strongly for improvements in the 1975 agreement.

It is to be expected that the new president will therefore be forced to show his militance in the 1978 negotiations and to remedy the deficiencies in the existing agreement which were referred to in the election debates.[9] The closeness of the last election and the spread of the rank-and-file slate to the Middle West and the Far West will increase Vacca's need to gain a substantial "victory" in the forthcoming negotiations. If Vacca is successful, the question may then be posed whether the NALC is ready to open merger negotiations with the APWU. Clearly, such a development must await the successful completion of the 1978 negotiations, greater internal stability within the NALC, and the streamlining of the APWU.[10]

The NALC differs from the APWU in that only a very small percent of its members are female (about 5 percent as compared to 33 percent of the APWU members).[11] It can be expected, however, in the years to come that both females and blacks will make up a larger proportion of NALC membership than they currently do. This will probably be a slow development because postal employment is not increasing and is not expected to increase substantially in the coming decade.

In both unions, however, the question of the primacy of bargaining over political action will come under constant review.

---

[8] 687 GERR A6–A7 (December 13, 1976).

[9] *Ibid.*

[10] One indication of the internal problems of the APWU and the NALC is the large number of discharge cases taken to arbitration. It is estimated by one arbitrator that postal unions lose 90 percent of these cases and that many of the cases are processed to arbitration without regard to their merits.

[11] Virginia A. Bergquist, *Women's Participation in Labor Organizations*, 97 Monthly Lab. Rev. 3 (October 1974).

Statistically, there is little doubt that the postal workers have done better than workers covered under the federal executive order during the years that postal workers have been separated from federal workers still covered by the order.[12] It seems more likely, therefore, that in both unions the forces pointing to the successes under the present system will prevail and that despite the importance of political action, emphasis will continue to be placed on achieving goals across the bargaining table rather than through congressional action. It is possible, however, that cost-cutting programs proposed by the management of the independent postal agency will be resisted by the unions through political action rather than by actions across the bargaining table. Postal unions may find it easier to obtain congressional support for such items as the continuation of Saturday mail delivery than to achieve such goals through bargaining.

The Federal Executive-Branch Unions

Without the postal unions, it is doubtful whether Presidents Kennedy and Nixon would have issued the famous executive orders creating and revising a labor-management framework for federal executive-branch employees. The slowness of the unions in this sector to take advantage of their opportunities during the 16 years since the first executive order reflects primarily the poor position from which these unions started. In 1962, unions of federal employees—with the exceptions of the long-established International Association of Machinists (IAM) and AFL-CIO Metal Trade's Council (MTC) units in shipyards and other industrial-type establishments—were underfinanced, understaffed, and relatively inactive. For the most part they were loosely tied together locals in different federal agencies which supported a small national office in Washington to pursue their goals through the traditional political paths.

The major unions in the federal service and their approximate estimated membership as of 1976 are: American Federation of Government Employees (AFGE), AFL-CIO (275,000 members); National Federation of Federal Employees (NFFE), indepen-

---

[12]See Chapter 4 in this volume by Daniel J. B. Mitchell.

dent (70,000 members); and National Treasury Employees Union (NTEU), independent (70,000 members).[13] Each of the unions is discussed separately in this section of the chapter.[14] Analysis of the annual report of the Civil Service Commission shows that these three unions represent approximately 75 percent of the federal employees covered by labor agreements. On the assumption that the ratio of the number of members to number of employees covered by agreements held by the three is a reasonable proxy for the relationship of membership to agreement-coverage among all federal unions, the 415,000 estimated membership of the three unions generates an estimate of 553,000 union members covered by the executive order.

This estimate of approximately 550,000 members is corroborated by a Civil Service Commission statistic showing that union dues were being withheld from 550,000 employees covered by the executive order.[15] It should be emphasized, as is explained subsequently, that membership statistics and representation data in the federal sector differ dramatically from those found in the private sector. Unions in the federal sector have won elections entitling them to represent 1.2 million employees, about 58 percent of those covered by the executive order. Less than half of these employees, however, are union members.

In addition to the three unions representing the largest number of federal employees, another 80 unions hold recognition rights, including the independent National Association of Government Employees (NAGE) which is strong in New England and which in recent years has organized workers in local government and in private firms doing government business.[16] In addition, there are the long-established IAM and the MTC, repre-

---

[13]Estimates of union membership used in this chapter were prepared by graduate research assistants Judith Flora and Dianne Kutell on the basis of union, BLS, and Civil Service Commission documents and phone conversations with representatives of these organizations.

[14]Seminar papers by George Heatley about the AFGE and by Dianne Kutell about the NFFE and NTEU were drawn upon heavily by the author in the preparation of the sections about these unions.

[15]Anthony F. Ingrassia, *Status Report on Federal Labor-Management Relations,* Civil Service J. 41 (July-September 1977).

[16]For example, NAGE recently won an election to represent 3200 professional Massachusetts state employees. It has a police affiliate, the International Brotherhood of Police Officers, representing local and state police; and, earlier in 1977, it merged with the independent Massachusetts State Employee Association and is challenging AFL-CIO unions in Massachusetts for the right to represent all groups of state employees. 728 GERR 16 (October 13, 1977).

senting approximately 30,000 and 60,000 federal employees, respectively—primarily wage-board employees in shipyards and other industrial-type situations.

The American Federation of Government Employees (AFGE, AFL-CIO)

AFGE was founded in 1932 by the AFL-CIO after the existing AFL-CIO union for federal employees (NFFE) withdrew from the AFL because of jurisdictional disputes and policy differences with AFL unions representing blue-collar craft workers. The union started with a membership of less than a thousand members in 34 locals, mainly located in the Washington, D.C., area.[17] Over the next 30 years it increased its membership to about 80,000 and, in the first six years of the executive order, experienced its most rapid growth to over 300,000 members.[18] Since that date, although it has continued to increase the number of employees it represents, its membership has declined slightly and was reported to be about 260,000 in 1976.[19]

The "free rider" problem of AFGE and other federal unions seems to be much greater than the problem faced by private-sector unions and unions of municipal employees. To some extent, of course, the federal executive order prohibition on compulsory payment of union dues could be cited as the obvious cause of the problem. Employees may vote for union representation and then be unwilling to pay dues voluntarily. But this explanation is not sufficient to explain the variations in the gap between membership and representation among the different unions which operate under a legal framework prohibiting compulsory payment of dues or service fees. Membership in the postal unions is probably as close to the number of employees represented as is found in private-sector union-shop situations despite the legal prohibition against compulsory union membership.

A second factor which may shed further light on this question is the relatively low number of employees who bother to vote in union representation elections. From 1971 to 1975, 57 percent

[17]Jack and Lorna Nevin, The Story of the American Federation of Government Employees (Washington: AFGE, 1976), 13.
[18]Report of the National Office, American Federation of Government Employees, to the 25th Biennial Convention, September 20–24, 1976, Las Vegas, Nevada, 4.
[19]Ibid.

of eligible voters participated in elections under the executive order as compared to 88 percent of the eligibles in NLRB private-sector elections and a similar figure for postal system elections.[20] It seems quite possible that the membership figures of many federal unions reflect the number of employees who voted for the union in the representation election, and the "gap" between membership and representation consists of those employees who did not vote and those who voted against the union.

Although the elimination of the prohibition against agency shops may be a necessary step if membership figures are to approach representation figures, it should be kept in mind that the possibility of compulsory payment of union dues or a service fee may tend to bring out many voters who will vote against the union in order to avoid the possibility of being obliged to pay dues in the future. AFGE might find it more difficult to win representation elections in such a situation. In any event, this large gap between membership and representation figures is an unusual aspect of industrial relations in the federal sector.

Until the mid-1970s, AFGE's internal political struggles were relatively mild. John Griner was president of AFGE from 1962 until 1972, when he resigned because of poor health. His successor, Clyde Webber, who had been the executive vice president since 1966, died in 1976. The new officers, President Kenneth Blaylock and Executive Vice President Joseph Gleason, are much younger than their predecessors and are expected to lead AFGE into a more militant posture than it has traditionally maintained.

Blaylock, who was 41 years old when he became president, is from Alabama and rose through various offices to that of national vice president from the southeast region of AFGE in 1972.[21] Contrary to the geographical dispersion pattern of members in traditional private-sector unions, AFGE's five-state southeast region contains more members than any other district —reflecting the concentration in the domain of powerful southern legislators of defense agency units employing large numbers of civilian workers.

Although the changing of top leadership brings to power

---

[20] Ingrassia, *supra* note 15, at 40.

[21] 677 GERR A4–A11 (October 4, 1976) reports on the 1976 AFGE convention. It is the source for the information presented about the AFGE in the following few paragraphs.

individuals who have announced that the business-as-usual policies of AFGE which used to prevail will now be ended, it is not
clear just what new policies will be adopted. For the most part,
the change at this point seems symbolic. Blaylock made an im-
passioned extemporaneous speech that swayed the delegates
sufficiently to obtain passage of a resolution favoring the extension of AFGE jurisdiction to include military personnel and
private-sector military contractors. An overwhelmingly adverse
referendum vote and hostile congressional reaction to unionization of the military, however, has forestalled AFGE action on
this front.[22]

Organization of private-sector contractors of the federal government and organization of overseas federal employees is getting under way. AFGE won its first NLRB election covering
custodial employees of a private contractor at a Virginia weapons center. Also, AFGE and the American Federation of Teachers (AFT) signed a pact permitting overseas organizers of each
union to sign up members for the other.[23]

Two other 1976 AFGE convention actions provide further
indications of the ways in which this union may be changing.
AFGE became the first nonpostal federal employee union to
establish a strike fund when it agreed to put 5 cents of a 50-cent
increase in monthly per capita into a strike fund. Although the
amount is small, the action illustrates the way in which AFGE
ideology is changing. On the question of creating the post of
national vice president (NVP) for women's affairs, the delegates
followed Blaylock's lead and rescinded the 1974 convention
action requiring delegates at the 1976 convention to fill such a
position.

Abolition of the position reflects a victory for those delegates
who argued that women should gain NVP positions on their own
and that a special NVP position would limit rather than improve
the opportunities for women. Allied to that argument was the
traditional claim that the creation of a spot for "women" would
then have to be followed by the creation of other special positions for blacks and other groups.

Women and blacks have held national offices and are dominant in many locals. Blaylock's opposition for president, Royal

---

[22]725 GERR 7–8 (September 12, 1977).
[23]*Ibid.*

L. Sims, is a black long-time leader of the AFGE Veterans Administration Center in Philadelphia, who became the first black
NVP in 1968. Sims led Blaylock in the presidential primary,
101,707 votes to 94,896 votes but lost in the runoff by about
16,000 votes when the eliminated candidates threw their support to Blaylock.

The key question to be answered by the more militant-sound-
ing AFGE leadership is whether it can persuade the more than
300,000 nonmembers which it presently represents to join the
union. Presumably, AFGE will pursue this goal politically in
order to remove the prohibition against union-security provisions and also will intensify its organizational efforts. Neither of
these goals is easily attainable in the short run. Federal employee unions seem to be enjoying less public support in 1977
than they did 10 years ago, and it is quite possible that during
this decade neither Congress nor the nonmembers will respond
favorably to AFGE efforts.

The National Federation of Federal Employees (NFFE, Independent)

NFFE started out in 1917 as the AFL-CIO union of federal-
government employees and has since gone through several significant changes in character. As noted previously, NFFE left the
AFL-CIO in 1931 because of jurisdictional and policy differences with the craft unions. NFFE supported the adoption of the
general-service schedule and a civil-service-type compensation
plan, while the crafts adhered to the wage-board approach and
the tying of individual craft rates to the prevailing private-sector
union rate for that craft.[24] When NFFE withdrew from the AFL-
CIO, it reportedly had almost 50,000 members. In the next 30
years, however, membership declined as AFGE made inroads in
this field.

When Executive Order 10988 was published in 1962, NFFE
condemned it and brought an unsuccessful court suit challenging the constitutionality of the President's action. Only after a
two-year losing battle accompanied by a further decline in membership did NFFE reverse its position. The reversal was brought
about by the newly elected NFFE president, Nathan T. Wolkomir, who defeated the incumbent who had opposed the execu-

---

[24]Murray Nesbitt, Labor Relations in the Federal Government Service (Washington:
The Bureau of National Affairs, Inc., 1976).

tive order.[25] Under Wolkomir's leadership, NFFE rebuilt its membership to its present level and increased the number of employees it represents from about 32,000 in 1967 to 133,000 in 1976. After 12 years in office, Wolkomir retired in 1976 and was succeeded by James M. Pierce, Jr. Pierce, who had been the union's education and training director, was elected by an overwhelming margin.[26]

NFFE is usually thought of as a rather conservative union—its initial opposition to Executive Order 10988 is an example of this trait. But just as it adjusted its course of action when opposition to 10988 proved fruitless, so at its 1976 convention it took actions that hinted of further change away from its traditional conservatism. For example, it eliminated the no-strike pledge which had been in its constitution since 1917. Also, it raised its per capita tax from $3 to $4 per month in order to obtain improved service from the national office. In the past, NFFE locals have negotiated their contracts with minimal service from the national office. Local autonomy has been one of the virtues to which NFFE representatives traditionally have pointed when competing with AFGE and other federal employee unions. It appears that NFFE may be changing its position on this question of local autonomy, probably because of the 1976 Executive Order 11838 amending Executive Order 11491 in order to facilitate consolidation of bargaining units.

Consolidation of bargaining units raises the question of NFFE cooperation with AFGE. Until 1976, Wolkomir had warned against joint action because of his fear that the majority union, AFGE, would swallow up its smaller rival, NFFE. Under its new president, NFFE may reconsider its position because of the problem of losing some power when negotiations move from the local level to the agency level. A speaker at the 1976 NFFE convention pointed out that AFGE, which represents 30,000 of the 37,000 Defense Supply Agency employees, may achieve de facto national bargaining rights for that agency, and NFFE locals will have no choice but to join with AFGE locals in joint-council-type bargaining if they are to have any influence on agency policy.[27]

Although there are no overt signs that NFFE is contemplating

---

[25] 54 GERR A7 (September 21, 1964).
[26] 676 GERR A1–A4 (September 27, 1976).
[27] 686 GERR A9–A10 (December 6, 1976).

merger with AFGE, the long-run possibility of such a move should not be ruled out. Philosophical differences between the two organizations have lessened and the tendency of government management to deal uniformly with both AFGE and NFFE across the bargaining table has tended to leave both unions with the same problems. The pressures arising from bargaining are likely to provide a strong impetus for joint action, and if joint action is successful, it may in turn give rise to considerations of merger on efficiency grounds.

The National Treasury Employees Union (NTEU, Independent)

The final federal employee union to be discussed here is NTEU, an unusual union started by the professionals in the Internal Revenue Service who have extended its occupational jurisdiction to cover clerical employees, and its agency jurisdiction to cover all of the Treasury Department and also employees of other agencies.

The predecessor organization to NTEU, the National Association of Collectors of Internal Revenue, was formed in 1938 by field employees in that agency who were seeking civil service status.[28] In the 1950s, as the Internal Revenue Service was restructured, the organization expanded its jurisdiction to cover all IRS employees and changed its name to the National Association of Internal Revenue Employees (NAIRE). In 1973 the present organization changed its name again to its present one, NTEU, in recognition of its further expansion within the Treasury Department. In 1976, NTEU represented about 90,000 employees, of whom about 60 percent are female and 70 percent are dues-paying members.[29]

The NTEU president is Vincent Connery, currently serving his third four-year term. In his last election, in 1975, Connery had only token opposition in contrast to the 1971 election when organized opposition accused him of being a dictator. The charge of dictatorial tactics reflects Connery's successful efforts to centralize authority and to hire professional staff members responsible to him. In contrast to NFFE membership, NTEU

---

[28] The NTEU Story (Washington: National Treasury Employees Union, undated).
[29] Information obtained by Dianne Kutell in an interview with Jerry Klepner, NTEU Director of Communications, April 9, 1977.

membership is concentrated in the northeastern section of the country and consists primarily of employees of one federal department. Internally, its major problem in the past ten years has been its conversion from a group of middle-level professionals to an agency-wide, industrial-type union.

As of 1977, NTEU seems to have resolved the problems which occupied much of its efforts in the past and is contemplating further expansion. In 1976, NTEU dislodged AFGE as the bargaining representative for most Customs Service employees, a move which was facilitated by the decision of the old National Customs Service Association to merge itself into NTEU.[30] At its 1977 convention, NTEU amended its constitution in order to permit it to accept any federal government employee as a member. It was reported that NTEU already represents all employees of the newly created Federal Energy Administration (these employees were in the Treasury Department prior to the establishment of the new cabinet-level department) and was considering plans to organize employees of the Immigration and Naturalization Service of the Justice Department.[31]

On the collective bargaining front, NTEU has been successful in consolidating local agreements into agency-wide agreements and has gained national recognition rights for all IRS employees. Factors such as its relatively militant membership, centralized authority, aggressive leadership, and successful efforts to move bargaining up from the local level to the agency-head level suggest that NTEU may continue to grow and will become a more important federal union in the future.

Unions in Education

The dramatic shift in image from the milquetoast-like teacher to the militant unionist which has accompanied the adoption of collective bargaining procedures by teachers at all levels of instruction is one of the well-publicized developments in public-sector labor relations. The three major unions in the field and their estimated membership are: the National Education Association (NEA, independent, membership about 1.7 million in 1977); American Federation of Teachers (AFT, AFL-CIO, mem-

[30]681 GERR A17 (November 1, 1976).
[31]722 GERR 3 (August 22, 1977).

bership about 450,000); and American Association of University Professors (AAUP, independent, membership about 60,000 active nonstudent members).[32]

In contrast to the federal sector, membership exceeds the extent of collective bargaining coverage. Most AAUP chapters do not engage in collective bargaining. Many NEA members are in locals in southern states where bargaining does not take place. And, because of the rivalry between the NEA and AFT in New York State in 1977, some teachers may be paying a service fee to one organization while maintaining membership in the other.

In education, as in other parts of local government, the national union usually is not involved in the collective bargaining process. The key decision-makers are either local union officers or officials of district councils, UniServe districts, or state councils. For this reason, national office-holders and national policy are less important in these organizations than in industrial unions in the private sector.

The National Education Association

The predecessor organization to the present-day NEA was founded in Philadelphia in 1875 by educational administrators and college professors. For most of its long existence, it has functioned as a professional organization promoting the cause of public education and the improvement of teaching. In the 15 years since1962 when the NEA was defeated by the AFT in the battle to represent New York City school teachers, however, the organization has undergone a sharp metamorphosis. Today in many sections of the country it is indistinguishable from the AFT in so far as its bargaining stance is concerned. In several respects, however, it still differs from the AFT.

First, as a matter of ideology the NEA has maintained that affiliation with the AFL-CIO is not desirable. Second, in states where bargaining is not well rooted, school administrators are influential in the affairs of the organization. Third, in part because of membership losses to the AFT in major cities in the Northeastern, Middle Atlantic, and North Central States, more

---

[32]Seminar papers by Sam Wheeler, John Daresh, and Glenn Neiner about the NEA, AFT, and AAUP, respectively, were relied upon heavily in the preparation of the sections of this chapter about those organizations.

conservative positions on policies are adopted than otherwise
would be the case.

For example, the largest state delegation at the 1977 NEA
convention was from Texas and this group and others from the
South had sufficient votes to defeat an amendment to the constitution which would have disqualified supervisors and administrators from active membership in the organization. This group
also defeated the proposal recommended by the NEA president
and board of directors to give paraprofessionals and teacher
aides full NEA membership rights. Both of these amendments
were favored by most of the classroom teachers in states in
which the locals engage in collective bargaining.[33]

The current president of the NEA, John Ryor, was reelected
to office by acclamation. He is the first person to be eligible for
reelection under the constitutional amendment that became
effective at the previous convention. The chief administrative
officer of NEA, however, is the executive director, Terry Herndon, although the constitutional amendment permitting the reelection of the president gives greater power to that office.
Under the leadership of Herndon and Ryor, the NEA has
launched organizational drives to represent teachers in New
York State and California. In addition, the NEA delegates, by a
roll-call vote of 3,357 to 1,969, voted to continue their financial
support of the collective bargaining program at a level equal at
least to the percent provided for in the 1977–1978 budget (20.8
percent, $10.1 million out of a total budget of $48.5 million).[34]

Key officials of the NEA are appointed to office rather than
elected directly by the rank and file or convention delegates. At
the national level, the key position is that of executive director.
It is filled by someone hired by the national board of directors
—a group of about 125 people elected by the state affiliates. The
board of directors meets quarterly and is subordinate only to the
biennial convention, called the representative assembly by the
NEA. The executive director is given guidance on the running
of the NEA by a 12-member committee, consisting of three
national officers and nine board members at large—all 12 of
whom are elected at the representative assembly and who serve
also on the board of directors.

[33]716 GERR 15–17 (July 11, 1977) reports on the activities of the 1977 convention
and provides a summary of current trends in the organization.
[34]Id., at 17.

Similarly, at the state level, state executive directors are appointed by state officers and boards of directors who in turn have been elected by delegates to state conventions. National staff members and state staff members in states without bargaining laws are concerned with the usual broad range of activities, other than bargaining, carried on by most unions—political and legislative activity, organizing, legal actions, education, research, affirmative action, and special-projects and crisis-related functions. In states where bargaining has statutory protection and is widespread, the state office may help local unions and UniServe districts, particularly in strike situations.

The UniServe district is a structural unit of the organization created in order to administer bargaining activities. Typically, there is a local union for each school district and each local union has a contract which it has negotiated with the school board. But most districts, except the largest ones with a thousand or more teachers, cannot pay the salaries of full-time negotiators—nor is there a need for a full-time staff representative for each small unit. By persuading independent local unions in the same general geographic area to combine forces in maintaining a UniServe office and staff, the NEA has created the mechanism for providing staff help in contract negotiation and administration.

The NEA is attempting to provide one UniServe staff representative for each 1,000 teachers. The staff-representative subsidy provided by the national and state organizations is sufficient to induce most small locals to join their UniServe district. The convention resolution overwhelmingly endorsing the UniServe-district concept and adequate funds to maintain it is an indication of the extent of support within the NEA nationally for an active bargaining program. Although the negotiators and state directors are appointed by elected officials of the organization, the usual path to these key offices is through the elected hierarchy.

The American Federation of Teachers (AFT, AFL-CIO)

The American Federation of Teachers was formed in 1916 by about two dozen teachers' groups across the country with a total membership of approximately 3,000 members. The Chicago Federation of Teachers, which had existed since the turn of the century and which had joined the AFL in 1913, was the key group in early AFT activities. Its longtime leader, Carl Megel, was president of the AFT from 1952 to 1964. In the 1960s when the New York City local of the AFT, the United Federation of Teachers (UFT), gained bargaining rights for New York City teachers after defeating the NEA affiliate in an election, the balance of power shifted from Chicago to New York, and Charles Cogen, past president of the New York group, became the AFT president. In 1974, Albert Shanker, who was then and who continues to be the president of the UFT and an AFL-CIO vice president, became president of the AFT. His decision to retain the presidency of the New York City local reflects the fact that the important bargaining decisions vitally affecting the life of the union are made at the local level.

The 450,000-member AFT is primarily the union of teachers in major cities and holds bargaining rights in New York, Chicago, Philadelphia, Detroit, Boston, Pittsburgh, Cleveland, Minneapolis, Denver, and Baltimore. Leaders of these locals serve as unpaid national officers and guide AFT activities between conventions. The only full-time national officer paid by national funds is the secretary-treasurer who directs the daily activities of the AFT. The president, Albert Shanker, and the 30 vice presidents who comprise the national executive board receive expenses but no salaries from the AFT. As local officials, however, these national AFT officers receive salaries from their locals and devote most of their time to local union activities. The AFT structure, like the NEA structure, reflects the importance of bargaining decisions made at the local level.

The AFT has approximately 1,900 local unions. The national office supplies the same wide range of nonbargaining services to its units as does the NEA. The national office also supplies the organizers and conducts the campaigns to persuade teachers to join the AFT instead of the NEA. In states that have AFT locals, the AFT maintains a state organization that handles legislative matters, participates in organizational drives, and helps local unions handle bargaining problems. In some areas, locals have banded together to form area councils. Since AFT strength is in its big-city locals, however, the elected officials and staff of these locals provide the essential services to most AFT members.

At its 1977 convention, the AFT, like the NEA, faced the question of organizing groups other than teachers. But unlike the NEA, which declined to give paraprofessionals full rights, the AFT passed a convention amendment permitting it to organize workers outside of schools and educational institutions. AFT already represents nonteacher groups in the field of education such as bus drivers and school cafeteria workers and now may attempt to organize such groups as civil service employees, library workers, lawyers, and employees in the health care field.[35]

The AFT maintains that it favors merger with the NEA, but the NEA continues to reject this idea although there has been cooperation and in some instances mergers of local AFT and NEA groups.[36] For example, the United Teachers, Los Angeles, which represents teachers in the Los Angeles school district, permits its members to maintain their membership in either the local AFT or NEA affiliate. Active competition for bargaining rights, however, continues to be the prime focus of each union.

In 1977, each group reported many successes and glossed over defeats by the other organization. It appears, for example, that the NEA gained bargaining rights for most California K-12 districts and won more units in the field of higher education, although the AFT captured the large Los Angeles community-college system. In New York State, where the statewide merged AFT-NEA affiliate had broken its NEA affiliation, the NEA was successful in recapturing only about 10 percent of the teachers while the AFT maintained bargaining rights for about 80 percent of them.[37] The AFT reported a big win in Ohio when the Cincinnati school teachers, who had been represented by the NEA, voted to join the AFT. Also, it won bargaining rights for a five-campus Illinois state college system. The AFT announced also that it will expand its southern organizing drive and that a prime target will be the 160,000 Texas school teachers, many of whom are NEA members at present.[38]

Although circumstances could change dramatically in the coming year or two, it seems more likely that the competition between the NEA and the AFT will continue in much the same vein as the present. The AFT will continue its attempts to ex-

---

[35]723 GERR 18 (August 29, 1977).

[36]Discussions about the prospect of merger have been conducted annually for the past three years by AFT and NEA leaders on National Public Radio debates moderated by John Merrow. A summary of the September 12, 1977, debate between Herndon and Shanker can be found in 727 GERR 18–20 (September 26, 1977).

[37]*Ibid.*

[38]723 GERR 17–22 (August 29, 1977) summarizes 1977 convention activities. Excerpts of AFT-officer convention reports are in the same issue, at 35–39.

pand beyond the big cities where it is presently strong, and the
NEA will attempt to strengthen its bargaining activities in areas
where bargaining previously has not been stressed. An important tool that the NEA is attempting to use more widely is coordinated bargaining. UniServe districts permit the NEA to organize its side of the table for multidistrict bargaining, but the
spread of this technique requires that the school boards on the
other side of the table agree to try this approach. At present,
management cooperation in such matters as exchange of information is more the order of the day than joint bargaining.

The American Association of University Professors (AAUP)

The attempts by the NEA and the AFT to extend their organizing efforts to the field of higher education have led the
AAUP to reconsider its traditional roles in the field of academic freedom, protection of individual rights, and promotion
of higher education, and to add collective bargaining as a legitimate means of improving the status of the profession. In 1966
the AAUP adopted a policy stating that it "should oppose the
extension of the principle of exclusive representation to faculty members in institutions of higher education. . . ."[39] In
1969 it reaffirmed its support of faculty governance but
"recognize[d] the significant role which collective bargaining
may play in bringing agreement between faculty and administration on economic and academic issues."[40] In 1972 the
AAUP abandoned its opposition to exclusive representation
and stated: "The AAUP will pursue collective bargaining, as a
major additional way of realizing the Association's goals in
higher education, and will allocate such resources and staff as
are necessary for a vigorous selective development of this activity beyond present levels."[41]

It is clear that the AAUP changed its policy because of the
pressure from local chapters on campuses where NEA or AFT
affiliates were likely to become sole representatives of the faculty
if the AAUP did not attempt to become the bargaining agent. At
the national level, AAUP created a department with a small staff

[39]AAUP Bulletin (Summer 1966), 229.
[40]AAUP Bulletin (Winter 1969), 490.
[41]AAUP Bulletin (Spring 1972). Pages 46–61 of this issue contain a summary of the
development of the positions on bargaining taken by the AAUP leadership and the
reasons for and against the change.

to provide assistance to locals that participated in representation elections and contract negotiations. For the most part, however, the local union had to carry out its bargaining function without the personal participation of the small national staff. Neither the dues level nor the organizational structure of the AAUP was designed with collective bargaining in mind, and a restructuring may be necessary if the AAUP is to be a vital force in this field.

Policy direction of the AAUP between conventions is determined by a 40-person council including top officers and three persons from each of the ten geographical districts into which the country is divided. Council members are not paid a salary by the AAUP, and they continue in their roles as faculty members. Day-to-day activities of the association are conducted by the full-time general secretary and his staff. Average dues of about $3 a month are paid to the national office; local and area groups are permitted to charge small additional amounts to cover their activities. In 1976, because of the needs of locals that had become bargaining representatives, the AAUP created the Collective Bargaining Congress, consisting of delegates from locals that bargain. These delegates elect a chairman who serves on the executive council. As of 1976, the congress included representatives from 44 locals and paid additional dues to the congress of 50 cents per member per annum.

The AAUP, which was formed in 1916 with less than a thousand members, had grown by 1970 to a professional organization with just under 80,000 active members. In the following years, however, it suffered a decline in membership and had about 60,000 active members in 1977. Of this number, about 15,000 are in the 44 bargaining units represented by the AAUP alone or by the AAUP jointly with either the NEA or the AFT. Most AAUP members who bargain are located in four-year colleges, while NEA and AFT are stronger in the two-year colleges. Since less than one fourth of the faculty members in the country are in collective bargaining units, it is anticipated that the rivalry between AAUP and the NEA and AFT will continue unabated. In the annual report on the situation, Joseph Garbarino notes that further expansion of bargaining among faculty groups is dependent primarily upon the passage of enabling legislation in states where at present faculty do not have statutory bargaining rights.[42] At the present stage of development, it appears that the AAUP is regarded more favorably than the NEA and AFT by the faculty at "prestige" universities, but on the other campuses the reverse is true.[43]

Unionism in Municipal and State Governments

Although the American Federation of State, County, and Municipal Employees (AFSCME), AFL-CIO, is the dominant union of local and state government employees outside of education, many other organizations represent sizable numbers of public employees. In many states there are heated organizational battles between different AFL-CIO unions. The struggle in Florida between AFSCME and the Laborers' International Union (LIU) and the argument of the AFT and AFSCME about jurisdiction over New York City school board employees other than teachers are illustrative of such conflicts.[44] In Massachusetts, AFSCME is allied with the Service Employees International Union (SEIU) in a contest against the State Employees Association which has affiliated with NAGE.[45] AFSCME and state employee associations (SEAs), most of which belong to the Assembly of Governmental Employees (AGE), compete strenuously for representation rights for state employees in various states. And, in some instances, public employees have turned to the International Brotherhood of Teamsters (IBT) for representation.

In the health care field, the American Nurses Association (ANA), like professional associations in education, has been drawn into the collective bargaining arena in order to maintain its representation function. The ANA bargains for private-sector nurses covered by the National Labor Relations Act as well as nurses employed by city, county, and state governments. In recent years, some groups of salaried doctors in both the private and public sectors have sought to bargain with their employers. Competition to represent the nonprofessional employees of hospitals and nursing homes in both the private and public sectors is increased by the efforts of the New York City-based

[42]Mimeographed release by Joseph Garbarino and John Lawler, *Faculty Union Activity in Higher Education—1977,* January 1978.
[43]Bill Aussieker and J. W. Garbarino, *Measuring Faculty Unionism: Quantity and Quality,* 12 Ind. Rels. 117 (May 1973).
[44]686 GERR B12 (December 6, 1976).
[45]635 GERR B17 (December 8, 1975).

hospital workers Local 1199 of the Retail, Wholesale and Department Store Union (RWDSU), AFL-CIO, which competes with AFSCME, SEIU, and LIU for bargaining rights.

In the protective-services field, it is clear that the International Association of Fire Fighters (IAFF), AFL-CIO, has little competition for the right to represent fire fighters, in contrast to the situation among police where several organizations are active.

The largest police group is the International Conference of Police Associations (ICPA), a loosely tied together confederation of individual, local, independent, police organizations. The next largest is the Fraternal Order of Police (FOP), a more cohesive group with its membership concentrated in Pennsylvania. In addition, AFSCME represents police in some cities, and the New England-based International Brotherhood of Police Officers (IBPO) division of NAGE claims to represent a substantial number of police officers.[46] Also, the SEIU has a small police union, the National Union of Police Officers (NUPO), whose strength is mainly in the Far West.[47]

Table 1 shows the estimated number of public-sector members of the more important unions mentioned in this section of the chapter, along with estimates of the size they will reach by 1985. It should be stressed that the estimates, although based on published data and information provided in telephone conversations with representatives of the unions and with Bureau of Labor Statistics personnel who deal with these statistics, should be regarded as very tentative approximations of membership statistics and trends. These membership statistics are included primarily to give the reader some idea of relative size and possible growth trends.

National membership figures can be misleading in specific situations because some unions tend to be strong in one region and weak in others. For example, SEIU has considerable strength in the California public sector and almost none in Wisconsin. Another factor making it more difficult to analyze public-sector unions is the degree to which bargaining is local in character. Local unions and district councils are relatively autonomous groups in so far as bargaining strategy is concerned, and may be going in many different directions. One unit

---

[46]Department of Labor news release, 77–701, August 15, 1977, states that the IBPO has more than 45,000 members.

[47]Hervey A. Juris and Peter Feuille, Police Unionism (Lexington, Mass.: D.C. Heath and Co., 1973), 28–29.

Table 1
Public-Sector Union Membership of Selected Unions[a]

	1975	Estimated Growth (%)	1985
Public safety			
International Association of Fire Fighters	160,000	20	192,000
International Conference of Police Associations	140,000	20	168,000
Fraternal Order of Police	115,000	20	138,000
State and local government			
American Nurses Association	50,000	20	60,000
American Federation of State, County, and Municipal Employees[b]	750,000	20	900,000
Service Employees International Union	180,000	30	234,000
Teamsters	100,000	30	130,000
Laborers	80,000	20	96,000
Assembly of Government Employees	600,000	10	660,000

[a] Prepared by Judith Flora and Diane Kutell, Research Assistants, University of Wisconsin, 1977–1978.

[b] Does not take into account the affiliation of the quarter-million member New York State Civil Service Employees Association with AFSCME and therefore understates AFSCME membership by that amount.

may be militant and favor striking, while another may prefer arbitration.

The role of AGE and its SEAs which represent state employees in 34 states and local employees in 17 states is an interesting one.[48] These associations have maintained themselves during the past decade when public-sector unions were expanding and, in states which have passed comprehensive bargaining legislation, have competed for bargaining rights. The conflict among these public employee organizations including the SEAs extends to classified professional employees at educational institutions including universities. It is quite likely that in the coming decade, because of the costs of this widespread competition, there will be some structural rearrangements. The ad hoc coalitions that have formed may well presage events of the future. Just as many observers predict the eventual merger of the AFT and NEA, so also the SEAs may join forces with AFSCME. As

[48] 723 GERR 11–14 (August 29, 1977).

of 1978, however, the dominant mood is still competitive rather than cooperative.

In May 1978, however, after this chapter had been written, the quarter-million-member Civil Service Employees Association of New York State affiliated with AFSCME. Although this occurred shortly after the CSEA was defeated by an AFT-led coalition in a major representation election involving professional employees and, as such, may be a special case, it also may signal the beginning of a national trend.

This review of public-sector unions is made more complicated by the shift of the local transit industry in the last 15 years from the private sector to the public sector. Practically all major city transit systems have gone public during this period and, strictly speaking, the unions in this industry which traditionally have not been thought of as public-sector unions should be included in that category.

The three major unions representing bus drivers and other local transit employees are the Amalgamated Transit Union (ATU) and the Transport Workers Union (TWU), each with approximately 140,000 members, and the local transit division of the United Transportation Union (UTU), which represents a smaller number of local transit workers than the other two unions. The ATU is the dominant union in the field nationally, but the TWU represents bus drivers in New York City, Philadelphia, San Francisco, and Miami, while the UTU represents drivers in several other cities including Los Angeles and surrounding communities.[49] Bargaining procedures and union policies in the local transit industry frequently are quite different from those covering other public employees of the same city or county but may in the future become more similar as public-transit labor relations is integrated into the public-sector labor relations policies of the employer.

Space limitations and the impossibility of analyzing in any depth the many unions active in the public sector have made it necessary to limit the following portion of the chapter to a relatively brief summary of AFSCME and to omit discussions of other unions. Information about them can be found in a variety of places but the easiest starting point is the previously men-

---

[49]James L. Stern, Richard U. Miller, Stephen A. Rubenfeld, Brian P. Heshizer, and Craig A. Olson, Labor Relations in Urban Mass Transit (Madison: Industrial Relations Research Institute, University of Wisconsin, 1977).

tioned volume by Jack Stieber, *Public Employee Unionism,* the basic reference in this field.

The American Federation of State, County and Municipal Employees Union (AFSCME), AFL-CIO

AFSCME was founded in the early 1930s by scattered groups of public employees who had affiliated individually with the AFL. The pioneering organization to do this in 1932 was the Wisconsin State Employees Association under the leadership of Arnold Zander, who subsequently became the first president of AFSCME. Originally, the individual units of local government employees were included within AFGE, but in 1936, AFSCME was chartered separately by the AFL.[50] At the time it had about 10,000 members, and by 1950 its membership had increased to over 80,000. When the AFL and CIO merged in the mid-fifties, the 30,000-member, public employee CIO affiliate merged with AFSCME. By 1960, the union had about 180,000 members and was entering a period of internal strife.

In 1964, Jerry Wurf, the executive director of the large New York City AFSCME District 37, defeated Arnold Zander for the AFSCME presidency. In his campaign, he argued that the union must devote more of its efforts to collective bargaining. Over the following 14 years, Wurf strengthened his position as president and increased his influence in his own union and among leaders of other private- and public-sector unions within and outside of the AFL-CIO. At its 1976 convention, Wurf and William Lucy (the secretary-treasurer, a black leader who previously had been Wurf's administrative assistant) were reelected overwhelmingly.[51] Between 1964 and 1977 AFSCME membership more than doubled and was about 750,000 at the end of 1977. With the addition of the quarter-million members of the New York State Civil Service Association in 1978, AFSCME became both a million-member union and the largest affiliate of the AFL-CIO.

---

[50]Information about the early history of AFSCME and its development is to be found in Leo Kramer, Labor's Paradox (New York: John Wiley & Sons, Inc., 1962); Richard Billings and John Greenya, Power to the Public Worker (Washington: E.B. Luce, 1974); Stieber, *supra* note 2; and an article by Jerry Wurf and Mary Hennessy about AFSCME in J. Joseph Loewenberg and Michael H. Moskow, eds., Collective Bargaining in Government (Englewood Cliffs, N.J.: Prentice-Hall, Inc., 1972). Seminar papers about AFSCME by Billie L. Johnson, Robert H. Runke, Greg Salzman, Maurice Sullivan, and Thomas G. Thurman also provided the author with further background information about AFSCME.
[51]662 GERR B10 (June 21, 1976).

Under Wurf's leadership, AFSCME had maintained friendly relations with NEA and other non-AFL-CIO groups. AFSCME and NEA are the dominant unions in The Coalition of Public Employees (CAPE) which, with NTEU and other groups, maintains an independent voice for public employees in competition with the AFL-CIO's Public Employee Department (PED). The IAFF, which formerly was in CAPE, is now active in PED and, along with the AFT and AFGE, make up the core of PED. AFSCME, however, withdrew its financial support of PED and was suspended from it in 1976.[52] The split voice of public employee unions at the national level carries over also to state and local levels as CAPE has formed coalitions at those levels as well.

Despite the spotlight on Jerry Wurf as the national leader, it should be kept in mind that bargaining is essentially a local matter and that the most important bargaining decisions are being made at the local level. The key decision-maker in AFSCME bargaining is the full-time representative helping the local negotiate the contract. In contrast to major steel and auto negotiations, national AFSCME leadership does not usually participate in these negotiations. In the major AFSCME negotiations, key decisions are usually made by the full-time executive director of the AFSCME district council in the area, with the approval of his bargaining team. Victor Gotbaum, executive director of the New York City AFSCME council, and his counterparts throughout the nation have considerable power and autonomy.

Analyses of different councils, however, reveal different patterns of operation. In some councils, staff members are elected (Philadelphia, for example). In others, staff members are appointed by the executive director. Some directors favor the appointment of college-trained or private-sector, union-trained, full-time staff, while others pick local activists who have demonstrated ability. The traditions of the district council and the composition of the membership provide partial explanations for these differences. Approximately half of AFSCME's membership is female or nonwhite and about one quarter of its membership is in the semiskilled and unskilled occupations in the health care field. These members may not aggressively seek union leadership roles and may prefer to rely upon staff professionals chosen from outside their ranks.

---

[52] 645 GERR B11–B14 (February 23, 1976).

The most important factor explaining the various postures of different councils is the absence or presence of bargaining legislation and the degree to which legislation, where it exists, facilitates employee organization. Historically, the public sector has frowned on compulsory union membership. More recently enacted legislation and court decisions, however, have looked favorably upon mandatory payment of dues or an equivalent service fee. In the absence of favorable legislation, most locals and councils must devote a major portion of their time to organizing and political activities. They need to increase their membership and activate it politically so that favorable legislation can be enacted at the state or local levels. In most instances, it is only after success on the legislative front that the union can turn its attention to serious bargaining.

Conclusions and Speculation About the Future

In 1970, the late E. Wight Bakke identified major trends in public-sector bargaining.[53] He predicted that unionization in the public sector would increase rapidly, that it would be militant in the foreseeable future, and that the achievement of power would be a major objective of union leaders for a considerable period. These predictions proved correct for the 1970–1978 period. The question becomes, will they continue to hold true in the coming decade?

Membership growth seems to be tapering off and, for several reasons, will probably be far smaller in the next ten years than in the past ten years.[54] Future organizing efforts will involve units in smaller cities and regions of the country not known for their sympathy for public-sector unions. Legislation in many southern states bans bargaining and in this way discourages unionization. Possibly, the spread of legislation authorizing agency-shop provisions or mandatory payment of fees to the bargaining agent, as in Hawaii, may increase membership; but, all in all, it seems more likely that the rate of growth will decrease. Furthermore, since the degree of public-sector unioniza-

---

[53]E. Wight Bakke, *Reflections on the Future of Bargaining in the Public Sector,* 93 Monthly Lab. Rev. 21 (July 1970).
[54]Union Recognition in the Federal Government, 1976, Civil Service Commission Bull. No. 711–37 reprinted in GERR RF 144 (June 20, 1977), and Labor Management Relations in State and Local Governments, 1975, State and Local Government Special Studies No. 81, U.S. Bureau of the Census, February 1977.

tion has already outstripped private-sector unionism, it does not seem likely that events in the private sector will fuel further quantum leaps by public-sector unions.

The decline in the union growth rate may stimulate efforts to reduce interunion organizing competition, although the private-sector experience subsequent to the merger of the AFL and CIO suggests that the elimination of competition may not necessarily bring substantial organizing victories. It is possible that no-raid agreements similar to those developed in the private sector will be more widely adopted in the public sector. One factor mitigating against this development, however, is the greater emphasis on local decision-making in the public sector. In the private sector, powerful national leaders were able to impose the no-raid pacts on local unions. National public-sector union leaders may not be able to do so because local affiliates are less dependent on the national union and less willing to tolerate invasions of their autonomy.

Although Bakke's prediction of continual union militance held up for the first half of the 1970s, it may prove less accurate for the coming five years primarily because of the stiffening resistance by public-sector managers to that militance and the idea that the payoff to militance is declining. In recent years, despite the union rhetoric favoring the right to strike of public employees, public-sector unions have lobbied heavily for state laws forcing employers to submit contract impasses to arbitration. About 20 states provide for arbitration, and less than 10 have given a limited legal right to strike to some or all public employees.[55]

As for Bakke's prediction that a major objective of union leaders "for a considerable period" will be to achieve collective power, it appears that a considerable period will stretch out for another decade. Bakke was not referring to the ability of public-sector union leaders to make their own leadership positions secure from internal challenge, but rather to the attempts of these leaders to obtain bargaining rights and labor agreements covering most workers in their jurisdictions. Although great strides have been made in that direction, there are still many problems to be resolved before public-sector unions will have achieved power nationally.

---

[55]See Chapter 6 in this volume by B.V.H. Schneider.

One problem that the public-sector union leaders have not been able to resolve is the establishment by the federal government of a national labor relations law analogous to that covering the private sector. The *National League of Cities* v. *Usery* Supreme Court decision has made this problem even more difficult than it seemed several years ago.[56] The attempt to get national legislation is also hampered by the fact that PED and CAPE support different bills.

One other interesting development which has an impact on public-sector union philosophy is the exemption from bargaining of supervisors and administrators, or the creation of separate supervisory bargaining units. In contrast to the private sector, public-sector administrators have in some instances started the union—AFSCME and NEA, for example—and in the NEA in the South are still influential. Higher level federal personnel who were active in AFGE have also been excluded from bargaining units under the 1969 executive order. In general, it appears that these exclusions have tended to make the organizations more militant, particularly in education where the principals have been excluded.

The challenge for the public-sector union leadership is clearly one of creating union loyalty among groups who up until now have not demonstrated this characteristic. Government employers have been less antagonistic to public-sector unionism in the past 15 years than their private-sector management counterparts were to industrial unions prior to World War II, and this may have facilitated union efforts. At present, however, the organizing climate does not seem as favorable as it has been because public-sector employees and their unions are no longer seen as the weak underdogs deserving of taxpayer sympathy and support. Resentment against tax increases and an impression that powerful public-sector unions are "ripping off" the public seem to be more prevalent, and increased management resistance to unionism supposedly reflects this trend.

Possibly the most intriguing speculation about the future of public-sector unions concerns the likelihood that major public-sector unions will merge and that they will form a single major confederation to represent their interests. This could involve a breakaway of some unions from the AFL-CIO and the formation

---

[56]See Chapter 7 in this volume by Joseph Grodin.

of a rival power center. Possibly, CAPE could provide the springboard for such a development. It is also possible that some working arrangement can be developed that will permit the merger of CAPE and PED and the creation of a cooperative arrangement with the AFL-CIO which might not involve membership of all of these unions in the AFL-CIO. Developments such as these are not likely in the short run, however, because leaders of the public-sector unions are still primarily concerned with the strengthening of their respective individual unions.

One final question about public-sector unions to be considered before concluding this chapter is whether the differences between the public and private sector are now seen as more important or less important than formerly. Differentiation by broad occupational groupings and industrial categories may seem more useful than comparisons based on status as a public- or private-sector employee. Clearly, professional and craft-union structures are more closely tied to occupational boundaries than to considerations of private- or public-sector status. Professors, nurses, and building trades craftsmen alike identify by occupation and belong to unions organized to serve their occupations. Many semiskilled and unskilled workers tend to identify by industrial category, such as local transit or hospital, and belong to unions active in those fields.

These characteristics make it difficult for general unions of public-sector employees such as AFGE at the federal level and AFSCME at the local level to fend off more particularistic unions. The general unions draw support for their position from legislators and public-sector personnel administrators because of considerations of equity and their desire to extend uniform treatment to different groups of public employees. The power of these groups and the general unions is considerable, but it is not clear that it will prevail against the contrary wishes of professional associations and occupation- and industry-based unions. Whichever view prevails, however, will have an important influence on the structure of public-sector unions in the future.

CHAPTER 3

MANAGEMENT ORGANIZATION FOR COLLECTIVE BARGAINING IN THE PUBLIC SECTOR*

MILTON DERBER†

The subject of this chapter is so wide-ranging in scope that detailed, comprehensive treatment is not possible. I have therefore made two arbitrary decisions on coverage. First, I have placed the primary focus on state and local government, with which I have been mainly concerned as a researcher and practitioner, devoting only a few pages at the end to the federal sector. Second, I have confined the discussion to five topics which have been of greatest interest and relevance to me and have disregarded others that might be judged of equal significance.

I start with an analysis of what may seem a peculiar question: who is public management? I hope to demonstrate that this is indeed a question of considerable practical as well as theoretical importance. The next major section examines the apparent trend toward centralization of management authority for bargaining. The third section explores the complicated problem of management internal organization and procedures for effective bargaining, including the utilization of bargaining specialists and their relations with the top policy-makers, line officials, the personnel staff, budget-makers, and the pertinent legislative body. Following this, I turn to the organizational problems confronting management in the contract-administration stage. And finally, I devote brief attention to the universally discussed matter of training members of the management hierarchy in labor relations concepts, skills, and knowledge.

*I am indebted to my colleague, Peter Feuille, and to R. Theodore Clark, Jr., for a number of valuable comments.
†University of Illinois at Urbana-Champaign.

Who Is Public Management?

From a collective bargaining perspective, the concept of public management poses problems not normally found in the private sector. The private employer is readily identified as an entity, and the line of management responsibility for bargaining is usually clear and direct. But in the public sector responsibility is generally divided or shared, and the formal responsibility often differs from the actual.

Constitutional, Political, and Bureaucratic Considerations

The reasons for such confusion and ambiguity are multiple.[1] One major factor is the constitutional system of checks and balances that distributes authority for policy-making and implementation among the legislative, executive, and judicial branches. Even the executive or legislative responsibilities may be legally shared among separately elected executive officers (e.g., the governor and the secretary of state) or among legislative bodies (e.g., the state legislature and home-rule municipal councils). Legislative bodies in turn often delegate rule-making authority to other agencies, such as a civil service commission, a school board, or a municipality. Arvid Anderson has pointed out that "the education law, civil service law, welfare laws, statutes affecting police and fire [sic], prevailing wage statutes, pension statutes, statutes affecting the fiscal authority of the municipal employer and the timetable for budgetmaking, all affect and may operate as constraints on the authority of the public employer."[2]

Another significant factor is that apart from the federal Congress and the state legislatures, few public agencies have either the authority or the means to raise all or most of the money they need to perform their functions. Furthermore, to an increasing extent, public bodies obtain their funds from a multiplicity of sources rather than a single source. When a lower level of government receives grants from a higher level, the transfer is often accompanied by constraints on the use of the funds or condi-

[1] See, for example, my article, *Who Negotiates for the Public Employer*, in Perspective in Public Employee Negotiation, ed. Keith Ocheltree (Chicago: Public Personnel Association, 1969), 52–53.

[2] *The Structure of Public Sector Bargaining*, in Public Workers and Public Unions, ed. Sam Zagoria (Englewood Cliffs, N.J.: Prentice-Hall, Inc., 1972), 43.

tions are specified about the qualifications or methods of the personnel involved.[3]

Finally, but not least in importance, political forces may shape the allocation of responsibility for collective bargaining. A strong mayor or governor typically prefers a centralized bargaining system under his direct control; a weak chief executive may be obliged to share responsibilities with other elected officials in executive or legislative or even administrative positions, resulting in a highly fragmented management approach. In some cases (e.g., where a union is linked to a party machine), the ultimate authority for bargaining may lie with a political leader or group that holds no formal governmental position but operates behind the scene.

The appointed bureaucracy or professional staff may also exercise widely varying degrees of responsibility in collective bargaining in relation to the elected officials who are formally their superiors. A city manager, a school superintendent, or the head of a municipal or state department, possessing a strong personality as well as labor relations expertise and long experience, may assume a dominant role in collective bargaining, whereas less well-endowed counterparts may have little or no role.

A number of these ambiguous strands were reflected in a March 1977 decision of the State of Washington Supreme Court.[4] The issue was whether, under the state public employee relations law, the state budget director was obliged to negotiate with an employee union over the state salary plan. The court held that the budget director was "the public employer" for wage bargaining because he had the power to review and approve the plan prepared in the first instance by the personnel board. On the other hand, the negotiations conducted by the budget director were only of a "meet and confer" nature and could not lead to an agreement binding the governor at whose pleasure the budget director served. Furthermore, the governor had to submit the salary plan for final action by the legislature.

---

[3]An example is the Urban Mass Transportation Act which specifies that before any federal funds are provided to a state or local government for the operation of a transit system, the U.S. Secretary of Labor must certify that arrangements have been made to protect the interests of affected employees, including the continuation of collective bargaining rights.

[4]*John Ortblad, et al.* v. *The State of Washington, et al.*, Case No. 44331, March 12, 1977. 712 GERR 8 (June 13, 1977).

Citizen Interest Groups

Public management's bargaining structure may also be strongly influenced by the activities of interest groups that believe they (as members of the sovereign public) are entitled to a voice in the collective bargaining process. In some instances the group may desire representation on management's bargaining team, in others the right to attend the bargaining sessions, in still others the opportunity to present their views to the bargaining team or to the legislative body prior to the approval of a collective agreement. Illustrations of such interest-group desires are found in laws in Montana, Oregon, and Florida requiring student representation in university negotiations and in the court petition of a Parents' Union to obtain the right to participate in negotiations during the 1972–1973 Philadelphia teachers' strike.[5]

Because general government services must be paid for by the public through the tax system, public management has a relationship to its public(s) that is very different from that of private management to its firm's customers. In the latter case, typically, a concerned customer can only exercise the choice of buying or not buying, but lacks the power to influence the private management's collective bargaining policies or procedures. In the former case, a concerned public may seek to replace the responsible managers or force a change in bargaining policies.

Thought about the public's role in negotiations has led Sam Zagoria, director of the Labor-Management Relations Service, a public employer organization, to advocate "giving either party by law the right to take [a] contested issue to public referendum, hitching the factfinders' recommendation on the next regular or special election ballot. In effect, the issue would be taken to the citizens of the community, the ultimate public employer, for them to decide whether they want to supersede the instructions implicit in their earlier election of municipal officials by giving them newer directives based on the issue before them."[6] At least three cities in Colorado have adopted the use of the public referendum as the terminal point for an impasse procedure; the public referendum mechanism was also used in San Francisco in November 1975 when Proposition B was passed by a two to one

---

[5] Richard P. Schick and Jean J. Couturier. The Public Interest in Government Labor Relations (Cambridge, Mass.: Ballinger Publishing Co., 1977), 45–67.

[6] Resolving Impasses by Public Referendum, 96 Monthly Lab. Rev. 5 (May 1973), 37–38.

margin abolishing a formula that tied pay for city craft workers
to the prevailing wage rate for similar occupations in private
industry.[7]

Frank P. Zeidler, former mayor of Milwaukee and a specialist
in public-sector labor relations, has noted that taxpayers often
believe that they are not represented at the bargaining table
because they are not sure that the public employer representatives represent them. "The taxpayer recognizes that the negotiator or negotiators for his side have several pressures at work
on them other than taxpayer interests."[8]

A Theory of Diffused Management Responsibility

The diffused character of public management has been
stressed by a number of students. Thomas Kochan, for example,
in a study of fire-service bargaining in 228 cities, observed that
"a number of semiautonomous management officials (both administrative and elected) often share decision-making power
over issues traditionally raised by unions in collective bargaining."[9] Community interest groups were also found by Kochan
(and others[10]) to become involved in the bargaining process.
Kochan concluded that multilateral bargaining was a function of
several variables, most notably the extent of internal conflict
among management officials and the degree to which employee
organizations use political pressure tactics. In short, the political context of municipal collective bargaining may lead to a
fragmented management authority structure in contrast to
the more unified management approach in private-sector bargaining.

One possible consequence of such fragmentation in management bargaining responsibility is the use by unions of the "end-
run." It is a rare public employee organization that does not

[7] 651 GERR B22 (April 5, 1976).
[8] *The Public Interest in Collective Bargaining*, in Perspective in Public Employee Negotiation, ed. Keith Ocheltree (Chicago: Public Personnel Association, 1969), 9.
[9] *A Theory of Multilateral Bargaining in City Governments*, 27 Ind. & Lab. Rels. Rev. 4 (July
1974), 526. *See also* Thomas A. Kochan, George P. Huber, and L. L. Cummings, *Determinants of Intraorganizational Conflict in Collective Bargaining in the Public Sector*, 20 Admin. Sci.
Quarterly 1 (March 1975), 10–23.
[10] Kenneth McLennan and Michael H. Moskow, *Multilateral Bargaining in the Public
Sector*, in Proceedings of the 21st Annual Meeting, Industrial Relations Research Association (Madison, Wis.: IRRA, 1968), 34–41; Hervey A. Juris and Peter Feuille, Police
Unionism: Power and Impact in Public Sector Bargaining (Lexington, Mass.: D.C. Heath
and Co., 1973), 45–52.

have friends and supporters among elected public officials. At every level of government the unions and associations devote, often considerable, resources (personnel, communication channels, financial contributions) in support of the election of particular candidates as well as in general lobbying. Sometimes these officials may "leak" information to employee representatives during or prior to bargaining. In other cases, if the employees cannot achieve their demands from the management negotiators, they may appeal informally to their elected friends to try to influence management positions or to secure more favorable consideration at a higher decision-making level. Numerous examples come to mind: the school board member who informs the teacher representatives of the board representative's bargaining strategy, the city council member who urges the finance committee to approve the police association's wage demands, the party professional who advises a county board to make bargaining concessions as a tradeoff for union support in a forthcoming election.[11]

Need for Legal Specification of Management Responsibility

Because of these potential negative results of fragmentation, there seems to be widespread agreement among practitioners and students that management responsibility for collective bargaining should be clearly specified in law or administrative guidelines, although no specific uniform rule may be feasible. Where the constitutional structure requires a sharing of responsibility, agreements entered into in one forum should be clearly contingent on action in another, with an obligation on the part of both sides to the initial agreement to support it fully and wholeheartedly in its progress through any other requisite decision-making forum.

Some states have attempted to provide a degree of specification in their public-employment collective bargaining laws. For example, New York's Taylor Law defines the various political units (state, county, municipality, special district, etc.) which fall within the meaning of the term "government" or "public em-

---

[11]For the observations of one experienced management negotiator, see R. Theodore Clark, Jr., *Politics and Public Employee Unionism: Some Recommendations for an Emerging Problem,* 44 U. Cincinnati L. Rev. 680–89 (1975).

ployer" and gives the Public Employment Relations Board the power to determine a "joint public employer" for bargaining purposes.

In addition, the law contains definitions of the terms "chief executive officer" and "legislative body of the government" in the case of school districts and it defines collective bargaining "agreements" as "the result of the exchange of mutual promises between the chief executive officer of a public employer and an employee organization . . . except as to any provisions which require approval by an appropriate legislative body."

The Connecticut Municipal Employee Relations act goes a step further. It specifies [Sec. 7–474(a)] that "the chief executive officer, whether elected or appointed, or his designated representative or representatives shall represent the municipal employer in collective bargaining. . . ." The act also mandates that where an agreement contains provisions conflicting with any charter, special act, ordinance, or regulation or certain hours and retirement statutes, the agreement must be referred to the appropriate legislative body within a set period and the latter must approve or reject the agreement within a given time. The Connecticut act defines as employer for collective bargaining "a district, school board, housing authority or other authority established by law, which by statute, charter, special act or ordinance has sole and exclusive control over the appointment of and the wages, hours and conditions of employment of its employees . . ." [Sec. 7–474 (d)].

The Hawaii public employee bargaining act not only defines 13 appropriate bargaining units within the state, but specifies in the case of multi-employer units who shall negotiate on behalf of the employers, how many representatives each employer may have, and how many votes each employer shall be entitled to [Sec. 89–6(b)].

Multi-Employer Arrangements

Although cities and states have sought to avoid fragmentation of bargaining units by consolidating occupations, departments, and agencies under a single bargaining authority, there has been surprisingly little interest among local management groups in establishing multi-employer bargaining units with corresponding management coordinating organizations.[12] Feuille et al. report a variety of interemployer arrangements to exchange bargaining information (partly to counter union whipsawing tactics), but the benefits of such arrangements have not persuaded these public agencies to give up their bargaining autonomy. Nor, despite some union pressures, especially in education, to widen bargaining units, does the prospect for a change in management attitude on this subject appear strong.

Supervisors as Part of Management

The problem of defining management for purposes of collective bargaining has one other aspect that merits note. This pertains to the drawing of management boundaries, i.e., which supervisory or managerial staff members are to be treated as "management" and therefore to be excluded from appropriate bargaining units or to be confined to special units separate from the employees they supervise. For the private sector, the federal Labor Management Relations Act defines management boundaries broadly, encompassing first-line supervisors who are excluded from the protective definition of "employee" under the act. In the public sector, however, employee organizations *historically* counted even middle and upper supervisory and managerial officials not only as members but often as leaders. This was particularly true in the specialized services of education, health care, fire fighting, and police protection, but it also applied to the general civil service. As a result there was strenuous resistance among some employee organizations, as well as some managers, against proposals to adopt private-sector policies on management boundaries.

One of the strongest attacks on the effort to maintain a distinction between the public and the private sector in this (and other) respects was made by former NLRB chairman, Edward B. Miller. In a speech to the National Public Employer Labor Relations Association, he assailed those public employers who

. . . seemed bent on proving they were different. Some public employers, for example, insisted on ignoring all the experience about

---

[12]See Richard Pegnetter, Multiemployer Bargaining in the Public Sector: Purposes and Experiences (Chicago: International Personnel Management Association, PERL 52, 1975); Peter Feuille, Hervey A. Juris, Ralph Jones, and Michael Jay Jedel, *Multiemployer Bargaining Among Local Governments,* in Proceedings of the 29th Annual Meeting, Industrial Relations Research Association (Madison, Wis.: IRRA, 1977), 123–31.

bargaining units which had been developed in the private sector under the National Labor Relations Act. . . .

We also saw units which included supervisors and managers. You probably read some of the same scholarly articles that I did wherein the ivory tower visionaries were regularly telling us that supervisory lines were "blurred" in the public sector. We were told that in schools and in police departments and in fire departments, existing associations of employees ignored these kinds of lines, and thus we would have to accept that when bargaining took place in this public institutional framework we would have to have units quite different from those in the private sector.[13]

Tim L. Bornstein of the University of Massachusetts similarly concluded, in discussing the fire department problem, that

in the long run, it is all but inevitable that your deputies and your captains, and perhaps even your lieutenants, will systematically be excluded from collective bargaining. The reason is that collective bargaining, which can be a very helpful, useful, constructive institution in the conduct of public affairs, has to operate according to rules which assure that both sides have a reasonable measure of leverage. And if, in a community, only the fire chief or one or two deputies are excluded from the bargaining unit, then who is left to assure that policy is carried out faithfully and effectively?[14]

Most states with public employee relations legislation have, indeed, incorporated a Taft-Hartley-type definition of supervisor as part of management into their laws, as has the federal government in its executive orders. In some branches of government, most notably education, top and middle managers, like superintendents and principals, have been obliged to abandon their dual role of management and employee.

Nonetheless, as Hayford and Sinicropi have concluded, after a comprehensive national survey, "The bargaining rights status of public sector supervisors is far from being settled. While it is clear that a [sic] federal employment experience has paralleled that of the private sector, several state legislatures and/ or administrative agencies have chosen a more expansive approach. . . ."[15] This approach has taken two principal forms: (1) many individuals with supervisory titles are not held to be supervisors for statutory purposes because they "are not really managers"; (2) "bona fide supervisors" are granted bargaining

---

[13]702 GERR 39–40 (April 4, 1977).
[14]718 GERR 12 (July 25, 1977).
[15]Stephen L. Hayford and Anthony V. Sinicropi, *Bargaining Rights Status of Public Sector Supervisors,* 15 Ind. Rels. 59 (February 1976).

rights but are usually placed in bargaining units separate from the employees whom they supervise.

A few cases may be illustrative. The Minnesota law provides that supervisory and confidential employees, principals, and assistant principals may form their own organizations and the latter may receive exclusive representation rights for the purpose of negotiating terms and conditions of employment as though they were essential employees, i.e., with the right to invoke binding arbitration [Sec. 179.65(6)]. Wisconsin's *municipal* employment relations act generally does not consider a supervisor to be a covered employee, but it distinguishes fire fighters from other municipal employees and explicitly defines supervisors as the chief and the officer directly below him in single-station communities and all officers above the rank of the highest ranking officer at each single station in municipalities with more than one station. Fire fighting and law enforcement supervisors may organize separate units for the purpose of negotiating with their municipal employers, although the statute's other provisions do not apply to them. Moreover, the Wisconsin Employment Relations Commission may require a supervisory unit of fire fighters or police to be separately organized from the local employee unit, but it may not prevent affiliation by a supervisory representative with the same parent state or national organization as the employee representative [Sec. 111.70(1)(b), (1)(o)(2), and (3)(d)].

Wisconsin's *state* employment relations act authorizes the WERC to establish two statewide units of professional and nonprofessional supervisory employees, but the certified representatives may not be affiliated with labor organizations representing other categories of nonsupervisory employees. Moreover the supervisory representatives may not bargain on any matter other than wages and specified fringe benefits [Sec. 111.81(3)(d)]. Thus far neither state supervisory unit has been involved in a certification election. Hawaii's public employee bargaining law, like Wisconsin's, specifies appropriate bargaining units, but it distinguishes between supervisory employees in blue-collar positions and those in white-collar positions. In New Jersey, the schools receive a bit of special attention in this area with the provision that the term "managerial executive" shall mean the superintendent of schools or his equivalent; and the law further provides that no supervisor shall have the right to be represented in collective negotiations by an employee organization that admits nonsupervisory personnel to membership "except where established practice, prior agreement or special circumstances, dictate the contrary" [Sec. 34:13A-5.3].

Practice often indicates even wider divergence. A 1977 survey in New York City noted that, among others, deputy chiefs in the fire and police departments, all supervisors below the level of borough superintendents in the sanitation department, and housing project managers in the housing authority belong to a union. The conclusion reached was that "many managers identify not with the City but with the union they belong to."[16]

The foregoing provisions and practices, and others like them, reflect the tensions and the ambiguities of public-sector management. On the one hand, many top executives (particularly those in elective positions) have failed to appreciate the importance of adequately motivating, training, and rewarding middle and lower managerial and supervisory personnel so as to bind them to the management side. On the other hand, many supervisory personnel have been impressed by the organizational achievements of the people whom they supervise and are determined to keep pace.

Centralization of Management Authority for Bargaining

The distribution of management responsibility for bargaining appears to be at least partly related to the structure of the bargaining unit. The wider and more comprehensive the bargaining unit, the greater the likelihood that management responsibility for bargaining will be centralized. When bargaining units are smaller, narrower, and more numerous, centralized authority is more difficult to maintain, and there is a tendency for responsibility to be dispersed (formally or informally) among a variety of agencies, departments, and institutions. Several empirical surveys support this thesis.

After an extensive study in 1968–1969 of local government in some 40 cities and towns (part of The Brookings Institution's Studies of Unionism in Government), John Burton concluded that "bargaining forces a centralization of authority within management which overcomes the fragmentation of control over

---

[16] *Reporter at Large,* The New Yorker (August 1, 1977), 38.

various [personnel] issues typical in a nonunionized unit of local government."[17] As bargaining develops, "Collective bargaining will shift authority for personnel issues to the executive branch at the expense of the legislative branch and the civil service system." And within the executive branch, "Authority for bargaining will be centralized and primary responsibility assigned to an individual or officer directly responsible to the chief executive."[18]

Similar conclusions were reached by this writer and by Ralph T. Jones in two separate 1974–1975 surveys of state government collective bargaining. Jones (after a study of eight widely spread states) perceived the appearance of a "life cycle" pattern wherein "management structure evolves into and through distinctive growth and maturity patterns characterized by an almost instinctive thrust toward increasing centralization."[19] His study found that state bargaining was initiated under a variety of environmental circumstances which greatly affected the first management structures. Vertical units involving department-level contracts resulted in decentralized administration within state management. Horizontal units resulted in centralized administration. "Whatever the initial structure, however, subsequent events lead to further centralization. Decentralized administration becomes inappropriate as statewide units are established. These in turn begin to fade as pressures for coalition bargaining surface."[20]

My own research in the 12 midwestern states discovered three main bargaining patterns in which the allocation of management bargaining authority, the nature of the bargaining unit, and the scope of bargaining issues were interrelated.[21] Where bargaining coverage was widespread and the scope of bargaining was

---

[17]John F. Burton, Jr., *Local Government Bargaining and Management Structure,* 11 Ind. Rels. 124 (May 1972).

[18]*Id.,* at 138.

[19]Ralph T. Jones, *Public Management's Internal Organizational Response to the Demands of Collective Bargaining,* draft final report prepared by Contract Research Corp., Belmont, Mass., for Labor-Management Services Administration, U.S. Department of Labor, Contract No. L–74–207, undated, mimeographed, p. 27.

[20]*Id.,* at 32. This trend toward centralized state government bargaining must be distinguished from multi-employer local government bargaining as discussed earlier.

[21]Milton Derber, Charles Maxey, and Kurt Wetzel, Public Management's Internal Organizational Response to the Demand of Collective Bargaining in the Twelve Midwestern States (Washington: U.S. Department of Labor, Labor-Management Services Administration, 1977). See also Milton Derber, Peter Pashler, and Mary Beth Ryan, Collective Bargaining by State Governments in Twelve Midwestern States (Champaign: Institute of Labor and Industrial Relations, University of Illinois, December 1974).

comprehensive (including pay, hours, and fringe benefits), government responsibility for bargaining tended to be centralized at the level of the governor or a civil service commission. Wisconsin, one of the pioneers in state government bargaining, illustrated the evolutionary process from widely dispersed, limited-scope management bargaining to a highly centralized system including the formal intermeshing of the executive and legislative roles. Iowa, influenced by its neighbor's experience, adopted a centralized bargaining system controlled by the governor's office from the outset. Other states with limited bargaining coverage and, typically, limited scope of issues reflected two different patterns. In some of these states (e.g., Missouri and North Dakota) responsibility was left to the heads of the agencies involved, and the chief executive followed a hands-off policy. In others of this group (e.g., Ohio, Nebraska) there was a centralized unit acting in behalf of the governor to maintain a measure of statewide uniformity. However, in such states a tradition of departmental autonomy often resisted the centralization effort. As bargaining units evolved to a statewide scale, the centralization process tended to be strengthened.

The relationship between management authority and bargaining structure suggested by the foregoing is by no means an iron law. In the cases of New York State and New York City, we find centralized managerial responsibility for bargaining with widely divergent bargaining-unit systems. The state has five broad horizontal units and three vertical units covering about 180,000 employees; the city has about 100 units (reduced from 400) covering some 250,000 employees. Bargaining for the state is conducted by the Governor's Office of Employee Relations; bargaining for the city is the responsibility of the Mayor's Office of Labor Relations. The history of management labor relations policy in both state and city is one of increasing centralization under the chief executive.[22] In the city, this centralization has occurred not only within the executive branch but also as between the executive and legislative branches. In the state, the legislature has retained its traditional power over appropria-

---

[22]For a history of the city's labor relations, see Raymond D. Horton, Municipal Labor Relations in New York City (New York: Praeger Publishers, 1972), and Raymond D. Horton, *Report to State Charter Revision Commission on Reforming New York City's Labor Relations Process,* 594 GERR E1-E8 (February 24, 1975). The state's structure is described by Donald H. Wollett, *State Government: Strategies for Negotiations in an Austere Environment —a Management Perspective,* in Proceedings of the 1976 Annual Spring Meeting, Industrial Relations Research Association (Madison, Wis.: IRRA, 1976).

tions but has invariably assented to the collective bargaining agreements.

Horton, Lewin, and Kuhn, however, have cautioned against overgeneralizing the centralization thesis. They offer three reasons for a "diversity" hypothesis:

> First, the formal dispersion of political power, particularly at the local government level in American cities, is so well-advanced that political "end-runs" around newly designated labor relations agencies and actors remain possible. Second, and closely related to the above point, one must distinguish between formal and informal power structures. The mere act of creating new labor relations institutions and delegating to them responsibilities to make decisions previously reached elsewhere in government does not mean, in fact, that the locus of control over decision-making also changes. Third, in certain cities where public employees are well-organized and politically strong, formal bargaining programs may result in a redistribution of power from public officials to municipal unions. This may represent a form of centralization, but not of the kind customarily anticipated by academics or public officials.[23]

A Lewin study of the evolution of management structure in the City and County of Los Angeles lends some support to the diversity thesis.[24] Despite an apparent formal centralization of public management authority in these two major governmental units, multiple sources of authority remain. In the city, the Personnel Department, departmental commissioners, the city council, and the council's personnel committee, as well as the city administrative officer (the chief negotiator) and the mayor have all been participants to one degree or another in municipal labor relations. In the county, where decision-making is more highly centralized than in the city, a five-member board of supervisors controls virtually all the departments. Nevertheless, the county administrative officer (the chief negotiator), the personnel department, and the board of supervisors share negotiating responsibility.

Management's Internal Organization for Bargaining

Centralization of management responsibility in collective bargaining was fostered by a mounting recognition that the bar-

[23]Raymond D. Horton, David Lewin, and James W. Kuhn, *Some Impacts of Collective Bargaining on Local Government*, 7 Administration & Society 509 (February 1976).

[24]David Lewin, *Local Government Labor Relations in Transition: The Case of Los Angeles*, 17 Lab. History 191 (Spring 1976).

gaining process demands professional skills, specialized knowledge, quick access to relevant data, and quantities of time and energy. After a few exposures to the process, many executives and legislators were happy to relinquish the function to others on their staffs. Most recruited bargaining specialists, on a part-time or full-time basis, to represent them in bargaining and to advise them on policy.

In his 1969 Brookings survey of municipal and county management, David Stanley found that the "largest group of cities and counties (in a sample of 15) are relying on their personnel or civil service staffs to assume labor relations responsibilities. Only large cities with a multiplicity of bargaining units have set up full-time labor specialists or units. More cities can be expected to follow their lead. . . . The larger more thoroughly unionized governments can be expected to move toward the industrial pattern—a department of labor relations headed by a vice mayor or an assistant manager for labor relations, who will supervise not only bargaining and employee relations but also selection and training activities."[25]

An Iowa study of the city manager's role in collective bargaining in 1975, shortly after the state enacted a comprehensive public-employee bargaining law, revealed a similar tendency.[26] Nine of 16 managers had initially assumed the role of chief negotiator, either because they had been explicitly hired with the function in mind (two cases) or were required to assume the responsibility by city charter or by an ordinance adopted by the city council. However, most of the group indicated that the excessive time demanded by negotiations and the difficulty of maintaining consistency across multiple bargaining units had led them to consider seriously the appointment of a full-time labor relations specialist. The other seven managers had decided, for lack of experience in bargaining, to delegate the function to a committee (typically the city's chief finance officer, a personnel officer, and several department heads) or had hired an outside consultant, usually a lawyer with labor relations expertise.

Functional specialization in bargaining has raised a number of interesting questions and problems for management generally.

---

[25]David T. Stanley, Managing Local Government Under Union Pressure (Washington: The Brookings Institution, 1972), 27–28.
[26]Peter A. Veglahn and Stephen L. Hayford, *An Investigation into the City Manager's Role in the Collective Bargaining Process,* 5 J. Coll. Negotiations in the Pub. Sector 289 (1976).

Where in the management structure should the bargaining specialists be located? What role should department administrators play in the bargaining process, and how should their department interests be protected? How should communication lines be maintained with legislators who must approve any agreed items or vote appropriations to finance the agreements? Once negotiations have been completed, who should be responsible for contract administration and the settlement of grievances?

The answers to these and related questions have varied widely not only at different levels of government but also within the same level. Contributory factors are numerous—the size and complexity of the bargaining unit, the legal framework, the distribution of political power, and the attitudes of management leaders, among others.

The Location of the Bargaining Specialist

Small governmental units (municipality, school board, or state institution) often hire a lawyer or industrial relations specialist on an ad hoc basis to represent management at the bargaining table. The consultant confers mainly with the chief executive (city manager or mayor) or a governing board, performs his function of negotiating an agreement with the union, and then withdraws from the scene. No systematic information is available on the characteristics or the role of these part-time representatives. General observation indicates that they are numerous, that they satisfy an essential need, and that a corps of such specialists have acquired multiple clients in various regions of the country.

Larger government units often appoint a full-time specialist as employee-relations director in the manner of a private corporation. Sometimes the labor relations director handles all personnel matters; sometimes personnel and labor relations are treated as separate functions. As a staff specialist, the labor relations director is usually responsible to a top administrative officer—the mayor or city manager, the civil service head, the superintendent of schools, the administrator of a hospital, the state director of administration or director of personnel, or the governor, as the case may be. Numerous variations may be cited.

In a national study of police unionism, Hervey A. Juris and Peter Feuille found that bargaining responsibility rested with the executive branch (mayor or city manager) or the city council.

In "strong mayor" cities (Buffalo, Boston, New York, New Haven, Seattle), the executive branch prepared the budget, the city negotiators received instructions from the mayor, and at critical times the latter would enter the negotiations himself. In "weak mayor" cities (Milwaukee, Omaha, Los Angeles), the council was the dominant management factor. In council-manager cities, although the labor relations specialists were attached to the city manager's office, the council typically provided negotiating directions or guidelines to them either directly (Oakland, Rochester, Vallejo) or through the manager (Cincinnati, Hartford, Dayton). In one instance, however, Juris/Feuille reported that the manager was able to persuade the council that "it was less costly politically to let him handle labor relations than to become involved themselves."[27]

In state government, as collective bargaining expanded, professional negotiators were employed increasingly to represent management at the bargaining table. In New York,[28] for example, Governor Rockefeller initiated the bargaining process shortly after the passage of the Taylor Law in 1967 by appointing a management negotiating team comprised of his secretary, the president of the Civil Service Commission, and the director of the budget. It became clear in the following two years that these three top officials were far too involved in other functions to carry the collective bargaining responsibility. As a consequence the governor requested the legislature to establish by law an Office of Employee Relations to bargain and administer contracts for the state. The director of the OER reported directly to the governor and became part of the governor's informal cabinet. He had a deputy director, who also served as director of the division of contract negotiation and administration, a research director who also served as director of the grievance division, and a legal counsel who served as the director of the legal division. Five assistant directors were responsible for preparation for negotiations and contract administration.

In Wisconsin, as in New York, comprehensive centralized bargaining followed the passage of a new bargaining law in 1971.[29] Bargaining responsibility for the state was conferred upon an Employment Relations Section established within the Depart-

---

[27]Juris and Feuille, *supra* note 10, esp. 62–63.
[28]Derived mainly from Jones, *supra* note 19, at App. A—State Report.
[29]Derber, Maxey, and Wetzel, *supra* note 21, at 6–7.

ment of Administration, with easy access through the DOA secretary, a cabinet member, to the governor. The Director of Employment Relations was designated the chief state negotiator. Together with a staff of five professionals, he developed management positions prior to bargaining, conducted bargaining, monitored all third-step (department) grievances, and represented management in all grievance cases submitted to arbitration. Whereas under an earlier law the Bureau of Personnel (which administered the merit system) acted as adviser to department negotiators, the post-1971 system separated responsibility for the labor relations function from that of the personnel function. In late 1977, following a comprehensive review of the state's personnel system, a bill was enacted which removed personnel functions from the Department of Administration and created a new Department of Employment Relations (headed by a secretary) with responsibility for the administration of the state civil service system, the affirmative action program, and collective bargaining [Sec. 230].

Minnesota provides an example of a shift in labor relations responsibility from an independent Civil Service Board to the governor, with a team of top management officials as the governor's surrogates.[30] Under an initial "meet and confer" law (1965), state employee relations were controlled by the civil service department, whose head was appointed by a part-time Civil Service Board. When a bargaining law was enacted in 1971, negotiating responsibility was given jointly to the Director of Civil Service and the Commissioner of Administration, a key member of the governor's cabinet. In 1972 two state negotiators were hired within the Civil Service Department. The following year (1973) statutory revisions changed the title of Director of Civil Service to Commissioner of Personnel, made him a gubernatorial appointee instead of an appointee of the Civil Service Board, and limited the power of the board mainly to merit-employment procedures and merit appeals.

In Oregon[31] more than a decade of experimentation and change has produced a comparatively weak central employee relations section located in the Executive Department but not strongly supported by the governor or the legislature. The su-

---

[30]*Id.*, at 10–12.
[31]Jones, *supra* note 19, at App. A—State Report.

pervisor of the employee relations section reports to the director of the Personnel Division who in turn reports to the director of the Executive Department. The ERS negotiators obtain their guidelines from the director of the Executive Department who consults with the governor. On occasion unions have made "end runs" to the governor to obtain concessions that the state negotiator has rejected. Agreements reached at the bargaining table may be altered at different levels—by either the Personnel Division (after a public hearing) or the Public Employment Relations Board if a merit-system rule is involved, by the governor, or (as has frequently happened) by the legislature. In addition, some 45 agencies or departments have the power to bargain on local issues such as work schedules, travel pay, supervisory appraisals, and maternity leave. All agency appointments must be reviewed and approved by the Personnel Division and the Executive Department director.

While the more highly developed collective bargaining systems have led to the employment of centrally located professional negotiators, as illustrated above, numerous municipal, county, and state agencies continue to rely on line or staff officers with little or no expertise or experience.

Relations with Line Officials

When responsibility for negotiations is assigned to a central labor relations office, or is retained by the chief executive, a major problem arises as to the involvement of the heads of the operating departments and agencies. At least two reasons support some degree of such involvement. One is the specialized knowledge possessed by the administrator. The other is the concern of the administrator with the impact of the labor agreement on the functioning of his agency. If an agreement is to be meaningfully applied, it must be understood and (for best results) accepted by the people who must live with its provisions. Not the least of the negotiator's problems in some jurisdictions is the hostility of managers at various levels to the idea of collective bargaining and their reluctance to help make it work. In some cases elaborate steps may be taken to frustrate bargaining.

The chief executive (mayor, city manager, school superintendent) who handles negotiations directly usually communicates informally with his main subordinates, asking for information or ideas as needed. Sometimes one or more line administrators may sit in on the negotiations. On the other hand, it is not uncommon for such officials to remain wholly in the dark about the negotiations and even to learn about them later than some of their unionized employees. The negative consequences for administrative morale and efficiency are obvious.

Professional management negotiators, whether at central or agency level, are usually sensitive to the internal communication problem. However, they have not always been successful in coping with it, either because of limitations of staff and time or because bargaining strategy impels them to hesitate to reveal their plans to others for fear of leaks. Moreover, in large and complex organizations (a major city, a large school district, or a state) size creates serious communications barriers. In addition, organizational politics, competition for power, interpersonal relations, differences in age and experience in office, geographical spread of offices, and a host of other internal factors may encourage close involvement with some officials and total neglect of others.

Juris and Feuille found that in the early days of collective bargaining, police managers in several cities (e.g., Dayton, Omaha) were excluded entirely from the bargaining process by the mayor's or city manager's office. This approach led to a lack of sufficient information to evaluate union proposals properly and had to be changed. In three other cities (Detroit, Los Angeles, Rochester) the police chief was granted total authority over nonwage issues, while the city labor relations bureau, the city administrative officer and city council, and the city manager's labor officer, respectively, bargained on cost items. This prevented tradeoffs between economic and noneconomic issues in bargaining and was also altered.[32]

Stanley cites the case[33] of a police negotiations where the city representatives agreed to a time-off provision without the prior knowledge of the police chief. The result was the loss of the equivalent of 11 men for a provision that the chief felt was thrown in by the union for bargaining purposes. Such an example can be attributed to inexperience or carelessness. But what is to be done when the negotiator is representing an organiza-

---

[32]Juris and Feuille, *supra* note 10, at 64–65.
[33]Stanley, *supra* note 25, at 28.

tion that has a multiplicity of departments and agencies? Is it
possible to develop a system that will avoid such misjudgments?

In Wisconsin, to cite one answer, the state negotiator set up
an Employment Relations Council consisting of 36 members,
one from each of the state's principal operating and staff units.
This council meets with the negotiating staff to review existing
agreements and rules, to help evaluate union demands and develop management positions, and to keep all departments informed of the progress in negotiations. Several of the departments most directly concerned with the particular negotiations
have representatives on the bargaining team. Despite the general approval of department officials with this system, the fear
was expressed by several that the needs of a particular department might be compromised during negotiations. Some smaller
and less influential departments believed that their needs would
be given less weight than those of larger departments.[34]

Relations with the Personnel Staff

If the labor relations and personnel functions are handled
by the same individuals or housed in the same office, communications involving the possible overlap between the collective bargaining agreement and personnel rules and regulations are not likely to be a problem. If, however, as often
happens the functions are separated, then the state or local
government negotiator and the personnel specialist must exercise considerable care to consult with each other, draw
upon their respective expertise, and avoid conflict between
rules and collective agreements.

Donald Wollett, New York state negotiator, tells of a situation
that occurred in 1976 when a blizzard prevented many employees from getting to work and the Director of State Opera-
tions decided that state offices should be shut down for the
day.[35] The question arose as to whether or not employees who
got to work were entitled to compensatory time off. Past practice
had been in the negative, but the DSO was persuaded to reverse
the policy. Since Wollett had a proposal on the bargaining table
to reduce personal-leave time and the DSO decision had the
effect of adding a day, his position at the bargaining table was
"fatally undermined."

---

[34]See Derber, Maxey, and Wetzel, *supra* note 21, at 45.
[35]Wollett, *supra* note 22, at 506.

The possibility of policy conflict becomes even more serious when civil service rules and regulations may be affected. The state of Michigan offers an atypical but instructive illustration.[36] In this situation departmental managers may "confer with" employee-association or union representatives over local working conditions; they are prohibited from altering the rules of the very strong Department of Civil Service (DCS). The DCS officers also hold conferences directly with employee representatives, but generally play what they perceive as a traditional civil service role by arbitrating the interests of both employees and management. Communications between the DCS and the line departments take the form of either a general policy memorandum or informal, individual department, Civil Service correspondence. Line officials reportedly feel that the "neutral" role of the DCS is not functioning on behalf of management and reduces the ability of the line to deal effectively with employees.

Where a strong collective bargaining office has been developed, it tends to dominate the personnel unit, although the latter often serves a valuable support role in providing information (statistical and qualitative).

Relations with the Budget-Makers

In smaller bargaining situations, the management bargainers typically are also responsible for fund-raising, i.e., voting tax levies. Bargaining and budgeting are closely integrated. This is illustrated by most school districts where the board and the superintendent fulfill the dual functions for management. In a large city or a state, however, the relationship becomes more complex.

The City of New York offers an example.[37] Initially (1960) collective bargaining was handled under the mayor's close surveillance by the chief examiner of the Bureau of the Budget, with the director of the Personnel Department playing a secondary role. However, as bargaining spread, a new mayor (in 1966) found it desirable to establish for bargaining purposes an independent specialized Office of Labor Relations which had no

---

[36]Derber, Maxey, and Wetzel, *supra* note 21, at 48.
[37]See Frederick O'R. Hayes, *Collective Bargaining and the Budget Director,* in Public Works and Public Unions, ed. Sam Zagoria (Englewood Cliffs, N.J.: Prentice-Hall, Inc., 1972), 89–100; Horton, *Report, supra* note 22.

responsibility for the budget or finance. The Bureau of the Budget and the Personnel Department were "virtually eliminated from the labor relations process." It became their responsibility simply to implement bargaining decisions that affected the budget and the civil service system. The result, as one budget director put it, was to turn budgeting "into a kind of roulette game." There was a total lack of synchronization between collective bargaining and the budgeting process. The operating budget was usually formulated and approved with only a rough (usually inadequate) estimate of bargaining costs.

As the Charter Revision Commission noted, "Much of the general looseness historically associated with preparation, adoption, and administration of the City's expense budget results from participants in the budgetary process, executive as well as legislative, having inadequate information about what is by far the single largest component of the expense budget—labor costs." One of the commission's major recommendations was to synchronize bargaining and budgeting by requiring all collective bargaining agreements to expire on June 30, settling all negotiations through agreement or binding arbitration by a specified date that would enable incorporation of the new costs flowing from the contracts into the expense-budget process, and prohibiting the comptroller from paying wage increases after the beginning of a fiscal year unless specified in a collective bargaining agreement signed prior to the cutoff date.

New York's experience was by no means unique. A 1971–1972 survey of some 30 state and local government units in Illinois found many similar problems emanating from the separate dynamics of the bargaining and budget-making processes.[38] The authors also recommended that bargaining and budget-making schedules have a common target date, but noted the need for flexibility to cope with inevitable deviations.

Stanley's study of local governments likewise revealed a variety of management efforts to synchronize bargaining and budgeting as well as to assure that bargaining decisions reflect budgeting realities.[39] Often, however, the budget people did not appear to have direct relations with the bargainers or participate in the bargaining process. Instead the mayor or city manager or

---

[38]Milton Derber, Ken Jennings, Ian McAndrew, and Martin Wagner, *Bargaining and Budget Making in Illinois Public Institutions*, 27 Ind. & Lab. Rels. Rev. 49 (October 1973).
[39]Stanley, *supra* note 26, at ch. 6.

council finance committee set guidelines for the bargainers on the basis of information provided by the budget department and political judgments of the elected officials.

Management efforts to integrate bargaining and budgeting have taken a number of different paths at the state government level. One pattern illustrated by Pennsylvania provides for close but informal contact between the Bureau of Labor Relations in the Office of Administration and the Bureau of the Budget in the Budget Department. No one from the budget bureau is appointed to the bargaining team, but that bureau is consulted at the top level in decision-making on state economic issues. In Wisconsin there is a similar relationship except that (until recently) both the employment relations section and the budget officer were located in the Department of Administration. In Minnesota the Commissioner of Finance, who is responsible for central budget functions, sits with the Commissioner of Personnel, the Commissioner of Administration, and the governor's executive secretary on a top-level committee that prepares the bargaining guidelines for the state negotiator. In Hawaii, to cite another variant, a representative of the Department of Budget and Finance serves as one of the governor's official representatives in all negotiations together with the state's chief negotiator and the Director of Personnel Services. The New York structure is similar to Hawaii's but more complex. Representatives of the Employee Compensation and Relations Unit within the Budget Division serve on the negotiating teams for each of the state's bargaining units. The ECRU estimates and analyzes the cost of union demands. It also serves as a training resource for departmental and agency budget examiners who assist the agencies in contract administration just as the ECRU staff itself assists the state negotiators in collective bargaining.[40]

It seems clear from the foregoing discussion that for management to neglect the interrelationships between bargaining and budget-making is to incur serious risks respecting the effectiveness of collective bargaining and the fiscal stability of government. Structure must be adapted to function. The negotiators and the budget-makers can contribute to each other's area of responsibility. Whether this communication is done formally or

---

[40]The data on Pennsylvania, Hawaii, and New York came from Jones, *supra* note 19. The data on Wisconsin and Minnesota came from Derber, Maxey, and Wetzel, *supra* note 21.

informally matters less than that it is recognized by public management as a necessary activity for both.

Relations with the Legislative Body

One of the distinctive features of public collective bargaining is that agreements about money (pay, fringe benefits) usually require legislative approval, and about certain nonfinancial matters (civil service rules and regulations) often do. As noted earlier, some legislative bodies have, for this reason, retained responsibility for collective bargaining rather than leaving it to top management officers. Most legislative bodies, however, have found the technical intricacies and time requirements of collective bargaining too demanding and have adopted a more limited role. Questions about the legislative role include a number of different aspects: whether the legislature should be involved in the preparation of the bargaining guidelines, whether it should be represented at the bargaining table, whether legislative leaders should approve the agreement before it is formally signed, whether the legislature should have the authority to revise the terms of an agreement or merely approve or disapprove, and whether it should remain wholly aloof from the collective bargaining process and simply act on relevant appropriations and legal rules.

In most school districts and many municipalities, the legislative body (school board or city council) is totally involved from preparation for bargaining to approval of the agreement and the voting of necessary funds. Members of the legislative body may even participate in the bargaining team, although as the specialized character of collective bargaining becomes increasingly appreciated, the legislators tend to withdraw to the background except in crises. At the other extreme are the cases in which the legislature (typically state legislatures and large city councils) try to disassociate themselves from the bargaining process and act on appropriations and other bills as in the days before bargaining. In between are the legislative bodies that accept a limited responsibility for collective bargaining by requiring the submission to them of negotiated agreements for approval or disapproval.

The argument for a shared responsibility for the legislative body and the executive branch is that both represent the community or public interest and therefore should coordinate their actions in relation to the employee organizations. A division between the two branches of government, it is found, will encourage "end runs" and undermine the effectiveness of the negotiators. An opposing view is that the public managers (including the chief executive) have a different role in government than legislators and that the latter must take into account the interests of both management and nonmanagement employees as well as the interests of other public groups that are not ordinarily represented at the bargaining table.

Such philosophic differences are usually overridden by pragmatic political considerations and the distribution of power. In New York City the virtual exclusion of the city council and the Board of Estimate from collective bargaining and the supremacy of the mayor have been attributed to the former's inability to develop strong public or official confidence.[41] In Chicago, the mayor's dominant role can be explained by his party's monopoly of power and the integration of most of the unions into the party machinery. At the state level, however, in both New York and Illinois, a vigorous two-party system has given the governor responsibility for bargaining, while the legislature retains the final voice on appropriations.

One of the most ingenious and atypical systems of linking the state negotiators from the executive branch with a closely divided two-party legislature is found in Wisconsin. There the collective bargaining law provides for the establishment of a Joint Legislative Committee on Employment Relations (JOCER) on which the leaders of both parties in both houses are represented. The state negotiator must consult prior to bargaining with this committee in order to secure tacit approval of his bargaining position. After negotiations with the union, he must return to the committee for its approval or disapproval of the tentative bargaining agreement. If the agreement is disapproved, he must return for further negotiations. The finally approved agreement can then expect quick appropriations support in the legislature without the likelihood of an "end run" by either party from the bargaining table. The JOCER system worked well until 1977 when a strike of state employees occurred and there was a breakdown in communications between

---

[41]Horton, *Report, supra* note 22, at E5. See Paul F. Gerhart, Political Activity by Public Employee Organizations at the Local Level: Threat or Promise (Chicago: International Personnel Management Association, 1974) for a broader discussion.

the negotiators and the legislators. A settlement was rejected by JOCER, and it became necessary for the bargainers and the union to renegotiate the agreement. To avoid a recurrence, the legislature subsequently tightened up the consultation procedure between the state negotiators and JOCER in the 1977 statute [Sec. 230].

Michigan, in contrast, has virtually insulated state employee relations from legislative impact by virtue of a constitutional provision that grants the state Civil Service Commission plenary power over all conditions of employment and authority to set wage rates and fringe benefits subject only to a veto of two-thirds vote in both houses of the legislature. There has not been such a veto since the rule was adopted in the mid-thirties.

Administering the Agreement

The ultimate success of collective bargaining lies in the manner in which the terms of a negotiated agreement are applied. Hence management must be as concerned with its organization for administrative purposes as it is for negotiation of the agreement. In small units, no serious problems need arise. The chief executive negotiator can readily communicate with line officers on the meaning of the agreement, and if issues emerge at the workplace the supervisors can quickly turn to the negotiator or his superior.

In the typical small school district, for example, the superintendent or one of his assistants provides the integrating role between the negotiating and the administrative process. Usually only a single level of supervision (the principal) lies between the superintendent's office and the teachers. Somewhat larger schools with a departmental structure may have a second level of supervision, but the principal ordinarily is responsible for day-to-day personnel problems. Matters can be readily referred to the superintendent's office or, if need be, to the school board.

The situation of the small municipality is much the same. The mayor or city manager is normally well versed in the agreement. If an aide, legal counsel, or personnel director conducts negotiations on their behalf, the tie is close. The operating heads of the municipal departments have quick access to the central office and should be able to obtain authoritative answers to questions about the meaning of the agreement.

If a conflict situation arises through misapplication of the agreement, the reason usually lies in interpersonal failings.

In larger governmental units (a complex school district, a major city, or an entire state), size and complexity do demand close attention to management's organization for administering the agreement. This cannot be left simply to informal interpersonal relations. The state of Illinois offers one type of integrative structure. Each department or agency (subject to the Civil Service Code) has assigned to it a personnel officer who is a member of the state Department of Personnel. This officer is also responsible to the operating head of the particular agency, or one of his chief assistants, so that he has dual lines of communication—one within the agency for the conduct of the agency's personnel business, the other to the state's central personnel office so as to implement state rules and regulations, including the terms of the applicable state collective bargaining agreement. It is the responsibility of the personnel officer to assist the agency's line officials in the day-to-day effectuation of the agreement through advice and information, including the settlement of employee grievances. These personnel officers are usually subordinate to the senior line officials; they are not power centers and can often be frustrated by line officials who are hostile to collective bargaining or reluctant to deal cooperatively with union representatives. The state's personnel network then is largely dependent upon the quality of its field representatives, particularly their ability to persuade operating officials that they can be valuable sources of information about personnel rules and regulations and useful aides in dealing with the union organization.

In other states the departmental or agency personnel or labor relations staffs are responsible exclusively to the operating units. The central labor relations office then has the difficult task of developing communications with a wide variety of individuals in whose selection it had no voice and over whose conduct it has no control. These field personnel people attach primary importance and loyalty to their employers. Even when the governor issues a memorandum mandating close cooperation with central personnel and strict adherence to the terms of applicable agreements, there may be considerable variation in practice. Some department heads are much more influential than others at the cabinet level and may be able to achieve more autonomy. The situation may be even more difficult when the governor, for one reason or another, fails to give the state labor negotiators the authority to control departmental action.

The University of Illinois study of state-government labor relations in the 12 midwestern states observes:

> Managerial decision making concerning collective bargaining must always be superimposed on a pre-existing management structure. Attempts to centralize such decision making in the form of either coordination or overt control often become problematic where there has been a tradition of decentralized decision making over personnel questions. While line departmental administrators typically seem to feel that collective bargaining requires the use of experts, such experts are rarely able to establish high levels of control over department decision making in the absence of strong support from senior executive officials. This kind of competition between line personnel and labor relations specialists is most notable in the states with limited-scope of bargaining such as Ohio, South Dakota, Kansas and Nebraska.[42]

In his study of eight state governments, Ralph Jones reported that there was generally "close coordination" between the central labor relations office and the line departments in transmitting information on new contract terms and case data.[43] Informational meetings were commonly held with departmental personnel. However, only Pennsylvania, New York, and Wisconsin published this information. "Some states, Pennsylvania and New York, for example, are well aware of the variations among line departments in interpreting and administering contracts." Published material such as comparative analyses of contracts and interpretations of arbitration awards were viewed as helping to resolve this problem.

With respect to grievance handling, the agreements invariably left the first two or three steps of the procedure to the departments. At the step before arbitration and at the arbitration or court stage, a central office unit (either the negotiators or a personnel section) typically assumed principal responsibility. However, there were exceptions. In New York, for example, the line department retained total responsibility for all grievances pertaining exclusively to the department. Additionally, it should be noted that not all state employee grievances arise under the terms of a collective bargaining agreement. Some (e.g., dismis-

---

[42]Derber, Maxey, and Wetzel, *supra* note 21, at 52.
[43]Jones, *supra* note 19, at 27.

sal, reduction in pay, demotion, suspension, reclassification, or geographical transfer) may be subject to a civil service appeals procedure. Others may be raised by employees outside of a bargaining unit for which a separate grievance procedure may apply. In these instances, the negotiators would have no voice.

At the level of the large city or county organization, the administration of agreements poses the same type of problems for management as in the states. In 1969 David Stanley found that "management's working level relationships with unions are normally maintained by department heads and lower-level supervisors on an informal basis."[44] However, he also noted that with collective bargaining, employee-management relationships "tend to become more formal and potentially more hostile."[45] The employee raising a grievance or asking for a change has become more of an adversary and less of a co-worker or subordinate, especially if he is accompanied by a union representative. Aware of the fact that the union can appeal to higher executive levels or to the city or county board, the line manager may become more cautious in his decisions and is more likely to "pass the buck" to the labor relations office or to the chief executive.

As noted above, the line officials must be kept informed of the provisions of collective agreements as well as of new arbitration awards and court decisions that may be applicable to their departments. Whether dependency relations develop between the department and the central labor relations office or whether the department works out a fairly autonomous relationship with local union officials (i.e., a type of "fractional bargaining") will depend on many personal and political factors.

Training

Given the comparatively short experience of most public-sector collective bargaining, it is not surprising that virtually every significant study of the impact of bargaining on management has emphasized the importance of training all levels of management in labor relations concepts, skills, and knowledge. Stanley writes: "It is obvious that almost any amount of supervisory

[44]*Id.*, at 29.
[45]*Id.*, at 58.

training in labor relations matters will be beneficial. Yet, most of the urban governments studied here (as of 1969) offer no organized training of this sort."[46] Stanley did report some exceptions, notably Detroit and Milwaukee, where hundreds of supervisors and executives had participated in short courses or conferences conducted mainly by the Civil Service Commission or area universities. Some of the programs were designed to train trainers. Where training was absent, the management officials attributed the lack to limited funds and staff and the existence of higher priority needs.

A mail questionnaire survey in 1972 by William D. Torrence elicited reports that eight of 17 responding state governments had education and training programs for state negotiators and 12 for middle-management and supervisory personnel.[47] The training programs for both categories combined had been in effect only about two years on the average. One state (Delaware) reported a program of ten years' duration. Thirteen subjects were covered in these programs (three states offered the entire list) ranging from collective bargaining and contract administration to communications skills, economics, and state negotiating legislation. There was no indication in the article as to the frequency or scope of the programs. Torrence repeated his survey in 1976 and, as might be expected, found an expansion of training activity.[48] Of 28 responding states, 15 indicated some type of education and training program for state negotiators and 22 for middle-management and supervisory personnel. Details about the programs were not particularly enlightening.

The University of Illinois study in 1974–1975 likewise found widespread concern about and interest in labor relations training at the level of state government but "little practical achievement."[49] Training needs and problems were reported not only for line management but also for central and departmental labor relations staff. None of the midwestern states had an adequate program. Even the most involved had to leave such training to the departments because the central labor relations office was

---

[46]Stanley, *supra* note 25, at 29.

[47]*Collective Bargaining and Labor Relations Training at State-Level Management,* 2 Pub. Personnel Mgt. 257 (July-August 1973).

[48]*State Government and Management Preparation for Labor Relations,* 49 State Govt. 224–25 (Autumn 1976).

[49]Derber, Maxey, and Wetzel, *supra* note 21, at 73.

not equipped to do the job. Strong civil service states like Michigan, Wisconsin, and Minnesota had well-established training units within their civil service sections, but they tended to emphasize the traditional occupational improvement or advancement subjects and to give very little attention to labor relations. The most effective training programs in labor relations involved the use of specialized university faculty. Government labor relations specialists generally lacked the time to do such training and typically confined their activities to one-day discussions on new collective bargaining agreement provisions.

A fairly typical expression of concern for more effective training was offered by Captain Willard Shafer, executive officer of the U.S. Naval Facilities Engineering Command's northern division. Shafer told the Society of Labor Relations Professionals that "a 'metamorphosis' is required on the part of federal managers in order for them to implement an effective labor relations program . . . [managers] run the risk of putting their foot in their mouth when dealing with unions if they have not been schooled."[50]

One of the most innovative projects reported in the literature is a labor-management training program jointly sponsored by the Department of Personnel, State of Minnesota, and AFSCME Council 6 and coordinated by the University of Minnesota's Industrial Relations Center.[51] The focus of the program was on the content of a new master agreement that had been recently negotiated after considerable turmoil. The aim was to reduce negative attitudes arising out of the negotiations and to reduce the frequency and severity of grievances arising under the agreement. A total of 1,474 employer representatives and 683 union representatives participated in 11 training sessions held throughout the state in June 1975. The program ratings by the participants were highly favorable.

Although the Minnesota project was not supported by funds available for training under the federal Intergovernmental Personnel Act, in recent years the IPA has served as an increasing source of financial support for labor relations training of management staff. This portion of the IPA program is administered

---

[50]693 GERR 4 (January 31, 1977).
[51]Michael Garvey and George E. O'Connell, *From Conflict to Cooperation: A Joint Labor-Management Training Program,* 5 Pub. Personnel Mgt. 347 (September-October 1976).

by the U.S. Civil Service Commission, which has not only been concerned with the training of federal negotiators and managers, but also with state and local programs.

Another important contributor to such training has been the Labor-Management Relations Service which is supported by the United States Conference of Mayors.[52] One distinctive LMRS program, partially supported by IPA funds, is an annual series of executive-level internships or fellowships in labor relations, whereby promising young staff members are assigned to experienced labor relations offices in other locales for three to four months' training. In 1977 the LMRS set up a week-long prefellowship training program to provide a general orientation to its fellows before they move to their assigned positions. The LMRS, together with other governmental organizations, has also sponsored innumerable conferences and workshops for state and local government officials and staff concerned with collective bargaining.

A variety of other agencies have become involved in the education and training arena for management (as well as labor and neutrals) in labor relations. These include the Public Employee Labor Relations Division of the U.S. Department of Labor's Labor-Management Services Administration (which has developed some valuable case simulation and role-playing materials), the National Civil Service League, the Public Employment Relations Research Institute, the Federal Mediation and Conciliation Service, the Society of Professionals in Dispute Resolution, the National Public Employer Labor Relations Association, and numerous university industrial relations institutes and centers. The number of conferences and workshops lasting from one day to one week has grown enormously.

Indeed, the time may have arrived when a general reassessment of labor relations training is in order. Although the innumerable conferences and short-courses have undoubtedly provided useful information and stimulating ideas to many management officials and staff, their long-run impact is dubious. What is necessary at this early stage of public-sector collective bargaining is a continuing program for all levels of management (staff and line) run by full-time training specialists. Such specialists would be attached to the labor relations or personnel offices of state governments or large state and local government agen-

---

[52]Until January 1, 1977, LMRS was also cosponsored by the National League of Cities and the National Association of Counties.

cies. The leading civil service and public personnel departments have had long years of experience in training public managers and other employees in human relations as well as occupational skills. Parallel programs are now necessary for labor relations. In particular, special emphasis should be placed on training trainers.

At the Federal Government Level

The preceding discussion has been concerned mainly with management in state and local government. Many of the concepts, propositions, and issues also apply to management in the federal government. The latter, however, has some distinctive features which merit comment although space limitations preclude a detailed examination.

From a collective bargaining perspective, the executive branch of the federal government, the nation's largest single employer, should be subdivided into at least three primary segments: (1) the quasi-autonomous postal service, with over 600,000 employees, which is covered by the 1970 Postal Reorganization Act and the Labor Management Relations Act; (2) the classified civil service, with over 1.3 million white-collar employees, which (with some minor exceptions) is covered by a series of presidential executive orders issued first by President John Kennedy on January 17, 1962, and subsequently by Presidents Nixon and Ford; and (3) the wage-board system, with some 570,000 blue-collar employees, which is also covered by the executive orders but which has a prior history of collective bargaining focused on area prevailing-wage rates.

Because both the postal and wage-board systems share many characteristics of private-sector collective bargaining, the discussion in this section will be devoted to the classified civil service. Executive Order 11491, as amended by 11616, 11636, and 11838, gives principal responsibility for implementation to four units: the Federal Labor Relations Council, the Federal Service Impasses Panel, the Assistant Secretary of Labor for Labor-Management Relations, and the Civil Service Commission.[53] Only the second of these, the impasses panel, is comprised of professional outside neutrals. The others are top-

---

[53]U.S. Federal Labor Relations Council, Labor-Management Relations in the Federal Service: Amendments to Executive Order 11491 with accompanying Report and Recommendations, Washington, 1975.

level members of the executive branch of the federal government. This latter fact has not only evoked strong union criticism of the executive-order system, but has also raised complaints about role ambiguity and confusion within the ranks of management.[54]

For example, the Federal Labor Relations Council, which "shall administer and interpret this Order, decide major policy issues, prescribe regulations, and from time to time report and make recommendations to the President," is comprised of the chairman of the Civil Service Commission, who also serves as FLRC chairman, the Secretary of Labor, and the director of the Office of Management and Budget. The Civil Service Commission, in addition, has the diverse responsibilities of providing "administrative support and services" to the council, establishing and maintaining (in conjunction with the OMB) a program for the policy guidance of agencies on labor-management relations in the federal service, continuously reviewing the operation of the labor-management relations program, providing technical advice and information to the agencies, assisting in the development of programs for training agency personnel and management officials in labor-management relations, and reporting to the FLRC on the state of the program and making recommendations for its improvement.

The Assistant Secretary of Labor for Labor-Management Relations also plays a major role in the implementation of the executive order, replicating in effect the NLRB's role in the private sector with respect to representation matters, unfair labor practices, and questions of negotiability and arbitrability. If the Labor Department itself is involved in a case falling within the Assistant Secretary's jurisdiction, the latter's duties are to be performed by a member of the Civil Service Commission designated by the chairman of the commission.

The processes of contract negotiations and administration are left to the managements of the separate departments and agencies, a widely dispersed system involving about 3,700 bargaining units (nearly 2,000 units in the Defense Department alone). The exclusion of basic pay and hours of work, as well as most fringe benefits, from the scope of bargaining under the executive order

---

[54]See, for example, *Who Is Handling Labor Relations for Uncle Sam?* in Selected Proceedings of the 1977 Convention of the Society of Federal Labor Relations Professionals, February 24–25, 1977, Washington, published in 6 Pub. Personnel Mgt. 313 (September-October 1977).

operating management, the framework within which they function must appear incredibly complex—the executive order itself, the Civil Service Commission's Federal Personnel Manual, the decisions and regulations of the Assistant Secretary of Labor and the Federal Labor Relations Council, the awards of arbitrators, and the agency personnel manuals, among others. As one leading personnel director put it, "It can be a frustrating system, with everybody from the General Accounting Office, the Office of Management and Budget, and the courts, in addition to the three principal bodies specifically charged with responsibilities under E.O. 11491, having a piece of the action."[55] "This complexity," he added, "was built deeply into the government structure long before we had a formal labor relations program, and collective bargaining was imposed largely on top of—not in lieu of—what already exists."[56]

After 16 years of experience with the evolving executive-order system, management organization for collective bargaining in the federal government does not suffer from a scarcity of resources such as often prevails in state and local government. Both the top-level managerial units (i.e., the Federal Labor Relations Council, the Civil Service Commission, and the Assistant Secretary of Labor's office) as well as the operating departments and agencies appear to be reasonably staffed (if not to the full satisfaction of the units), and a great deal of attention has been given to the development and improvement of communications network and training programs. A Society of Federal Labor Relations Professionals, comprised of management, union, and third parties, has functioned since 1972 for the purpose of exchanging ideas and information and debating policy issues.

The Civil Service Commission in 1977 provided, through its Labor Relations Training Center, 17 interagency labor relations courses, including six general series courses (such as "Labor Relations for Supervisors and Managers") and 17 specialty workshop courses (such as "Advanced Collective Bargaining Negotiations").[57] More than 9200 managers and management representatives participated in 1976 in these interagency pro-

---

[55]William C. Valdes, staff director of the Office of Civilian Personnel Policy in the Office of the Assistant Secretary of Defense, in Selected Proceedings, *supra* note 54, at 316.
[56]*Id.*, at 319.
[57]Reported by Kenneth L. Steen, director of the U.S. Civil Service Commission's Labor Relations Training Center, *id.*, at 300.

grams and in on-site programs developed with individual agencies. The commission has been a leader in training nationally not only for federal management, but for state and local managements as well. In addition, the Federal Mediation and Conciliation Service provided in 1976 some 140 training sessions in the federal sector, many of which took the form of joint training between first-line supervisors and union officers and stewards.[58]

Nonetheless, Thomas R. Colosi, vice president of the American Arbitration Association, has expressed doubts about the adequacy of the government's training activities. After adding the eight professional trainers of the Civil Service Commission in Washington, the 20 distributed in 10 regional training centers, and the 20 labor relations professionals in the Commission's Office of Labor-Management Relations together with the training personnel of the departments and agencies, he concluded that both the number of trainers and the number of management personnel reached by them were seriously below what was necessary. What was needed, he asserted, was an "umbrella organization or system" to collect, digest, and disseminate the huge flow of labor-management relations information and a substantial expansion of training by the federal government.[59]

However, the essence of the problem of management organization for collective bargaining appears to lie in the previously noted deficiencies of the executive-order system itself rather than in the measures taken to implement it. The role of the Civil Service Commission is particularly ambiguous. It is concurrently a major rule-maker on both collective bargaining and personnel issues, an overseer of rule implementation, an advisor to and coordinator of the operating agencies, a supplier of information and training, and a protector in traditional civil service terms of the interests of employees. It would be pretentious for this author to attempt to offer a facile solution to so complex an organizational problem in which are intertwined political and bureaucratic power considerations as well as structural factors of vast size and diversity. It might be helpful, however, if functional responsibility for management policy-making and administration was more clearly specified by the President, if the

[58]Reported by John F. McDermott, FMCS Commissioner, *id.*, at 307.
[59]*Id.*, at 310–12.

desired mix of centralized and decentralized authority for bargaining was prescribed, and if each responsible agency was confined to activities of a compatible nature.

Conclusion

As the preceding discussion indicates, public management has been confronted with a variety of structural and procedural problems emanating from the rapid growth of public unionism and collective bargaining since the middle sixties. Experimentation, consciously contrived or unplanned, has been rife throughout the country and at all levels of government. A large number of outside labor relations specialists have been attracted by the challenges and rewards. Both personnel staff and line administrators from within have sought to develop new, needed skills by formal training and trial and error experience. Old management structures and practices have been discarded or revised; new ones have been introduced. But the time period has been short (few systems go back more than a decade), and the problems are complex. Hence most of the basic issues remain at least partially unresolved despite a noticeable advance in knowledge and understanding and a substantial development in bargaining expertise.

CHAPTER 4

THE IMPACT OF COLLECTIVE BARGAINING ON COMPENSATION IN THE PUBLIC SECTOR*

Daniel J. B. Mitchell†

Overview of Government Wage Determination

The general absence of a profit motive in government has led observers to expect that there would be significant differences in pay policy relative to the private economy. Pay policy, of course, can encompass a variety of fringe benefits as well as wages. Thus, pay policy between sectors can vary in the mix of benefits as well as in the absolute magnitude of compensation.

There are some notable differences in the composition of compensation packages between the public and private sectors. Consider, for example, the relative proportions of fringe vs. wage and salary compensation at the state and federal levels compared with the private sector, as shown on Table 1. (The table does not include local governments which are discussed later.) It is evident that both the state and federal governments devote relatively more compensation to indirect and deferred methods of pay than does the private sector. In 1972, state governments paid only 74.9 percent of their compensation package in the form of pay for work time, compared with 80.5 percent in private, nonfarm enterprises.

The federal contrast is even more impressive. In 1974, pay for working time in the federal government was only 68.9 percent of total compensation costs. This was less than the 75.2-percent figure reported for the larger firms included in the PATC (professional, administrative, technical, and clerical pay) survey from which federal pay levels are set. Since smaller firms tend

*Research for this chapter was undertaken while the author was Associate Director of the Institute of Industrial Relations, University of California, Los Angeles. Research support was received from the Institute. Steven Stambaugh provided research assistance. Helpful comments were received from James Stern, Benjamin Aaron, Joseph Grodin, David Lewin, Paul Prasow, and others.
†University of California, Los Angeles and The Brookings Institution.

Table 1

Composition of State and Federal Government Compensation Compared with Private Nonfarm Sector

	State Government 1972	Private Nonfarm Sector 1972	Federal Government 1974 Including Postal Service	Federal Government 1974 Excluding Postal Service	Private Nonfarm Sector 1974 PATC Survey	Private Nonfarm Sector 1974 Total
Pay for working time	74.9%	80.5%	68.9%	68.5%	75.2%	78.2%
Pay for leaves (except sick leave)	8.9	5.6	9.8	10.0	7.5	6.0
Pay for retirement	9.1	7.0	14.5	14.7	9.2	8.1
Social security[a]	3.0	3.7	.2	.2	4.5	4.4
Other plans	6.1	3.3	14.3	14.5	4.8	3.7
Pay for life insurance and health and welfare	6.8	4.7	6.3	6.2	5.8	4.9
Workers' compensation	.5	.9	.8	.9	.6	1.0
Other plans	6.3	3.8	2.8	2.9	5.2	3.9
Pay for unemployment	.2	1.0	.5	.6	1.0	1.1
Unemployment insurance	.1	.9	.4	.5	.8	.9
Other plans	—*	.2	.1	.1	.2	.2
Pay for other plans	.1	1.1	.1	.1	.8	1.7
Total compensation	100.0	100.0	100.0	100.0	100.0	100.0
Excluding legally required payments	96.5	94.6	98.6	98.4	94.1	93.5

Source: U.S. Bureau of Labor Statistics [68, 69, 64, 67].
Note: Details need not add to totals due to rounding.
* Less than .05 percent.
[a] Includes railroad retirement.

to devote less compensation to fringes, it is still less than the 78.2-percent figure for the overall private nonfarm sector. The contrast between the government and private sector is even greater when it is recognized that "legally required" fringes are not really required of government.[1]

Fringe benefits may have the effect of hindering voluntary job mobility. This is especially true of pensions, even with vesting. Hence, state and federal government employers tailor their compensation programs to hold down turnover, intentionally or not. Unfortunately, detailed data of the type shown in Table 1 are not available for the period before unionization of the public sector was a major factor, and not for local governments. Data from the national-income accounts suggest that local employers, as a group, devote a *smaller* portion of total compensation to deferred benefits than do state governments or private employers.[2] Many local employers are small, and it may be that, as in private employment, size and fringes are correlated.

Government jobs have historically offered job security. The unemployment rate for government workers in the trough year of 1975 was 4.0 percent, compared with 9.2 percent for private nonfarm wage and salary earners. Although federal employment totals have occasionally declined slightly in the postwar period, state and local employment has persistently expanded. This

---

[1]Note that social security coverage is voluntary for state and local governments. Workers' compensation and unemployment insurance are voluntary for federal and state governments. Local governments could be required to participate in these programs by states.

[2]According to the national-income accounts, in 1972, 88.1 percent of total compensation in the private nonfarm sector went to wages and salaries. In contrast, for state and local compensation combined, the figure was 88.9 percent. Thus, the private nonfarm sector was devoting slightly *more* to fringes in relative terms than state and local governments taken together. Data from U.S. Bureau of Economic Analysis [63, pp. 197, 201]. Table 1, which does not break down compensation in the same way as the national-income accounts, suggests that state governments devoted more to fringes than did private nonfarm employers. Thus, it may be inferred that local governments must be devoting less to fringes than either state or private employers. There is a problem of potential statistical illusion here since public employers commonly require employee contributions to pension funds and other such plans. To make public and private comparisons, total contributions—whether from employer or employee—should really be considered. However, the national-income-accounts data (and Bureau of Labor Statistics data) include only employer contributions. According to the Bureau of the Census, employee contributions to "state-administered" retirement funds represent a larger share of total contributions than they do in "locally-administered" systems. This indicates that the gap between state employers and local employers is even larger than the national-income-accounts data would suggest. However, the issue is clouded by the fact that local governments are often hooked into "state-administered" systems and contribute a significant proportion of revenue to such funds. The lack of hard data is a common problem in the public sector. A general review of available data can be found in U.S. Council on Wage and Price Stability [70].

does not mean that government employees are never laid off. But it does suggest that the probability of this happening is less than in the private sector. For example, nonfarm male wage earners in January 1973 had 4.3 median years on their current job. Within that group, those working in public administration reported 6.7 years. For women, a similar gap exists: 2.8 years vs. 3.8 years (see Hayghe [32]).

The structure of government compensation has several implications. First, it suggests that pay comparisons between government and private wages alone may understate government compensation relative to private. Second, it suggests that public-sector unions face a different environment than existed in the early days of mass unionization in the private sector. Fringes and job security are already present. Although unions may demand improvements in these items, the principle of having them is not at issue. This is probably true of the unmeasurable concept of due process. Public employers routinely have formalized grievance procedures.

The Theory of Government Wage Policy

The phrase "wage policy" can be understood as a consistent practice of paying more or less than the typical wage for a given type of job. All employers have such policies, whether consciously arrived at or not. Not surprisingly, there is a literature that explicitly considers alternative wage policies. In a sense, this literature can be related to private-sector research that stresses the role of relative pay differentials as a device to deal with costly turnover. However, where the private-sector literature suggests an employer's wage decision is basically socially optimal (with all the usual assumptions), the public-sector literature is based on "perverse" incentives. For example, Reder considers the possibility of a wage premium to employees as a payoff for political activity ("vote production").[3] More generally, it is held that government does not have the discipline of the market and that wage determination is excessively diffused and decentralized (Love and Sulzner [50]).

Such theorizing is usually aimed at explaining excessive wage rates in government. However, lack of market discipline could

---

[3]See his essay in Hamermesh [31].

also result in errors of underpayment. Thus, the literature is supplemented by examples of actual practices which bias wage policy upward, such as prevailing-wage clauses that require *at least* the going private wage (Hersch and Rufolo [34]; Leshin [43]). In the background hovers vote-getting from civil servants, union pressure, etc.

Those with experience in government can easily cite upward-biasing policies. For example, it was this author's experience in the federal sector that a civil servant's salary was primarily a function of his previous salary and the salaries of those he or she supervised. Each office manager has an incentive to inflate the job description of subordinate employees and therefore their classifications. A change of position may also result in a jump in grade. Thus, salaries of individuals can drift upward, even though salary grades are tied to prevailing wages.[4]

Despite anecdotal evidence, observations on wage policy at one level of government need not apply to others, or to all occupations within a branch of government. One study, by Sharon P. Smith [56], used data on a sample of individuals in the Washington, D.C., area to study the issue with regard to federal pay. Smith estimated wage equations from *1960* and *1970 Census of Population* for federal and private workers. Explanatory variables included such characteristics as education, experience, race, sex, and marital status. A positive differential for both years was found in favor of federal employees. Curiously, despite the considerable attention devoted by Smith to the federal prevailing-wage system as an inflationary influence, the relative economic "rents" received by federal workers did not appear to widen significantly from 1960 (before the system) to 1970 (after it was in use).

Smith's methodology centered on explaining the wages of individuals by their characteristics. As is well known, there is considerable unexplained variance left after such a procedure. Rates of return to particular characteristics are known to vary by occupation, and federal salaries are based on both occupation and individual characteristics. Thus, a case can be made for applying the Smith methodology on an occupational basis, an exercise described below.

---

[4]Average federal salaries have historically risen faster than basic salary scales. For example, from October 1967 to April 1976, federal average salaries rose by almost 82 percent, while basic scales rose by slightly over 65 percent. See LeRoy [42].

Published *1970 Census of Population* data on characteristics of 58 occupations found in each of the federal, state, and local sectors, as well as in the private economy, were selected. Occupations with no private counterpart were not included, whereas individuals in such occupations would have been included in the Smith study. Regression equations were estimated explaining median occupational earnings for males in the three levels of government and the total economy by various occupational characteristics.[5] Two comparisons were then made between government and total-economy pay (see Table 2). First, a "gross" comparison of the simple average pay for the 58 occupations was made with the corresponding simple average in the total economy. This comparison produced higher pay in the federal sector as compared with the total economy, but negative differentials in the state and local sectors.

Second, the total-economy equation was applied to each gov-

Table 2
Three Measures of Government Pay Compared with Total-Economy Pay, 58 Occupations

	Difference Between Government and Total Pay	
	Dollars Per Year	Differential as Percent of Average Pay in Sector
Gross		
Federal	$ 894	+9.6%
State	−755	−9.8
Local	−430	−5.4
Adjusted based on total equation		
Federal	172	+1.8
State	−1239	−16.1
Local	−133	−1.7

Note: See text for derivation of figures.

---

[5]Occupations such as police and postal workers were omitted from the selection. However, some occupations included mainly government workers, e.g., fire fighters (only about 3½ percent not in government). In such cases, the contrast was mainly between levels of government. The selected occupations account for about 48 percent of local government male employment, 57 percent of state government male employment, 34 percent of federal government male employment, and 38 percent of total male wage and salary employment. Data were drawn from Census volumes on *Government Workers* and *Occupational Characteristics* [61]. Characteristics considered were median years of schooling, male median age, percent male, male percent white, male percent working 30 or more hours per week for 50–52 weeks. The first two characteristics are intended to capture human capital from schooling and experience. The next two reflect both discrimination in wages and occupational crowding of nonwhites and women. The last adjusts for hours worked. Dependent variable is median annual wage and salary income. Each variable was calculated separately for each sector.

ernment sector and an "adjusted" average pay level was produced. In this adjusted comparison, federal pay again exceeded
the total economy, and the other sectors exhibited negative
differentials. Thus, at the federal level, the occupational method
produced results at least qualitatively in line with those of Smith.
However, it appeared that federal findings could not be generalized to other levels of government.

Some research suggests that at the local level of government
there is not a consistent tendency to overpay or underpay, but
rather a tendency to overpay at the bottom of the wage scale and
underpay at the top (see Fogel and Lewin [21]; Lewin [44]).
Overpayment at the bottom is primarily the result of social concerns and employee pressure. Underpayment at the top results
from political concern about payment of salaries well above
those received by the average taxpayer. A study of municipal pay
in 11 large cities in 1970–1971 is sometimes cited as evidence
for the tendency of cities to overpay in nonsupervisory occupations (Perloff [54]). More recent evidence for 24 cities tends to
support these findings (Field and Keller [20]). However, both
studies indicate considerable variation in the public/private differential.

If there is a tendency for wage policy to vary over the occupational hierarchy, it might be detectable from the Census figures
discussed above. Table 3 presents two tests of this tendency.
Equations were estimated regressing the ratio of public-sector
to total-economy pay against total-economy pay for the 58 selected occupations. The first set of equations used the gross
ratio unadjusted for occupational characteristics. As can be seen
on the table, at each level of government there was a systematic
tendency to pay above the total economy for low-paid occupations and below the total economy for the higher paid. However,
the tendency evaporates when the occupational characteristics
—using the total-economy equation—are used to adjust the
public-to-total ratios, at the federal and state levels. No significant relation was found for the federal adjusted ratio. At the
state level, underpayment persisted throughout the range, but
was *less* pronounced at the upper wage levels. In keeping with
the results reported by earlier writers, local occupations show a
persistent tendency to be "overpaid" at the bottom and "under-
paid" at the top, even after adjustment.

There are three major implications for collective bargaining
in the public sector suggested by the occupational data. First,

Table 3
**Predicted Percentage Public- to Total Economy-Wage Differential
at Different Wage Levels**

Occupation with Median Male Pay in Total Economy of:	Unadjusted for Occupational Characteristics			Adjusted for Occupational Characteristics		
	Federal	State	Local	Federal	State	Local
$ 3,000	+72%	+17%	+12%	—[a]	−26%	+9%
$14,000	−29	−26	−16	—[a]	−7	−8

Note: See text for derivation of figures.
[a] No significant relation observed.

federal employees have not done badly, despite the absence of collective bargaining over wages for nonpostal workers. Of course, federal unions are involved at various stages in the prevailing-wage process, and they affect wages indirectly.[6] Perhaps this explains why nonpostal federal unions have been reasonably satisfied with a right to bargain only on nonwage issues.

Second, at the local level, where a tendency to give more at the bottom than at the top seems to prevail, it would be interesting to explore further the union impact on wage structure. Does pressure at the bottom result from more widespread unionization at that level? Are local government unions consciously trying to narrow differentials? Will there eventually be a revolt at the top as has occurred in the private sector where percentage differentials are narrowed by periodic cents-per-hour increases? Or has the observed compression always been a feature of local government, predating collective bargaining?[7]

Third, there is still much to be learned about the interaction effect of collective bargaining and public operation on wages. Census data unfortunately do not indicate who is unionized and who is not. However, a start in examining the public-ownership effect has been made by Hamermesh, who compared unionized public and private transit workers' salaries, and found a higher public wage.[8]

---

[6]See Donoian [16] and L. Earl Lewis [48] for descriptions of prevailing-wage processes at the time the data for the 1970 Census [61] were gathered. Recent procedures are discussed in William M. Smith [57].

[7]Compression should cause queuing for jobs at the bottom and vacancies at the top. In the private sector, it might be assumed that the situation would be self-correcting over a period of time. However, wage rigidities in the face of shortages and surpluses in government have been noted in other contexts. See Doherty [15] for evidence relating to teachers.

[8]See the chapter by Hamermesh in Hamermesh [31]. A different view can be found in Barnum [6].

Relative Trends in Public Wages

The danger of cross-sectional analysis is that temporary conditions may be confused with long-term tendencies. Unfortunately, there is a relative paucity of long-term, time-series data on the public sector. However, the national-income accounts provide figures on compensation per full-time employee equivalent at various levels of government and for the private sector going back to 1929. In some cases, it is possible to obtain data including fringes. Table 4 shows the ratio of government- to total domestic-economy pay—using wage and fringe data combined where possible—for selected years during 1929–1975. It is important to note that there is no reason that the ratio should normally be equal to unity, since it is uncorrected for occupational mix and other relevant characteristics.

It is apparent that the ratio of government to domestic pay can vary considerably. The figures suggest, for example, that the slide into the great depression favored government salaries, which proved more resistant to cuts than did private wages. On the other hand, during World War II, labor market pressures—despite the presence of wage controls over private wages only—drove up private wages relative to public, except in the nonpostal federal sector where presumably the war effort created demand for civilian employees. Nonpostal federal wages either advanced or at least kept pace in relation to other domestic

Table 4
Ratio of Public- to Domestic-Sector Wages, 1929–1975

Year	Federal Civil Servants[a]	Federal Enterprises[b]	State and Local Civil Servants			State and Local Enterprises[b]
			Total[b]	Educational Employees[a]	Noneducational Employees[a]	
1929	1.35	1.34	1.06	1.01	1.08	1.11
1932	1.60	1.58	1.27	1.23	1.27	1.33
1935	1.03	1.56	1.13	1.12	1.11	1.27
1940	.88	1.40	1.14	1.09	1.18	1.19
1945	1.20	1.09	.88	.85	.90	1.05
1950	1.20	1.10	.91	.92	.90	1.02
1955	1.23	1.03	.92	.92	.90	1.02
1960	1.26	1.03	.95	.99	.89	1.00
1965	1.35	1.08	.96	1.01	.90	1.02
1970	1.42	1.11	1.02	1.06	.96	1.05
1975	1.40	1.23	.99	1.03	.97	1.03

Source: Calculated from U.S. Bureau of Economic Analysis [63].
[a] Based on wages and salaries per full-time-equivalent employee.
[b] Based on total compensation per full-time-equivalent employee.

wages throughout the postwar period. Wages in federal enterprises (chiefly the post office) declined in relative terms during
the 1940s and 1950s, but began to accelerate relative to the
private sector in the 1960s. In the early 1970s, when other
government workers tended to slip slightly in relative status, the
federal-enterprise sector showed considerable gains. It is difficult not to associate this recent development with the adoption
of collective bargaining for postal workers.

One question that could be asked is whether there is any
statistically significant relation between the rate of change of
government pay and the business cycle. There has been comparatively little work on time-series wage equations for the public sector to date. The chief exception is a study by Annable [3]
where government wage change was related to private wage
change and a tax revenue measure. Thus, as an experiment,
several government wage equations were estimated for the public and total domestic sector. These were essentially modified
Phillips curves—with all the well-known pitfalls of interpretation
—except that the activity variable has been generated out of
GNP data rather than unemployment data. Results appear on
Table 5. In qualitative terms, both public and private wage
changes seem responsive in the expected positive manner to
economic activity, represented by the ratio of real GNP to its
trend *(RGNP)*. However, government wages exhibit a sluggishness in responding to changing economic conditions. While
domestic-sector wage changes are positively related to the rate
of change in real GNP *(PGNP)*, public-sector wage changes
show no significant relations. A combination of bureaucracy and
legislative lethargy probably accounts for this sluggishness. The
rate of price inflation *(PPB)* generates comparable responses in
the domestic sector and for federal civil servants.[9] But at other
levels of government the response, while positive, is either
smaller or not statistically significant.

Phillips-type curves are known to be unstable. However, the
finding that government wages are not immune from general
economic conditions is important. Also of interest is the behavior of the residuals (actual values minus estimated values) during recent years. In general over the period 1965–1975, public-

---

[9] *RGNP* is the ratio of GNP in 1972 dollars to its exponential trend estimated over
1929–1975, *PGNP* is the rate of change in GNP in 1972 dollars from year to year in
percentage points, and *PPB* is the rate of change in the deflator for the private business
sector from year to year in percentage points.

Table 5
Annual Compensation Change Regressions[a]

	Domestic Sector	Federal Civil Servants	Federal Enterprises	State and Local Civil Servants	State and Local Enterprises
Constant	−14.31*	−48.17*	−19.73	−15.33	−14.25
RGNP	17.17*	51.66*	24.65*	20.36*	18.30*
PGNP	.14*	.14	−.02	−.06	−.02
PPB	.67*	.70*	.14	.16	.35*
Rho	.31	.04	.13	.53	.14
R^2	.95	.51	.18	.60	.68
D-W	2.03	1.75	1.96	2.09	2.08

[a] Dependent variable is annual rate of change of total compensation per full-time-equivalent employee (wage and salary compensation for federal civil servants) in percentage points. Period of estimation is 1931 to 1975. Equations estimated using Cochrane-Orcutt iterative technique. Independent variables are defined in the text and note 9.

* Significant at 5-percent level.

and domestic-sector wages tended to experience somewhat faster rates of wage inflation than expected. The only exception was federal civil servants, a finding suggesting that the recent wage premiums detected for federal employees were generated by "normal" events rather than a special development.[10]

In general, the limited empirical evidence presented in this section suggests that time-series analysis would be a useful approach for future research on government wage determination and the effects of unions on wage and nonwage items. Specialized data series for particular groups of workers can often be assembled. For example, Lequin [41] found evidence of a collective bargaining impact using time-series data on salaries of Montreal teachers. Of particular interest would be evidence on whether collective bargaining has an effect on the structure of the wage response to external economic developments. It has been argued that union wage rates are "stickier" than nonunion rates in the private sector, causing the union/nonunion differential to vary with the business cycle. Does this same effect occur in government? Or are government wages already so sticky that they act like union wages in the private sector?

---

[10]For the total domestic economy, the residuals (actual minus predicted values) averaged .4 percent for compensation and .2 percent for wages. At the federal level, the residuals were −.1 percent for civil servants and 2.5 percent for enterprise workers. At the state and local level, residuals were 1.0 percent for civil servants (.7 percent for education workers and 1.7 percent for noneducational employees) and 1.3 percent for enterprise workers.

The Union Impact in the Public Sector

Public-sector unions as a group are clearly somewhat different from those in the private sector. Some do not think of themselves as unions at all, but rather view themselves as professional associations who engage in collective bargaining. Some had a history that predates any interest in collective bargaining. The remnants of the past heritage are not entirely absent from current attitudes or actions. But they are in contrast with "typical" private-sector labor organizations.

Public-sector management tends to be more constrained and restrained than its private-sector counterparts when it comes to union activities. Many states have enacted statutes protecting the right of civil servants to engage in union activities. Public-sector managers have fewer prerogatives to lose than their private-sector counterparts, owing to civil service rules. While it would be incorrect to state that no hostility to unionization exists, it would also be inaccurate to compare the difficulties that modern public-sector unions have in organizing with those experienced in the private sector in the 1930s or before.[11]

Recent survey information from the Bureau of Labor Statistics permits a contrast between state and local government contracts with larger private-sector agreements. Summary data are provided in Table 6. Some obvious contrasts can be seen. First, it is apparent that public and private contracts tend to cover different types of workers. Blue-collar workers—the traditional union base—predominate in the private sector but not in the public, suggesting that public-sector unions face the task of *converting* employees to militant action. Although this may be less of a hurdle than it was, say, 15 years ago, it is still a barrier.

Public-sector unions, in part due to legal constraints, are less likely to have union-security arrangements, especially union-shop clauses. This may have a weakening effect on the unions' bargaining position. On the other hand, it may put pressure on union officials to deliver attractive settlements. Thus, there are conflicting pressures on public-sector unions with regard to

---

[11]A case in point is the Rodda Act in California which established a mechanism for collective bargaining in public education. While the Rodda Act contains unfair labor practices similar to those of the Wagner Act, allegations of employer interference with employee rights to organize have been rare under Rodda. Source: informal comments by Reginald Alleyne, chairman of the Educational Employment Relations Board, at seminars at the UCLA Institute of Industrial Relations, February 3, 1977, and April 8, 1977.

Table 6
**Comparison of State and Local Government
and Private-Sector Collective Agreements
(Percent of Contracts with Specified Feature)**

	State and Local Government[a]	"Major" Private Sector[b]
Type of worker covered		
Blue-collar only	31.0%	78.9%
Blue-collar and others	19.0	11.8
Others only	42.0	9.3
Unknown	8.0	—
Duration of agreement		
0–12 months	25.5	4.3
13–24 months	44.3	21.4
25–36 months	26.8	67.7
37–48 months	1.8	4.8
Over 48 months	1.8	1.9
Escalator provision	15.3	37.1
Grievance arbitration	75.8	97.5
Binding	56.0	n.a.
Union-security provision	33.5	81.9
Union shop or modified union shop	10.3	68.1
Agency shop or modified agency shop	13.5	6.9
Maintenance of membership,	9.8	3.8

Source: U.S. Bureau of Labor Statistics [66, 65].
[a] Sample of 400 agreements as of January 1, 1974.
[b] Sample of 1550 agreements as of July 1, 1974. Excludes railroads and airlines. Agreements cover at least 1000 workers.

their degree of aggressiveness at the bargaining table. There is nothing in the data, however, that suggests that public-sector unions will be more aggressive than those in private employment.

It may well be that negotiating activities for public-sector unions are more costly than those in the private sector due to greater frequency. Table 6 indicates that contract durations tend to be shorter in the public sector. And cost-of-living escalator provisions—which help make long-term contracts possible—are rarer. The tendency toward short-term agreements probably is explained mainly by the budgetary cycle in government and the difficulty in making future commitments. Longer term contracts will become more common as bargaining matures. But, the current frequent negotiations process is probably not a factor that would increase union bargaining strength, and it might well have a weakening effect.

Grievance arbitration is found in virtually all private-sector contracts. It is common—but less so—in the public sector, presumably because existing civil service mechanisms provide grievance procedures. Arbitration is often not binding in the public sector, since governments are reluctant to yield final sovereignty. But this divergence from private practice is likely to narrow in the future. The constrained scope of bargaining in the public sector provides fewer avenues for compromise. Combined with frequent bargaining and lesser union security, this factor would seem to suggest a greater potential for conflict in the public than in the private sector. Yet strikes per unionized employee—despite more frequent expirations—are decidedly lower in public employment relative to private. This could be a sign of lesser union aggressiveness *or* lesser management resistance.[12] Since contract data do not indicate which generalization is valid, it is best to turn to empirical studies of the impact of unionism on public-sector wages.

Some Empirical Evidence

There have been many studies during the past decade that attempt to measure the impact of collective bargaining on government wages. The well-known work of H. G. Lewis [47] in the early 1960s on the effects of "unionism" in the private sector is often cited in recent empirical work on the public sector. Sometimes the "bottom line" of the Lewis study—the famous 10–15 percent estimate for the average private union/nonunion differential—is cited to put whatever results the researcher has obtained for the public sector into perspective. Less frequently are the methodological issues raised by Lewis considered.

Lewis was concerned about two interrelated issues: defining the effect of unions and measuring it. Unions affect not only the wages of their members, but also nonunion wages. A variety of effects on nonunion wages are possible. For example, nonunion employers may raise wages "voluntarily" in the hope of warding off unionization—the so-called "threat effect." An increase in the wage of union workers may lead to attempts through the product market or labor market to substitute nonunion labor. Such an increase in the demand for nonunion workers might raise their pay levels. On the other hand, some nonunion workers may be complementary in demand with union workers; if a union wage increase lowers the demand for union workers, it

---

[12]For further analysis of public strikes, see the chapter by Burton and Krider in Hamermesh [31].

may also lower demand (and pay) for these nonunion groups. Also to be considered are "teeter-totter" effects. If unions increase wages, they may create displacement of workers among affected employers. These displaced workers may then drive down wages in other areas in which they seek employment.

A key point of Lewis's analysis is that if union and nonunion wages are compared, the observed effect will not be the direct impact of unions on the wage of their members relative to what it would have been in the absence of unions. Rather, it will be the sum of direct and indirect effects. These considerations probably account for Lewis's use of the peculiar term "unionism" to define what was behind the effects he was measuring.

The issue of measurement is really one of interpretation. Lewis interpreted the coefficient obtained from regressing a wage measure against some index of the degree of unionization. The coefficient can be viewed as an estimate of the average wage of union workers relative to the average wage of nonunion workers in the groups under observation. Much of Lewis's analysis was a discussion of the conditions under which the estimate would be biased upward or downward.

An important conclusion by Lewis was that the coefficient obtained does not necessarily measure the *marginal* effect of unionization on union wages. For example, suppose unionization is measured by the ratio of union to total employment in groups under observation. And suppose that all union workers have a 10-percent wage premium above nonunion workers, regardless of the proportion unionized. If the wage variable in each group is a weighted average of the union and nonunion wage, and if nonunion workers' wages are not affected by union wages, a positive correlation between unionization and wages will be observed. To make the example simpler, suppose the nonunion wage is always $200 per week so that the union premium is always $20. In a group with no union members (unionization ratio = 0), the average wage will be $200. In a group with 50-percent unionization (unionization ratio = .5), the average wage will be $210. And in totally unionized groups (unionization ratio = 1.0), the average wage will be $220. A simple regression of average wages (W) against the unionization rate (U) will produce a coefficient of U of $20 and a constant term of $200. The $20 coefficient is an accurate estimate of the average union/nonunion wage differential. But, by definition, the marginal effect of unionization on union wages is zero. By assumption, an increase in unionization in a group from, say, 50 to 51 percent has no effect on the $20 premium enjoyed by union workers.

A second important conclusion is that even as a measure of the average union/nonunion wage effect, the coefficient of U may well be biased. Consider the following (rather implausible) assumption that the indirect effect of boosting union wages had a sufficient negative indirect effect on nonunion wages so that the weighted average of each group always worked out to $200. The coefficient of U would then be zero, a clearly downward-biased estimate of a positive union/nonunion wage differential. More plausibly, a *tendency* for nonunion wages to be lowered by union wage effects will tend to bias down the estimate of the average union/nonunion wage.

Similarly, a tendency for the union impact on union wages to be positively associated with unionization will bias upward the estimate of the average union/nonunion wage effect. Suppose that unionization had no effect on nonunion wages in the earlier example but that it had an increasing effect on union wages so that union wages would rise by $20 only if $U = 1$ (total unionization), but would be less than $20 for lower rates of unionization down to $0 when $U = 0$. Assume that the observation groups cover the entire range from $U = 0$ to $U = 1$. The regression coefficient of U will be about $20, but the average union/nonunion wage effect will be less than $20.[13]

Having outlined the circumstances under which bias would occur, Lewis analyzed various empirical studies and made subjective estimates of the bias based on other information concerning the way the particular labor market functioned. It is important to note, however, that even without such adjustment, the regression coefficient of U can be used to detect the *presence* of a union impact, although the magnitude of the impact cannot be precisely determined. The coefficient might be biased downward sufficiently to obscure the impact. But if unions have no effect on union wages, and presumably therefore no effect on nonunion wages, it is unlikely that a positive coefficient of U will be estimated.

---

[13]Under the assumptions in the text, the maximum union/nonunion differential of $20 occurs when $U = 1$. Since U is generally less than 1, the average differential will be less than $20. In effect, there is a curvilinear relationship between U and the average wage with end-points at $U = 0$ and $U = 1$ of $0 and $20. Hence, forcing a linear fit into this relation will give a slope of $20, if observations are scattered across the range.

Table 7 presents the results of some simple experiments using state cross-sectional data from the 1972 *Census of Governments* [62]. These results will help put into perspective the more elaborate studies on union wage impact to be discussed below. The average monthly wage of teachers and all other employees on a full-time–equivalent basis was regressed against the proportion of employees unionized at both the state and the local levels. A crude attempt to standardize for local labor market conditions was made through the inclusion of average hourly earnings in manufacturing in the state (*AHE*) as an index of expected pay levels.[14] Other experiments (not shown) were

Table 7
Cross-Section Regression Results

	Constant	*AHE*	*U*	*CN*	*MC*	R^2	Mean of Dependent Variable
State government							
Teachers	999*	49	93	—	—	.04	1206
Others	216*	104*	259*	—	—	.64	689
Local government							
Teachers (1)	253	193*	−147	—	—	.45	862
(2)	272*	138*	—	214*	—	.56	845
(3)	324*	113*	—	—	255*	.52	845
Others	98	113*	348*	—	—	.74	618

Note: Dependent variable is average monthly earnings in October 1972 of full-time-equivalent employees of the specified employee group. *AHE* = average hourly earnings in manufacturing in the state involved, *U* = ratio of unionized full-time employees to total full-time employment, *CN* = ratio of school districts with collective negotiations to total school districts, *MC* = ratio of school districts with meet-and-confer arrangements to total school districts.
Source: Employment and Earnings, 1972 Census of Governments [62].
* Significant at the 5-percent level.

---

[14] It could be objected that the manufacturing wage *AHE* is not well suited as an index of an "opportunity wage" for government employees. Obviously, this depends on which type of employees are discussed. The nonteacher equations contain blue-collar backgrounds. Moreover, the manufacturing wage has the virtue of being readily available and has been used in previous studies of this type. See Schmenner [55], Ehrenberg [18], Ehrenberg and Goldstein [19], and Lewin and Keith [46]. Experiments were tried with state average quarterly earnings of employees in business services—a white-collar-oriented variable—without success.
The equations were run in absolute dollar terms, rather than the more common logarithmic format, so that the coefficients could be more easily interpreted. Since the equations are cross-sectional, the need for a logarithmic form is less than it would be in time-series work. A logarithmic form basically assumes that the union impact is best captured as a percentage differential rather than an absolute differential. Although Lewis worked in logarithmic form, it is easy to transform his basic results, following a simplified proof by Ashenfelter [4, p. 195]. Let W_u = union wage, W_n = nonunion wage, W^* = wage that would have prevailed in the absence of a union effect, W_T = observed wage (mixture of union and nonunion) in each group, $D_n = W_n - W^*$, $M = W_u - W_n$, AW_u = average union wage for all groups, AW_n = average nonunion wage, and $AM = AW_u - AW_n$. Then:

tried using political-legal and other economic variables along with the unionization index.[15]

At the state level, the estimated equation for "teachers" was basically unsuccessful in terms of predictive ability. State-employed teachers represent a hodgepodge of university faculty and specialized personnel. Many of these are part of a nation-wide employment market, so that state average wages would not be expected to be related to their wage levels. In the other three categories, however, local wages were positively associated with government salaries. No association between unionization (U) and average salaries appeared for local teachers. For other employees at both the state and local level, some association was noted. The large magnitudes of the coefficients of U in those cases, when compared to mean salaries in the classifications, suggest that an upward-biasing influence is present if the estimate is interpreted as the average union/nonunion differential.

The Lewis model suggests that one factor which could cause a substantial upward bias in the results would be a tendency for the union effect on wages to become larger as the proportion of unionized workers increases. This supposition seems entirely reasonable, since greater unionization would permit more effective political pressure on government officials, as well as more "muscle" at the bargaining table. Some spillover effects to nonunion workers may also be at work. Threat effects, which Lewis discussed, are not likely to be the primary cause, however, although they are not entirely absent. Since public-sector management already has limited prerogatives, the strategy of paying union wages to avoid unionization probably has a smaller payoff than in the private sector. But, since union security is not as widespread in the public sector as it is in the private, some nonunion workers receive union wages because they are in bargaining units. It is unlikely that nonunion government workers outside bargaining units experience significant negative effects

---

(a) $$W_T = UW_u + (1 - U)W_n = W_n + UM$$
Since $W_n = W^* + D_n$ and $M = AM + M - AM$, equation (a) can be rewritten as:
(b) $$W_T = W^* + D_n + U(M - AM) = W^* + U(AM) + Z$$
where $Z = D_n + U(M - AM)$. W^* can be estimated as a linear function of AHE. If Z is uncorrelated with U, then the coefficient of U will be an unbiased estimate of AM, the average union/nonunion wage effect. It should be noted that the methodology applied in the text is comparable—except for the year studied—to that found in Kasper [35]. Kasper's study applied only to teachers, but did use state cross-sectional data. For criticism of this technique, see Baird and Landon [5].

[15]All equations estimated omit Hawaii due to the difference in the structure of responsibility for local education in that state compared with others.

from the unionization of others. Especially in the two categories that have positive and significant coefficients for U, many employees can find similar work in the large private sector, so that displacement of union workers is not likely to lead to teeter-totter effects for nonunion employees.

In short, the regressions for nonteachers suggest that a union effect is present, although the magnitude for the average union/nonunion differential is certainly less than the $239 and $348 monthly wage coefficients for U. The lack of a detectable effect for teachers could be consistent with studies showing small effects of teacher unionization. However, another explanation may be at work. The largest teacher representative, the National Education Association, for many years rejected union-type activities. In many areas it still operates with something less than full-fledged collective bargaining. Thus, unionization is probably not a good index of union impact under collective bargaining.

As an experiment, two indexes that were available from the *Census of Governments* were substituted for U. These were the proportion of school districts with collective negotiations in the state (CN), and the proportion of school districts with meet-and-confer procedures (MC). Both measures are underestimates of the proportion of *employees* covered by such arrangements, since unionization is concentrated in large districts; thus the coefficients of CN and MC are further upward-biased. Moreover, only states with reporting school districts could be included.[16]

Both measures, CN and MC, produce positive and significant coefficients. Given the further upward bias of these measures, it seems likely that the $214 and $255 estimates would be substantially lowered if estimation were possible on an employee rather than a district basis. In percentage terms—because of the higher average wage of teachers—these estimates are already below the levels of the estimates for other employees. While the magnitude of the bias cannot be determined, it appears that collective bargaining and/or unionization does have a wage-raising effect for affected workers in the public sector.

As noted earlier, an important conclusion of the Lewis analysis is that the finding of a positive coefficient of U, or a related index such as MC or CN, could not necessarily be interpreted

---

[16]Omitted states are Alaska, Hawaii, Maryland, North Carolina, and Virginia.

as an indication of a marginal relationship between that index and the impact on union wages. Even if there were no such marginal association, the coefficient could still be positive. The use of an average index to measure the impact of unions avoids the problem of having to specify the precise structural relationships that connect wages and unions. However, it is reasonable to suppose that there is in fact some positive marginal association between the proportion of workers unionized (or covered by collective bargaining agreements) and the magnitude of the impact.

Future research on the union wage impact in the public sector could usefully pursue the marginal impact of unionization (or other appropriate indexes). Certainly, it would be more useful to public employers to have an estimate of what would happen to their wage costs if their workers became, say, 75-percent unionized than simply to know that the average union/nonunion differential covering units ranging from 0- to 100-percent unionization has been Y dollars or X percent. Another way of stating this point is simply to note that it is important to have some notion of the structural relationships that underlie the average effects which are observed.[17]

Previous Literature

Literature related to the union impact in the public sector can be divided into two groups. First, there are studies in which a major goal is the measurement of impact on compensation. Second, there are "structural" studies that attempt to define the channels through which the union impact occurs. The literature in this area has mushroomed, and it would be impossible to attempt a review on an article-by-article basis of the studies that have been published to date. In this section, the objective is simply to characterize these studies.

The target groups for study have varied; teachers seem to be

---

[17]Under certain assumptions, the coefficients of U (or CN or MC) can be viewed as measures of the marginal impact. For example, in the case where all workers, union and nonunion, in an observation group receive the union wage (due to unit determination, powerful threat effects, or whatever), the coefficients are estimates of the marginal relationship. Thus, the coefficient of U for state nonteachers of $239 could be interpreted as indicating that each percentage increase in U is accompanied by a $2.39 monthly wage increase under these assumptions. Experiments with alternative assumptions indicated that the coefficients of Table 7 do not vary substantially across a range of plausible suppositions.

138 PUBLIC-SECTOR BARGAINING

a popular one. Teacher unionization is a major part of total unionization at the local government level. And by concentrating on a particular occupation, researchers can avoid the need for elaborate standardization procedures. Fire fighters, and to some extent police, have also been target groups. But some studies have used more aggregate groupings of employees. In general, compensation studies have in fact been limited to wages and salaries and have omitted fringes. This is unfortunate especially since one study (Staller [58]) which looked at the union impact on total compensation in public employment found the effect to be especially concentrated on fringes.

In most cases, the dependent variable has been some measure of absolute wages rather than the rate of change of wages. The standard notion that in the long run unions create a differential in absolute pay undoubtedly accounts for this emphasis. But, since public-sector unionization is relatively new, experiments using the rate of increase of pay cannot necessarily be faulted (see, for example, Freund [24]; Lipsky and Drotning [49]). In the case of fire fighters, where weekly hours have been a working-conditions issue, hours have been used as dependent variables. In principle, unions might be willing to trade off wage increases for improvements in hours (Ehrenberg [18]; Ashenfelter [4]). The student/teacher ratio is a similar variable for teachers that has been examined (Hall and Carroll [29]).

Where pay is the dependent variable, an issue arises over the appropriate measure to use. Specifically, should some official pay *rate* be used, such as a starting salary or maximum salary? Or should average earnings be used? Examples of each appear in the literature, and some authors use both. There is no "right" answer. If earnings are used, factors such as changes in the mix of employees (age, occupation, education, etc.) can affect the dependent variable, and it may not be possible to standardize for these factors through other means. If unions do push up wages, employers may respond by improving labor quality. Thus, standardization for quality may artificially reduce the observed union wage impact. This dilemma can be escaped by using official wage rates. However, if unions affect wages partially through changing the operation of progression plans and de facto entry levels, the union impact might again be obscured.

The impact of public-sector unions on pay structure is itself an interesting topic. Use of minimum and maximum pay rates for particular occupations as dependent variables permits analysis of one aspect of structure. Explicit research on relative wages of groups of employees has been reported (Moore [52]). Further work in this area would be useful. It would be interesting to know whether occupational differentials are affected by craft vs. industrial unionism.[18]

It is difficult to categorize the many independent variables that have been utilized in the literature. A measure of an external or opportunity wage for the target group is often used. Presumably, the going-wage level in the area affects the wages governments pay, with or without unions. Such a measure can be loosely thought of as a supply variable, although it may contain other information. A variety of demand variables related to community income or wealth levels have been used. And more direct measures of the "ability to pay," based on tax and expenditure data, have been tried. But there is always a danger of reverse causation lurking in such data. Perhaps high wages lead to high taxes.

A complicating factor with which some studies have dealt is the presence of employer monopsony power. If government employers have monopsony power, and if unions form in response to this power, the union impact on pay may be obscured. If unions are partially successful in offsetting monopsony, it might still appear that unionization and pay are negatively correlated. Introducing an index of potential monopsony helps alleviate this problem. Teachers seem to be a popular subject for monopsony study, but monopsony variables have been introduced in studies of other occupations (see Landon and Baird [40]; Schmenner [55]; Hall and Vanderporten [39]; Lipsky and Drotning [49]; Fottler [22]).

Some researchers have attempted to include "noneconomic" variables as explanatory factors. Aspects of the legal environment relating to public-sector bargaining rights may be tried. The vaguer concept of a favorable political climate with regard to unions and their activities is also applied on occasion. In terms of wage determination, public-sector employees may be more prone than private employees to political climate. Some studies have also considered whether government structure, for example, city-manager system, affected union impact. Some

---

[18]Hamermesh suggests that when public-sector craft workers are organized by AFSCME, their wage differential relative to other workers is narrower than when they are organized by traditional craft unions. See his chapter in Hamermesh [31].

types of government might be supposed to be better equipped than others for bargaining.[19]

Finally, there is a question of the measure to be used to detect the presence of a union influence. Some studies use unionization, that is, indexes based on the proportions of workers who belong to unions or who are represented by unions. Others rely on indexes of the formal relationship such as the presence of a collective bargaining agreement. Still others use both types of indexes. There is no correct a priori rule of measurement. Unions might affect wages even if no agreement exists, through lobbying or informal negotiations. On the other hand, it might be the case empirically that unions do not have much effect without the existence of a formal bargaining procedure. Or it could be that the presence of a formal arrangement simply adds to the effect unions have without it.

There is sometimes sufficient intercorrelation of independent variables to create doubt about the specific justifications researchers provide for each variable they consider. Readers may sometimes wonder whether the models presented were not created after considerable experimentation with the data to determine what "worked." However, the codes of academia preclude further discussion of this issue. Most models manage to end up with a single-equation form for estimation.

The structuralist literature is mainly associated with Thomas Kochan. Kochan's work is basically a quantification of the seemingly unquantifiable.[20] Indexes are created for such concepts as the occurrence of multilateral bargaining, a phenomenon associated with public-sector bargaining due to the fragmented structure of management authority. Other such indexes have measured liberality of public policy with respect to bargaining rights of employees (suggesting that legal climate is not necessarily to be considered an exogenous variable) and the many complicated clauses in union contracts.

It is difficult to summarize the conclusions of the variegated statistical literature on public-sector bargaining. In terms of union impact, some of the related literature suggest that the

[19]Ehrenberg and Goldstein [19], Schmenner [55], and Ehrenberg [18]. The variable types considered in the text are not exhaustive of the many types that have been tried. For example, Thornton [59] considers union affiliation, as do Gerhart [25], Kasper [35], and Baird and Landon [5]. Lewin and Keith [46] consider police-fire parity.

[20]Kochan [36, 37, 38] and Kochan and Wheeler [39]. Of course, Kochan is not the only researcher in this field. For example, see Gerhart [25].

elasticity of demand for labor in the public sector is relatively low.[21] This characteristic should be favorable for unions since it suggests that substitution possibilities are limited. However, the statistical studies on union or collective bargaining impact produce mixed results. Some find significant pay boosts associated with unions; others find little if any effect.[22] There is some evidence that the interaction of unionization and public ownership raises wages.[23] But there is also counterevidence that unions are less effective in wage-raising in public enterprises relative to private (Fottler [22]).

At the least, it can be concluded that unions and collective bargaining may raise pay in the public sector and influence working conditions. The magnitude of the effect may be large in some cases, small in others, and is sometimes nil. This finding is not earthshaking, but it is not very different from the general conclusion of comparable literature on private-sector unionization. Despite the special features of public-sector labor relations, there does not appear to be justification for the viewpoint that unionization must inevitably lead to a looted treasury.

Collective Bargaining and Financial Problems of State and Local Governments

In a loose sense, it is obvious that state and local governments —which cannot print money—have a motive to resist bargaining demands by their employees. But despite this motivation, there has been concern in recent years over the impact of collective bargaining settlements on the financial health of state and local governments.[24] It can be suspected that this concern is partially a reaction to the relative newness of public-sector bargaining. But it is impossible to deny that under certain circumstances, collective bargaining could be the "straw that breaks the camel's back."

However, the issue of pay increases as a cause of financial distress needs to be put in perspective. According to Table 4, state and local civil servants increased their total compensation per full-time-equivalent employee from 88 to 99 percent of

---

[21]Ehrenberg [17] and the chapter by Ehrenberg and Ashenfelter in Hamermesh [31].
[22]A summary of the impact literature can be found in Lewin [45].
[23]See the Hamermesh chapter in Hamermesh [31].
[24]See the chapter by Nisbet in Chickering [10]. A lesser degree of alarm can be found in Wellington and Winter [71] and Doherty [14].

domestic-sector pay from 1945 to 1975. If state and local pay had risen at the same rate as pay in the total domestic sector, public payrolls would have been about 12 to 13 percent lower in 1975 than they actually were, and state and local revenues could have been 6 to 7 percent lower. In contrast, if state and local civil servant employment had grown at the same rate as domestic-sector employment during 1945–1975 (38.8 percent on a full-time-equivalent basis) instead of their actual growth rate (261.4 percent), state and local payrolls would be reduced by over 60 percent. Thus, the chief source of pressure for revenue in terms of labor policy has come from the employment side rather than the wage side. Pressure for expansion of government activities and programs stemmed mainly from forces exogenous to collective bargaining.[25]

Analysis of the Bargaining Process

Theories of the bargaining process, even in the private sector, quickly run into trouble. On the employer side in the private sector, there is at least the goal of profit-maximization on which to rely. It provides a demand curve for labor along which the parties bargain. And it suggests that employers make some sort of cost-benefit analysis with regard to particular strategies. However, the union side is not so neat. Unions are conglomerations of interests. Moreover, they do not necessarily act as if they in fact operate along a demand curve with an implicit wage-employment tradeoff.

In the public sector, the process of bargaining is more difficult to model theoretically. The goals of employers are difficult to understand; they represent a conglomeration of interest pressures even more complex than those that reside in a union. Employers have demand curves for labor, to be sure, but how to derive these curves in any useful expositional way remains a mystery.[26] At present, studies of the budget-formulation pro-

---

[25]Discussion of the effect of collective bargaining on financial stability has often been conducted with New York City in mind. However, the New York case appears to have resulted from a combination of forces including irresponsible budgeting, a declining tax base, demographic changes, etc. Collective bargaining may have speeded the New York City crisis, but it would have come eventually. For references, see Gramlich [28], de Torres [60], Debs [12], and Anderson [2].

[26]There is a literature that attempts to derive conclusions about the behavior of public employers from assumptions about their motivations. For example, Carlsson and Robinson [9] draw conclusions about substitution between high-quality and low-quality workers by public employers. Unfortunately, their model relies heavily on the theory of the

cess are more likely to provide fruitful hypotheses than abstract modeling.

Burton [8] has described the tendency for budgetary authority to be fragmented, especially between the legislative and executive branches. This fragmentation is obviously a complicating factor for collective bargaining since it may not be clear who has final authority to represent the management side. According to Burton, the authority over budgetary commitments on wages is gradually shifted toward the executive branch by collective bargaining. Kochan [36, 38] views decentralized, multilateral bargaining authority as something that plays into the hands of unions, who engage in "end-run" tactics, thereby obtaining from one level of government what was denied at another.[27]

Because management decision-making processes can be murky in the public sector, one alternative for researchers is to try to generalize the "rules of thumb" that seem to emerge. One study (Gerwin [26]) has attempted to simulate management behavior in terms of decision rules involving the timing of wage increases, the mix of fringes vs. wages, and the magnitudes granted. The characterization of management behavior as a series of decision rules, of course, tends to divert attention from how the rules were initially formulated. Still, if the same approach worked well for a variety of employers, it could at least be supposed that similar formulation processes were at work. This is an area, therefore, in which replication studies would be useful.

In the private sector, unions can often afford to ignore detailed information on the employer's financial condition and rely on employer resistance to prevent "excessive" wage demands from eroding employment opportunities. A similar situation may be arising in public collective bargaining. One study, for example, reported that unions seem to ignore budgetary information, while management is clearly sensitive to it, in formulating wage proposals (Derber et al. [13]). Thus, in this respect public and private behavior may not be greatly divergent.

There have been many studies of the attitudes and behavior

---

firm and avoids the issue of measurement of output and productivity. Moreover, the behavioral assumptions about governments are peculiar. The most striking conclusion, that labor might be a Giffen good (demand rises as wages increase) turns out to depend heavily on the assumption that vacancies are not allowed to occur. For other criticisms, see Craft [11]. See also Owen [53].

[27]See also Love and Sulzner [50] and McLennan and Moskow [51].

of union members in the private sector. A similar literature is being developed for public-sector unions. But, on the union side, there is less reason to suspect that the act of bargaining with a public employer should result in differences between private-sector members and public-sector members. However, there are particular occupations that are unique to, or concentrated in, the public sector. Members of these occupational groups may have different motivational patterns.[28]

In any case, research on the development of the management side in the public sector is important. The management role is as essential to the bargaining game as having someone on the other side of the net in tennis. One suspects that as a general rule the management side in the public sector is currently less prepared for bargaining than is the labor side. Some public-sector unions have already gained experience in the private sector. Others bring to new bargaining units lessons learned in dealings with other government employers. Management, however, learns primarily by doing, and until knowledge of the bargaining process is widespread within management, it will be difficult to make statements about the economic impact of public-sector unions with long-term predictive validity.

Bibliography

1. Joseph A. Alutto and James A. Belasco. "Determinants of Attitudinal Militancy Among Nurses and Teachers." *Industrial and Labor Relations Review* 27 (January 1974): 216–27.

2. Arvid Anderson. "Local Government—Bargaining and the Fiscal Crisis: Money, Unions, Politics, and the Public Interest." *Labor Law Journal* 27 (August 1976): 512–20.

3. James E. Annable, Jr. "A Theory of Wage Determination in Public Employment." *Quarterly Review of Economics and Business* 14 (Winter 1974): 43–58.

4. Orley Ashenfelter. "The Effect of Unionization on Wages in the Public Sector: The Case of Fire Fighters." *Industrial and Labor Relations Review* 24 (January 1971): 191–202.

5. Robert N. Baird and John H. Landon. "The Effect of Collective Bargaining on Public School Teachers' Salaries," and

---

[28]See Fox and Wince [23], Alutto and Belasco [1], Belasco and Alutto [7], and Hellriegel, French, and Paterson [33]. The public may also be a relevant actor to consider. See Goldberg [27].

Hirschel Kasper, "Reply." *Industrial and Labor Relations Review* 25 (April 1972): 410–23.

6. Darold T. Barnum. "From Private to Public: Labor Relations in Urban Transit." *Industrial and Labor Relations Review* 25 (October 1971): 95–115.

7. James A. Belasco and Joseph A. Alutto. "Organizational Impacts of Teacher Negotiations." *Industrial Relations* 9 (October 1969): 67–79.

8. John F. Burton, Jr. "Local Government Bargaining and Management Structure." *Industrial Relations* 11 (May 1972): 123–40.

9. Robert J. Carlsson and James W. Robinson. "Toward a Public Employment Wage Theory." *Industrial and Labor Relations Review* 22 (January 1969): 243–48.

10. A. Lawrence Chickering, ed. *Public Employee Unions: A Study of the Crisis in the Public Sector.* San Francisco: Institute for Contemporary Studies, 1976.

11. James A. Craft, "Toward a Public Employment Wage Theory: Comment," and Robert J. Carlsson and James W. Robinson, "Reply." *Industrial and Labor Relations Review* 23 (October 1969): 89–100.

12. Richard A. Debs. "New York City's Economy—Some Longer Term Issues." *Federal Reserve Bank of New York Monthly Review* 57 (November 1975): 258–60.

13. Milton Derber et al. "Bargaining and Budget Making in Illinois Public Institutions." *Industrial and Labor Relations Review* 27 (October 1973): 49–62.

14. Robert E. Doherty. "Public Employee Bargaining and the Conferral of Public Benefits." *Labor Law Journal* 22 (August 1971): 485–91.

15. ———. "Teacher Bargaining, Resource Allocation and Representative Rule." In *Proceedings* of the 22nd Annual Meeting, Industrial Relations Research Association. Madison, Wis.: IRRA, 1969. Pp. 248–56.

16. Harry A. Donoian. "A New Approach to Setting the Pay of Federal Blue-Collar Workers." *Monthly Labor Review* 94 (April 1969): 30–34.

17. Ronald G. Ehrenberg. "The Demand for State and Local Government Employees." *American Economic Review* 63 (June 1973): 366–79.

18. ———. "Municipal Government Structure, Unionization,

and the Wages of Fire Fighters." *Industrial and Labor Relations Review* 27 (October 1973): 36–48.
19. Ronald G. Ehrenberg and Gerald S. Goldstein. "A Model of Public Sector Wage Determination." *Journal of Urban Economics* 2 (July 1975): 223–45.
20. Charles Field V and Richard L. Keller. "How Salaries of Large Cities Compare with Industry and Federal Pay." *Monthly Labor Review* 99 (November 1976): 23–28.
21. Walter Fogel and David Lewin. "Wage Determination in the Public Sector." *Industrial and Labor Relations Review* 27 (April 1974): 410–31.
22. Myron D. Fottler. "The Union Impact on Hospital Wages." *Industrial and Labor Relations Review* 30 (April 1977): 342–55.
23. William S. Fox and Michael H. Wince. "The Structure and Determinants of Occupational Militancy Among Public School Teachers." *Industrial and Labor Relations Review* 30 (October 1976): 47–58.
24. James L. Freund. "Market and Union Influences on Municipal Employee Wages." *Industrial and Labor Relations Review* 27 (April 1974): 391–404.
25. Paul F. Gerhart. "Determinants of Bargaining Outcomes in Local Government Labor Negotiations." *Industrial and Labor Relations Review* 29 (April 1976): 331–51.
26. Donald Gerwin. "Compensation Decisions in Public Organizations." *Industrial Relations* 8 (February 1969): 174–84.
27. Albert I. Goldberg. "The Local Community and Teacher Strike Solidarity." *Industrial Relations* 13 (October 1974): 288–98.
28. Edward M. Gramlich. "The New York City Fiscal Crisis: What Happened and What Is to Be Done?" *American Economic Review* 66 (May 1976): 415–29.
29. W. Clayton Hall and Norman E. Carroll. "The Effect of Teachers' Organization on Salaries and Class Size." *Industrial and Labor Relations Review* 26 (January 1973): 834–41.
30. W. Clayton Hall and Bruce Vanderporten. "Unionization, Monopsony Power, and Police Salaries." *Industrial Relations* 16 (February 1977): 94–100.
31. Daniel S. Hamermesh, ed. *Labor in the Public and Nonprofit Sectors.* Princeton, N.J.: Princeton University Press, 1975.
32. Howard Hayghe. "Job Tenure of Workers, January 1973." *Monthly Labor Review* 97 (December 1974): 53–57.
33. Don Hellriegel, Wendell French, and Richard B. Peterson.

"Collective Negotiations and Teachers: A Behavioral Analysis." *Industrial and Labor Relations Review* 23 (April 1970): 380–96.
34. Werner Z. Hirsch and Anthony M. Rufolo. "A Model of Municipal Labor Markets." *Journal of Urban Economics* 2 (October 1975): 333–48.
35. Hirschel Kasper. "The Effects of Collective Bargaining on Public School Teachers' Salaries." *Industrial and Labor Relations Review* 24 (October 1970): 57–72.
36. Thomas A. Kochan. "City Government Bargaining: A Path Analysis." *Industrial Relations* 14 (February 1975): 90–101.
37. _____. "Correlates of State Public Employee Bargaining Laws." *Industrial Relations* 12 (October 1973): 322–37.
38. _____. "A Theory of Multilateral Collective Bargaining in City Governments." *Industrial and Labor Relations Review* 27 (July 1974): 525–42.
39. Thomas A. Kochan and Hoyt N. Wheeler. "Municipal Collective Bargaining: A Model and Analysis of Bargaining Outcomes." *Industrial and Labor Relations Review* 28 (October 1975): 46–66.
40. John H. Landon and Robert N. Baird. "Monopsony in the Market for Public School Teachers." *American Economic Review* 61 (December 1971): 966–71.
41. Jacques-André Lequin. "The Impact of Collective Bargaining on Wages: The Case of Montreal Teachers." Unpublished research paper, Graduate School of Management, University of California, Los Angeles, Spring 1977.
42. Douglas LeRoy. "Basic Salary Scales for U.S. General Schedule Employees Rose 5.1 Percent in October 1976." *Current Wage Developments* 29 (March 1977): 34–41.
43. Geraldine Leshin. *The Prevailing Wage Concept in Public Sector Collective Bargaining.* Los Angeles: Institute of Industrial Relations, University of California, Los Angeles, 1977.
44. David Lewin. "Aspects of Wage Determination in Local Government Employment." *Public Administration Review* 34 (March/April 1974): 149–55.
45. _____. "Public Sector Labor Relations." *Labor History* 18 (Winter 1977): 133–44.
46. David Lewin and John H. Keith. "Managerial Responses to Perceived Labor Shortages." *Criminology* 14 (May 1978): 65–92.
47. H. G. Lewis. *Unionism and Relative Wages in the United States:*

An Empirical Inquiry. Chicago: University of Chicago Press, 1963.

48. L. Earl Lewis. "Federal Pay Comparability Procedures." *Monthly Labor Review* 92 (February 1969): 10–13.

49. David B. Lipsky and John E. Drotning. "The Influence of Collective Bargaining on Teachers' Salaries in New York State." *Industrial and Labor Relations Review* 27 (October 1973): 18–35.

50. Thomas M. Love and George T. Sulzner. "Political Implications of Public Employee Bargaining." *Industrial Relations* 11 (February 1972): 18–33.

51. Kenneth McLennan and Michael H. Moskow. "Impasse Resolution, the Community, and Bargaining in the Public Sector." In *Proceedings* of the 21st Annual Meeting, Industrial Relations Research Association. Madison, Wis.: IRRA, 1968. Pp. 31–40.

52. Gary A. Moore. "The Effect of Collective Bargaining on Internal Salary Structures in the Public Schools." *Industrial and Labor Relations Review* 29 (April 1976): 352–62.

53. John D. Owen. "Toward a Public Employment Wage Theory: Some Econometric Evidence on Teacher Quality." *Industrial and Labor Relations Review* 25 (January 1972): 213–22.

54. Steven H. Perloff. "Comparing Municipal Salaries with Industry and Federal Pay." *Monthly Labor Review* 94 (October 1971): 46–50.

55. Roger W. Schmenner. "The Determination of Municipal Employee Wages." *Review of Economics and Statistics* 55 (February 1973): 83–90.

56. Sharon P. Smith. "Pay Differentials Between Federal Government and Private Sector Workers." *Industrial and Labor Relations Review* 29 (January 1976): 179–97.

57. William M. Smith. "Federal Pay Procedures and the Comparability Survey." *Monthly Labor Review* 99 (April 1976): 27–31.

58. Jerome M. Staller. "Collective Bargaining: Its Effect on Faculty at Two-Year Public Colleges." In *Proceedings,* National Center for the Study of Collective Bargaining in Higher Education, Baruch College-CUNY (April 1975): 74–87.

59. Robert J. Thornton. "The Effects of Collective Bargaining on Teachers' Salaries." *Quarterly Review of Economics and Business* 11 (Winter 1971): 37–46.

60. Juan de Torres. "New York City Is Really Something Different!" *Conference Board Record* 13 (January 1976): 2–7.
61. U.S. Bureau of the Census. *1970 Census of Population.* Washington: U.S. Government Printing Office, 1972–1973. Volumes on *Government Workers* and *Occupational Characteristics.*
62. _____. *1972 Census of Governments.* Washington: U.S. Government Printing Office, 1973–1975. Volumes including *Management-Labor Relations in State and Local Governments* and *Compendium of Public Employment.*
63. U.S. Bureau of Economic Analysis. *The National Income and Product Accounts of the United States, 1929–74.* Washington: U.S. Government Printing Office, 1977.
64. U.S. Bureau of Labor Statistics. *Changes in Compensation Structure of Federal Government and Private Industry, 1972–74.* Summary 77–2, February 1977.
65. _____. *Characteristics of Major Collective Bargaining Agreements, July 1, 1974.* Washington: U.S. Government Printing Office, 1975.
66. _____. *Collective Bargaining Agreements for State and County Government Employees.* Washington: U.S. Government Printing Office, 1976.
67. _____. *Employee Compensation in the Private Nonfarm Economy, 1974.* Summary 76-12, January 1977.
68. _____. *Handbook of Labor Statistics 1975.* Washington: U.S. Government Printing Office, 1975.
69. _____. *State Government Employee Compensation, 1972.* Washington: U.S. Government Printing Office, 1976.
70. U.S. Council on Wage and Price Stability. *State and Local Government Employee Compensation Data Needs.* Staff Report. Washington: October 1976.
71. Harry H. Wellington and Ralph K. Winter, Jr. *The Unions and the Cities.* Washington: The Brookings Institution, 1971.

Chapter 5

DYNAMICS OF DISPUTE RESOLUTION IN THE PUBLIC SECTOR*

Thomas A. Kochan†

Introduction

The central theme running throughout this chapter's analysis of the dynamics of dispute resolution in the public sector is that the challenges became greater as the majority of states moved through their first decade of experience under collective bargaining statutes. Thus, the transition to the second decade is characterized by (1) political and economic environments that produce disputes of greater intensity and complexity, (2) highly sophisticated bargaining representatives who are able to pursue aggressively the interests of their organizations through the various stages of dispute resolution, and (3) more assertive union members, management negotiators, politicians, and public interest groups. These developments follow the decade of experimentation with numerous dispute-resolution procedures designed to substitute for the right to strike—procedures so varied and so often changed that by now we have had some experience with most of the commonly discussed alternative systems.

Two important assumptions underlie the analysis: (1) the factors causing collective bargaining impasses are diverse, and (2) there is no "one best way" for resolving all types of disputes. Thus, after reviewing the record of the strike and its alternatives

*Funds for this research were provided by NSF Grant No. APR-17120 and by the New York State School of Industrial and Labor Relations, Cornell University. The conclusions expressed in this chapter do not represent the official positions of either institution. I would like to thank Mark Blondman and Bruce Crawford for their research assistance and John F. Burton, Jr., David B. Lipsky, Charles Morris, and the editors of this volume for helpful comments on an earlier version.
†Cornell University.

during this first decade of bargaining, the chapter will conclude with a description of the options available to policy-makers holding different normative premises or assumptions regarding the appropriateness of alternative processes—fact-finding, arbitration, and the strike.

Historical Evolution of Attitudes Toward Strikes

The attitudes of the public and of political leaders toward the right of governmental employees to strike in the half-century predating the establishment of collective bargaining in the public sector is perhaps best captured by the often-quoted statement of Calvin Coolidge during the 1919 Boston police strike: "There is no right to strike against the public safety by anybody, anywhere, at anytime."[1] Other public officials of different political persuasions held similar and equally strong views. Franklin D. Roosevelt, for example, argued that strikes and militant actions against government were "unthinkable and intolerable."[2] The courts, on their part, reflected the antistrike views of most elected officials, consistently ruling that public employees lacked any rights to strike.[3] Thus, the predominant view during the first half of this century was that strikes were a form of organized anarchy and, therefore, represented a direct assault on the sovereignty of government. Since strikes were viewed as a necessary component of any collective bargaining system, it followed that the collective bargaining process was inappropriate for public employees.

Public-employee unions had little choice but to accept this prevalent view of strikes. Most of the major unions either had constitutional prohibitions against the right of their members to strike or banned strikes through some official policy statement. Spero and Capozzola argue that these union positions reflected less of a philosophical agreement with the sovereignty doctrine than a recognition of the futility of strikes in the face of such hostile public and political attitudes toward direct actions by public-employee organizations.[4]

---

[1]Sterling Spero, Government as Employer (New York: Remsen Press, 1948), 280.
[2]Id., at 2.
[3]Sterling Spero and John M. Capozzola, The Urban Community and Its Unionized Bureaucracies (New York: Dunellen, 1973), 257.
[4]Id., at 243.

Breaking from the Traditional Premises

For reasons discussed in more detail in other chapters of this volume, events of the 1960s created pressures for changing the traditional view of the legitimacy of collective bargaining for public employees, necessitating a reexamination of the normative or philosophical opposition to unionization and bargaining rights for this large and important segment of the work force. As attitudes changed and the political power of public employees increased, policy-makers in the majority of states were required to fashion more pragmatic responses to the conflicts that are inherent in collective bargaining. The search for a new policy toward strikes centered on three broad options.

The first argued for transferring the strike-based bargaining system from the private to the public sector. The central themes underlying this approach were that (1) the right to strike is essential to the success of the bargaining process, and (2) strike bans are unsuccessful in preventing strikes. Kheel probably expressed this argument best after reviewing bargaining in New York City during the first 16 months following passage of the Taylor Law, a law that does not grant the right to strike:

> In September, 1967, the teachers in New York City struck for 14 days; in the early hours of 1968 a transit strike was narrowly averted after negotiations in which the Act's procedures were set aside, and an implicit strike threat informed the bargaining with appropriate urgency. In February, the sanitation service of New York City was interrupted for nine days. Other important city workers, including police and firemen, have either threatened strikes or resorted to some form of job action.[5]

Kheel's solution was simply to ". . . acknowledge the failure of unilateral determination, however disguised by unreal promises of joint negotiation, and turn instead to true collective bargaining, even though this must include the possibility of a strike."[6] Most unions concurred in Kheel's view in the early stages of public-sector bargaining. In 1968, for example, the International Association of Fire Fighters (IAFF) dropped the ban on strikes from its constitution. Only a few states adopted this approach, however, and those that did limited strike rights to selected local government employees and to

---

[5]282 GERR F2 (February 3, 1969).
[6]*Id.*, at F6.

situations following the exhaustion of various impasse procedures.

A second and almost diametrically opposed point of view argued that strikes are inappropriate weapons of economic conflict in the public sector under any circumstances. This approach placed less weight on the function of the strike for a viable bargaining process and greater weight on the costs of the strike-based system to our democratic institutions of government. A variety of themes support this approach, ranging from the traditional sovereignty argument to beliefs that the right to strike gives public employees the economic and political power to coerce elected officials into settlements injurious to the public interest.[7] A separate argument supporting this view is that public-sector strikes disrupt essential public services and, therefore, should not be tolerated. Most early advisory committees and state legislatures took this approach.[8]

A third approach argued for the right to strike only for nonessential employees. Its advocates accepted the premise that the right to strike was important to the bargaining process and rejected the arguments of those who felt that strikes would uniformly tip the balance of economic and political power in favor of public employees. Advocates of this position likewise rejected the sovereignty argument as being outdated and impractical, given the growth of public-sector unions. They also questioned the view that strikes were a form of "economic" protest and that other forms of pressure were more legitimate because they were essentially "political" tactics. Instead they argued that any pressure tactic was a form of political protest and that the strike was no more coercive than direct political threats or tradeoffs of political support for bargaining concessions.[9]

Although these three basic positions remain popular today, the views of the various groups have shifted somewhat since the initiation of public-sector bargaining. The most important shift

---

[7]See, for example, Harry H. Wellington and Ralph K. Winter, Jr., The Unions and the Cities (Washington: The Brookings Institution, 1971).

[8]See, for example, Governor's Committee on Public Employee Relations: Final Report (Albany: State of New York, March 31, 1966), at 16–19. For a review of the recommendations of a number of these early study commissions, see Report of Task Force on State and Local Government Labor Relations (Chicago: Public Personnel Association, date), at 91–92, and 1970 Task Force Supplement, at 20–22.

[9]See, for example, John F. Burton, Jr., *Can Public Employees Be Given the Right to Strike?* 21 Lab. L. J. 472 (August 1970).

that occurred in the last decade was the decline in interest of police and fire fighters in the right to strike and their increased preference for various forms of compulsory arbitration. The IAFF, for example, now strongly endorses enactment of arbitration statutes. This shift in preference developed after several IAFF locals experienced a good deal of public backlash and a decline in political support following a strike. Faced with only two realistic alternatives—fact-finding and arbitration—the IAFF chose the latter. Their experience with fact-finding during the 1960s helped them to recognize the need to put the ultimate decision in the hands of a neutral rather than the employer.[10] Police and fire fighter organizations have lobbied intensely for arbitration, and at least 18 states have adopted it in one form or another for these groups. Two states, Iowa and Wisconsin, have extended arbitration procedures to other municipal employees as well. Ironically, while most management spokesmen still prefer fact-finding, when forced to choose between arbitration and the right to strike, a number of professional management groups have voiced support for the latter option.[11] As will be shown in a later section, the increased management support for the strike option reflects an increased willingness of elected officials and the public to take a strike.

In the 1970s, "final-offer" arbitration, an idea proposed by Carl Stevens[12] for avoiding the "chilling" effects of conventional arbitration, was adopted in several states. Final-offer arbitration is now in force for police and fire fighters in five states, for other local and state government employees in Iowa, and for local government employees in Wisconsin.

State legislatures have also exhibited a modest increased tolerance for the right to strike. Presently (early 1978), eight states (Alaska, Hawaii, Minnesota, Montana, Oregon, Pennsylvania, Vermont, and Wisconsin) grant strike rights in one form or another to selected employee groups. Furthermore, in some states such as Michigan, employees appear to have gained a de

---

[10]For a representative example of the views of most IAFF officials on the merits of fact-finding vs. arbitration, see The Proceedings of the Symposium on Police and Firefighter Arbitration in New York State, December 1–3, 1976 (Albany: New York State Public Employment Relations Board, 1976), at 29–32.

[11]R. Theodore Clark, Jr., *Legislated Interest Arbitration—A Management Perspective,* in Proceedings of the 27th Annual Meeting, Industrial Relations Research Association (Madison, Wis.: IRRA, 1974), 320–23.

[12]Carl M. Stevens, *Is Compulsory Arbitration Compatible with Bargaining?* 5 Ind. Rels. 38 (May 1966).

facto right to strike without a change in legislation, because injunctions and other sanctions against illegal strikes are not ordinarily imposed. All states, however, continue to prohibit strikes by essential-service employees such as police and fire fighters either by express laws or by language limiting strikes that threaten public health and safety.

A number of states have recently built more options into their impasse procedures. For example, the New Jersey police and fire fighter arbitration law allows the parties to choose from a menu of options including final-offer by package, final-offer by issue, final-offer on some issues and conventional arbitration on others, or conventional arbitration on all issues. The new 1978 Wisconsin law allows the parties to choose between final-offer arbitration and the right to strike in local government disputes not involving police and fire fighters.[13] Iowa's 1974 final-offer arbitration law allows the parties to fashion their own local impasse procedures.[14] These multiple-option approaches assume that the parties who design their own procedure (1) can match the procedure to fit the types of disputes they encounter, and (2) will be more committed to making it work than if the procedure is mandated by state law. On the other hand, the multiple-option approach has been criticized for adding undue complexity and confusion to the bargaining process; some critics have sarcastically called it "an academic's dream and a practitioner's nightmare." In addition, the approach embodies the risk of incorporating some options that may be inconsistent with the intent, if not the letter, of the state law. In Iowa, for example, the state Public Employment Relations Board has ruled that local options must provide finality in order to be equivalent to the procedure outlined in the state law. Most of the local procedures that have been negotiated have simply changed the time limits, the methods of selecting arbitrators, or the sequence of procedures preceding arbitration. (Some have eliminated fact-finding as an intermediate step.)[15] Some local options have changed the criteria or standards for decision-making. One innovative local option provides that if mediation fails to resolve the dispute, the local school board will provide finality by issuing a binding

---

[13]1977 Senate Bill 15, amending Sec. 111.70 of the Wisconsin Municipal Employment Relations Act.

[14]Iowa Public Employment Act of 1974.

[15]Thomas P. Gilroy and Jack A. Lipovac, *Impasse Procedure Utilization: Year One Under the Iowa Statute,* 6 J. Coll. Negotiations in the Pub. Sector 184 (1977).

decision!¹⁶ In the early years of the Taylor Law in New York State, at least 29 cities, counties, and school districts exercised the local-option provisions in the law. However, many of these alternative procedures have since been abandoned after the parties found that they injected more confusion and local expense than they were worth. Only 14 remain, and only a few, such as New York City's, are still active.

Another recent trend, this one consistent with the general pressure to reduce secrecy in government, has been toward the idea of "sunshine" bargaining, that is, opening bargaining sessions to the public. Statutes in Florida, Iowa, and Wisconsin now provide for it, and it has been tried on a voluntary basis in a number of jurisdictions. The experience reported to date, however, does not suggest that much light is shed on the bargaining process by opening it to the public. In fact, a fundamental law of sunshine bargaining might be suggested: the more people who show up to observe bargaining, the less there will be to see. That is, the more the negotiators perform for an audience, the less substantive the bargaining that will occur and the greater the pressures that will build to move the real negotiations to some cloistered arena. Furthermore, once the process turns to internal caucuses, mediation, or an executive session in arbitration, the public is again closed out of the process. Thus, the public again misses the critical forums where the real bargaining and decision-making takes place.

Two final points need to be made in summarizing the evolution of dispute-resolution policies over the first decade of public-sector bargaining. First, although a number of states passed arbitration statutes initially on a two- or three-year experimental basis, as yet no state has repealed an arbitration (or a right-to-strike) law and returned to fact-finding. Thus, the move from milder to stronger forms of third-party intervention or from a no-strike to a modified strike-based system may set in motion an irreversible dynamic. Once employees are provided these rights, it is unlikely that the clock can be turned back to an earlier day. Second, while the multiplicity of systems that have evolved for different employee groups in the same state may to some extent reflect differences in the essentiality of services, it is more

¹⁶David Bishop, Voluntary Impasse Procedures Under the Iowa Public Employment Act of 1974, term paper, New York State School of Industrial and Labor Relations, May 25, 1977.

likely that the differences reflect variations in the political influence of these groups.[17] While this is understandable, we might question whether political power is the most appropriate basis for choosing a dispute-resolution system for any group of employees. If the research community wishes to question the current distribution of procedures and to guide policy-makers in future deliberations, we must provide an accurate and concise assessment of the dispute-resolution experience under the various alternative systems that were tried during the first decade so that future choices can reflect the lessons of this experience. Attention will now turn to this task.

Strike Activity over the First Decade

The variety of initial and subsequent approaches adapted in response to the pressures for bargaining rights provided an ideal laboratory for experimentation and learning about the performance of collective bargaining under alternative dispute-resolution systems. Throughout the remainder of this chapter, these experiences will be evaluated with the available empirical evidence. Data from the first decade of bargaining will be used to describe the current state of affairs as well as to illustrate the limitations of the research and data that have attempted to take advantage of the laboratory for research and experimentation.

Aggregate Strike Experience, 1960–1976

The aggregate increase in public-sector strike activity between 1960 and 1975 is presented in Table 1. Strike activity accelerated most rapidly between 1966 and 1976. The relatively stable 1960–1966 period represents the final years in the pre-collective-bargaining era for most states. The number of strikes varied over these six years from a low of 28 to a high of 42.[18] In 1966, 132 strikes occurred, and the upward movement continued to a record 428 in 1975. The Bureau of Labor Statistics (BLS) reported that 2.2 percent of all public employees participated in a strike in 1975, a figure equal to the comparable

---

[17]For an analysis of the factors associated with variation in public-employee bargaining laws, see Thomas A. Kochan, *Correlates of State Public Employee Bargaining Laws*, 12 Ind. Rels. 322 (October 1973).

[18]The strike data are taken from the Bureau of Labor Statistics report, Work Stoppages in Government, various years.

rate for private-sector employees for that year. That year was somewhat atypical, however. In 1976, as in most previous years, all of the measures of strike impact, duration, and percentage of working-time lost ranged between one fourth and one half of the comparable private-sector figures. For example, the average duration of public-sector strikes (measured as average number of days workers were on strike) has been consistently less than half the duration of private-sector strikes. Since 1960, strikes by state employees averaged 5.6 days, and strikes by local employees averaged 7.4 days; the average duration of strikes for workers in all industries was 15.5 days. Similarly, the total percent of work-time lost due to strikes in the public sector remains considerably below the comparable private-sector rate. In 1976, 0.19 percent of total working time in the private sector was lost due to strikes, compared to 0.04 in the government sector. Even in 1975, a high year for governmental strikes, these same figures are 0.16 for the private sector and 0.06 for the government sector.

Ninety-two percent of all governmental strikes occurred at the local level between 1960 and 1975. State employees accounted for 7.5 percent of the strikes; federal employees accounted for only 0.5 percent. Thus, public-sector strikes are predominantly local and state government phenomena.

It is difficult to compare trends in strikes across occupational groups since the BLS only began reporting these data in 1971. The data show that between 1971 and 1975 approximately 55 percent of all strikes took place in public education. Strikes by fire fighters and law enforcement employees accounted for about 7 percent of the total. Sanitation workers accounted for approximately 6 percent, and no other occupation group accounted for more than 5 percent of the total number of strikes.

These aggregate figures tell us little about the performance of collective bargaining in avoiding strikes in the private and public sectors because the number of contract expirations in the public sector in a given year is unknown. The comparisons of the impact and the duration data do suggest, however, that the average public-sector strike is considerably shorter and has less impact than its private-sector counterpart, perhaps indicating that the sanctions against public-sector strikes, the essentiality of the services provided, and/or the intense public and legal pressure brought to bear on striking workers and management have limited the duration and impact of strikes. The effects are

Table 1
Work Stoppages by Level of Government, 1960–1976
(Workers Involved and Days Idle in Thousands)

Year	Total[a] Number of Stoppages	Total Workers Involved	Total Days Idle During Year	Federal Number of Stoppages	Federal Workers Involved	Federal Days Idle During Year	State Number of Stoppages	State Workers Involved	State Days Idle During Year	Local[b] Number of Stoppages	Local Workers Involved	Local Days Idle During Year
1960	36	28.6	58.4	—	—	—	3	1.0	1.2	33	27.6	67.7
1961	28	6.6	15.3	—	—	—	—	—	—	28	6.6	15.3
1962	28	31.1	79.1	5	4.2	33.8	2	1.7	2.3	21	25.3	43.1
1963	29	4.8	15.4	—	—	—	2	.3	2.2	27	4.6	67.7
1964	41	22.7	70.8	—	—	—	4	.3	3.2	37	22.5	57.7
1965	42	11.9	146.0	—	—	—	—	—	1.9[d]	42	11.9	145.0
1966	142	105.0	455.0	—	—	—	9	3.1	6.0	133	102.0	449.0
1967	181	132.0	1250.0	—	—	—	12	4.7	16.3	169	127.0	1230.0
1968	254	201.8	2545.2	3	1.7	9.6	16	9.3	42.8	235	190.9	2492.8
1969	411	160.0	745.7	2	.6	1.1	37	20.5	152.4	372	139.0	592.2
1970	412	333.5	2023.2	3	155.8	648.3	23	8.8	44.6	386	168.9	1330.5
1971	329	152.6	901.4	2	1.0	8.1	23	14.5	81.8	304	137.1	811.6
1972	375	142.1	1257.3	—	—	—	40	27.4	273.7	335	114.7	983.5
1973	387	196.4	2303.9	1	.5	4.6	29	12.3	133.0	357	183.7	2166.3
1974	384	160.7	1404.2	2	.5	1.4	34	24.7	86.4	348	135.4	1316.3
1975	478	318.5	2204.4	—	—	—	32	66.6	300.5	446	252.0	1903.9
1976	378	180.7	1690.7	1	—[c]	—[c]	25	33.8	148.2	352	146.8	1542.6

Source: Bureau of Labor Statistics, Work Stoppages in Government 1975, Rep. No. 483, Table 1. 1976 data are preliminary.

Note: Because of rounding, sums of individual items may not equal totals.

[a]The Bureau of Labor Statistics has published data on strikes in government in its annual reports since 1942. Before that year, they had been included in a miscellaneous category—other nonmanufacturing industries. From 1942 through 1957, data refer only to strikes in administrative, protective, and sanitary services of government. Stoppages in establishments owned by governments were classified in their appropriate industry; for example, public schools and libraries were included in education services, not in government. Beginning in 1958, stoppages in such establishments were included under the government classifications. Stoppages in publicly owned utilities, transportation, and schools were reclassified back to 1947, but a complete reclassification was not attempted. After 1957, dashes denote zeros.

[b]Includes all stoppages at the county, city, and special-district levels.

[c]Fewer than 100.

[d]Idleness in 1965 resulted from two stoppages that began in 1964.

similar to those of strike controls employed by the War Labor
Board during World War II.[19] Whether the strike bans and
procedures reduce the frequency of strikes cannot be determined from these aggregate data. To deal with this question we
must turn to more disaggregated comparisons across policy alternatives within the public sector.

Policy Options and Strike Frequency

A number of studies have attempted to examine the incidence
of strikes for specific occupational groups in the public sector.
Two central questions underlie all of these analyses: (1) Has the
passage of collective bargaining laws increased or decreased the
rate of strike activity? (2) How effective are alternative dispute-
resolution procedures in deterring strikes? Before the impact of
public-policy variables on strike activity can be estimated, it is
necessary to control for differences in state and local economic
and political environments, for the degree of public-sector unionization, and for other nonpolicy-related causes of strikes.
After controlling for the environmental and unionization context
of local governments, Burton and Krider found a "mild tendency" for 1968 and 1971 strike activity to be higher in states with
laws requiring or permitting bargaining or establishing meet-
and-confer procedures.[20] They also found that strikes were just
as frequent in states where bargaining was illegal. They concluded, therefore, that while statutes providing the right to bargain collectively or meet and confer perhaps have a "mild tendency to encourage strikes," laws that prohibit bargaining have
little power to reduce the rate of strikes. Furthermore, their
analysis showed no significant consistent effect for strike penalties or for policies providing fact-finding or mediation. Again,
there was some evidence that a statutory provision for mediation
or fact-finding tended to increase the rate of strike activity.

Incidence of Teacher Strikes

The Burton and Krider study excluded public-school teachers. However, Colton's study of teacher strikes between 1963

---

[19]Herbert R. Northrup, Compulsory Arbitration and Government Intervention in
Labor Disputes (Washington: Labor Policy Association, 1966), 21.
[20]John F. Burton, Jr., and Charles E. Krider, *The Incidence of Strikes in Public Employment*,
in Labor in the Public and Nonprofit Sectors, ed. Daniel S. Hamermesh (Princeton, N.J.:
Princeton University Press, 1975), 161–70.

and 1973 produced very similar results.[21] He analyzed the number of strikes in the three years prior to and immediately following the passage of a collective bargaining law for teachers in 28 states. Ten states experienced no change in the incidence of teacher strikes, five experienced a slight decrease in the number of strikes, nine experienced an increase of from one to six teacher strikes, and four states (Michigan, New York, New Jersey, and Pennsylvania) experienced increases in strikes ranging from a low of 12 (New York) to a high of 86 (Pennsylvania). The reason for the large increase in Pennsylvania is quite obvious— teachers were given the right to strike under the new law. The author cautions, however, that these statistics do not control for differences in the economic or political environments of these states, and he further points out that the four states that experienced the largest increases in strike activity following the passage of a collective bargaining law are all large, highly organized, densely populated, northeastern states. Thus, these environmental characteristics may be more important than the nature of the law as causes of strikes. This interpretation is further reinforced by other data presented in this study. Sixty percent of all teacher strikes between 1963 and 1975 occurred in four states, two of which (Michigan and Pennsylvania) had a collective bargaining statute for teachers and two (Illinois and Ohio) that had no statute. Thus, these descriptive statistics on teacher strikes provide conclusions quite similar to the multivariate analyses of local strikes discussed above. The passage of a law has apparently fewer consistent effects than the nature of the environment in which bargaining occurs.[22]

Fire and Police Strikes

Wheeler examined all fire fighter strikes reported by the BLS between 1969 and 1972 and found that there were no strikes in states with compulsory arbitration, 10 strikes in states with fact-finding procedures, and 18 strikes in states with no formalized impasse-resolution procedures.[23] The absence of fire fighter strikes under compulsory arbitration appears to have continued

---

[21]703 GERR 31–35 (April 11, 1977).
[22]The same conclusion was drawn by an author of a more recent analysis of public-sector strikes. See James L. Perry, *Public Policy and Public Employee Strikes*, 16 Ind. Rels. 273 (October 1977).
[23]Hoyt N. Wheeler, *An Analysis of Firefighter Strikes*, 26 Lab. L. J. 17 (January 1975).

up through February 1977 even though more states have enacted arbitration statutes over this time period. The IAFF research department has tabulated a total of 70 fire fighter strikes between September 1966 and January 1977. Of these 70, only one (a 5½-hour strike in New York City in 1973) occurred where a compulsory-arbitration statute was in effect.[24] Again, these data do not control for differences in the state environments, the degree of unionization, the number of contracts negotiated, or any other causal variables. The lack of fire fighter strikes under arbitration is even more surprising, however, when one considers that these procedures are found in highly unionized states with a large number of public-employee unions and relatively high strike rates for nonuniformed-service employees (e.g., Pennsylvania, New York, Michigan, Massachusetts, Wisconsin, etc.).

The data on police strikes are somewhat less conclusive. Of the 93 police strikes reported by BLS between 1972 and 1975, 21, or 28.8 percent, occurred in states where police operate under a compulsory-arbitration statute.[25] (During this time period, approximately 25 percent of the states had such a law for police.) Of the 21 reported strikes, however, 13 occurred in Pennsylvania. In fact, strikes by police in Pennsylvania accounted for all of the strikes under a compulsory-arbitration law in two of these years, four of the strikes in the third year, and two out of eight strikes in the fourth year. Thus, the record for compulsory arbitration, at least as reported by BLS, is again quite good except for Pennsylvania. Why the strike rate for Pennsylvania police is higher than others under arbitration cannot be conclusively determined from these data. In fact, many of the strikes apparently were short slowdowns, sickouts, or ticket-writing actions that BLS counted as strikes, since another study has reported that no strikes occurred in Pennsylvania under the arbitration statute between 1968 and 1974.[26]

In any event, the evidence is quite clear that for fire fighters, and perhaps for police, arbitration deterred strikes more effec-

---

[24]Internal memorandum, Department of Research, International Association of Fire Fighters, February 1977.
[25]Bureau of Labor Statistics, Work Stoppages in Government, Reports 434, 437, 453, and 483, 1972–1975.
[26]James L. Stern et al., Final-Offer Arbitration (Lexington, Mass.: D.C. Heath and Co., 1975), 32.

tively than did fact-finding or the absence of legislation during the first decade of bargaining in the public sector.

Dynamics of Strikes

Have strikes proven to be the effective political and economic weapon that some of the early critics of the strike option predicted? The paucity of empirical evidence or theory concerning nonpolicy causes of public-sector strikes or their effects makes this question difficult to answer, but we will address it in this section by examining some of the case studies and news reports of public-sector strikes, giving attention to possible causes of strikes as well as the response of elected officials and the public to the pressures generated by strikes.

Most case studies of strikes focus on the political and social contexts of the dispute and the bargaining power or militancy of the union.[27] Some have drawn on the premises underlying the studies of multilateral bargaining to argue that since collective bargaining is essentially a subset of the larger political processes of the community, strikes or protracted impasses are likely to be partially caused by the same factors that lead to open political conflict on other issues.[28] Thus, strikes should be most likely found in the most politically complex communities—where diverse political interests share power over decision-making and where unions are both militant and politically influential. More recently, the willingness of public-sector management to resist union pressure and to hold the line on wage increases has been noted as a prominent cause of public-sector strikes or impasses.

A recent study of determinants of police and fire fighter impasses attempted to combine these *ad hoc* hypotheses into a predictive model. The model suggested that impasses (and presumably strikes) are caused by a combination of pressures from (1) the economic, political, or legal environments; (2) the structural and organizational context of bargaining; (3) the interper-

---

[27]See, for example, Richard P. Schick and Jean J. Couturier, The Public Interest in Government Labor Relations (Cambridge, Mass.: Ballinger Publishing Co., 1977).

[28]See, for example, Kenneth McLennan and Michael H. Moskow, *Multilateral Bargaining in the Public Sector,* in Proceedings of the 21st Annual Meeting, Industrial Relations Research Association (Madison, Wis.: IRRA, 1968), 31–41; Peter Feuille, *Police Labor Relations and Multilateralism,* in Proceedings of the 26th Annual Meeting, Industrial Relations Research Association (Madison, Wis.: IRRA, 1973), 170–77; or Thomas A. Kochan, *A Theory of Multilateral Collective Bargaining in City Governments,* 27 Ind. & Lab. Rels. Rev. 525 (July 1974).

sonal relationships between the parties; (4) the personal characteristics of the negotiators; and (5) the history of previous
rounds of bargaining.[29] As in previous studies of strikes and/or
impasses,[30] it was found that although economic pressures were
important components of many disputes, the economic environment did not effectively distinguish between parties who
reached an impasse and those who settled on their own. Economic disputes, however, were more protracted and difficult to
resolve short of the final stages of the impasse procedure. The
profile of political and organizational factors suggested by the
multilateral bargaining models were correlated with impasses
and, when treated as a group, proved to be important predictors
of impasses. Finally, the existence of interpersonal hostilities
between the parties, the use of hired professional or highly
experienced negotiators, and a history of previous impasses all
increased the probability of an impasse in a given round of
bargaining. The major conclusion derived from this study was
that to understand the probability of disputes arising out of
public-sector negotiations, one must consider these multiple
sources of impasse. The more of these potential sources of
impasse that are present in a given situation and the greater the
magnitude of each, the more likely it is that a protracted impasse
and perhaps a serious strike threat will occur. Although the
framework has yet to be systematically tested to see if the same
factors cause both strikes and impasses, its utility can be illustrated by outlining briefly the contexts of several recent strikes
by public employees.

The 1977 strike by state employees in Wisconsin illustrated
how these multiple pressures combine to produce a protracted
strike.[31] In the previous round of bargaining, the contract was
settled through an "end-run" around the management negotiators. The agreement was worked out in consultations between
the governor and Jerry Wurf, president of the American Federation of State, County, and Municipal Employees (AFSCME).

---

[29]Thomas A. Kochan and Jean Baderschneider, *Dependence on Impasse Procedures: Police
and Firefighters in New York State,* 31 Ind. & Lab. Rels. Rev. 431 (July 1978).
[30]Burton and Krider, *supra* note 20. For a review of studies of impasses that have failed
to find significant effects for the economic variables, see John C. Anderson and Thomas
A. Kochan, *Impasse Resolution in the Canadian Federal Service: Effects of the Bargaining Process,*
30 Ind. & Lab. Rels. Rev. 283 (April 1977), 287–90.
[31]The information on the Wisconsin state employees' strike and the Milwaukee teachers' strike is taken from newspaper articles in the Wisconsin State Journal and the
Milwaukee Sentinel during the course of these disputes.

The memory of this end-run carried over and conditioned the attitudes and expectations of the negotiators on both sides of the table in 1977.

The bargaining process was further complicated by the agreement to open negotiations to the public. Newspaper reports of the early stages highlighted the verbal sparring that was taking place, as the union negotiators repeatedly protested that the management negotiators lacked adequate authority to bargain. The background for these statements was a complex political situation. A new interim governor took office at about the time the contract expired. The management structure for bargaining consisted of a negotiating team supervised by the secretary of the Department of Administration, the governor, and a bipartisan committee of the state legislature.

Most of the sources of impasse discussed above were factors in this dispute. The parties had a history of difficult bargaining; in the past the governor and other political officials who were not present at the bargaining table ended up becoming involved. The decision-making structure on the management side was highly complicated, with a number of different officials sharing power. Intense political rivalries and differences existed among some of these management officials; the union and management negotiators distrusted each other; the membership and officers of the union displayed their militancy from the start by making preparations for a strike; and the importance, scope, and visibility of the bargaining process ensured that it would become a major political issue in the state. The presence of all of these conditions clearly suggested that bargaining would be difficult, and the probability of an impasse and a strike loomed large.

The resolution of this dispute lived up to the expectations. It was settled after: (1) a 15-day strike during which the governor declared a state of emergency, called out the National Guard, and transferred physically and mentally handicapped patients from state to private institutions; (2) the union rejected the Wisconsin Employment Relations Commission mediators because they were perceived to be part of the state administration; (3) an injunction was issued against the strikers; (4) an out-of-state, *ad hoc* mediator was brought in; (5) national officials of AFSCME and the governor became involved in direct negotiations; (6) the joint legislative committee rejected the settlement that ended the strike; (7) further negotiations and mediation took place involving the governor, representatives of the legislative committee, and the union; (8) the strike settlement was modified and approved by the legislature; and (9) the attorney general pursued contempt proceedings against striking workers over the objections of the governor.

The importance of multiple political, organizational, and interpersonal pressures is also illustrated by the 1976 strike by Milwaukee teachers. These negotiations followed a federal court desegregation order. During the course of negotiations, a serious political split erupted among members of the board of education. A similar split between the black teachers' caucus and the white majority in control of the union provided further complications. During bargaining prior to the strike, the teachers charged that the board did not have the real decision-makers at the bargaining table and was engaging in surface bargaining. Mediation efforts prior to the strike were ineffective. After the strike began, the process turned into an extremely complex, multiparty dispute involving mediators from the Wisconsin Employment Relations Commission, a representative of the governor, and the court-appointed special master charged with implementing the desegregation plan. Thus, it was necessary to mediate disputes not only between the two major parties, but also among factions within the parties. At one point, the special master for the desegregation plan threatened to obtain a federal court injunction to end the strike on the grounds that it was inhibiting the desegregation effort. The final settlement involved intensive negotiations among the multiple interest groups, all operating under the threat of intervention by a federal court.

Other case studies of strikes document the importance of multiple causes of strikes. Kervin, for example, concluded that the bitter seven-week strike by teachers in metropolitan Toronto was caused by a complex set of interacting economic, internal political, and interpersonal pressures.[32] This strike ended only after a special act of the Ontario legislature sent the teachers back to work and provided for an arbitrated settlement.

If this model and case-study evidence is accurate, then public-sector strikes cannot be explained simply as exercises of the

---

[32]John B. Kervin, The 1975 Metro Toronto Teacher-Board Negotiations and Strike (Toronto: Centre for Industrial Relations, University of Toronto, 1977).

economic or political muscle of unions seeking to exploit a weak public management. Rather, they are a function of the complex political and organizational contexts of public-sector bargaining.

The response of public employers to strikes varies considerably. For example, a number of long and unsuccessful teacher strikes in rural or suburban communities illustrate the limitations of the strike weapon in a political environment that is hostile to unions. The 1974 Hortonville, Wisconsin, and Timberlane, New Hampshire, teachers' strikes are examples where communities chose to break the strikes by hiring substitute teachers and keeping the schools open.[33] The 42-day teachers' strike in Lakeland, New York, a conservative suburban community, is a vivid illustration of a community's willingness to back its school board in a protracted conflict. Four weeks into the strike, the community voted by a 4–1 margin to reject a proposal (supported by the union) to submit the dispute to binding arbitration.[34]

It is also increasingly apparent that public management has stiffened its resistance to strikes in some larger cities where unions have traditionally been politically powerful. For example, in Buffalo, New York, the school board held out for three weeks before agreeing to end a strike by referring the dispute to binding arbitration. Similarly, the 1976 San Francisco craft workers' 38-day strike ended with only an agreement to refer the dispute to a committee of union representatives and elected officials. This dispute centered over a management proposal to eliminate a prevailing-pay plan. Thus, like the 1977 Yonkers, New York, teachers' strike, it arose over aggressive management efforts to eliminate a costly contract provision or practice. Still other examples of strikes in large cities that backfired for public-employee unions can be found. Six months after AFSCME declared that its 1977 strike against the City of Atlanta was officially lost, the union was reported to be struggling to maintain its majority status.[35] The subtitle of an article, "What Ever Happened to the Chicago Social Workers?" describes the plight of one union that struck in the absence of (1) legal protections for collective bargaining, (2) the ability to impose meaningful eco-

---

[33]662 GERR E1-E6 (June 21, 1976); 553 GERR B21 (May 6, 1974).
[34]736 GERR 17–20 (November 28, 1977).
[35]733 GERR 14 (November 7, 1977).

nomic costs on the employer, or (3) any political influence.[36] Clearly, therefore, not all strikes have served as the potent economic or political weapon that opponents of the right to strike predicted. Indeed, in a growing number of cases, strikes appear to be defensive reactions to increased management aggressiveness in bargaining.

One other interesting feature of public-sector strikes is that many of them end without a formal agreement but, as illustrated above, with a promise to continue bargaining or to submit the dispute to some dispute-resolution procedure. Approximately 50 percent of the strikes in California between 1970 and 1974 were reported to have ended this way[37]—many of them having been protest actions designed to stimulate more intensive bargaining. BLS data on strikes between October 1974 and October 1975 indicate that only 43.7 percent of all state and local strikes were ended by agreement between the parties, another 25.7 percent were ended by either mediation or agreement to submit the dispute to some other procedure, and approximately 17 percent were ended by employees voluntarily returning to work, mass dismissal, or some other unclassified means.[38]

Court injunctions have been used frequently in an effort to end strikes, but their effectiveness varies. While injunctions were obtained in about a third of the 104 strikes in California between 1970 and 1974, only about 5 percent of them were ended by the injunctions.[39] The same study found that employers were reluctant to take punitive action against strikers; action was initiated in only 16 cases, most of which were eventually dropped.[40] BLS data for 1975 show that about 13 percent of all state and local strikes in 1975 were ended by court injunctions.[41] In general, court injunctions appear to be more effective in ending smaller strikes or strikes where the union is weak; they have been less successful in ending larger strikes by more powerful unions. As in the Milwaukee teachers' strike described above, however, an injunction may serve to shorten the strike by

---

[36]Arnold R. Weber, *Paradise Lost; or What Ever Happened to the Chicago Social Workers?* 22 Ind. & Lab. Rels. Rev. 323 (April 1969).

[37]Bonnie G. Cebulski, *A Five-Year Study of California Public Employee Strikes,* 32 California Pub. Emp. Bull. 3 (June 1975).

[38]Labor-Management Relations in State and Local Governments: 1975, State and Local Government Special Studies No. 81 (Washington: U.S. Government Printing Office, 1977), 5.

[39]Cebulski, *supra* note 37, at 3.

[40]*Ibid.*

[41]Labor-Management Relations, *supra* note 38, at 5.

increasing the pressure on the union to negotiate a settlement. Indeed, one study found that a majority of teacher strikes that occurred between 1960 and 1967 ended within two days of the issuance of an injunction.[42]

Although it is difficult to draw firm conclusions regarding the impact of public-sector strikes, the fragmentary evidence reviewed above suggests at least the following tentative conclusions. First, the effectiveness of the strike as a union tactic is dependent on the political power and influence of the public employees. Strikes by unions in small, conservative, or rural communities have met with strong community resistance and have often ended by injunction or after the union has been seriously weakened. Second, the likelihood of a serious strike threat and of an actual strike is greatest in large, politically complex jurisdictions where unions have traditionally been politically active, powerful, and militant. Third, injunctions have had little success in ending strikes by large, powerful unions. Fourth, employers and the public have become more willing to resist strike pressures recently as economic conditions of cities and states have deteriorated and the political pendulum has shifted against public employees. Fifth, not all strikes are caused by unions seeking major substantive improvements in bargaining. Increasing numbers of strikes appear to be defensive reactions by unions facing management efforts to reduce benefits or eliminate provisions agreed to in earlier years. Nor do all strikes end with agreements favorable to the union. In fact, some appear to end with no settlement at all, but rather with an agreement to go back to bargaining or to some procedural form of dispute resolution.

All of these tentative conclusions suggest that the effectiveness of the strike as a political or economic weapon varies considerably across localities, employee groups, and over time. The experience to date has not supported the hypothesis that strikes uniformly tip the balance of power in favor of public employees. Even the short-run successes of some of the early public-sector strikes have led to political backlashes that have strengthened the public will to resist future strikes.

---

[42]Spero and Capozzola, *supra* note 3, at 259.

Performance of Dispute-Resolution Procedures

Since impasse procedures are designed to avoid strikes, the central criterion for evaluating their effectiveness revolves around the issue discussed in the previous section, namely, their relative effectiveness in deterring strike activity. In addition, however, the collective bargaining system in the United States has historically placed a premium on the process of "free" collective bargaining. That is, there is a deeply shared ethos among scholars, policy-makers, and practitioners that values the ability of the parties to settle their own disputes without the intervention of an outside third party. Thus, one of the central objectives of any dispute-resolution procedure is to minimize the dependence of the parties on impasse procedures.[43] But some observers fear that the absence of an effective strike threat reduces the motivation to bargain and ultimately results in a process in which the parties become overdependent on the alternative procedures. This has been discussed in the literature as the "chilling" or the "narcotic" effects.[44] To the extent that these two problems occur in the bargaining system, we would expect over time to find (1) an increase in reliance on the procedures, and (2) less meaningful bargaining taking place prior to the intervention of third parties.

The same problems exist in evaluating the impact of impasse procedures on the bargaining process as were present in attempting to make aggregate comparisons of strike activity across different types of laws and procedures. The absence of adequate controls for other factors affecting the use of impasse procedures limits the conclusiveness of most analyses. A number of studies of experiences in specific jurisdictions or states can be used, however, to reach a number of tentative conclusions regarding the performance of these alternatives over the first decade of bargaining.

---

[43]See, for example, the statement of the Taylor committee on this issue in Final Report, *supra* note 8, at 33.

[44]For a discussion, see Hoyt N. Wheeler, *Compulsory Arbitration: A Narcotic Effect,* 14 Ind. Rels. 117 (February 1975); Peter Feuille, *Final Offer Arbitration and the Chilling Effect,* 14 Ind. Rels. 302 (October 1975); Anderson and Kochan, *supra* note 30, at 283–301; or Thomas A. Kochan, Mordehai Mironi, Ronald G. Ehrenberg, Jean Baderschneider, and Todd Jick, Dispute Resolution Under Factfinding and Arbitration: An Empirical Analysis (New York: American Arbitration Association, 1978).

Dependence on Procedures: A Narcotic Effect?

There are at least two points in the sequence of impasse-resolution efforts that are often used for comparing the degree of dependence on the procedures. The first point is the rate of initial impasses filed. Most impasse procedures start with an effort at mediation. This point of the procedure is analogous to the rate of reliance on mediation in the private sector. The second point is the percentage of negotiations that require issuance of either a fact-finding report or an arbitration award.

Since the majority of jurisdictions outlaw the right to strike, it is not surprising that the rate of impasses is higher than the rate of reliance on mediation in the private sector. Similarly, the rates of going to either fact-finding or arbitration appear to be higher than the average rate of strikes in private-sector bargaining. For example, the Federal Mediation and Conciliation Service (FMCS) annual reports for the years 1967 through 1976 show that between 8 and 10 percent of all 30-day notifications of a contract expiration require a formal meeting with a mediator. Approximately 15 to 20 percent of the contracts in the private-sector covered by FMCS require either a formal mediation meeting or informal discussions with the parties over the telephone.[45] Of the 30-day notifications, only between 2 and 3 percent of the negotiations end up in a strike.[46]

Although the rates of initial impasses and the use of fact-finding and arbitration in the public sector vary widely, every study examined for this chapter shows a higher rate of intervention than do private-sector data. Consequently, the relevant question becomes not *whether* the absence of the right to strike will lead to greater intervention by third parties, but rather the *magnitude* of the difference that is associated with alternative forms of dispute-resolution procedures.

In a comparison of the rate of reliance on fact-finding vs. arbitration in fire fighter cases during the 1971–1972 time period, Wheeler found that fact-finding was initiated 21.5 percent of the time. Arbitration was initiated in 37.3 percent of the cases operating under a conventional-arbitration statute. Similarly, 12.0 percent of the cases under fact-finding required a report, compared to 26.8 percent of the cases under arbitration that

---

[45]Annual Reports of the Federal Mediation and Conciliation Service, 1967–1976.
[46]*Ibid.*

required an award.[47] (No final-offer-arbitration statutes were in effect during the period covered by this study.)

Feuille's study reviewed the performance of conventional arbitration and final-offer-arbitration procedures in a number of different settings.[48] No consistent difference was found in the percentage of cases initiating these different procedures; however, a lower percentage of arbitration awards was issued under the final-offer than under the conventional-arbitration procedures. Specifically, the median percentage of cases ending in an arbitration award under the 11 different conventional-arbitration statutes was 25 percent. The range varied from a low of 14 percent to a high of an estimated 40–50 percent. The median for the four final-offer statutes analyzed was between 10 and 12 percent, with a range from a low of 6 percent to a high of 33 percent.[49]

In a recent study, the impasse histories of police and fire fighters in New York State were compared with those of police and fire fighters in Wisconsin and Massachusetts.[50] The Wisconsin-New York comparisons provide the most complete information and the most instructive findings. Wisconsin had fact-finding as its basic impasse procedure for police and fire fighters until 1972 when the law was changed to final-offer arbitration on the total package. New York had fact-finding until 1974 when it changed to conventional arbitration. The results showed that (1) Wisconsin police and fire fighters went to impasse and received fact-finding reports in a far smaller percentage of cases between 1968 and 1972 (6 percent compared to 26 percent) than did their counterparts in New York, and (2) both Wisconsin and New York experienced increases in impasses and in the number of cases going to the final step of their procedures after they changed to their respective forms of arbitration. For example, in Wisconsin during the first two years of the final-offer procedure, approximately 34 percent of the negotiations went to impasse and approximately 10 percent were resolved by an arbitration award. These percentages increased in the second two years (1974–1976) under final-offer arbitration to an impasse rate of between 48 and 55 percent and an arbitration rate of between 12.7 and

[47]Wheeler, *supra* note 44.
[48]Feuille, *supra* note 44.
[49]*Id.*, at 306.
[50]Kochan et al., *supra* note 44.

14.6 percent of all negotiations. In contrast, after the arbitration amendments were passed in New York, approximately 76 percent of police negotiations and 53 percent of fire fighter negotiations went to impasse, while 32 percent of the police negotiations ended in an arbitration award compared to 26 percent of the fire fighter negotiations. Analysis of these data showed that both states experienced comparable increases in the number of impasses and of cases going to the final step of the procedures. Thus, even though large differences in the rate of impasses and arbitration awards exist across these two states, the differences appear to be due to something other than the difference between final-offer and conventional arbitration.

A similar effect appeared to occur as the Massachusetts police and fire fighter procedures changed from fact-finding to final-offer arbitration in 1974. Like Wisconsin and New York, Massachusetts experienced an increase in the percentage of cases going to an impasse after the change in the statute. A study by Somers showed that in the last year under fact-finding, an estimated 29.5 percent of police and fire negotiations reached an impasse, compared to 42.4 percent of negotiations during the first year under the arbitration statute. Only 8.6 percent of all negotiations under the final-offer procedure required the issuance of an arbitration award.[51] Thus, here again final-offer arbitration did not appear to reduce the rate of initial impasses, but was more successful than conventional arbitration in achieving settlements prior to the imposition of an award.

In addition to the general increase in impasse rates over time, analysis of the New York data showed evidence of a narcotic effect. That is, those units that went to impasse in the first round had a higher probability than others of being repeat-users in the second and third rounds of bargaining. Thus, a pattern of repeated usage was clearly developing over time in this system. Similar analyses of bargaining histories of teachers in New York State and of federal employees in Canada have found repeated use of the procedures by the same units over successive rounds of bargaining.[52] Thus, at least three studies that have tracked the

---

[51]Paul Somers, *An Evaluation of Final-Offer Arbitration in Massachusetts*, 6 J. Coll. Negotiations in the Pub. Sector 193 (1977).

[52]John E. Drotning and David B. Lipsky, *The Relations Between Teacher Salaries and the Use of Impasse Procedures Under New York's Taylor Law: 1968–1972*, 6 J. Coll. Negotiations in the Pub. Sector 229 (1977); Anderson and Kochan, *supra* note 30.

history of the same units over several rounds of bargaining have identified somewhat of a narcotic effect building up within the dispute-resolution systems over time.

The one characteristic that is most often found to be positively associated with dependence on impasse procedures is the size of the jurisdiction.[53] In their three-state study of final-offer arbitration, Stern et al. reported higher rates of impasse usage in the larger cities in all of the states.[54] In Michigan, for example, it was reported that while cities under 10,000 population make up 28 percent of all cities negotiating, they have received only 13 percent of all arbitration awards. On the other hand, the 7 percent of cities with more than 100,000 population have received 23 percent of all awards.[55] In Wisconsin, it was reported that the small rural municipalities were less dependent on the intervention of third parties than were either the larger cities or the suburban areas surrounding Milwaukee.[56]

The evidence of the repeated dependence on third-party intervention in the larger jurisdictions in New York State is even more striking. The five largest cities in the state (excluding New York City), that is, Buffalo, Yonkers, Rochester, Syracuse, and Albany, have reached an impasse with their police and fire fighters in about 90 percent of their negotiations between 1968 and 1976,[57] and have resorted to fact-finding and beyond in more than 70 percent of all negotiations. Buffalo, the largest city and the one with the most severe financial problems and the most politicized bargaining environment, has gone to fact-finding or beyond (or arbitration after the change in the law in 1974) with both police and fire fighters in *each* of the five times it negotiated with these groups during this time period. The record of the city with teachers and other occupational groups in similarly bleak. Over these years, sickouts, threatened slowdowns, court challenges of arbitration awards, and improper-practice charges have been common characteristics of bargaining in Buffalo.

While the systematic data from large cities in other states are

[53]This is consistent with other studies that show size to be positively associated with other measures of industrial conflict. See, for example, Sherill Cleland, The Influence of Plant Size on Industrial Relations (Princeton, N.J.: Industrial Relations Section, Princeton University, 1955), 53.
[54]Stern et al., *supra* note 26.
[55]*Id.*, at 52–53.
[56]*Id.*, at 95.
[57]These results are summarized in Kochan et al, *supra* note 44.

not available, it is quite clear that cities such as Detroit, Milwaukee, Pittsburgh, Philadelphia,[58] San Francisco, and Boston as well as other major metropolitan centers have also been frequent users of impasse procedures. Clearly, these large cities have proven to be tough environments to instill effective bargaining without reliance on impasse procedures or the threat of a strike. These jurisdictions have more of the political, organizational, interpersonal, and personal characteristics that cause impasses—unions are more militant and willing to use political pressure and job actions, management is more politicized and subject to internal disputes and power struggles, negotiators are more experienced and skillful in utilizing pressure to achieve their goals in bargaining, and, finally, most of these cities have been experiencing severe financial difficulties in recent years.[59]

A number of very tentative conclusions can be drawn from the above analyses regarding the reliance on impasse procedures during the first decade of public-sector bargaining. First, a higher percentage of cases have reached impasses under both conventional and final-offer arbitration than under fact-finding procedures. It should be noted, however, that all of the states examined experienced an increase in the rate of cases going to impasse over time. Consequently, our comparisons of fact-finding with final-offer and conventional arbitration are confounded with time. To the extent that the increasing reliance on procedures is a function of time rather than a function of a change in the law, these comparisons overstate the differences between the two procedures. Second, no significant differences in the number of initial impasses were found in cases where final-offer arbitration was compared to conventional arbitration. However, fewer cases resulted in an arbitration award under final-offer arbitration than under conventional arbitration. Third, a narcotic effect has been observed in a number of jurisdictions operating under both fact-finding and arbitration. Fourth, large jurisdictions tend to rely heavily on whatever dispute-resolution procedure is available.

---

[58]A recent study reported that the City of Philadelphia has gone to arbitration in each of its seven rounds of negotiations with its police and fire fighter bargaining units between 1970 and 1977. See Philadelphia's Experience Under the Pennsylvania Police and Fire Arbitration Law (Philadelphia: Pennsylvania Economy League, 1977).

[59]Kochan et al., *supra* note 44.

The Chilling Effect

Most theories of the bargaining process suggest that hard bargaining or movement will occur when the costs of continuing the dispute exceed the costs of making a compromise or a concession to settle the dispute.[60] In short, the parties are expected to make significant compromises toward an agreement only when under pressure to do so. This explains why most intensive bargaining appears to occur in the final days or hours prior to a strike deadline. In the public sector where the strike is constrained, we should expect it to be even more difficult to get hard bargaining in negotiations prior to an initial impasse. To the extent that multiple steps are built into the impasse procedures that proceed from milder to stronger forms of intervention (e.g., mediation followed by fact-finding and/or arbitration), the "final hour" or moment of truth is even farther removed from the initial bargaining process. Thus, while policymakers hope that the existence of impasse procedures will not "chill" bargaining, our theories of bargaining suggest that this is exactly what should happen.

A number of studies have attempted to assess the amount of hard bargaining or movement that takes place prior to impasses. Some of the early studies of this issue provided reasonably optimistic findings.[61] More recently, studies of the actual movement or compromising behavior have reported greater evidence of a chilling effect in negotiations. For example, a comparison of fact-finding in Wisconsin and New York in 1972 revealed that 80 percent of the parties rated bargaining prior to fact-finding as either slight or nonexistent,[62] and a multivariate study of fire fighter bargaining found a number of cases in which no movement off the initial positions took place prior to an impasse.[63] Similar results were obtained in an analysis of police and fire fighter bargaining in New York State: unions and employers

[60]See, for example, Neil W. Chamberlain and James W. Kuhn, Collective Bargaining, 3d ed. (New York: McGraw-Hill Book Co., 1965), 171–73.

[61]See, for example, James L. Stern, Edward B. Krinsky, and Jeffrey B. Tener, Factfinding Under Wisconsin Law, 1966 (Madison: University of Wisconsin Extension, 1966); or Byron Yaffe and Howard Goldblatt, Factfinding in New York State Public Employment: More Promise Than Illusion (Ithaca: New York State School of Industrial and Labor Relations, Cornell University, 1971).

[62]William Word, Factfinding in Public Employee Negotiations, 95 Monthly Lab. Rev. 6 (February 1972).

[63]Hoyt N. Wheeler, How Compulsory Arbitration Affects Compromise Activity 17 Ind. Rels. 80 (February 1978).

held back concessions from their resistance points or bottom-line positions, and the parties reported that no or very little movement occurred prior to impasse under both fact-finding and arbitration statutes.[64] Even more disconcerting was the disclosure that less movement (and a higher probability of impasse) occurred in negotiations involving more experienced negotiators.

Thus, there is at least some direct evidence that as the parties gained more experience with bargaining, they became *less* willing to engage in meaningful negotiations prior to impasse. While these findings may not be generalizable to all of the public sector, they do suggest that the chilling phenomenon has become a significant problem in these jurisdictions. Furthermore, the studies reviewed above suggest that the chilling effect may have become more serious in the latter half of the first decade of bargaining, after the parties became more experienced with negotiating under dispute-resolution procedures.

Dynamics of Mediation, Fact-Finding, and Arbitration

In this section some of the dynamics of the three major procedural mechanisms used to resolve public-sector impasses —mediation, fact-finding, and compulsory arbitration—will be described. The theories underlying each procedure will first be outlined in order to identify the expectations that scholars and policy-makers had for each technique when they were first proposed, debated, and implemented. Then the performance of each technique in the public sector will be reviewed in order to illustrate the extent to which these a priori expectations were fulfilled in practice. Emphasis will be placed on the ways in which these procedures were modified and adapted over time to fit different situations and jurisdictions.

The Mediation Process

Mediation is perhaps the most widely used and least understood dispute-resolution procedure in collective bargaining. It is the first form of intervention in most disputes in both the private and public sectors. Yet there are few empirical studies

---

[64]Kochan et al, *supra* note 44.

of the mediation process. The few theoretical statements that can be drawn from studies of the private-sector mediation process suggest that mediation can be most successful when (1) the negotiations cycle has progressed to the point where the parties are under the greatest pressure to settle; (2) the mediator is acceptable to and trusted by the parties; (3) the real bottom-line positions of the parties either overlap or are not far apart; and (4) the obstacles to a settlement reflect a breakdown in the communication process more than a real substantive difference on the economic or political issues involved.[65] The application of mediation as the initial step in impasse procedures in the public sector raises an additional important policy question: How effective is mediation when followed by fact-finding, conventional arbitration, final-offer arbitration, the right to strike, or some other form of dispute resolution?

The above hypotheses were formalized into a model of the mediation process and tested using the New York police and fire fighter sample.[66] Specifically, the effectiveness of mediation under fact-finding and conventional arbitration was compared, controlling for the effects of (1) different sources of impasse, (2) characteristics of the mediator, and (3) the strategies employed by the mediator. The sample was drawn from the last round of negotiations by police and fire fighters under New York State's fact-finding statute and the first round of bargaining under conventional arbitration. Approximately 30 percent of the impasses that went to mediation were resolved at this stage prior to passing the dispute on to the next stage of the procedure. After controlling for the other factors outlined above, it was estimated that the change in the law from fact-finding to arbitration increased the effectiveness of mediation, or the probability of settlement, between 13 and 18 percent. That is, there was a marginal increase in the number of settlements achieved under the arbitration statute as compared to what would have been expected had fact-finding remained in effect. This marginal increase, however, was limited to small jurisdictions that were experiencing a catch-up effect in their wage settlements. Man-

---

[65]See Carl M. Stevens, *Mediation and the Role of the Neutral,* in Frontiers of Collective Bargaining, eds. John T. Dunlop and Neil W. Chamberlain (New York: Harper & Row, 1967), 271–90. See also Carl M. Stevens, Strategy and Collective Bargaining Negotiations (New York: McGraw-Hill Book Co., 1963), 122–46; and Kenneth Kressel, Labor Mediation: Exploratory Survey (Albany, N.Y.: Association of Labor Mediation Agencies, 1972).
[66]Kochan et al., *supra* note 44, at ch. 5.

agement negotiators in these jurisdictions, because they recognized that arbitration would very likely impose a relatively high wage settlement, were under pressure to avoid it, and the mediators recognized that they could use the threat of arbitration to induce the management negotiators to make significant movement. Thus, the estimates of the effect of the change in the law probably suggest more about the impact of the threat of going to a procedure in which one party will be at a severe disadvantage than they imply about the inherent differences between mediation under fact-finding and under conventional arbitration.

The net effects of the change in the law were less important than the effects of some of the control variables examined. Specifically, the mediation process at this initial stage of the impasse procedure was *most* effective in resolving impasses where (1) the negotiators—especially the union negotiators—lacked experience; (2) the negotiations process broke down because one of the parties was overcommitted to a particular position; (3) a dispute was below average in intensity or difficulty, that is, the magnitude and number of sources of impasse were relatively small; (4) the parties were motivated to reach a settlement; and (5) an aggressive, experienced, and high-quality (as perceived by the parties) mediator was involved. On the other hand, mediation was *least* successful in situations (1) where the underlying dispute arose because of an employer's inability to pay; (2) where the parties had a history of going to impasse and to the later stages of the dispute-resolution procedure; and (3) where the jurisdiction was among the largest. Some of the larger jurisdictions chose to skip the mediation process entirely since it was clear that any effort to resolve the dispute through mediation at the early stage of the impasse procedure was futile.

Other studies of the mediation process in the public sector have shown higher rates of settlement through mediation in the earlier stages of bargaining. For example, the early experience in Wisconsin under fact-finding was that more than 50 percent of the disputes were resolved through mediation. Under Wisconsin's final-offer statute, 70 percent of the cases going to mediation between 1973 and 1976 were settled at this step.[67] According to statistics published by the New York State Public

---

[67] *Id.*, at ch. 3.

Employment Relations Board, from 30 to 42 percent of all mediation cases involving teachers were settled at this initial stage of
the procedure between 1968 and 1972. Furthermore, the same
source reports that from 42 to 57 percent of all PERB cases were
settled at the mediation stage over these five years. The data
show a small drop in the percentage of cases settled by mediation in the later years and again reflect the tendency for the
parties to go further into the procedures in this more recent
time period.[68]

A group of mediators discussing the relative effectiveness of
mediation under fact-finding, conventional arbitration, and
final-offer arbitration indicated that, in general, mediation appears to be more meaningful under final-offer arbitration than
under either of the other alternatives. This perception is consistent with the finding noted above that the percentage of cases
going on to an award under final-offer arbitration in Massachusetts, Wisconsin, and Michigan were all less than the percentage
of cases going to conventional arbitration in New York State.
Thus, there does appear to be a stronger incentive effect associated with mediation under final-offer than under conventional arbitration. This effect is weakened, however, the farther
the mediation process is removed from the arbitration step of
the procedure (e.g., compare mediation in Wisconsin where
arbitration follows immediately with mediation in Massachusetts
where fact-finding follows mediation before final-offer arbitration).[69] It is further weakened when mediation is an expected
part of the arbitration process (e.g., compare Wisconsin and
Massachusetts where few disputes are mediated at the arbitration stage with Michigan where mediation in arbitration settled
64 percent of arbitration cases in 1973 and 1974).[70]

It was reported that the conferees also felt that mediation was
more effective under conventional arbitration than under fact-
finding. This was contrary to the view of the Michigan mediators
interviewed as part of that study. There it was reported that the
parties felt that some of the life had gone out of mediation under
arbitration that had been present in earlier years under fact-
finding.[71]

As noted above, it would be a mistake to assume that mediation in the public sector takes place only at the initial stages of

---

[68]Annual Reports of the New York State Public Employment Relations Board, 1975.
[69]Stern et al., *supra* note 26, at 124.
[70]*Id.*, at 54.
[71]*Id.*, at 62–63.

the impasse-resolution procedure. On the contrary, over time the distinctions between mediation, fact-finding, and arbitration have become blurred in the sense that mediation is often employed during, and sometimes even after, the fact-finding and arbitration processes have become initiated. A number of people have debated the wisdom and appropriateness of mixing the fact-finding and mediation processes or the mediation and arbitration processes.[72] Some have argued that if we want to preserve the integrity of fact-finding and arbitration and provide a greater incentive to settle in mediation prior to going to these procedures, mediation should be discouraged or prohibited once these more formal impasse procedures are invoked. This position was adopted as the official policy of the Michigan Employment Relations Commission in the early years of bargaining in that state. Studies in Michigan, however, have shown that despite the official policy, fact-finders mediated in the majority of disputes.[73] In New York, the distinction between mediation and fact-finding not only has become blurred in practice, but has become institutionalized by a change in the way in which neutrals are assigned to cases. New York State's PERB no longer assigns a mediator at the first stage of the impasse procedure; instead a fact-finder is assigned under the assumption that he or she will attempt to mediate the dispute prior to conducting a formal hearing. Thus one additional step at which mediation traditionally occurs is eliminated, thereby not only saving time and money but also reducing the parties' incentive to delay and hold back concessions. The disadvantage of combining the two procedures is that the parties may hold back information from the mediator because they fear it will jeopardize their positions if the dispute goes to fact-finding. The more the parties hold back information and fail to put their strongest effort forward in mediation, the less likely the dispute will be settled prior to the fact-finding hearing. Although there has been considerable debate over whether mediation is more effective under this type of an arrangement or where the mediator will not be the fact-finder, there is little systematic evidence one way or the other.

In some cases mediation occurs after fact-finding. Again, in

---

[72]For a review of these debates, see Ralph T. Jones, Public Sector Labor Relations: An Evaluation of Policy Related Research (Belmont, Mass.: Contract Research Corp., 1975), 162–67.

[73]Jack Stieber and Benjamin Wolkinson, *Fact-Finding Viewed by Factfinders: The Michigan Experience,* paper presented to the 1975 meetings of the Society of Professionals in Dispute Resolution, 4.

the State of New York it has become common for the parties to request and require post-fact-finding mediation, or what has been labeled "superconciliation." The term itself illustrates the difference between mediation at the initial stage of impasse and at the later stage of the negotiations where the process involves a much more aggressive intervention strategy by the neutral. In superconciliation the parties are at the final stage of bargaining and are faced with the threat of arbitration, a legislative hearing, a strike, or simply continued impasse. There is less room for delaying or holding back concessions because there is no next step in the procedure. Thus, the mediator can exert pressure on the parties to face reality, make concessions, or change their expectations.

Finally, there is "med-arb," a term that has been popularized as the public-sector bargaining process has evolved.[74] As the term implies, mediation occurs in the arbitration process itself—especially in tripartite arbitration. Some neutrals have argued for procedures in which the mediator serves as the arbitrator if the parties fail to reach an agreement through his mediation efforts. While we have few examples of this option built into the statutory impasse procedures (Wisconsin's new law provides for it), the strategy is widely used by arbitrators on an *ad hoc* basis. The dynamics of this process will be discussed in a later section.

The Fact-Finding Process

Every discussion of fact-finding in the public sector has noted that the term is a misnomer. The fact-finding process involves more than the searching-out of the factual basis of the parties' positions; it also involves an effort to identify an acceptable compromise settlement. Most studies have found that fact-finders tend to give the greatest weight to some variant of comparability. The criteria of ability to pay, cost of living, interest and welfare of the public, and "good" labor relations practice tend to follow in mixed order as secondary factors.[75] Underlying

---

[74]Sam Kagel and John Kagel, *Using Two New Arbitration Techniques,* 95 Monthly Lab. Rev. 11 (November 1972).

[75]Howard S. Block, *Criteria in Public Sector Interest Disputes,* in Arbitration and the Public Interest, Proceedings of the 24th Annual Meeting, National Academy of Arbitrators (Washington: BNA Books, 1971), 165; or Richard Pegnetter, *Fact-Finding and the Teacher Salary Disputes: The 1969 Experience in New York State,* 24 Ind. & Lab. Rels. Rev. 165 (January 1971).

the application of these criteria, however, is a search for an acceptable compromise. Thus, the effort to frame a recommendation that the parties will accept or use as the basis for negotiating an agreement captures the heart of the fact-finding process in the public sector. In a sense, when applied in this fashion, fact-finding is little more than mediation with written recommendations.

In a review of the early experience of bargaining under fact-finding, McKelvey found that most initial assessments of this process were quite favorable. She questioned, however, whether these early successes would prove illusory as the parties became more experienced and accustomed to bargaining under this procedure. In short, she feared that the fact-finding process would become less effective over time.[76]

Although the majority of states that have enacted bargaining legislation still have fact-finding as an important part of their impasse procedures for nonuniformed services, the bulk of the evidence suggests that its effectiveness, both in avoiding strikes and in achieving settlements, has atrophied over time. For example, Gatewood's study of fact-finding in teacher disputes in Wisconsin found that of the 44 teachers' strikes between 1968 and 1974, only 11 were preceded by fact-finding, and in only two of 18 teacher strikes in 1974 was fact-finding used before the teachers turned to the strike as a tactic for reaching an agreement.[77] The data in the Gatewood study also documented an increased rate of rejection of fact-finding reports over time. The deterioration of the efficacy of the process was part of the motivation underlying Wisconsin's adoption of final-offer arbitration for fire fighters and police in 1972 and, more recently, of the final-offer/strike option for other state employees.[78] The move to arbitration in Wisconsin along with the adoption of arbitration for police and fire fighters in other states that had fact-finding procedures in the early years of bargaining provides perhaps the strongest evidence that the half-life of the fact-finding procedure in the public sector has been rather short.

Yet approximately half of the states with arbitration statutes covering police and fire fighters have kept fact-finding as an

---

[76]Jean T. McKelvey, *Factfinding: Promise or Illusion*, 22 Ind. & Lab. Rels. Rev. 543 (July 1969).

[77]Lucian Gatewood, *Factfinding in Teacher Disputes: The Wisconsin Experience*, 97 Monthly Lab. Rev. 47 (October 1974).

[78]See Report of the Wisconsin Study Commission on Public Employee Labor Relations (Madison, Wis.: Legislative Reference Bureau, 1976).

intermediate stage in their procedures. The question arises, therefore, what role does fact-finding play in an arbitration statute? Does it serve as an effective intermediate step with a unique function, or does arbitration simply become an instant replay of the fact-finding process? In New York State between 1974 and 1976, approximately 20 percent of the police and fire fighter cases that went to fact-finding were resolved at that stage.[79] For those cases that were not resolved, however, the arbitration awards tended to follow the fact-finders' recommendations very closely. In 70 percent of the cases examined, the salary award was identical to the fact-finder's recommendation; where there were differences, the magnitude was relatively small. The major reasons indicated by arbitrators for deviating from a fact-finder's recommendation were that economic conditions had changed since the recommendation was issued, new information on comparable settlements was available to the arbitrator, or the parties found the fact-finder's recommendation to be unacceptable and therefore some modifications were necessary in order to increase the acceptability of the arbitration award.

The New York State PERB attempted to have the arbitrators use a "show cause" approach to the arbitration hearing, that is, they wanted the parties to identify what was wrong with the fact-finder's report. However, the parties objected to this approach and demanded the right to present their cases *de novo*. Yet in the executive sessions of tripartite arbitration panels, most of the arbitrators adopted a show-cause approach as a means of trying to either negotiate a settlement or resolve the disputed issues around the fact-finder's recommendations. Many of them were somewhat uncomfortable with having to second-guess the recommendations of another neutral, recognizing that in some future case *they* might be the fact-finder and someone else serving as an arbitrator might be second-guessing their opinions.

Thus, in New York State arbitration did look very much like an instant replay of fact-finding. Presumably, if the show-cause approach to arbitration following fact-finding could be effectively implemented, the role of fact-finding under an arbitration statute could be strengthened and improved. Fact-finding followed by final-offer arbitration might be still another way to

---

[79]Kochan et al., *supra* note 44, at ch. 3.

strengthen its role in an interest-arbitration system. While the disadvantages of fact-finding in the New York procedure were found to outweigh its contributions to the dispute-resolution system, there may be ways of designing an important role for this procedure under alternative arbitration schemes.

The Arbitration Process

One of the major questions facing designers of arbitration procedures centers on the pros and cons of tripartite vs. single-arbitrator systems. Advocates of tripartite arbitration argue that it allows the parties greater control over the outcomes of the award, reduces the risk of obtaining an unworkable award, facilitates mediation in arbitration, and increases the commitment of the parties to the award. Opponents argue, on the other hand, that the public interest may be compromised by the involvement of the parties, bargaining and mediation in the earlier stages of the procedures will be less vigorous because mediation is available again, and the procedure is more time-consuming and cumbersome.

There is clear evidence that tripartite arbitration does become an extension of bargaining and mediation. Approximately 60 percent of all arbitration awards issued in the first two years under the New York statute were unanimous.[80] Furthermore, interviews with the parties to these arbitration panels clearly documented the heavy emphasis on negotiation and mediation in the executive sessions. The same has been true in tripartite arbitration under the Michigan final-offer statute since a high proportion of cases are settled in arbitration prior to an award. Thus, the med-arb process is a prominent component of tripartite arbitration structures in the public sector.

The pressure for negotiation in mediation and arbitration sessions is most evident in the larger jurisdictions when the economic and political stakes in the outcomes of the awards are the greatest and where the parties are militant enough to pose a threat to the "finality" of an award through strikes, refusals to implement the award, or court appeals. The 1976–1977 dispute between New York City and its police officers is a case in point. There the central issues were wages and a management pro-

---

[80]*Id.*, at ch. 8.

posal to change the number of hours worked and the deployment of personnel in patrol cars. The dispute went through several job actions, strike threats, mediation efforts, written mediation recommendations, court appeals, and an impasse-panel recommendation; ultimately it was placed before an arbitrator. After the arbitration award was written but before it was made public, the arbitrator gave the parties one more opportunity to negotiate a settlement. At this final stage, the parties were successful in reaching a negotiated accommodation. This case is instructive for a number of reasons. First, it shows that where the issues are complex, the stakes high, and the parties militant, negotiations continue through every stage of the impasse-resolution process. Second, it suggests that when the dispute involves a major change in operating procedures, arbitrators are reluctant to impose their own solutions. Third, it also illustrates the need to fashion an acceptable award when one (or both) of the parties is militant enough to seriously threaten to overturn or ignore the award. Fourth, it suggests the difficulty of adopting a "judicial" approach to complex interest disputes. There simply is no one best answer to these types of complex problems, nor is it very easy to identify what the "public interest" would dictate as the outcome of this type of dispute.[81]

A number of studies have examined how arbitrators use statutory criteria in framing an award. The most common finding is that comparability is used rather extensively, with cost of living or ability to pay taking top priority only in unusual circumstances.[82] As in fact-finding, however, the criteria are not applied in any consistent fashion. Instead of serving as uniform standards, these and other criteria, such as general labor relations practices, interests and welfare of the public, etc., appear to be used as general guides that are considered and applied on a case-by-case basis and used by the parties to rationalize their positions in arbitration. These findings again illustrate the premium that neutrals and partisans place on shaping an award that is acceptable to the parties.

Some commentators have expressed the fear that the arbitrators' stress on comparability as a decision criterion will make it difficult for either party to achieve a major innovation in arbitra-

---

[81]For an argument supporting a more judicial approach to arbitration, see Raymond D. Horton, *Arbitration, Arbitrators, and the Public Interest,* 27 Ind. & Lab. Rels. Rev. 497 (July 1975).

[82]See, for example, Kochan et al., *supra* note 44, at ch. 8; or Jones, *supra* note 72.

tion. If this is true, arbitration may also have a limited half-life as the parties find that there are few gains left to achieve without breaking new ground. There is some evidence that this problem has emerged in the Canadian federal sector where a union has the option of arbitration or the right to strike.[83] In that system, the preference for arbitration declined among unions once they had achieved comparable contract provisions. The point of diminishing returns may have contributed to the decision of more units to shift to the strike route. As yet, there is little evidence of this problem arising in the U.S. systems. It is, however, an issue that merits attention in future studies.

Beyond the Procedural Debate

The design of a dispute-resolution system requires balancing the multiple objectives of avoiding strikes, minimizing third-party dependence and maximizing good-faith bargaining, protecting the public interest and the accountability of elected officials, and, in the long run, building the commitment of the parties and the public to a bargaining system that forces the parties to confront their problems effectively.

The record of various forms of dispute resolution that have been tried over the first decade of public-sector bargaining suggests that no "one best way" or optimal procedure for achieving all of these objectives has yet been identified. Thus, in this final section a number of comments will be made to interpret the results discussed earlier in this chapter in order to identify the tradeoffs that are associated with alternative systems.

Those wishing to provide as iron-clad a no-strike system as possible will probably need to embrace some form of compulsory arbitration. While no system can guarantee the complete absence of strikes, the record of strike avoidance, at least for police and fire fighters, so far has been better under arbitration than under fact-finding or in the absence of legislation. Whether this same experience will generalize to other occupational groups will be known only if more states extend these rights to a broader array of employee groups. There also is no way to determine at this point whether final-offer and conventional arbitration differ in their strike-avoidance potential.

---

[83]Anderson and Kochan, *supra* note 30, at 292–93.

For those concerned about the chilling effect of arbitration, the evidence from Massachusetts and Wisconsin suggests that the best choice is a system providing mediation followed closely by final-offer arbitration with a single arbitrator who is constrained from mediating at the arbitration stage. Under this type of system, a relatively high proportion of disputes will likely go to mediation; however, the mediation process should be relatively successful in reducing the number of cases that are passed on to arbitration. The mediation process, therefore, is the focal point of this system for resolving impasses.

A variant of this system—a tripartite arbitration structure—can be designed for those who wish to increase the parties' control over the final outcome. Even greater control can be imposed by using the issue-by-issue method of final-offer selection in a tripartite structure. This system builds the potential for further mediation into the arbitration stage of the procedure and would likely result in a similarly high percentage of negotiations reaching impasse, a lower settlement rate in mediation prior to arbitration, and a higher settlement rate in arbitration without an award. Another variant on this system for those who are opposed to final-offer arbitration—conventional arbitration with a tripartite structure—would be expected to have relatively similar effects, except that we might observe a higher rate of unanimous awards rather than mediated settlements without an award.

All of the above options assume that a high priority is placed on avoiding strikes. Relaxing this priority a bit relative to other objectives opens a wide array of additional options. For example, if one wishes to deal with the fear that arbitration stifles innovation or the ability to make major breakthroughs in collective bargaining, the dual impasse routes of arbitration or the right to strike can be built into the law. If the Canadian experience under this system generalizes to other jurisdictions, then we would expect that over time (1) the weak bargaining units lacking an effective strike threat will stay within the arbitration route as long as they can benefit from a "catch-up" argument, (2) the strong bargaining units with an ability and willingness to strike will prefer the strike option, (3) the rate of impasse will be relatively high in order to get to the critical pressure point in the procedure, and (4) the parties may switch from one option to the other over time as they grow dissatisfied with the outcomes from one route. A variant on this option, which makes it more difficult for the stronger party to dominate the choice of the routes, is found in the Wisconsin statute, where both parties must agree on the strike route or else the arbitration route becomes automatic.

A more liberal strike-based system might adopt the approach of Hawaii and several other states by allowing strikes after mediation and/or fact-finding have been exhausted, subject to a limitation in cases affecting public health and safety. Although experience under these statutes has not been very thoroughly analyzed, some evidence from Hawaii and Pennsylvania suggests that a reasonably high rate of impasses can be expected.[84] The number of strikes is likely to vary considerably depending on the nature of the economic and political environments and the characteristics of the relationships between the parties. For example, a higher strike rate might be expected in relationships involving strong, militant unions in complex political environments under a system of this type than under one where there was no statutory right to strike. Strikes that do occur might also tend to be of longer duration here than in jurisdictions where the strike is illegal.

Finally, those who are philosophically opposed both to the right to strike and to any form of compulsory arbitration can still rely on the most commonly used system—mediation followed by fact-finding. While it might be difficult, if not impossible, to return to this system once arbitration or the right to strike has been provided, this approach still may be useful as a first step in establishing bargaining rights in jurisdictions where the parties are unfamiliar with collective bargaining and dispute resolution. Since the states that have yet to establish bargaining rights are largely located in environments where there is less reason to expect a rapid rise of militant unionism, the process of fact-finding with recommendations may have a longer half-life than it had in some of the states that adopted and then abandoned this system in the first decade of public-sector bargaining.

In summary, a variety of options are available to public policy-makers, depending on the weights they assign to different policy objectives. Although each alternative offers a slightly different approach, in practice their similarities may outweigh their differences. As Rehmus recently noted, the parties have adapted the

---

[84]See Peter Feuille, *Symposium Introduction: Public Sector Impasses,* 16 Ind. Rels. 265 (October 1977).

various dispute-settlement procedures in ways that suggest that the dispute-resolution process has come full circle.[85] Instead of the distinct steps envisioned by most states that start with negotiations, proceed to mediation, and then go to fact-finding and/or arbitration, the parties and neutrals have found ways to mix each of these processes together in combinations that fit the needs of their particular dispute. Thus, we have fact-finding followed by mediation, med-arb, arbitration followed by negotiations, strikes followed by fact-finding, mediation and/or arbitration, etc. Over time, as more experience is gained with these strategies and better data become available on their performance, we can understand more fully the potentials and limitations of all of the options. The more we learn, the more we are likely to be convinced of the futility of searching for the "one best way" or the "optimal" system for resolving all collective bargaining disputes. Instead, we should become better equipped to design alternative systems to meet different policy objectives or to adapt to changing circumstances.

---

[85]Charles Rehmus, *A Circular View of Government Intervention*, in Symposium on Police and Firefighter Arbitration in New York State (Albany, N.Y.: Public Employment Relations Board, 1977), 165–78.

CHAPTER 6

PUBLIC-SECTOR LABOR LEGISLATION—
AN EVOLUTIONARY ANALYSIS*

B. V. H. SCHNEIDER†

A reading of the history of employer-employee relations in
the public service shows a consistent thread of concern that
collective bargaining as we know it in the private sector is ir-
reconcilable with the nature of government. This concern has
been expressed in a variety of specific ways over the years, but
in general it says that the complete transplantation of traditional
collective bargaining into the governmental process would im-
pair the decision-making power of elected officials as they seek
to represent the public interest.

Resistance to collective bargaining in the name of the public
interest, however expressed, often represents little more than a
simple reluctance of an employer to share authority. Such a
reaction is familiar in the private sector. But the problem is a
larger one in the public sector. The political nature of government and its special relation to the public create a unique employment environment, one in which sovereignty and delegation of authority have been critical considerations in the creation
of public-sector labor relations law.

Early thought on the subject concluded that such mechanisms
as exclusive recognition, binding agreements, and the strike or
lockout were not transferable from the private to the public
sector. Ida Klaus reported in 1959 that many governmental units
had permitted their employees freedom of association and had
accorded some degree of recognition to organizations of employees in the determination of employment conditions, but *at no
level* had any government adopted "a thoroughgoing and systematic code of labor relations at all comparable in fundamental
policy, basic guarantees and rights, and procedures for their

*The following people assisted in the preparation of this chapter: David J. Bowen,
Bonnie Cebulski Bogue, Hazel Grove, Sharon Melnyk, Clara Stern, and Marla Taylor.
†University of California, Berkeley.

enforcement, with those of prevailing labor-relations laws in the private sector."[1] Such a system was generally viewed as inconsistent with government's sovereign decision-making status.

Nonetheless, when it became impossible to prevent strikes or to ignore the demands of public workers for participation in the setting of their terms of employment, policy-makers turned hesitantly to the private-sector model. At a loss for workable alternative policy instruments, they diluted, stretched, and bent the system in attempts to make it fit government needs and employee expectations in hundreds of public agencies and dozens of states. The result has been piecemeal adoption of traditional procedures.

The process has not been smooth or complete. The history of labor relations in the public sector is characterized by continuing tension between the drive for collective bargaining, interpreted as equity by public employees, and the resistance of government as it strives to protect and guarantee its right to make unfettered decisions. From this comes the overriding "labor relations problem" in the public sector: the need to separate or reconcile the sovereign authority of government and the bilateral authority inherent in the grant of collective bargaining rights.

Accommodation has been achieved in regard to many elements of traditional (i.e., private-sector-like) collective bargaining. In others, such as impasse resolution, the tension is unresolved, although the search for solution has been intense.

In no case has a law been adopted which reproduces the National Labor Relations Act, although many approximate it. By 1977, 33 states had enacted collective bargaining statutes covering all or some occupational groups,[2] four had authorized bar-

[1] *Labor Relations in the Public Service: Exploration and Experiment,* 10 Syracuse L. Rev. 184 (1959).

[2] For purposes of this general listing, collective bargaining is defined as at least a legal compulsion on the employer to meet and confer on request on pay and conditions of employment. Alabama Code Recompiled, Title 37 § 450(3) (1967) (firemen); Alaska Statutes, Title 23 § 23.40.070–23.40.260 (1972) as amended 1977 (public employees generally), Title 14 § 14.20.550–14.20.610 (1970) as amended 1975 (teachers); California Annotated Codes, Government, Title 1 § 3500–3510 (1961) as amended 1973 (local employees), § 3512–3524 (1977) § 3525–3536 (1971) as amended 1977 (state employees), § 3540–3549.3 (1975) as amended 1977 (public school employees), Labor § 1960–1963 (1959) (firemen); Connecticut Gen. Stat. Annotated, Title 7, Ch. 113, § 7-467-7-479 (1965) as amended 1977 (local), Title 10, Ch. 166, § 10-153a–10-153g (1961) as amended 1977 (teachers), Title 5, Ch. 68, § 5-270–5-280 (1975) as amended 1977 (state); Delaware Code Annotated, Title 19, Ch. 13, § 1301–1302 (1965) (public employees generally), Title 14, Ch. 40, § 4001–4013 (1969) (teachers): Florida Stat. Annotated, § 447.201–447.609 (1974) as amended 1977 (all public employees); Hawaii Revised Stat., Ch. 89, § 89-1–89-21 (1970) as amended 1977 (all public employees); Idaho Code, Ch. 18, § 44-1801–44-1811 (1970) as amended 1977 (firemen), Ch. 12, §

gaining by statute for certain groups under restrictive circumstances,[3] and one had extended the right by executive order.[4] What problems have arisen in the movement toward the pri-

---

33-1271–33-1276 (1971) as amended 1977 (teachers); Indiana Stat. Annotated, Code Ed., Title 20, § 20-7.5-1-1–20-7.5-1-14 (1973) as amended 1974 (teachers), Title 22, § 22-6-4-1–22-6-4-13 (1975) (state and local); Iowa Code Annotated, Sec. 20, § 20.1–20.27 (1974) (all public employees), Sec. 90, § 90.15–90.27 (1959) (firemen arb.); Kansas Stat. Annotated, Ch. 75, § 75-4321–75-4337 (1971) as amended 1977 (public employees generally), Ch. 72, § 72-5413–72-5425 (1970) as amended 1977 (teachers); Maine Rev. Stat. Annotated, Title 26, Ch. 9-A, § 961–973 (1969) as amended 1976 (local), Ch. 9-B, § 979–979-0 (1974) as amended 1976 (state), Ch. 12, § 1021–1034 (1975) as amended 1977 (university employees); Massachusetts General Laws Annotated, Ch. 150E, § 1–15 (1973) as amended 1977 (all public employees), Ch. 1078, § 4–4A (1973) as amended 1977 (police and fire arb.); Michigan Compiled Laws Annotated, § 423.201–423.216 (1947) as amended 1977 (public employees generally), § 423.231–423.247 (1969) as amended 1978 (police and fire arb.); Minnesota Stat. Annotated, § 179.61–179.76 (1971) as amended 1977 (public employees generally); Missouri Annotated Stat., Title 8, Ch. 105, § 105.500–105.530 (1967) as amended 1969 (all except police and teachers); Montana Rev. Codes, Title 59, § 59-1601–59-1617 (1973) as amended 1977 (public employees generally), Title 41, § 41-2201–41-2210 (1969) (nurses); Nebraska Rev. Stat., 1943, Ch. 48, Art. 8, § 48-801–48-838 (1947) as amended 1977 (public employees generally), Ch. 79, § 79-1287–79-1295 (1967) (teachers); Nevada Rev. Stat., Title 23, Ch. 288, § 288.-010–288.280 (1969) as amended 1977 (local, teachers, and state nurses); New Hampshire Rev. Stat. Annotated, Ch. 273-A, § 273-A:1–273-A:16 (1975) (all public employees); New Jersey Stat. Annotated, Title 34, Ch. 13A, § 34:13A-1–34:13A-13 (1941) as amended 1974 (all public employees), Ch. 85, § 1–9 (1977) (police and fire arb.); New York Consolidated Laws Annotated, Civil Service, Art. 14, § 200–214 (1967) as amended 1977 (all public employees); North Dakota Century Code, Title 34, Ch. 34-11, § 34-11-01–34-11-05 (1951) (public employees—mediation), Title 15, Ch. 15-38.1, § 15-38.-1-01–15-38.1-15 (1969) (teachers); Oklahoma Stat. Annotated, Title 11, § 548.1–548.14 (1971) as amended 1972 (local, police, and fire), Title 70, § 509.1–509.10 (1971) (school employees); Oregon Rev. Stat. Ch. 243, § 243.650–243.782 (1963) as amended 1975 (all public employees); Pennsylvania Stat. Annotated, Title 43, Ch. 19, § 1101.101–1101.-2301 (1970) as amended 1976 (public employees generally), Ch. 7, § 217.1–217.10 (1968) (police and firemen), Title 53, § 39951, Art. V (a-e) (1967) (transit); Rhode Island Gen. Laws 1956, Title 36, Ch. 11, § 36-11-1–36-11-11 (1958) as amended 1973 (state), Title 28, Ch. 9.4, § 28-9.4-1–28-9.4-19 (1967) (local), Ch. 9.3, § 28-9.3-1–28-9.3-16 (1966) as amended 1975 (teachers), Ch. 9.1, § 28-9.1-1–28-9.1-16 (1961) as amended 1976 (firemen), Ch. 9.2, § 28-9.2-1–28-9.2-16 (1963) as amended 1976 (police); South Dakota Compiled Laws 1967, Title 3, Ch. 3-18, § 3-18-1–3-18-17 (1969) as amended 1974 (public employees generally); Tennessee Code Annotated, Title 49, § 1–19 (1978) (teachers); Vermont Stat. Annotated, Title 3, Ch. 27, § 901–1007 (1969) as amended 1977 (state), Title 21, Ch. 22, § 1721–1735 (1973) as amended 1976 (local), Title 16, Ch. 27, § 1981–2010 (1969) (teachers); Washington Rev. Code Ann., Title 41, Ch. 41.56, § 41.56.010–41.56.950 (1967) as amended 1976 (public employees generally), Title 41, Ch. 41.59, § 41.59.010–41.59.950 (1975) (teachers), Title 28B, Ch. 28B.52, § 28B.52.010–28B.52.200 (1971) as amended 1975 (community college academic employees), Ch. 28B.16, § 28B.16.010–28B.16.930 (1969) as amended 1977 (higher education), Title 53, Ch. 53.18, § 53.18.010–53.18.060 (1967) as amended 1975 (port employees); Wisconsin Stat. Annotated, Title 13, Ch. 111, § 111.80–111.97 (1965) as amended 1976 (state), § 111.70, 111.71 (1959) as amended 1977 (local), § 111.77 (1971) as amended 1977 (police and firemen); Wyoming Stat., 1957, Title 27, Ch. 14, § 27-265–27-273 (1965) (firemen).

[3]Georgia Code Annotated, Title 54, Ch. 54-13, § 54-1301–54-1315 (1971) (firemen); Kentucky Rev. Stat., Ch. 345, § 345.010–345.130 (1972) as amended 1976 (firemen), Ch. 78, § 78.400, 78.470, 78.480 (police); Maryland Annotated Code of the Pub. Gen. Laws, Art. 77, § 160A (1974) as amended 1975 (class. school employees), Ch. 14-½, § 160 (1969) as amended 1972 (teachers); Texas Civil Stat., Title 83, Art. 5154c-1, § 1–20 (1973) (police and firemen).

[4]Illinois, Executive Order No. 6, September 4, 1973 (state employees).

vate model? Which appear to have been solved? What problems remain? Using a broad brush, this chapter traces policy development on four major elements of collective bargaining—the right to bargain, impasse resolution, scope of bargaining, and union security.

The Right to Bargain

There was a time—spanning several decades before World War II—when even the act of joining or attempting to form a union for the purpose of self-protection was viewed with grave misgivings in many parts of the public sector. The right of public employees to associate might be constitutionally protected (although the law was not always clear on this), but such a right could not supersede the government employer's obligation to protect "the public interest." Although sovereign immunity had been delimited in other areas, government authority in labor relations was viewed as absolute. In the absence of law specific to the subject, governments were successful in claiming in the courts that collective bargaining would amount to an abrogation of governmental discretion, that organization of personnel and determination of pay and conditions were government functions, and that governmental functions might not be delegated. Bargaining, agreements, and/or force (strikes) would be "intolerable" invasions of the sovereign's absolute authority to act in the public interest.[5]

But World War II and its aftermath brought dramatic changes in circumstances and attitudes. The demand for more government services, sharp increases in the numbers of public employees, and inflation led to the growth of more militant and durable public-employee organizations, a rash of more effective

---

[5]The classic works on the early history of public-employee organizations and the problems that arose in the government context are Sterling D. Spero, Government as Employer, originally published in 1948 (Carbondale: Southern Illinois University Press, 1972), and Morton R. Godine, The Labor Problem in the Public Service (Cambridge, Mass.: Harvard University Press, 1951). Both are essential reading for those interested in the roots of public-employee organizations, which extend well back into the 19th century. It would be a serious error to assume, as much current work in this field does, that public-employee organizations were nonexistent or virtually impotent prior to World War II. Operating under constraints which normally foreclosed anything resembling a model collective bargaining situation, they nonetheless pursued a variety of protective activities and, as David Ziskind has so well documented, were not reluctant to strike: One Thousand Strikes of Government Employees (New York: Arno, 1971) (reprint of 1940 ed.).

strikes than had ever been experienced before, and, coincidentally but importantly, a resurgence of interest in the reform of public personnel administration.[6]

Public Policy and the Strike

Previously there had been no compelling reason for a review of public policy on the relationship between a government employer and its employees. Now, however, public and political concern over strikes gave rise to the first attempts to deal legislatively with a new labor problem in the public service.[7] In 1947, eight states passed antistrike laws.[8] In the same year, the Taft-Hartley Act banned strikes in the federal service and made such action a possible felony. Penalties in the state laws tended to be stiff, ranging from termination and ineligibility for reemployment for 12 months, to fines and imprisonment, to definition of striking as a misdemeanor. New York's Condon-Wadlin Act required that rehired workers be placed on probation for five years and receive no pay increases for three years.

In spite of the harshness of the antistrike laws, a new trend was discernible. Some of the laws gave statutory recognition to the right of employees to communicate their views on employment conditions (Michigan, Ohio, Pennsylvania). Nebraska, in addition, created the industrial relations court to hear labor disputes and issue decisions regarding proprietary activities of the state. In Minnesota, public hospitals were covered by a law (1947) allowing for negotiations, exclusive representation, mediation, and binding arbitration in tradeoff for a strike prohibition.

By 1950, the limitations of antistrike laws had become apparent. Many local governments had established bargaining arrangements with unions. Strikes were settled and penalties were ignored[9] as political bodies attempted to accommodate union aggressiveness and public demands for peace. An important straw in the wind was a recommendation of the first Hoover

---

[6]O. Glenn Stahl, Public Personnel Administration (New York: Harper & Row, 1962), 38–41.

[7]See Spero, *supra* note 5, at 16-43. Local government (excluding teachers) strikes: 1942, 39; 1943, 51; 1944, 34; 1945, 32; 1946, 61. Work Stoppages in Government, 1972, BLS Report 434 (1974). Teachers' strikes rose from two in 1942 to 20 in 1947. 90 Monthly Lab. Rev. 44 (August 1967).

[8]Michigan, Missouri, Nebraska, New York, Ohio, Pennsylvania, Texas, and Washington. Virginia led the way in 1946.

[9]Public Employee Labor Relations, Ill. Legislative Council, Pub. 132 (1958), 12–13.

Commission in 1949 that "the heads of departments and agencies should be required to provide for the positive participation of employees in the formulation and improvement of federal personnel policies and practices."[10]

Cooperation in the Public Interest

Then, in the fifties, came the second major public policy breakthrough: laws which reconceptualized the "labor problem"—i.e., strikes—as solvable by structured systems of labor-management cooperation. Cooperation as an assumption, if not a personnel technique, has a long history in the civil services. When service to the people is the objective, joint problem-solving is implied and the need for it was certainly made explicit so far as service was concerned when employee organization was first condemned. "Cooperation in the public interest" was now resurrected to cope with demands by employees for a hand in determining employment conditions.

Starting with Illinois and North Dakota in 1951, six states passed laws which supported formal bilateralism for some groups of employees.[11] Each established the rights of employees to join employee organizations. North Dakota and Minnesota placed an *obligation* on the employer to meet with representatives on employment problems. Illinois, New Hampshire, Wisconsin, and Alaska *authorized* employers to bargain collectively or to meet and confer. No law included a provision for exclusive representation or administrative machinery, although exclusive representation was practiced occasionally locally here and there and was standard practice in the Illinois state service.[12] At the other end of the spectrum were laws by which Alabama barred state employees from joining labor organizations and North Carolina prohibited police and fire employees from joining a national labor organization.

In the early sixties, California, Massachusetts, Oregon, and Rhode Island statutorily granted the right to organize. While California required all public employers to "meet and confer on request," Connecticut (municipal), Massachusetts (municipal),

---

[10]Kenneth O. Warner and Mary L. Hennessy, Public Management at the Bargaining Table (Chicago: Public Personnel Association, 1967), 398.
[11]Illinois and North Dakota (1951), New Hampshire (1955), Minnesota (1957), Wisconsin (1959), Alaska (1959).
[12]Richard C. McFadden, Labor-Management Relations in the Illinois State Service (Urbana: Institute of Labor and Industrial Relations, University of Illinois, 1954), 18–21.

Oregon (municipal), and Rhode Island (police and fire) authorized "collective bargaining" on a permissive basis. No guidelines or standards were included.

Beginning of Collective Bargaining

The stand that any form of bargaining in the public sector was impossible was crumbling in the face of experience and political expediency. General acceptance of the concept of a legal duty on the part of the employer to bargain in good faith was brought nearer by two events in 1962—federal Executive Order 10988 and a new law in Wisconsin.

Executive Order 10988, limited as its scope of bargaining was, had the effect of legitimatizing formal negotiating procedures, unit determination, exclusive recognition, and unfair-practice procedures in the public sector.[13] The order also strongly emphasized participation for the good of the service. It wove together the objectives of the civil service cooperation principle with procedural elements of the NLRA. Its preamble states, in part: "participation of employees in the formulation and implementation of personnel policies affecting them contributes to effective conduct of public business," "the efficient administration of the Government and the well-being of employees require that orderly and constructive relationships be maintained between employee organizations and management officials," and "effective employee management cooperation in the public service requires a clear statement of the respective rights and obligations of employee organizations and agency management. . . ."

Of major importance in terms of impact was the adoption of exclusive representation and written agreements—steps toward the conventional private-sector bargaining model and away from the "government is different" syndrome which would have seemed inconceivable 10 years earlier. Some court decisions in the forties had held that it was an abuse of discretion for a public employer to grant exclusive recognition to an employee representative if all employees concerned were not supporters of the representative. This position was slowly abandoned when governments began to move past the view that bargaining involves

[13]For a description of the executive order and the history of employer-employee relations in the federal service, see B.V.H. Schneider, *Collective Bargaining and the Federal Civil Service,* 3 Ind. Rels. 97 (May 1964).

an impermissible illegal delegation of authority and came to rest
on the rationale that agreements are an exercise of discretion
rather than a delegation of authority.[14] Once written agreements were seen as a desirable, if not inevitable, consequence
of formalized relationships, exclusive representation became a
logical prerequisite to orderly procedure. The prerequisite was
that "fair" representation be guaranteed, as it was in the executive order, by proof of majority support, by equal representation
of all employees, and by assurance that individual representa-
tions could still be made to the employer.

The other public policy springboard of 1962 was the implementation of Wisconsin's pioneering law for municipal
employees. It provided the sort of structure which the executive order did not—(1) a central administrative body, similar
to the NLRB, to enforce and apply policies and procedures,
and (2) a means for resolving impasses (mediation and fact-
finding). Although exclusive representation was not specifically mentioned, the Wisconsin Employment Relations Board
was mandated to hold elections and certify employee representatives, and employers were required to reduce agreements to writing in the case of negotiations with a majority
representative.

NLRA Structure Minus the Strike

The years 1965–1967 brought a watershed in public-sector
employment relations. Six more states—Connecticut, Delaware,
Massachusetts, Michigan, Minnesota, and New York—moved by
statute to a modified NLRA model, including a compulsion on
the employer to bargain with certain groups of employees, machinery to administer and enforce procedures, and mediation–
fact-finding mechanisms for the resolution of negotiations disputes. All included strike prohibitions.[15]

What were the reasons for this rush to an NLRA-type framework? Environmental conditions were of paramount impor-

---

[14]See Richard F. Dole, Jr., *State and Local Public Employee Collective Bargaining in the
Absence of Explicit Legislative Authorization*, 54 Iowa L. Rev. 539 (February 1969); see also,
State ex rel Missey v. *City of Cabool*, 70 LRRM 3394 (1969), in which the Missouri Supreme
Court ruled that the state's law allowing exclusive representation was not unconstitu-
tional.

[15]Eleven other states adopted provisions or amended existing statutes to allow or
mandate bargaining for certain groups: Alabama, Florida, Maine, Missouri, Montana,
Nebraska, Oregon, Rhode Island, Vermont, Washington, Wyoming.

tance. All seven states had influential labor movements and/or liberal political traditions, and a long history of public-sector employee organizations. Ad hoc bargaining arrangements had been developing steadily over the years. Perhaps the most critical factor of the time was the political-public realization that strikes were not a temporary postwar phenomenon or a condition which could be eradicated by law.[16] A statement of the American Federation of State, County, and Municipal Employees (AFSCME) in 1966 set forth the union's insistence on the right to strike as essential to free collective bargaining. In July 1967, the traditionally conservative NEA convention approved a policy statement that recognized strikes of NEA affiliates as likely to occur and worthy of support.[17] Clearly something more had to be done to counter the threat posed by the strike.

The situation in New York State in the mid-sixties exemplifies the kind of process going on somewhat less dramatically elsewhere. A critical trigger was the notoriety given the New York City transit strike in January 1966, Governor Rockefeller's appointment of the Taylor Committee the same month, and the committee's subsequent findings.[18] The committee's terms of reference focused on the twin policy goals which had been evolving since World War II: "protecting the public against the disruption of vital public services, while at the same time protecting the rights of public employees."[19] The committee, in its final report, came to grips with sovereignty and described the word as "scarcely an apt term to apply to a system of representative democratic government, such as our own, which is responsive to the electorate. It is more realistic to inquire as to the manner in which public employees can participate in establishing their employment terms within the framework of our political democracy."[20] More importantly, the committee articulated

---

[16]A total of 133 local government strikes were recorded in 1966. Work Stoppages in Government, 1972, BLS Report 434 (1974), 3.

[17]90 Monthly Lab. Rev. III (September 1967). Thirty public-school strikes occurred in 1966, the largest number ever recorded. See 90 Monthly Lab. Rev. 44 (August 1967).

[18]Other important influences were a New York City welfare workers' strike in 1965 which was ended by the use of mediation and fact-finding; the ignoring of Condon-Wadlin strike penalties following New York City teachers' strikes; the waiving by legislation of strike penalties in various instances, including the New York City transit strike. See 89 Monthly Lab. Rev. III-IV (April 1966) and 90 Monthly Lab. Rev. 25 (December 1967).

[19]New York Governor's Committee (Taylor) on Public Employee Relations, Final Report (March 31, 1966), 9.

[20]Id., at 15. (For an interesting example of the speed with which opinion changed on this subject, see Railway Mail Assn. v. Murphy, 44 N.Y. Supp. [2d] 601 [1943], which

the tradeoff which was to characterize public-sector legislation for the next few years: "It is elementary justice to assure public employees, who are stopped from using the strike, that they have the right to negotiate collectively."[21] The upshot was recommendations for procedures based loosely on the NLRA model, but adapted to public-sector differences—notably the substitution of mediation, fact-finding, and strike penalties for the right to strike.

By 1967, public policy in 21 states allowed participation of public employees in the determination of their pay and conditions of employment. Coverage of all public employees in a state was the exception, but coverage was slowly expanding and formal procedures and structures were increasingly common. The strike was still firmly rejected as incompatible with the nature of the government employer. Modified bargaining systems were intended to make the strike unnecessary, and mediation–fact-finding procedures were expected to evolve into an acceptable substitute.

Impasse Resolution and the Strike

When the Taylor Committee contended that the strike was inappropriate in the public sector, it based this view on two points. First, the strike is incompatible with the orderly functioning of our democratic form of representative government, in which relative *political,* rather than economic, power is the final determinant. Second, while admitting that some public employees are in nonessential services and others are engaged in work comparable to that performed in the private sector, it concluded that "a differentiation between essential and nonessential governmental services would be the subject of such intense and never-ending controversy as to be administratively impossible."[22] It also dispensed with compulsory arbitration as an option: "There is serious doubt whether it would be legal because of the obligation of the designated executive heads of government departments or agencies not to delegate certain

states in part, "To tolerate or recognize any combination of Civil Service employees of the Government as a labor organization or union is not only incompatible with the spirit of democracy, but inconsistent with every principle upon which our Government is founded.")

[21]*Id.,* at 20.
[22]*Id.,* at 18–19.

fiscal and other duties. Moreover, it is our opinion that such a course would be detrimental to the cause of developing effective collective negotiations."[23]

Pennsylvania proceeded to take a radically different line, moving directly from its 1947 no-strike statute to compulsory tripartite arbitration for police and fire fighters in 1968,[24] to a comprehensive law and a circumscribed right to strike for other public employees in 1970.[25] The commission that recommended the new approach stated: "Twenty years of experience [under a no-strike law] has taught us that such a policy is unreasonable and unenforceable, particularly when coupled with ineffective or nonexistent collective bargaining. It is based upon a philosophy that one may not strike against the sovereign. But today's sovereign is engaged not only in government but in a great variety of other activities. The consequences of a strike by a policeman are very different from those of a gardener in a public park."[26]

Apparently collective bargaining was an idea whose time had definitely come in Pennsylvania; the commission reported that it could recall no witness who opposed the concept.[27] Furthermore, "essentiality" as an insurmountable barrier to the right to strike was dismissed: "The collective bargaining process will be strengthened if this qualified right to strike is recognized. It will be some curb on the possible intransigence of an employer; and the limitations on the right to strike will serve notice on the employer that there are limits to the hardships that he can impose. . . . Strikes can only be effective so long as they have public support. . . . We look upon the limited and carefully defined right to strike as a safety valve that will in fact prevent strikes."[28]

The question which the New York committee and Pennsyl-

---

[23] *Id.*, at 46.

[24] Preceded by a public referendum.

[25] Also covered by compulsory arbitration are prison and mental hospital guards and court employees. Voluntary arbitration is allowed other groups except on matters requiring legislation. Strikes are prohibited during statutory bargaining procedures (including mediation and fact-finding), and in the event they create a danger or threat to health, safety, or welfare. The power to determine the latter is vested in the courts, as is the authority to issue injunctions.

[26] Governor's Commission to Revise the Public Employee Law of Pennsylvania, Report and Recommendations (June 1968), 7.

[27] *Id.*, at 9.

[28] *Id.*, at 13–14. Hawaii took the same step in 1970 and for roughly the same reasons.

vania commission attempted to deal with—given the limitations imposed by the governmental environment, how do you accommodate the pressure for finality in collective bargaining?—continues to absorb the parties, politicians, and public. More research has been carried on in this area than in any other in the field of public-sector labor relations. Legislative solutions, proposed and applied, have been imaginative and often daring.

Writing in 1967, only three years before passage of Pennsylvania's strike law, Andrew W. J. Thomson observed that no legislature "has yet permitted its employees to strike, and public opinion seems to indicate that such a development is not likely in the foreseeable future. The furthest that any legislative body has gone is to prohibit specifically only strikes which endanger the health, safety or welfare of the public as in Vermont. . . ."[29] A similar view was put forward by Ida Klaus who saw government as unyielding on the strike in part because of the unwillingness of the public to accept any action that would sanction strikes by public employees.[30] Both writers emphasized the difficulty of distinguishing between essential and nonessential services, the practical and philosophical point at which the New York and Pennsylvania legislatures chose to diverge, as noted above.

It is hardly surprising that heavy emphasis and high hopes were placed on mediation and fact-finding as procedural substitutes for strikes and lockouts. In 1973, Charles Rehmus reported that over 20 state statutes provided for fact-finding for some or all their public employees. He stated the reason for the attractiveness of the procedure: "If the issues in dispute and the recommendations for their resolution are clearly set forth and are well reasoned then the recommendations will be persuasive to all concerned."[31]

The problem with mediation and fact-finding, of course, is that they are not always persuasive, leaving the parties with the "finality" choices of an employer's unilateral action or an illegal employees' strike. In fact, it appears that only 16 states now provide for fact-finding as a last step for one or more groups.

---

[29]Andrew W.J. Thomson, Strikes and Strike Penalties in Public Employment (Ithaca: New York State School of Industrial and Labor Relations, Cornell University, 1967), 8.

[30]Ida Klaus, *A Look Ahead*, in Labor-Management Relations in the Public Service, Pt. 6 (Honolulu: Industrial Relations Center, University of Hawaii, September 1968), 775–76.

[31]Charles Rehmus, *The Fact Finder's Role*, in The Public Interest and the Role of the Neutral in Dispute Settlement (Albany, N.Y.: Society of Professionals in Dispute Resolution, 1973), 37.

The trend has been toward mechanisms that will avoid the inequity connotations of a unilateral employer action and the antipublic interest considerations implicit in a strike.

The Right to Strike

Given the historical aversion to the strike in the public sector, one of the most interesting developments over the seventies has been the statutory granting of this right in eight states.[32] The reasons seem to be basically those touched on by the Pennsylvania committee: a belief that bargaining will thereby be strengthened and a belief that true essentiality can be defined, and should be, to protect the interests of both public employees and the public. It is the latter objective which has most strongly marked these statutes. In no case is the right to strike unfettered. In all cases, a threat to the public health, safety, and/or welfare triggers a "no-strike" mechanism. In all cases, certain prestrike impasse procedures must be complied with. Some of these involve the passage of considerable time.[33] Others involve other kinds of devices to bring public pressure into the picture and to force harder bargaining. For example, after impasse, the new Wisconsin law requires each party to submit a single final offer, which becomes a public document; a public hearing must be held if five citizens request one; if *both* parties withdraw their final offers, the labor organization may strike after giving 10 days' notice unless a court finds that a strike would pose an imminent threat to public health or safety. Essentiality is doubly protected in five of these eight states by provision of compulsory arbitration for some group or groups of employees.[34]

The Trend Toward Compulsory Arbitration

Far more marked than the trend toward strike rights has been the trend toward compulsory arbitration of bargaining impasses. In 1965, Maine and Wyoming provided compulsory arbitration for fire fighters. Two years later, Delaware allowed voluntary binding arbitration on all issues but wages, and Rhode

[32]Alaska (1974), Hawaii (1970), Minnesota (1975), Montana (1969), Oregon (1973), Pennsylvania (1970), Vermont (1967), Wisconsin (1977).

[33]For example, in Hawaii the legislated procedure forbids a strike for 90 days from the date of impasse.

[34]The Hawaii, Montana, and Vermont laws do not include compulsory arbitration for any group.

Island, in education negotiations, had compulsory arbitration on all matters not involving the expenditure of money. In spite of a widely expressed concern of both employers and many AFL-CIO unions over the transfer of authority to third parties, by 1977, 18 states[35] had laws including compulsory arbitration in some form for some group or groups of employees. All but two include police and fire fighters.[36] Eight of the 20 involve a variation on conventional arbitration, for example, last-best-offer by package or issue by issue, systems designed to shift responsibility for final terms to the parties and away from the arbitrator, thereby extending the bargaining process.[37]

The overriding expressed consideration in the passage of these laws has been the need to develop "peaceful" procedures for resolving impasses. This objective appears over and over again in statutory policy statements and in the arguments of proponents of compulsory arbitration. By shifting finality to a third party, compulsory arbitration is intended to create a substitute both for the strike and for employer unilateralism. At one stroke a sort of balance is created between the parties by divesting them of their ultimate weapons, equity is achieved by settling impasses through a quasi-judicial forum, and the public interest is protected in that we have real collective bargaining, no strikes, and fair awards.

Few would argue that we have achieved this ideal. Compulsory arbitration is challenged most often on three grounds: (1) it does not deter strikes, (2) it has a chilling effect on the bargaining process, and (3) it involves an unacceptable delegation of governmental authority.

---

[35]Alaska, Connecticut, Indiana, Iowa, Maine, Massachusetts, Michigan, Minnesota, Nebraska, Nevada, New Jersey, New York, Oregon, Pennsylvania, Rhode Island, Washington, Wisconsin, Wyoming. The list includes Indiana whose law covering most non-teaching employees was declared unconstitutional by the state supreme court on July 12, 1977 (*IEERB, et al.* v. *Benton Community School Corp.*, Ind. Sup. Ct. No. 776 S. 203; 719 GERR 9-11 [September 11, 1977]); the issue was judicial review of representation-related decisions by the state administering agency; the law has been rewritten to include review and is expected to pass this year. Arbitration laws in South Dakota and Utah were declared unconstitutional in 1975 and 1977, respectively; see note 41, *infra.*

[36]The exceptions are Maine (fire fighters only) and Wyoming (fire fighters only).

[37]For examples, see Peter Feuille, Final Offer Arbitration (Chicago: International Personnel Management Association, 1977); Ralph T. Jones, Public Sector Labor Relations: An Evaluation of Policy-Related Research (Washington: National Science Foundation, 1975); Gary Long and Peter Feuille, *Final Offer Arbitration: Sudden Death in Eugene,* 27 Ind. & Lab. Rels. Rev. 186 (January 1974); Charles M. Rehmus, *Legislated Interest Arbitration,* in Proceedings of the 27th Annual Meeting, Industrial Relations Research Association (Madison, Wis.: IRRA, 1974); James L. Stern et al., Final-Offer Arbitration (Lexington, Mass.: D.C. Heath and Co., 1975); Fred Witney, *Final Offer Arbitration: The Indianapolis Experience,* 96 Monthly Lab. Rev. 20 (May 1973).

Does it deter strikes? The evidence is inconclusive, although it appears that arbitration has reduced strikes in some states.[38] Illegal strikes occur where they are illegal under all circumstances and where they are legal under some circumstances, without regard to the presence or absence of the arbitration option.[39] Research on strikes has so far produced little evidence that public policy can be correlated with strike incidence. Environmental and structural factors peculiar to particular states appear to determine strike behavior.[40]

Does arbitration discourage true bargaining? The arguments on both sides of this proposition have been well-covered elsewhere.[41] Suffice it to say here that the trend in public-sector law toward arbitration suggests that "chill" is a factor that can be dealt with or lived with.

Far more important—because it goes to the heart of the public-sector employment-relations problem stated at the outset of this chapter—is the question of delegation of authority. So far nine state supreme courts have upheld compulsory arbitration statutes against claims that they improperly delegate legislative power, and two state supreme courts have declared such statutes unconstitutional.[42] The decisions upholding constitutionality

---

[38]See Chapter 5 in this volume by Thomas A. Kochan.

[39]For strike data by state for 1975, see 71:1011 GERR RF (March 14, 1977).

[40]John F. Burton, Jr., and Charles Krider, *The Role and Consequences of Strikes by Public Employees*, 79 Yale L.J. 418 (1970), and *The Incidence of Strikes in Public Employment*, in Labor in the Public and Nonprofit Sectors, ed. Daniel S. Hamermesh (Princeton, N.J.: Princeton University Press, 1975); and contributions by James L. Perry and Jack E. Klauser in *Symposium: Public Sector Impasses*, 16 Ind. Rels. 273 (October 1977).

[41]See, for example, Robert G. Howlett, *Contract Negotiation Arbitration in the Public Sector*, 42 Cincinnati L. Rev. 47 (1973); Peter Feuille, *Final Offer Arbitration and the Chilling Effect*, 14 Ind. Rels. 302 (October 1975); Stern et al., *supra* note 37, at 182; Hoyt N. Wheeler, *How Compulsory Arbitration Affects Compromise Activity*, 17 Ind. Rels. 80 (February 1978).

[42]See Chapter 7 in this volume by Joseph R. Grodin. DECLARED CONSTITUTIONAL: *City of Biddeford by its Board of Education* v. *Biddeford Teachers Assn. et al.*, Maine Sup. Jud. Ct. (April 30, 1973), 83 LRRM 2098 (1973); *Town of Arlington* v. *Board of Conciliation and Arbitration, et al.*, Mass. Sup. Jud. Ct. (August 10, 1976), 352 N.E.2d 914, 93 LRRM 2494 (1976); *Dearborn Fire Fighters Union Local No. 412, IAFF* v. *City of Dearborn* and *Police Officers Assn. of Dearborn* v. *City of Dearborn*. Nos. 54308 and 54309, Mich. Sup. Ct. (June 24, 1975), *aff'g* 81:2826, 231 N.W.2d 226, 90 LRRM 2002 (1975); *School District of Seward Education Assn.* v. *School District of Seward in Co. of Seward*, No. 38267, Neb. Sup. Ct. (July 21, 1972), 80 LRRM 3393 (1972); *City of Amsterdam, N.Y.* v. *Helsby, et al.*, N.Y. Ct. App. (June 5, 1975), appeal from 88:3208, 89 LRRM 2871 (1975); *Harney, et al.* v. *Russo et al. comprising the Borough Council of Borough of East Lansdowne*, No. 291, Pa. Sup. Ct. (June 27, 1969), 71 LRRM 2817 (1969); *City of Warwick, et al.* v. *Warwick Regular Firemen's Assn.*, No. 616, R.I. Sup. Ct. (July 31, 1969), 71 LRRM 3192 (1969); *City of Spokane (Wash.), et al.* v. *Spokane Police Guild, et al.*, No. 43945 (September 2, 1976), 553 P.2d 1316, 93 LRRM 2373 (1976); *State of Wyoming on the Relations of Fire Fighters Local No. 946, IAFF, et al.* v. *City of Laramie, Wyoming, et al.*, No. 3633 (February 15, 1968), 68 LRRM 2038 (1968). DECLARED UNCONSTITUTIONAL: *City of Sioux Falls* v. *Sioux*

have most often found that there is a public interest in preventing strikes, that illegal delegation does not occur when there are statutory provisions of explicit standards and guidelines for arbitrators and procedural safeguards in the form of court review, and that the power to tax has not been transferred in that an arbitration act is regulatory, and does not in itself impose a burden or charge.

But, as Joseph Grodin points out, "Whatever impact collective bargaining and strikes may have upon the political process . . . there is a qualitative difference between that impact and the effect of interest arbitration."[43] His concern is that a system of legislatively mandated interest arbitration may intrude upon the central democratic premise that governmental policy is to be determined by persons responsible, directly or indirectly, to the electorate. "Even if it is assumed that arbitration generally deters strikes and that its impact on collective bargaining is benign or can be made benign, considerations of political responsibility remain. These considerations do not necessarily argue against a system of arbitration, but they do suggest that it be structured and limited in such a way as to preserve both the appearance and the reality of the democratic process in relation to important aspects of social planning."[44]

The search for a satisfactory means of achieving finality goes on. Neither the strike nor compulsory arbitration is a comfortable theoretical fit, but arbitration has got the nod at the moment because, I would speculate, it is controllable in form (it is "judicial," thereby satisfying an equity consideration) and it carries less emotional content than the strike.

New York's safety-service law was renewed last year despite a strong push by the governor for substitution of legislative review for binding awards.[45] Massachusetts's law was renewed regardless of widely publicized charges of the Massachusetts League of Cities and Towns that use was excessive and that awards were running 14-percent higher than negotiated settle-

Falls Fire Fighters Local 814, et al., Nos. 11406, 11411, and 11424, S.D. Sup. Ct. (October 9, 1975), 90 LRRM 2945 (1975); *Salt Lake City, et al.* v. *International Assn. of Fire Fighters Locals 1645, 593, 2064*, No. 14689, Utah Sup. Ct. (April 25, 1977).

[43]Joseph R. Grodin, *Political Aspects of Public Sector Interest Arbitration* 1 Ind. Rels L.J. 4 (Spring 1976).

[44]*Id.*, at 24.

[45]See Donald H. Wollett, *Revenue Sharing, Whipsawing, and the Domino Effect of Arbitration,* in Public Sector Labor Relations: At the Crossroads (Amherst: University of Massachusetts, 1977), 192–94.

ments.[46] The New Jersey Study Commission, whose findings preceded the passage of a police-fire arbitration bill last year, found that "arbitration to compel finality, seems to be, at this time, the single position that would be acceptable to the most persons. . . ."[47] Wisconsin's extension of the arbitration option to all employees was described by one close participant as a result of prior lack of any feature in the law to resolve a dispute without recourse to work stoppages, plus a doubling of illegal strikes over the past five years.[48]

Currently, public discontent in California over illegal strikes among public school teachers has led to legislative examination of means by which such strikes might be eliminated. In Pennsylvania, similar dissatisfaction with the number of legal strikes is in part the reason for appointment of a governor's commission to study existing law. On the other hand, in New York, a senate research committee is studying the feasibility of moderating strike penalties.

Compulsory arbitration is seen by many as the best available instrument for maximizing the potentialities of the collective bargaining process and minimizing illegal strikes and employer unilateralism.[49] In this sense, its proponents believe that compulsory arbitration is "in the public interest." Whether today's "best available instrument" is good enough to survive changing conceptions of the public interest is something else again. Continuing economic constraints, for example, may yet cause governments, management, employee organizations, and the public to reevaluate the professional neutral as the channel through which they choose to see final decisions made. The pendulum may then swing to greater experimentation with the legal strike.

Scope of Bargaining

If public policy on dispute resolution is still clearly in a state of evolution, this is even more true of statutory treatment of the

---

[46]Boston Municipal Research Bureau, Special Rep. 63 (March 3, 1977).

[47]New Jersey Public Employer-Employee Relations Study Commission, Report to the Governor and the Legislature (February 2, 1976), 4.

[48]Gary R. Johnson, *Compulsory Binding Arbitration—Beyond the Crossroads*, In Public Sector Labor Relations: At the Crossroads, *supra* note 45, at 103.

[49]See Arvid Anderson et al., *Impasse Resolution in Public Sector Collective Bargaining—An Examination of Compulsory Interest Arbitration in New York*, 51 St. John's L. Rev. 453 (Spring 1977).

scope of bargaining. We can see some consistency in the formation of policy regarding impasses. Trends are discernible, although a strong national consensus is absent. The question of scope of bargaining, however, resists orderly analysis. Some similarities are apparent in statutory development, but what is in fact bargainable is in large part being determined by the parties, administering agencies, and the courts, and the results have been quite different from state to state. This is not surprising when one considers private-sector experience. Scope is the area of labor relations in which the most vital interests of the parties and their constituencies are continually engaged. Scope in its manifestation as a bargain represents a delicate power balance. Even where scope is most narrowly defined by law, the self-interest of the parties will tend to push toward pragmatic solutions, regardless of legal restrictions. Decades of controversy have attended the gradual creation of a definition of legal scope in the private sector, and the process is still going on. This process is barely under way in the public sector.

With the adoption of public-sector bargaining systems, three substantive questions arose: What should be the status of laws which provide conflicting methods of determining wages, hours, and other terms and conditions of employment (e.g., civil service and merit systems)? What rights should the government as management reserve to itself? How can bilateral decision-making on certain issues be reconciled with the responsibility of government to the general public? It is not possible here to explore at length the way the states and the parties have tried to come to grips with these questions, but the following sketch does indicate that the subject of scope cannot be detached from considerations of the impact of bilateral decision-making on accountability.

Early Experience

In the fifties and sixties, many of the states that had statutes defined the scope of meet-and-confer or bargaining broadly in the manner of the NLRA, "wages, hours and other terms and conditions of employment." In his study for the New York Public Employment Relations Board (PERB) in 1970, Irving Sabghir found that statutory limitations on scope were not common. Those states which specifically restricted scope did so in the areas of management policies and civil service items, such as merit, recruitment, and classification. Furthermore, Sabghir could find no correlation between the types of bargaining relationship specified and scope provisions: "Thus, some meet and confer laws have a restrictive scope of bargaining provision and many which mandate a bargaining relationship are silent on the scope of bargaining."[50] By 1972, Lee C. Shaw[51] reported that a significant number of states were specifically exempting civil service systems and the merit principle from scope[52] or were limiting scope by enumerating certain management rights or prerogatives.[53]

As employee organizations grew stronger and collective bargaining became more sophisticated, closer attention began to be paid to the potential effects of bargaining on the political process.[54] By 1973, Patricia Blair found that 23 states had legislation containing language similar or identical to that used in the NLRA.[55] Her concern was of a specific character, but one important to the broad, controversial area of delegation of authority. She found that the expansive NLRA definition of scope was frequently combined with a definition of the public employer which excluded the state's legislative body, thereby requiring the courts, when construing the NLRA definition, to make decisions which could reallocate the distribution of power between state legislatures and executive officials and between state and local governments. This effect was created by interjecting laws authorizing or requiring bargaining into a structure of diffused power over public-employee working conditions.

The problem was not unrecognized in the states. In order to avoid such delegation, nine legislatures had provided that bargaining agreements could not supersede state laws and/or that public employers might conclude agreements on matters within

[50] The Scope of Bargaining in Public Sector Collective Bargaining, New York State PERB (October 1970), 5–21. An argument for completely unrestricted scope is made by Donald H. Wollett, *The Bargaining Process in the Public Sector: What Is Bargainable?* 51 Oregon L. Rev. 177 (1971).
[51] *The Development of State and Federal Laws,* in Public Workers and Public Unions (Englewood Cliffs, N.J.: Prentice-Hall, Inc., 1972).
[52] *Id.,* at 30. For example, Connecticut, Hawaii, Kansas, Maine, Rhode Island, Vermont, Washington, Wisconsin.
[53] *Ibid.* For example, Hawaii, Kansas, Nevada, New Hampshire, Wisconsin.
[54] See particularly Harry H. Wellington and Ralph K. Winter, Jr., The Unions and the Cities (Washington: The Brookings Institution, 1971); Clyde W. Summers, *Public Employee Bargaining: A Political Perspective,* 83 Yale L.J. 1156 (1974), and *Public Sector Bargaining, Problems of Governmental Decisionmaking,* 44 Cincinnati L. Rev. 669 (1975).
[55] *State Legislative Control Over the Conditions of Public Employment: Defining the Scope of Collective Bargaining for State and Municipal Employees,* 26 Vanderbilt L. Rev. 7 (January 1973).

their existing delegations of power. Blair pointed out the critical incongruity: Although these laws "will ensure against judicial interpretations that either expand existing delegations of power . . . or other laws that regulate public working conditions, this type of statutory scheme will restrict the scope of bargaining to less than that which prevails in the private sector. Restricting the number of subjects open to the collective bargaining process decreases the likelihood that collective bargaining will be an effective dispute settlement device, which is, of course, a primary reason for introducing bargaining into the public service."[56]

Two states—Connecticut (municipal) and Delaware (all except teachers)—had faced up to the delegation conflict in part by statutorily expanding the authority of state and local officials to conclude nonmonetary agreements that superseded state laws which had established conditions within the statutory definition of bargainable subjects. In neither case, however, did the law transfer legislative power that was previously undelegated and exercisable only by the legislature.[57]

Meanwhile, lively action was taking place at the court and administrative-agency levels, as employee organizations pressed to bargain over all matters affecting working conditions, and employers, with or without a statutory management-rights clause, struggled to limit scope in their favor.[58] According to the American Bar Association Labor Relations Committee report of 1975, the "trend has been to deem most topics bargainable, unless it can be demonstrated that the 'extent and quality of service' to be rendered or 'basic policy decisions as to the implementation of a mission of a government agency' is at stake. Even then the tendency is to find that the impact of managerial decisions on wages or working conditions is nevertheless a mandatory subject of bargaining."[59]

---

[56]*Id.,* at 17–18.
[57]*Id.,* at 20–21.
[58]For a useful description of scope trends in Michigan, New Jersey, New York, Pennsylvania, Texas, and Wisconsin, see Walter J. Gershenfeld, J. Joseph Loewenberg, and Bernard Ingster, Scope of Public-Sector Bargaining (Lexington, Mass.: D.C. Heath and Co., 1977).
[59]Part I, at 261.

Recent Experience

Confusion and controversy over "competing systems," i.e., civil service and merit laws and the scope of collective bargaining, appear to have lessened in recent years. Wage, hour, and condition items have been shifted into scope, but the merit principle itself has been little affected.[60] New Hampshire's new law for state employees excludes the merit system from bargaining; the Pennsylvania law was amended to allow contracts between the governor and state employees to supersede conflicting civil service rules on promotions and furloughs. California's 1977 law for state employees defines scope in the standard way and then lists relevant existing conflicting code sections which may be superseded by agreement. A new law for teachers in Washington provides that a negotiated agreement prevails over employer policy or regulation.

Another statutory trend from 1975 to 1977 has been toward inclusion of management-rights provisions in the laws. "The implicit theory is that certain subjects are so central to public policy and the public decisionmaking process that they cannot be determined bilaterally without involvement of others affected regardless of the advantages perceived by management. . . ."[61] Nevada narrowed its scope for teachers by redefining class size, student discipline, staffing levels, and workloads as management rights. Florida, Iowa, and New Hampshire (state) included strong management-rights provisions in new laws. California's new law for teachers met the problem by specifically defining the phrase, "terms and conditions of employment,"[62] and reserving all other matters to management decision. Approximately 28 states now have management-rights exclusions from the scope of negotiations in one or more of their public-sector labor laws.

In spite of more and more statutory clarifications, legal tests

---

[60]On this subject, see John F. Burton, *Local Government Bargaining and Management,* 11 Ind. Rels. 123 (May 1972); David Lewin, *Local Government Labor Relations in Transition: The Case of Los Angeles,* 17 Lab. Hist. 191 (Spring 1976); David Lewin and Raymond D. Horton, *The Impact of Collective Bargaining on the Merit System in Government,* 30 Arb. J. 199 (September 1975); Public Management's Internal Response to the Demands of Collective Bargaining in Twelve Midwestern States, U.S. Department of Labor (1977); Donald Vial, *The Scope of Bargaining Controversy: Substantive Issues vs. Procedural Hangups,* 15 Calif. Publ. Emp. Rels. 2 (November 1972).

[61]American Bar Association, Labor Relations Law Committee Report, II (1976), at 390.

[62]Health and welfare benefits, leave and transfer policies, safety, class size, evaluation procedures, union security, and grievance procedures.

continue to be the predominant means of sorting out what is, and what is not, bargainable. R. Theodore Clark, Jr., has made an impressive effort to come to grips analytically with what he describes as the "staggering number of scope decisions [which] appear to be all over the lot."[63] As in the private sector, the mandatory-permissive-illegal approach to subjects of bargaining has been widely used in the public sector. But because of the existence of conflicting systems, it is first necessary to determine whether it is legal for an employer to agree to a given subject. If it is, then it is necessary to determine whether the item is mandatory or permissible.[64] The mandatory-permissive dichotomy is applicable under almost all the statutes.[65] Although salary and hours have raised some problems, the phrase, "other terms and conditions of employment," has caused by far the most difficulty in resolving negotiability disputes. Several statutes which provide for NLRA-type scope also specify management prerogatives. This reservation creates, in many instances, an overlap problem, i.e., a given subject is arguably both a term or condition of employment and a prerogative which should be reserved to management. In fact, a management-prerogative provision need not exist at all for the management-reserved-rights doctrine to come into play.[66] (A classic example of such overlap is class size, which is both a working condition and an important element of educational policy.)

Two standards have been adopted by various state PERBs and courts to resolve this conflict. Several courts have settled the overlap problem by classifying a subject as mandatory if it is *significantly related* to wages, hours, and other terms and conditions of employment. By this standard, class size and welfare caseloads have been determined to be mandatory subjects.[67]

---

[63]R. Theodore Clark, Jr., *The Scope of the Duty to Bargain in Public Employment*, in Labor Relations Law and the Public Sector, ed. Andria S. Knapp (Chicago: American Bar Association, 1977). For a further discussion of recent scope litigation, see Joan Weitzman, Developments in Public Sector Labor Relations in the U.S., Occasional Paper (Ithaca: Institute of Public Employment, New York State School of Industrial and Labor Relations, Cornell University, January 1976), 23–29.

[64]A mandatory subject of bargaining is a subject on which the parties are required to negotiate, and a permissive subject is one which they may negotiate but which neither party can insist on to the point of impasse.

[65]Clark, *supra* note 63, at 85.

[66]*Fibreboard Paper Products Corp.* v. *NLRB*, 379 U.S. 223 (1964).

[67]*Washoe County School Dist.*, Item #3 (Nevada Local Government Employee-Management Relations Board, 1971), *aff'd* 90 Nev. 442, 530 P.2d 114 (1974); *Los Angeles Co. Department of Public Social Services and Dept. of Personnel*, UFC 55.3 (1971), *aff'd* 33 Cal. App.3d 1, 108 Cal. Rptr. 625 (1971).

Clark sees this standard as inadequate because it does not properly recognize the competing interests at stake; undue weight is given to conditions of employment. However, a *balancing* test is rapidly emerging that acknowledges the overlap problem and involves a consideration of competing political interests. Courts in several states appear to be following a balancing standard adopted by the Kansas Supreme Court:[68]

> It does little good, we think, to speak of negotiability in terms of "policy" versus something which is not "policy." Salaries are a matter of policy, and so are vacations and sick leaves. Yet we cannot doubt the authority of the board to negotiate and bind itself on these questions. The key, as we see it, is how direct the impact of an issue is on the well being of the individual teachers, as opposed to its effect on the operation of the school system as a whole. The line may be hard to draw, but *in the absence of more assistance from the legislature the courts must do the best they can.* (Emphasis added.)

More on the Accountability Factor

Concerns over the scope of bargaining and government discretion and accountability arise in a context somewhat different from that of 20 or 30 years ago. Collective bargaining on wages, hours, and working conditions has become public policy, i.e., it is now widely accepted as an institution and process consistent with the public's interest in equitable solution of labor problems. This shift has transformed the earlier concept of the government solely as sovereign into government as a dual entity: as employer and as sovereign. In the first role we see the government delegating authority to bargain and frequently to reach binding agreements, shifting pay-hours-conditions items from civil service laws and personnel rules to the bargaining table, and concerning itself with its prerogatives as a manager.

In its other role, as sovereign, the government retains the ultimate right to act and therefore the responsibility to resolve conflicts over issues which may be seen to fall within scope yet which are also seen to concern wider political/public interests. There may be no question but that government must act in this capacity, but in the poorly defined, slippery area of scope of bargaining in public-sector labor relations, the question is, when and how?

---

[68]*National Education Association of Shawnee Mission, Inc.* v. *Board of Education,* 212 Kan. 741, 512 P.2d 426, 84 LRRM 2230 (1973).

Where statutory guidelines have been established, it is clear that role separation is taking place in an expeditious fashion. For example, the impetus behind the move to more detailed management-rights provisions in statutes is in large part a desire to wall off subjects considered inappropriate to insulated bilateral action, such as the mission of an agency or the extent and quality of service. But it is impossible to draw comprehensive and rational lines that will permanently prevent conflict between the elected official's need to be responsive to the "public interest" and the demands of public employees for influence over their conditions of employment. The pressure for such lines has been, and undoubtedly will continue to be, an ongoing characteristic of public-sector labor relations.

Sunshine laws are an excellent example of how strain in this area can produce experimentation and divergence from the private model. The adoption of open-meeting or sunshine laws demonstrates an active need to somehow "regulate" the content of public-sector labor relations vis-à-vis the "public interest," and in this case the "public interest" is increasingly associated with budget-allocation matters, as well as questions of mission. The rationale appears to be that identifying and restricting unacceptable bargaining items is insufficient; the bargaining process should be open to the public, thereby ensuring access, exposure, and accountability.[69]

The public-sector labor laws of four states now require some sort of sunshine—California, Florida, Minnesota, and Wisconsin. California's laws for public schools (1975) and state employees (1977) both include provisions that require that initial proposals be presented at a public meeting and become a public record, that a reasonable time must then elapse before negotiating to enable the public to become informed and express itself at a public meeting called by the employer, and that subsequent new proposals must be made public. Florida's law, passed in 1974 and amended in 1977, requires that all negotiations be conducted in public. Minnesota (1971) requires that all negotiations and mediation sessions be public unless otherwise provided by the director of mediation services. One of Wisconsin's 1977 amendments requires that meetings held between the par-

---

[69]See Summers, "Public Employee Bargaining," *supra* note 53, at 1197–99. For an informative review of the stands taken on such laws, see Russell A. Smith, Harry T. Edwards, and R. Theodore Clark, Jr., Labor Relations Law in the Public Sector: Cases and Materials (New York: Bobbs-Merrill, 1974), 570–594.

ties for the purpose of presenting initial proposals be open to the public (a requirement that subsequent meetings be open unless both parties agree to close them was vetoed).[70]

The only state with experience is Florida.[71] Wisconsin and California (state employees) provisions are quite new; Minnesota practice has been to bar the public from the majority of negotiation and mediation sessions. Some community groups in California have complained at the failure of local school boards to implement public-notice provisions contained in the state's act covering public schools; although the administering agency has adopted a complaint procedure, it has so far avoided issuing guidelines on local implementation, pending evidence of voluntary compliance.[72]

Some variations on the open-meeting or public-disclosure concept which have surfaced are voluntary agreements by the parties to hold open negotiations,[73] statutory provisions which mandate student input into negotiations in institutions of higher education,[74] and local public referenda.[75]

Another example of how tension can arise from the bilateral authority/sovereign authority constraint is exemplified in the concern of many public employees, particularly professionals, with "mission" and "quality of service." It is perhaps surprising that as these issues are being withdrawn or excluded from bargaining scope, there has been so little examination of the feasibility of alternate statutory formal joint-consultation schemes. Public employees traditionally have played a major consultative role in the provision of public services. The current lack of interest in formal consultation systems can probably be credited to the fact that the fight to transfer former informal consultation items to bargaining scope is far from decided in many states. At

---

[70]Although all 50 states have public-disclosure laws of some sort, the practice has been to exempt labor negotiations. See, for example, 731 GERR 15 (October 24, 1977) on recent experience in Iowa. See also, reports on recent developments in Richard P. Schick and Jean J. Couturier, The Public Interest in Government Labor Relations (Cambridge, Mass.: Ballinger Publishing Co., 1977), and American Bar Association, Labor Relations Law Committee Reports for (1975), 273–73; (1976), 405–408; and (1977), 220–24.

[71]See Sunshine Laws in the Public Sector, Pts. I and II, Midwest Monitor (Bloomington: Indiana University, September/October and November/December 1977); Labor-Management Reporting Service (November 1976).

[72]See 34 CPER 28–30, 52–56 (September 1977); California School Boards Association, California Reporter on Public Employee Relations (March 1977), 14–16; Public Employment Relations Reporter (November 1977), 7.

[73]Sunshine Laws, supra note 71, at 4.

[74]Florida, Maine, Montana, Oregon.

[75]For experience in San Francisco, see 35 CPER 19 (December 1977). The LMRSs of October and December 1977 report on experiments in three Colorado towns.

the moment, only statutes in California and Indiana provide for some form of participation on specific subjects which are not bargainable, and then only for teachers.

Union Security

Prior to the introduction of formal public-sector collective bargaining structures, the only form of union security was voluntary dues deduction. But once exclusive representation was accepted, with its companion obligation to represent all employees in a unit, union-security devices became a major employee-organization goal. One of the more interesting statutory developments of the seventies has been the rapid acceptance of union-security provisions, ranging from the fair-share service fee to, in a few cases, anything short of the closed shop.[76]

The arguments presented in favor of union security are similar to those marshaled to support the transfer of other elements of traditional collective bargaining to the public sector, equity and stability: (1) as long as the exclusive representative must represent all employees in a unit equally, all employees should be obliged to pay their share of the cost of such services, and (2) the goal of constructive collective bargaining and peaceful settlements is substantially forwarded when a union has the security that flows from support of its full unit constituency. These arguments are identical to those used to justify union security in the private sector. Although the issue has not been unattended by controversy, it would appear that the private-sector position on union security has been widely accepted by the government employer.[77]

Seventeen state statutes presently include provision for some form of union security (beyond voluntary dues deduction) for all or some groups of employees. Six states allow the union

---

[76]Useful sources of information on union security in the public sector are Smith, Edwards, and Clark, *supra* note 68, at 595–654; Knapp, ed., Labor Relations Law, *supra* note 63, at 145–77; and American Bar Association, Labor Relations Law Committee Reports for 1975, 1976, and 1977.

[77]Consensus on the issue is apparent in the private sector. A 1970 survey by BNA showed that approximately 83 percent of a sample of all contracts in industry generally provided for the union shop, agency shop, or for maintenance of membership. If contracts in right-to-work states are excluded, the proportion rises to 95 percent. Basic Patterns in Union Contracts (February 1971), 87:1.

shop.[78] Two have maintenance-of-membership provisions.[79] Five provide for the agency shop,[80] while six provide for a service fee or fair-share arrangement.[81]

In the majority of cases, the union-security mechanism is a negotiable item, but there are some notable exceptions, where public policy has moved past the private-sector model and calls for the automatic grant of union security to an exclusive representative. This is presently the case in five states.[82] A variation on the mandatory requirement occurs in three states where union security is granted following a vote of unit members.[83]

With the exception of Vermont's (1969), all union-security statutory provisions were adopted in the seventies. However, local agreements on the subject became fairly common in some states before the enactment or amendment of laws. For example, in 1972 the Michigan Education Association stated that it had agency shops in about half of its 530 contracts.[84] In 1969, union attorney I. J. Gromfine reported union shops in transit agreements in the cities of Chicago, Boston, Pittsburgh, St. Louis, and Memphis, among others; union-security agreements with public agencies in Michigan, New York, Missouri, Vermont, Indiana, and Illinois; union shops for police and fire department employees in Rhode Island and Con-

---

[78]See *supra* note 2 for statute citations. Alaska (all but teachers), Kentucky (fire fighters), Maine (higher education), Oregon (all), Vermont (municipal), Washington (all). The Oregon Court of Appeals ruled on August 22, 1977, that statutory reference to an "all-union" type of security agreement was a drafting error and that although fair-share arrangements are permissible, union shops are prohibited because under the statute employers may not discriminate to encourage or discourage union membership (*Oregon State Employees Assn.* v. *Oregon State University,* Oregon Ct. App. No. C-93-76, CA 8129; 728 GERR 10 [October 3, 1977]). The Washington Supreme Court ruled on October 27, 1977, that although the statute required "membership," the word "membership" is clearly defined as an obligation limited to contribution of dues in exchange for representation rights (*Assn. of Capitol Powerhouse Engineers* v. *Division of Buildings and Grounds, State of Washington; Dept. of General Administration, State Personnel Board, and Washington Federation of State Employees,* Wash. Sup. Ct. No. 44211).
[79]California (state employees), Pennsylvania (all but police and fire fighters).
[80]California (public schools), Massachusetts (all), Michigan (all), Montana (all), Rhode Island (state employees).
[81]Connecticut (state employees), Hawaii (all), Minnesota (all), New York (all), Washington (state employees), Wisconsin (all).
[82]Connecticut (state), Hawaii (all), Minnesota (all; fair share not to exceed 85 percent of regular dues), New York (state), Rhode Island (state).
[83]A majority vote of unit members is required in Massachusetts (all) and Washington (state, higher education); in Wisconsin (state), the required margin is two-thirds of those voting.
[84]512 GERR E1 (July 16, 1973).

necticut.[85] In some cases, such as in Michigan, the topic was held to be within the scope of bargaining.[86] More often, such agreements were the result of local innovation, normally correlated with high proportions of membership.[87]

Two major objections to union security in the public sector are grounded in the character of government employment: (1) dismissal for failure to join and/or pay fees to an exclusive representative violates civil service tenure laws based on merit principles; and (2) the right to associate is constitutionally protected against government infringement.

Tenure Laws

Approximately 37 states have teacher-tenure laws which prevent discharge except for enumerated causes. "A state legislature may be unable to amend . . . to authorize discharge for failure to abide by a union security agreement because tenured teachers whose contracts were in existence prior to passage of any such amendment may be protected . . . by the impairment of contracts clause of the United States Constitution (Art. I § 10)."[88] Court interpretations have varied on this point. However, Blair speculates that the U.S. Supreme Court's reasoning in *Railway Employees' Dept.* v. *Hanson*[89] supports a conclusion that state authorization of union-security agreements for teachers would promote peace in public schools, thereby qualifying as an appropriate exercise of the state police power facilitating the efficient administration of public schools.[90]

In fact, many tenure laws have been construed as merely limiting the powers of school boards to discharge tenured

---

[85]At New York University's 22nd Conference on Labor. Reported in 304 GERR E9 (July 7, 1969).

[86]*Oakland County Sheriff, et al.*, 1968 MERC Op. 1.

[87]A large local jurisdiction in California has had a union-shop agreement for over 20 years in spite of unconducive statutory and case law. The agreement has never been challenged, partly, the participants believe, because no employee has ever been reluctant to join and partly because the agency has escaped the attention of California's active right-to-work committee. For experience with the agency shop in California local government, where it has been declared illegal under the existing statute, see David Smith, *The Agency Shop: An Old Issue in a New Environment*, 17 CPER 2–12 (June 1973).

[88]Patricia Blair, *Union Security Agreements in Public Employment*, 60 Cornell L. Rev. 199 (1975).

[89]351 U.S. 225 (1956). That is, that congressional authorization of union shops was appropriate under the Commerce Clause to promote industrial peace.

[90]Blair, *supra* note 88, at 202.

teachers, rather than conferring contractual rights; these laws may be amended or repealed at any time. Other laws that could be construed as granting contractual rights provide for discharge for "good or just cause," a term which could be interpreted to include a refusal to abide by a statutory requirement regarding union security.[91] This occurred in Michigan as early as 1969 when a discharge under an agency-shop clause was ruled valid as a discharge for "reasonable and just cause" under the state's tenure act.[92] New York may have avoided the tenure conflict problem in its amendment of the Taylor Law last year. There is no mention of agency shop or fair share. The parties may negotiate an "agency shop fee deduction." If an employee doesn't get the money in the first place, he can't refuse to pay a fee and thereby make himself vulnerable to discharge.

The Constitutional Issue

Of more general interest are the constitutional issues recently dealt with by the U.S. Supreme Court in *Abood.*[93] Do union-security arrangements violate the public employee's constitutionally protected freedom of association? A person may not be compelled by the government to join an organization. This bar is embodied in the First Amendment which creates the right to associate or decline to associate. The right to associate is secured only against governmental infringement, and the Fourteenth Amendment extends that restraint to state and local governments.

When the *Abood* case reached the U.S. Supreme Court, the Michigan provision specifically permitted a union and a local government employer to agree to an agency-shop arrange-

---

[91]*Id.*, at 207–208.

[92]*Applegate* v. *Grand Blanc Community Schools,* Michigan Teacher Tenure Commission Case No. 69–8 (February 26, 1969). The question of legal tenure and union-security agreements is still unresolved in Michigan. On February 9, 1978, the state's Tenure Commission ruled 3–2 that a teacher could not be fired because "nonpayment of 'agency shop' fees or dues does not meet the standards of reasonable and just cause for discharge within the meaning of the Tenure Act." For discussion, see 749 GERR 13–14 (March 6, 1978).

[93]*Abood, et al.* v. *Detroit Board of Education,* 97 S.Ct. 1782, 431 U.S. 209, 95 LRRM 2411 (1977). An analysis of the decision and a description of recent experience in California appears in Bonnie G. Cebulski, *The Agency Shop: California Perspectives on a Landmark Decision,* 34 CPER 2–8 (September 1977).

ment, whereby every employee represented by a union—even though not a union member—must pay to the union, as a condition of employment, a service fee equal in amount to union dues. The issue before the Court was: ". . . whether this arrangement violates the constitutional rights of government employees who object to public sector unions as such or to various union activities financed by the compulsory service fees."

The Court ruled that negotiated agency-shop provisions are constitutionally valid as long as employees may refuse to pay that portion of the fees which the union uses for ideological purposes unrelated to its duties as exclusive bargaining representative.

On the validity of the agency shop, the Court relied on the private sector cases, *Hanson*[94] and *IAM* v. *Street,*[95] and reiterated its view that such First Amendment "interference as exists is constitutionally justified by the legislative assessment of the important contribution" of union-security arrangements to labor relations systems. "The desirability of labor peace is no less important in the public sector, nor is the risk of 'free riders' any smaller."

On the second issue—whether the union can constitutionally use compulsory fees for purposes other than collective bargaining—the Court accepted the teachers' argument that their right to associate was being violated and held that being compelled to contribute to the support of an ideological cause as a condition of employment violates rights of freedom of association and speech.

Of particular interest is the teachers' argument that collective bargaining in the public sector is inherently political and, therefore, the First and Fourteenth Amendments forbid coerced support of political activities. The Court answered that the constitutional inquiry evoked is whether a public employee has a "weightier First Amendment interest than a private employee"; the Court found that the public employee does not. "The differences between public and private sector collective bargaining

---

[94]See *supra* note 89.
[95]*Intl. Assn. of Machinists* v. *Street,* 367 U.S. 740, 48 LRRM 2345 (1961).

simply do not translate into differences in First Amendment rights."

Neither the civil service tenure nor the constitutional arguments would appear to present barriers to the continued spread of union-security arrangements in the public sector.

Conclusion

The trend of law and public opinion in the United States has been toward more egalitarian interpretations of how employees and management should function within labor relations systems. But in the public sector, unlike the private, the equity goal constantly has had to be reconciled with the need to maintain the sovereignty of government. The descriptive material above traces some of the successes and failures of the reconciliation process.

In a significant number of states, the duty to bargain, exclusive representation, binding agreements, and union-security arrangements are now viewed as acceptable means to labor peace rather than as unacceptable "invasions of government authority." A similar core of acceptance underlies those more rudimentary systems that merely compel the employer to meet and confer with majority representatives. The trend is unmistakably toward bilateral responsibility for pay, hours, and working conditions.

This is not to suggest that all clashes with the sovereignty concept are likely to be resolved in due course. The nature of the conflict, rooted as it is in ideology, guarantees that the tension between sovereignty and bilateral authority can only be ameliorated, not eliminated. We will continue to see manifestations of the conflict whenever government's perceived need to have the last word intensifies (as is the case now regarding various scope issues, strikes, and compulsory arbitration).

Viewing public-sector labor relations in this manner points up the institutional barriers to full implementation of the traditional private-sector system, but fails to account for other factors influencing public-sector labor law. Economic conditions, for example, are of major importance. Following

World War II, inflation, rising real incomes, the increased demand for government services and hence for government employees, and the improvement in private-sector pay and benefits relative to those in the public sector all contributed to militancy, public sympathy, and the subsequent passage of collective bargaining laws. Demands for "equal treatment" fell on fertile soil.

The enigmatic economic circumstances of recent years have had a different impact. Continued inflation, a relative decline in real incomes, unemployment, and concerns over public budgets have created an environment in which the demands of public employees are often greeted with public indifference, if not hostility. Where legislation has created a bilateral system of some kind, the public response appears to argue that public employees are as "equal" as they ought to be, at least for the time being. Where no statutory systems have been adopted (a handful of states mainly in the South and Southwest), economic pressures undoubtedly reinforce existing disinclination to experiment with increased labor rights.

Not only are public employees vulnerable in the area of labor relations legislation, their proximity to government makes them ready instruments (and targets) of wider public policy in times of general economic stress. For example, in spite of a highly sophisticated fair-comparison pay scheme, federal employees have been subjected to pay caps "in the national interest" and apparently will be again this year. Similar instances of government's response to public economic concerns abound at the local level.

One might speculate that these same economic factors, operating to alter public attitudes and political responses, account for current inactivity on the subject of a national public-sector labor law. *National League of Cities* v. *Usery*[96] destroyed confidence that a national law could be declared constitutional under the commerce power, but it did not affect the possibility that Congress's taxing and spending powers could be used to require state compliance with national labor relations legislation.[97] The

---

[96]*National League of Cities, et al.* v. *Usery, et al.*, 96 S. Ct. 2465, 426 U.S. 833 (June 24, 1976).

[97]See *City of Macon* v. *Marshall*, No. 77–155–Mac (October 28, 1977), 96 LRRM 2797, in which a federal district court ruled in a case arising under the Urban Mass Transportation Act that the federal government may condition the distribution of tax money to local governments on their meeting certain requirements, including the granting of collective bargaining rights to employees.

historical development of both public and private labor law suggests that the limbo in which a national public-sector law now resides may have more to do with attitudes of the moment than with loftier questions of constitutionality.[98]

---

[98]An important test of the durability of collective bargaining in the public sector may be in the making in California. The impact of Proposition 13, the property-tax-reduction measure passed in June 1978, has been substantially muted for 1978-1979 by the transfer of over $5 million in state surplus funds to local agencies. Whether supplementary funding of such a magnitude can be continued is at present unknown, but forecasts are pessimistic. Collective bargaining was adapted to the public sector and its political characteristics over a period of general affluence, when it could be hypothesized that the public was more amenable to such an innovation than might have been the case under other circumstances. California may provide the first large-scale experiment in whether the mechanism is also viable in an environment of scarcity and public sensitivity to the costs of government.

CHAPTER 7

JUDICIAL RESPONSE TO PUBLIC-SECTOR ARBITRATION

JOSEPH R. GRODIN*

Binding arbitration of grievances that arise during the term of a labor agreement, once the exception in the public sector, is rapidly becoming the norm. A 1975 Bureau of Labor Statistics survey indicates that nine of every ten agreements contain some form of contractual grievance procedure, and of these, 79 percent culminate in arbitration.[1] By now the percentage that provide for arbitration is undoubtedly greater. Binding arbitration of interest disputes (that is, disputes arising out of negotiations for a new agreement) has also proliferated. A recent review reports that 34 states and a number of local governments have enacted legislation either mandating or authorizing binding interest arbitration for some or all public employees.[2]

Nor surprisingly, these phenomena have spawned a good deal of litigation in the courts. Parties have disputed over such matters as the validity of statutes or agreements calling for arbitration, over the role of the courts in determining prior to arbitration whether particular issues are arbitrable, over the role of courts in reviewing arbitration awards, and over the relationship of arbitration to constitutional or statutory principles external to the agreement. As in other areas of public-sector labor law, the litigation typically turns on interpretation of statutory provisions that vary widely from state to state, so that it is impossible to generalize about "the law" of the subject. Looming beneath the surface questions of interpretation, however, are issues of public policy that often transcend the language of particular enactments and to that extent are susceptible to a comparative,

---

*Hastings College of Law, University of California.
[1]U.S. Department of Labor, Bureau of Labor Statistics, Grievance and Arbitration Procedures in State and Local Agreements, Bull. No. 1833 (Washington: 1975).
[2]Comment, *Binding Interest Arbitration in the Public Sector: Is It Constitutional?* 18 Wm. & Mary L. Rev. 787 (1977).

if not generalized, examination of judicial response. That, at any rate, is the premise of this chapter. The focus will be on state law, since problems arising out of federal-employee labor relations seldom reach the courts.

Grievance Arbitration

The U.S. Supreme Court decisions in the famous *Steelworkers* trilogy cases of 1960[3] marked the beginning of what David Feller has called the "golden age of arbitration" in the private sector.[4] Not only were agreements to arbitrate contract grievances valid and enforceable,[5] they were favored to the extent that special rules were devised for their protection and nurture. In determining whether a particular dispute fell within their scope, courts were not to pass upon the merits, but only to determine whether the party seeking arbitration was making a claim which "on its face is governed by the contract." An order to arbitrate such a claim was not to be denied "unless it may be said with positive assurance that the arbitration clause is not susceptible to an interpretation that covers the asserted dispute."[6] Finally, so long as the arbitrator's award can be characterized as drawing its "essence" from the agreement, the award is final and not subject to judicial review.[7]

The policy premises underlying these principles of judicial deference stemmed from the Court's perception of the role of arbitration in labor relations—a role different from and more expansive than in the commercial arena, reflecting the unique characteristics of the collective bargaining agreement. While commercial arbitration is the "substitute for litigation," labor arbitration is the "substitute for industrial strife," the agreement to arbitrate being the quid pro quo for the agreement not to strike. The labor agreement itself is "more than a contract,"

---

[3] *Steelworkers* v. *American Mfg. Co.*, 363 U.S. 564, 46 LRRM 2414 (1960); *Steelworkers* v. *Warrior & Gulf Navigation Co.*, 363 U.S. 574, 46 LRRM 2416 (1960); *Steelworkers* v. *Enterprise Wheel & Car Corp.*, 363 U.S. 593, 46 LRRM 2423 (1960).

[4] Feller, *The Coming End of Arbitration's Golden Age*, in Arbitration—1976, Proceedings of the 29th Annual Meeting, National Academy of Arbitrators (Washington: BNA Books, 1976), 97.

[5] The validity and enforceability under federal law agreements to arbitrate were established prior to the trilogy cases in *Textile Workers Union* v. *Lincoln Mills*, 353 U.S. 448, 40 LRRM 2113 (1957).

[6] *Steelworkers* v. *Warrior & Gulf Navigation Co.*, *supra* note 3.

[7] *Steelworkers* v. *Enterprise Wheel & Car Corp.*, *supra* note 3.

said the Court; it is a "generalized code to govern a myriad of cases which the draftsmen cannot wholly anticipate," an "effort to erect a system of industrial self-government" with grievance machinery at its core and arbitration as a dynamic process, "part and parcel of the collective bargaining process itself." It is for these reasons that disputes should be presumed arbitrable unless the parties have clearly provided otherwise. The processing of even unmeritorious grievances may have "therapeutic value." And the arbitrator is not simply a judge without robes. Chosen for his experience, his personal judgment, and his knowledge of the "common law of the shop," he performs functions "not normal to the courts," and indeed "foreign to the competence of the courts." It is his judgment that the parties have bargained for. These are the considerations which led to the rule that courts should withhold judgment on the merits in deciding whether to order arbitration, and should decline to review the merits of an award once rendered.

Feller has expressed concern whether trilogy principles, premised as they are on the private nature of the collective bargaining relationship, can survive the steady intrusion of public law into the collective bargaining arena.[8] His thesis is that as arbitrators feel increasingly obliged to consider external law such as Title VII, OSHA, or the NLRA itself, judges will feel less inclined to defer to their special competence.

But if the "golden age of arbitration" is becoming tarnished in the private sector, what of the public sector where arbitration has just barely taken hold? Private-sector collective bargaining in the U.S. grew in an environment relatively free of statutory control; it supplanted a system in which terms and conditions of employment were determined largely by the individual "contract" of employment. In the public sector, on the other hand, collective bargaining arrived upon a scene saturated with public-law concepts. Government acts by definition through legislation or administrative regulation, and the authority of a particular governing body is in turn restricted or channeled by charter provision, statute, or constitution. Civil service systems and constitutional provisions accorded rights and procedures unknown to the private sector in its pre-collective-bargaining phase. Moreover, while the consequences of bargaining in the private

---

[8]Feller, *supra* note 4. See also Feller, *Arbitration: The Days of Its Glory Are Numbered,* 2 Jud. Rel. L.J. 97 (1977).

sector has public impact, our traditions of free enterprise view that impact as being largely beyond public control, whereas the consequences of bargaining (and therefore arbitration) in the public sector are seen within a democratic framework as being part of the public domain. Under such circumstances, will courts be willing to view public-sector grievance arbitration, through trilogy-colored lenses, as an essentially autonomous institution? Questions might also be raised as to the applicability of certain other premises underlying trilogy principles. Since there is little in the history of public-sector labor relations corresponding to the midterm work stoppages that characterized the prearbitration period in the private sector, can it be said that public-sector grievance arbitration functions as the "substitute for industrial strife"? Since most arbitrators come to public-sector grievance arbitration from the private sector, should it be presumed that they possess special competence with respect to the "common law of the shop"? Indeed, in view of the infancy of public-sector bargaining and the background of unilateral determination of employment conditions through ordinances and rules, does there exist a "common law of the shop" as to which special competence can be developed? Is the trilogy view of the collective bargaining agreement as an essentially open-ended process an appropriate model for the public sector? I do not mean to suggest the answers to these questions, nor to indicate that the answers should necessarily determine judicial response to public-sector grievance arbitration. On the contrary, I intend to argue that whatever the answers to these questions, grievance arbitration has a highly significant role to play in the public sector, and that courts should accommodate to it in much the same way that they have in the private sector. I mean only to indicate that these are substantial questions, the answers to which are by no means self-evident, and that it is reasonable to expect that courts will be troubled by such questions as they approach the task of delineating the judicial role in relation to the arbitral process. The decisions are in accord with that expectation.

Validity of Agreements to Arbitrate

While it is sometimes said that courts at common law disapproved the arbitration of public-sector labor grievances as an unlawful delegation of governmental power,[9] close examination of the cases cited in support of that proposition reveal either that the court was not talking about arbitration at all,[10] or that it confused grievance arbitration with interest arbitration,[11] or that its objection to arbitration stemmed from the court's view that the underlying collective bargaining agreement was itself beyond the authority of the public entity.[12] In any event, once legislatures in many states came to give their blessing to collective bargaining in the public sector, courts began to accept grievance arbitration as an appropriate means of giving effect to an otherwise valid contract even in the absence of express statutory authority. In the leading *City of Rhinelander*[13] case, for example, the Wisconsin Supreme Court held that a statute which authorized binding agreements by implication permitted binding agreements to arbitrate grievances, and it brushed aside the city's arguments based on sovereignty and home rule with the observation that the arguments failed to distinguish between grievance and interest arbitration. Similarly, in *Associated Teachers of Huntington,*[14] the New York Court of Appeals found that legislative authorization for unions to represent employees "in the administration of grievances" necessarily implies the legitimacy of arbitration, since (quoting from one of the trilogy cases) "arbitration is, of course, part and parcel of the administration of grievances."[15] And like its sister tribunal in Wisconsin, the New York court dealt summarily with the school board's contention that its province was being invaded:

> Nor can we agree that a board of education is better qualified than an arbitrator to decide whether a teacher in its employ should be dismissed for incompetency or misconduct. It may not be gainsaid that arbitrators, selected because of their impartiality and their inti-

---

[9]See, e.g., Note, *Legality and Propriety of Agreements to Arbitrate Major and Minor Disputes in Public Employment,* 54 Cornell L. Rev. 129, 130 (1968).

[10]E.g., *Mugford* v. *Mayor and City Council,* 185 Md. 266, 44 A.2d 745, 17 LRRM 690 (1945). Cited in Willingsworth, *Grievance Arbitration in Public Employment,* 13 Arb. J. (U.S.) 3, 7 (1958) as the "leading case."

[11]*Cleveland* v. *Division 268,* 15 Ohio Supp. 76 (1975), distinguished on that ground in *Madison* v. *Frank Lloyd Wright Foundation,* 20 Wis.2d 361, 122 N.W.2d 409 (1963).

[12]E.g., *Hayes* v. *Association of Classroom Teachers,* 76 LRRM 2140 (Cal. Super. 1970). Even in the absence of statute, some courts held collective bargaining agreements and grievance arbitration to be valid. E.g., *Norwalk Teachers Association* v. *Board of Education,* 138 Conn. 369, 83 A.2d 583, 28 LRRM 2408 (1951).

[13]*AFSCME Local 1226* v. *City of Rhinelander,* 35 Wis.2d 209, 151 N.W.2d 30, 65 LRRM 2793 (1967).

[14]*Board of Education* v. *Associated Teachers of Huntington, Inc.,* 30 N.Y.2d 122, 282 N.E.2d 109, 79 LRRM 2881 (1972).

[15]*Id.,* at 2885.

mate knowledge of school board matters, are fully qualified to decide issues such as those under consideration."[16]

Many of the modern statutes explicitly authorize, and in at least two cases actually mandate, provisions for binding grievance arbitration.[17] Thus, except in Delaware where the statute forbids third-party decisions in the case of school districts,[18] or in states where collective bargaining agreements are not yet permitted,[19] there appears to be no question as to the general validity of agreements to arbitrate public-sector labor grievances.

There are, however, a number of cases, particularly recent ones, in which courts have refused to enforce arbitration agreements, or have set aside arbitration awards, on the stated ground that some law or public policy external to the agreement precludes the public agency from "bargaining away" or "delegating" its authority or discretion with respect to the particular issue in dispute. In states where agreement is limited to mandatory subjects of bargaining, the limitation may be found in the statutory definition of bargaining scope;[20] in states where agreement is not so restricted, the limitation must be located elsewhere.[21] While the New York Court of Appeals, for example, spoke expansively in *Huntington* of the parties' freedom to contract over terms and conditions of employment "except in cases where some other applicable statutory provision explicitly and definitively prohibits the public employer from making an agreement," and in a subsequent decision declared that "arbitration is considered so preferable

[16]*Id.*, at 2886.

[17]See Aaron, *The Impact of Public Employment Grievance Settlement on the Labor Arbitration Process,* in The Future of Labor Arbitration in America (New York: American Arbitration Association, 1976), 11–12. Professor Aaron reports that as of September 1975 some 28 states and the District of Columbia had included some form of grievance procedure in their statutes.

[18]Del. Code Sec. 4008(c).

[19]This was the situation, for example, with respect to bargaining between school districts and teachers in California prior to 1975. *Hayes* v. *Association of Classroom Teachers, supra* note 12.

[20]*Dunellen Board of Education* v. *Dunellen Education Association,* 74 N.J. 17, 311 A.2d 737, 85 LRRM 2131 (1973) (school board could not be required to arbitrate dispute over consolidation of chairmanships of two departments, that being a matter of "educational policy" and therefore excluded from the scope of bargaining); *Gorder* v. *Matanuska-Susitna School District,* 84 LRRM 2683 (Alaska Sup. Ct. 1973) (discharge of probationary teacher not a matter involving continuous employment).

[21]See Clark, *The Scope of the Duty to Bargain in Public Employment,* in National Institute on Labor Relations, Law in the Public Sector, ed. Knapp, 81, 85.

a means of settling labor disputes that it can be said that public policy impels its use,"[22] the same court two years later suggested that because of the "governmental interests and public concerns" which may be involved in school matters, "public policy, whether derived from, and whether explicit or implicit in statute or decisional law, or in neither, may also restrict the freedom to arbitrate."[23] That suggestion found its way into holdings in subsequent decisions to the effect that while a school board may commit itself to arbitrate over the application to probationary teachers of agreed-upon tenure-evaluation procedures, it may not arbitrate over the tenure decision itself,[24] or (more recently) over whether school-board members were precluded by agreement from inspecting the files of individual teachers,[25] in both cases on the ground that such a commitment would be contrary to policy, which the court found to be implied in applicable statutes, that the board's discretion over such matters not be subject to such limitations. The Supreme Judicial Court of Massachusetts has followed New York's lead in holding that a school committee "may not delegate to an arbitrator its authority to make decisions concerning tenure,"[26] but the pattern of decisions is by no means consistent or symmetrical. Courts in Pennsylvania,[27] Michigan,[28] Maine,[29] Vermont,[30] and

---

[22]*Associated Teachers of Huntington* v. *Board of Education,* 33 N.Y.2d 229, 306 N.E.2d 791, 85 LRRM 2795 (1973), known as the "second Huntington case."

[23]*Susquehanna Valley Central School District* v. *Susquehanna Valley Teachers Association,* 37 N.Y.2d 614, 90 LRRM 614 (1975). The suggestion was dicta, the court holding that the school district was obligated to arbitrate a grievance concerning staff reduction.

[24]*Cohoes City School District* v. *Cohoes Teachers Association,* 40 N.Y.2d 774, 358 N.E.2d 878, 94 LRRM 2192 (1976).

[25]*Great Neck Free School District* v. *Areman,* 41 N.Y.2d 527, 362 N.E.2d 843, 95 LRRM 2165 (1977). Cf., *Board of Education* v. *Yonkers Federation of Teachers,* 40 N.Y.2d 268, 386 N.Y.S.2d 657, 92 LRRM 3328 (N.Y. Ct. App. 1976) (upholding arbitration of layoffs under contractual "job security" clause, but suggesting decision might be otherwise if clause were not of "relatively brief" duration, or had been negotiated in a time of financial emergency or between parties of unequal bargaining power, or if clause did not explicitly protect teachers from layoff due to budgetary conditions).

[26]*School Committee of Danvers* v. *Tyman,* 360 N.E.2d 977, 94 LRRM 977 (1977). New Jersey's Supreme Court takes a similar view. *Newark Teachers Union* v. *Board of Education,* 95 LRRM 2525 (1977).

[27]*Board of Education* v. *Philadelphia Federation of Teachers,* 346 A.2d 35, 90 LRRM 2879 (1975).

[28]*Kaleva-Norman-Dickson School District No. 6* v. *Kaleva-Norman-Dickson School Teachers Association,* 393 Mich. 593, 227 N.W.2d 500, 89 LRRM 2078 (1975) (upholding propriety of arbitrating nonrenewal of probationary teacher's contract, but without considering delegation issue). Cf., *Brown* v. *Holton Public Schools,* 258 N.W.2d 51, 96 LRRM 2884 (1977) (holding school board's decision not to renew probationary teacher's contract was not arbitrable under the agreement).

[29]Cf., *Board of Directors* v. *Merrymeeting Educators' Assn.,* 354 A.2d 169, 92 LRRM 2268 (Me. Sup. Ct. 1976) (issue of validity not raised).

[30]*Danville Board of School Directors* v. *Fibield,* 315 A.2d 473, 85 LRRM 2939 (Vt. Sup. Ct. 1974).

Wisconsin,[31] for example, appear to accept arbitration over tenure decisions, whereas the Illinois Supreme Court holds that even the application of contractual evaluation procedures is an impermissible subject for arbitration.[32] The Massachusetts high court has sustained the use of arbitration in a dispute over whether a school committee properly denied applications of school principals for transfer from one school to another, characterizing the issue as going to the "manner" of filling vacancies and therefore as not intruding upon the authority of the committee to exercise its discretion in individual cases,[33] whereas the Minnesota Supreme Court has declared that while a school district need not bargain over its "policy" of transferring teachers, the application of that policy to individual transfers is properly an arbitrable matter.[34]

The argument based on nondelegable discretion or authority has rarely been successful outside the field of education, but there are exceptions. The Supreme Court of Michigan, though apparently approving arbitration of disputes involving the nonrenewal of a probationary teacher's contract[35] and discharge of a police officer,[36] balked at arbitration over the dismissal of probation officers serving under the supervision of judges of the Recorders' court.[37] In a 4–3 opinion, a majority of the court, stressing the "sensitive" nature of the probation officer's function, argued that arbitration "could result in reinstatement of a probation officer in which the court could no longer place trust or confidence." One member of the majority, in a separate concurring opinion, even suggested that a statute which provided

[31]*Joint School District No. 10* v. *Jefferson Educ. Assn.*, 253 N.W.2d 536, 95 LRRM 3117 (Wis. Sup. Ct. 1977).

[32]*Board of Trustees of Junior College District No. 508* v. *Cook County College Teachers Union*, 343 N.E.2d 473, 92 LRRM 2380 (1976).

[33]*Bradley* v. *School Committee of Boston*, 364 N.E.2d 1229, 96 LRRM 2542 (1977). The Massachusetts high court has also sustained the use of arbitration in a dispute over a school committee's failure to hire sufficient substitutes to maintain agreed-upon limits on class size and teaching loads, where the committee acted not out of educational policy but because of financial strictures imposed by the mayor. *Boston Teachers Union* v. *School Committee of Boston*, 350 N.E.2d 707, 93 LRRM 2205 (1976). That court has held it beyond the authority of a school committee to agree to arbitrate over a decision to abolish a supervisory position, *Hanover School Committee* v. *Curry*, 343 A.2d 144, 92 LRRM 2338 (1976), though an arbitrator's award with respect to such a dispute was sustained insofar as it ordered compensation to the supervisor whose position was abolished, *Braintree School Committee* v. *Raymond*, 343 A.2d 145, 92 LRRM 2339 (1976).

[34]*Minneapolis Federation of Teachers* v. *Minneapolis Special School District*, 95 LRRM 2359 (1977).

[35]*Kaleva-Norman-Dickson School District No. 6* v. *Kaleva-Norman-Dickson School Teachers Assn.*, *supra* note 28.

[36]*Pontiac Police Officers Assn.* v. *City of Pontiac*, 246 N.W.2d 831, 94 LRRM 2175 (Mich. Sup. Ct. 1976).

[37]*AFSCME* v. *Recorders Court Judges*, 248 N.W.2d 220, 94 LRRM 2392 (1976).

for arbitration of such disputes, in the absence of "standards" for decision, would pose a serious constitutional issue involving delegation of governmental authority. And in California, a court of appeals has held that the City of Berkeley could not agree to arbitrate the dismissal of a city employee because its charter (which the court believed to be unaffected by the state public-employee bargaining law) vests the city manager with power to appoint, discipline, and remove all city employees, and in the court's opinion that power could not be "delegated" to an arbitrator.[38] While the case involved a police officer, the logic of the opinion would extend to any city employee, and to any city with a similar charter provision.

The high court in Massachusetts has suggested that the divergence of judicial opinion reflects "varying traditions and statutory provisions among the states."[39] There is clearly merit to that suggestion, but it is difficult to account for the results in terms of those factors alone. The tradition in all states prior to collective bargaining was that public bodies exercised virtually unfettered discretion with respect to nearly everything; the question is the extent to which that tradition should be deemed to survive a system of bilateralism imposed by law. And while the answer to that question is theoretically to be found in applicable statutes, the language of most of the statutes is singularly opaque. A statute that vests a school board with power to appoint for tenure "any or all of the persons recommended" by the superintendent of schools,[40] for example, does not necessarily imply that the power may not be limited through collective bargaining, or that the limitations may not be enforced through arbitration. If those results are found to be reflected in the statute, it is because in this, as in many areas of the law, the statute ultimately mirrors the policy predilections of the courts.

What those policy predilections are is not always easy to determine from the opinions. Analytically, the cases may be said to involve the validity of substantive contractual limitations

[38] *Taylor* v. *Crane* (1977), hearing granted.
[39] *School Committee of Danvers* v. *Tyman, supra* note 26, at 3184. The court's reference was to the varying opinions in the tenure cases.
[40] New York Education Law, Sec. 2509. This was the statute the New York Court of Appeals held to preempt arbitration in *Cohoes, supra* note 24. Compare *Board of Police Commissioners* v. *White,* 93 LRRM 2637 (Conn. Sup. Ct. 1976) (charter provision granting board of police commissioners power to remove police officers for cause held not to conflict with contractual provisions for arbitration).

upon the authority of the governing body rather than the validity of arbitration per se. From this point of view, if a public entity agrees to a particular limitation upon its authority, it should make no difference whether the limitation is to be enforced through arbitration or through the courts. It is difficult to resist the conclusion, however, that judicial perception of the nature of arbitration plays a role in the decisions. The word "delegation," for example, is not one that would be used in describing a system of norms to be judicially enforced, and the cases cited by the New York Court of Appeals as precedents for the proposition that some agreements to arbitrate ought not to be enforced are custody cases in which it was held that public policy required determination of the dispute by a judge.[41] What the judicial perception of the arbitral function is, and how it relates to the decisions rejecting arbitration of particular disputes, are matters best approached after completion of the survey.

Judicial Determination of Arbitrability

Assuming that the dispute is one which the parties may lawfully agree to arbitrate, a question may arise as to whether they have in fact done so. When this question arises in advance of arbitration in the private sector, courts are bound by the twin trilogy principles precluding consideration of the merits and requiring the presumption of an affirmative answer.

Until quite recently, most state courts which have had occasion to pass on arbitrability issues have looked to trilogy principles for guidance, and most have applied those principles consistent with their underlying policy.[42] Some courts, however, have intruded rather deeply into the merits in determining particular disputes to be nonarbitrable. The Connecticut Supreme Court, for example, held that although an agreement made reference to existing retirement plans, a dispute concerning those plans was not arbitrable under the agreement because the court considered it "impossible to say that the substantive provisions

---

[41] *Susquehanna Valley Central School District* v. *Susquehanna Valley Teachers Assn.*, *supra* note 23.

[42] E.g., *Kaleva-Norman-Dickson School District* v. *Teachers Assn.*, *supra* note 28; *City School District* v. *Poughkeepsie Public School Teachers*, 89 LRRM 2422 (N.Y. App. 1974). For discussion of the New York cases, see DeWolf, *The Enforcement of the Labor Agreement in the Public Sector: The New York Experience* 39 Albany L. Rev. 393 (1975).

of the pension plan were made part of the agreement."[43] And an appellate court in Oregon held that teachers were not entitled to arbitrate a dispute over provisions of state administrative rules specifying class size, despite contract language which arguably incorporated those rules, on the ground that the "only rational interpretation" of the contract limited its scope to policies of the school district itself.[44]

Some courts have gone so far as to reverse the usual presumption of arbitrability. The highest court in Maine in effect took that position in a case involving arbitration over nonrenewal of probationary teacher contracts,[45] but decisions such as that are perhaps explainable in terms of judicial doubts concerning the validity of an agreement to arbitrate the particular dispute. More far-reaching is the New York Court of Appeals' recent decision in *Acting Superintendent of Schools* v. *United Liverpool Faculty Association.*[46] In that case, a union sought to compel arbitration of a grievance alleging that the school board violated the collective bargaining agreement by refusing to allow a female teacher to return to work after sick leave unless she submitted to a complete medical examination by the school district's male physician, instead of permitting her to be examined by a female physician as she requested. The arbitration clause covered only "claimed violation, misinterpretation, or inequitable application of existing laws, rules, procedure, regulations, administrative orders or work rules of the District which relate to or involve Teachers' health or safety, physical facilities, materials or equipment furnished to teachers, or supervision of teachers," and the union argued that the dispute involved a claimed violation or inequitable application of existing laws and rules relating to the teacher's health. The agreement excluded from arbitration, however, "any matter involving a Teacher's rate of compensation, retirement benefits, disciplinary proceeding," and the district claimed that the dispute fell into the excluded category.

---

[43]*Policemen's and Firemen's Retirement Board, et al., City of New Haven* v. *Sullivan*, 376 A.2d 399, 95 LRRM 2351 (Conn. Sup. Ct. 1977).

[44]*Portland Association of Teachers* v. *School District No. 1*, 555 P.2d 943, 93 LRRM 2879 (Ore. App. 1976).

[45]*Chassie* v. *Directors*, 356 A.2d 708, 92 LRRM 3359 (1976) (if the parties had intended to arbitrate such an issue, "certainly plainer language should have been employed"). Cf., *Brown* v. *Holton Public Schools, supra* note 28 (court, applying trilogy language, concluded with "positive assurance" that contract language protecting teachers against unjust discharge was "not susceptible of an application" to the nonrenewal of a probationary teacher's contract).

[46]42 N.Y.2d 509, 399 N.Y.S.2d 189, 96 LRRM 2779 (1977).

There was no doubt that the district could lawfully have agreed to arbitrate the dispute, and the court so held. There was also no doubt that under trilogy principles the dispute would be held arbitrable, and the court impliedly conceded as much. The school board advanced an argument that the teacher waived her right to seek arbitration by filing an appeal under the state Education Law with the commissioner of education, and three judges of the court would have decided against arbitrability on that ground alone. A majority of the court, however, chose the occasion to announce new guiding principles for the determination of arbitrability in the public sector. Referring to the differences in perspective and approach that had evolved between commercial and labor arbitration, the former requiring (in New York) an "express, unequivocal agreement" to arbitrate the particular dispute, and the latter calling for application of trilogy principles, the court reasoned that arbitration agreements pursuant to the Taylor Law cannot properly be characterized under either category:

> In the field of public employment, as distinguished from labor relations in the private sector, the public policy favoring arbitration—of recent origin—does not yet carry the same historical or general acceptance, nor, as evidenced in part by some of the litigation in our Court, has there so far been a similar demonstration of the efficacy of arbitration as a means for resolving controversies in governmental employment. Accordingly, it cannot be inferred as a practical matter that the parties to collective bargaining agreements in the public sector always intend to adopt the broadest permissible arbitration clauses. Indeed, inasmuch as the responsibilities of the elected representatives of the tax-paying public are overarching and fundamentally nondelegable, it must be taken, in the absence of clear, unequivocal agreement to the contrary, that the board of education did *not* intend to refer differences which might arise to the arbitration forum. Such reference is not to be based on implication.

The guiding principle that emerged from the court's analysis was, in fact, the principle applicable to commercial arbitration: "the agreement to arbitrate must be express, direct and unequivocal as to the issues or disputes to be submitted to arbitration; anything less will lead to a denial of arbitration." The court concluded that a "very reasonable assertion can be made that this particular controversy falls within both the included and the excluded categories" and on that basis, and in light of the principle announced, concluded that arbitration should be stayed.

Judicial Review of the Award

The trilogy principle of arbitral finality so long as the award draws its "essence" from the contract has been explicitly adopted by some state courts,[47] and statutory provisions in a number of states narrowly constrain the scope of judicial review.[48] The language which the courts use when asked to review arbitral awards is thus generally in accord with federal principles, but the application of that language is in some cases highly dubious, reflecting a significantly greater tendency to substitute the court's judgment for that of the arbitrator.

In some cases courts have set awards aside on the ground that the contract, or at least the contract as interpreted by the arbitrator, intrudes impermissibly upon an area of authority or discretion committed to the public agency by law or public policy. This category of cases has previously been discussed. In others, courts have set awards aside on the ground that the contract as interpreted is in substantive conflict with the result dictated by an applicable law external to the agreement—as, for example, where the award enforces a contractual provision for parity pay found to conflict with the state public-employee bargaining law;[49] or orders reinstatement of an employee discharged for failing to reside within the city, contrary to the provisions of a city ordinance found to be controlling;[50] or directs payment of full pay to teachers during sabbatical leave in the face of a statute construed by the court as limiting sabbatical pay to one half.[51] These cases involve the extent to which a collective bargaining

---

[47]E.g., *Board of Directors* v. *Merrymeeting Educators' Assn., supra* note 29; *Darien Education Assn.* v. *Board of Education*, 374 A.2d 1081, 94 LRRM 2895 (Conn. Sup. Ct. 1977). Cf., *Beaver County Community College* v. *Faculty*, 96 LRRM 2375 (Pa. Sup. Ct. 1977) (applying statutory standard permitting review for awards "against the law," to require determination as to whether arbitrator's position could be "rationally derived from the agreement").

[48]E.g., Wis. Stat. Ann. (Supp. 1973), Sec. 111.86.

[49]*Fire Fighters Local 1219* v. *Connecticut Labor Relations Board*, 370 A.2d 952 (Conn. Sup. Ct. 1977).

[50]*Wisconsin Employment Relations Commission* v. *Teamsters Local No. 563*, 250 N.W.2d 696, 94 LRRM 2849 (Wis. Sup. Ct. 1977).

[51]*Allegheny Valley School District* v. *Allegheny Education Assn.*, 360 A.2d 762, 92 LRRM 3536 (Pa. Comm. Ct. 1976). See also *Conley* v. *Joyce*, 366 A.2d 1292 (Pa. Comm. Ct. 1976) (award regarding overtime pay modified to conform to statute); *Niagara Wheatfield Administrators Assn.* v. *Niagara Wheatfield Central School District*, 389 N.Y.S.2d 667, 94 LRRM 2682 (N.Y. App. Div. 1976) (award requiring continuance of fringe benefits after expiration of agreement modified to require continuance for reasonable time only, on grounds contract as arbitrator construed it was contrary to public policy). Cf., *Boston Teachers Union* v. *School Committee, supra* note 23 (invalidating award which required payment of money to union scholarship fund as remedy for contract violation).

agreement is permitted to supersede the provisions of an otherwise applicable statute or ordinance, and while one may quarrel
with the answer that the court gives in a particular case, the
proposition that the award should be set aside if the law be given
superseding effect is unobjectionable. Far more debatable are
the cases in which courts have set aside awards on grounds that
the arbitrator has in some respect exceeded his authority under
the agreement itself. While varying contract language and factual situations make generalizations difficult, several illustrative
patterns emerge.

First, the courts appear less inclined to defer to an arbitration
award where there exists a statute covering the subject matter,
even if the statute is not deemed preemptive. In one case, for
example, an arbitrator ruled that a school district, in determining the placement of teachers on salary schedules, was obligated
by contract to give newly hired teachers credit for teaching
experience outside the district. A state statute provided credit
only for teaching experience in the district. The court held that
while it was permissible for the parties to agree upon benefits
in excess of those provided by statute, an agreement to do so
must be expressed in a "clear and unmistakable manner," and
since it found no such expression in the agreement, it set aside
the award.[52] Such decisions reflect, perhaps, the unwillingness
of courts to accept the full implications of collective bargaining
and arbitration in an area still permeated by legislation.

Second, courts in the public sector appear less tolerant than
those in the private sector of awards that rely on past practice
to establish obligations not expressed in the agreement. In *Milwaukee Professional Fire Fighters* v. *City of Milwaukee*,[53] for example,
an arbitrator relied upon past practice to find that the city's
change in policies with respect to the scheduling of vacation
days, days off, and special-duty overtime work for fire fighters
was in violation of the agreement, and ordered that past practice
be resumed. The Wisconsin Supreme Court held that the arbitrator's reliance on past practice "did not draw its essence from
the agreement" because it was based upon his understanding of
the "wishes of the parties" rather than upon the agreement

[52]*Leechburg Area School District* v. *Leechburg Educational Assn.*, 355 A.2d 608, 92 LRRM
2368 (Pa. Comm. Ct. 1976). See also *Board of Education* v. *Champaign Education Association*,
304 N.E.2d 138 (1973).
[53]253 N.W.2d 481, 95 LRRM 2684 (Wis Sup. Ct. 1977). See also *County of Allegheny*
v. *Allegheny County Prison Employees*, 96 LRRM 3396 (Pa. Sup. Ct.1977).

itself. Where the arbitrator relied upon past practice to impose obligations at variance with the express terms of the agreement, judicial reaction is even more likely to be negative. In *Civil Service Employees Association* v. *City of Steuben,*[54] an arbitrator ruled that the county was precluded by past practice of many years from attempting to enforce a contract clause requiring that social workers obtain prior approval in writing in order to secure travel reimbursement from their homes to the homes of clients. The Appellate Division of the New York Supreme Court refused to enforce the award, stating that the arbitrator had "deliberately and intentionally" considered matters outside the agreement, and thereby "in effect wrote a new contract for the parties." While there are private-sector cases to similar effect, the prevailing view is to the contrary, and cases such as these may reflect a judicial assumption that in the public sector it is to be expected that limitations on managerial authority will be express rather than implied.

Finally, even where the arbitrator's award is based upon express contract language, courts in some cases have displayed a greater propensity than in the private sector to overturn the arbitrator's interpretation. In *Simpson* v. *North Collins Central School District,*[55] for example, an arbitrator interpreted a contractual provision requiring "just cause" for dismissal to require fair evaluation procedures for probationary teachers under consideration for tenure. Although the New York Court of Appeals had upheld the validity of arbitration over the application of evaluation procedures, as distinguished from arbitration over the substantive tenure decision, the Appellate Division of the New York Supreme Court found the arbitrator's interpretation of the agreement to be "irrational," and the imposition of what the court characterized as "ex post facto procedural standards" to be "tantamount to the making of a new contract for the parties."

---

[54]377 N.Y.S.2d 849, 91 LRRM 2916 (N.Y. App. Div. 1976). See *Lansing Fire Fighters Assn.* v. *City of Lansing,* 97 LRRM 2857 (Mich. Cir. Ct. 1976) (arbitrator ruled city obligated by past practice to pay employees who retire during contract year a full food allowance, despite contract clause providing for pro rata amounts to employees who serve less than 12 months regular full-time duty. Held: Arbitrator exceeded his authority).

[55]392 N.Y.S.2d 106, 95 LRRM 2083 (N.Y. App. Div. 1977). See also *Fairchild* v. *West Rutland School District,* 376 A.2d 28, 95 LRRM 3006 (Vt. Sup. Ct. 1977) (arbitrator exceeded his authority by applying dismissal provisions of agreement to failure of school board to renew probationary teacher's contract). *Contra: Joint School Dist. No. 10* v. *Jefferson Education Assn., supra* note 31.

Multiple Rights, Multiple Forums

In any system of grievance arbitration, private or public, questions arise as to the relationship between arbitration and other procedures for enforcement of rights created by the agreement or by external legal norms. Space does not permit a full exploration of this topic here,[56] but attempt will be made to give some indication of the various contexts in which such questions arise in the public sector and of the nature of judicial response.

With respect to rights created by the agreement itself, it is well established in the private sector that the arbitral procedures are exclusive as regards disputes that the parties have agreed to arbitrate, and resort to the courts is generally not permitted. This is true not only for the employer and the union, but for the employee as well, unless the union is shown to have violated its duty of fair representation. There would appear to be no reason for not applying these principles to the public sector as well, and in general the courts appear to have accepted them.[57]

With respect to rights based on norms external to the agreement, the problem is more complex. Questions concerning the relationship of arbitration to rights and remedies created by such legislation as Title VII of the Civil Rights Act of 1964 and the National Labor Relations Act have been the subject of frequent litigation in the private sector with varying results.[58] In the public sector, the problem of relationship is accentuated by the multiplicity of statutory provisions which antedated collective bargaining and which provide employees with certain rights and remedies (e.g., protection against arbitrary discipline) that more closely parallel the typical content of collective bargaining agreements. May an employee pursue such rights and remedies independently, or is he limited to the procedures which his union has agreed to? In some states the answer is contained in the collective

---

[56]For more extensive treatment, see Aaron, *supra* note 17; Note, *Public Sector Grievance Procedures, Due Process and the Duty of Fair Representation*, 89 Harvard L. Rev. 752 (1976).

[57]See Note, *supra* note 56, at 782. The editors argue that due process may require a higher standard for the union's duty of fair representation. But see *Dade County Classroom Teachers Assn. v. Ryan*, 225 So.2d 903, 71 LRRM 2958 (Fla. Sup. Ct. 1969) (nonconsenting teachers need not submit to union-controlled grievance procedure). See generally, Note, *The Privilege of Exclusive Recognition and Minority Union Rights in Public Employment*, 55 Cornell L. Rev. 1004 (1970).

[58]*Supra* note 56.

bargaining statute itself,[59] but in the absence of statutory guidance, courts have generally opted for a policy of coexistence: employees may elect to pursue statutory remedies despite the availability of contractual remedies,[60] and may even be permitted to pursue relief in one forum after losing in another.[61]

Such a coexistence policy may reflect judicial concern with the constitutional dimension of arbitration in public employment. Public employees enjoy some degree of constitutional protection for freedom of expression, privilege against self-incrimination, privacy, and where "property rights" are deemed to exist, procedural due process. Thus, questions may arise as to whether employee constitutional rights are adequately safeguarded by a system which (a) restricts the employee to the arbitral forum, (b) makes his utilization of that forum dependent upon his union's willingness to take the case to arbitration, and (c) precludes judicial review of the arbitral award except on very narrow grounds.[62] Litigation involving such questions to date has been minimal, the principal case being *Antinore* v. *State*[63] in which the Appellate Division of the New York Supreme Court upheld the constitutionality of New York's Civil Service Law permitting the substitution through collective bargaining agreement of arbitral for statutory remedies in discharge and discipline cases on the ground that the union, as the employee's representative, could waive on his behalf whatever substantive and procedural constitutional rights he might have. The court's reasoning on that score is debatable,[64] and probably not the last word on the subject. In the early *Huntington* case, the New York Court of Appeals suggested in a footnote that where rights external to the agreement were involved, judicial review might

---

[59]E.g., Me. Rev. Stat. Ann. tit. 26 § 979 ( ) (1964) (". . . any such grievance procedure shall be exclusive and shall supersede any otherwise applicable grievance procedure provided by law"); N.Y. Civil Service Law, § 74(4) (1973) (civil service remedies subject to terms of agreement).

[60]E.g., *Board of Education* v. *Associated Teachers of Huntington, supra* note 14.

[61]E.g., *City School District* v. *Poughkeepsie Public School Teachers, supra* note 42 (school district obligated to activate at union's request over denial of teacher's transfer request, though teacher had maintained appeal to commissioner of education and lost). Cf. *Alexander* v. *Gardner-Denver*, 415 U.S. 36, 7 FEP Cases 81 (1974), holding arbitration award no bar to pursuit of remedies under Civil Rights Act.

[62]For argument in favor of an affirmative answer, conditioned upon the imposition of higher standards upon unions in the screening of grievances, see Note, *supra* note 56.

[63]371 N.Y.S.2d 213 (App. Div. 1975), aff'd w/o op., 40 N.Y.2d 921, 389 N.Y.S.2d 576, 94 LRRM 2224 (1976).

[64]See Aaron, *Procedural Due Process and the Duty of Fair Representation in Public Sector Grievances*, in National Institute on Labor Relations, Law in the Public Sector, ed. Knapp, 179, 184.

extend to determining whether the arbitration proceeding was fair and regular.[65] Such a standard, whether or not it goes far enough to meet constitutional requirements, clearly goes further than the normal scope of judicial review. Benjamin Aaron's prediction that judicial review of grievance-arbitration decisions in the public sector is likely to be "broader in scope than that prevailing in the private sector, especially in cases involving discipline or discharge"[66] seems clearly on target.

Interest Arbitration

Interest arbitration, involving the binding determination of contract terms, has some private-sector roots, but is mainly a public-sector phenomenon, developed in response to the legal prohibition against strikes by public employees.[67] While a number of statutes authorize interest arbitration by agreement between a public entity and a union, in fact such agreements are rare, and most interest arbitration takes place pursuant to legislative mandate.[68] Thus, while grievance arbitration is primarily consensual and based upon procedure and criteria contained in agreements, interest arbitration is primarily statutory and based upon procedure and criteria specified by law. The differences go deeper than that, however. The grievance arbitrator's business is to pass upon the claims of the respective parties to rights under the agreement, and while his decisions may entail discretion, that discretion is typically channeled within a relatively narrow range of criteria and touches upon only a relatively small portion of the parties' relationships to one another. The interest arbitrator's business is to make a contract for the parties, at least with respect to the issues in dispute, and while the governing statute or agreement may prescribe standards to guide his determination, these are typically designed so as to allow discretion

---

[65] *Board of Education* v. *Associated Teachers of Huntington, supra* note 14. Footnote 8 of one opinion reads, "We assume, of course, that the arbitration procedure is fair and regular and free from any procedural inferences that might invalidate the award." (Cf., e.g., *Spielberg Mfg. Co.*, 112 NLRB 1080, 36 LRRM 1152 [1955].) Under the *Spielberg* doctrine, the NLRB will review arbitration awards involving mixed questions of contractual violations to determine not only procedural regularity, but also compatibility with statutory policies. As recently applied, the doctrine requires that the arbitrators have considered the statutory issue.

[66] Aaron, *supra* note 17, at 46–47.

[67] See Morris, *The Role of Interest Arbitration in a Collective Bargaining System*, in The Future of Labor Arbitration in America (New York: American Arbitration Association, 1976), 197.

[68] *Id.*, at 230.

to be exercised over a broad range. At the risk of some oversimplification, the difference is between norm application and norm creation.

Validity of Interest Arbitration

Statutes mandating interest arbitration for public employees have been challenged on a variety of state constitutional grounds, most of them involving either the relationship of state to local authority, the relationship of arbitration to the legislative process, or a combination of the two. The first category of challenge—that the statute intrudes impermissibly upon the autonomy of a "home rule" city or county—has been uniformly rejected by the courts and need not concern us here.[69] The second category, involving the relationship of arbitration to the legislative process, may take a variety of forms: that the statute constitutes an unlawful delegation of legislative power to private parties, that the statute contains insufficient standards or safeguards to guide or check arbitral discretion, that it represents an unconstitutional delegation of the taxing power, or that the method by which arbitrators are chosen violates the "one man, one vote" principle.[70] The third category of challenge stems from the provisions, known as "ripper clauses," found in 18 state constitutions and prohibiting the legislature from delegating to a "special or private body" any power to interfere with "municipal moneys or to perform municipal functions."[71]

Prior to 1975, Pennsylvania was the only state in which interest arbitration was held constitutionally impermissible, and that was on the basis of a ripper clause that has subsequently been amended to permit arbitration.[72] After that amendment, the state interest-arbitration statute was sustained.[73] The Supreme Court of Wyoming upheld that state's interest-arbitration statute despite a ripper clause in the state's constitution,[74] and the courts of Rhode Island,[75] Maine,[76] and Nebraska[77] (which have

---

[69]Note, *Binding Interest Arbitration in the Public Sector: Is It Constitutional?* 18 Wm. & Mary L. Rev. 787, 814 (1977).

[70]*Id.*, at 818.

[71]*Id.*, at 797.

[72]*Erie Fire Fighters Local 293* v. *Gardner,* 406 Pa. 395, 178 A.2d 691 (1962).

[73]*Harney* v. *Russo,* 435 Pa. 183, 255 A.2d 560, 71 LRRM 2817 (1969).

[74]*State ex rel. Fire Fighters Local 946* v. *City of Laramie,* 437 P.2d 295, 68 LRRM 2038 (1968).

[75]*City of Warwick* v. *Warwick Regular Firemen's Assn.,* 106 R.I. 109, 256 A.2d 206, 71 LRRM 3192 (1969).

[76]*City of Biddeford* v. *Biddeford Teachers Assn.,* 204 A.2d 387, 83 LRRM 2098 (Me. 1973).

[77]*School Dist. of Seward Education Assn.* v. *School Dist. of Seward,* 188 Neb. 772, 199

no ripper clauses) rejected constitutional challenges based on other grounds. The Supreme Court of Maine was equally divided on the question of unlawful delegation, but since the lower court had sustained the statute, the effect of the division was to affirm. Thus, by the end of 1974 the score stood 5–0 in favor of constitutionality. Since that time, interest arbitration's constitutional batting average has dropped somewhat. The highest courts in New York,[78] Massachusetts,[79] Washington,[80] and Michigan[81] have sustained the constitutionality of interest arbitration in those states, but the latter was by an equally divided court; and courts in South Dakota,[82] Colorado,[83] Utah,[84] and Maryland[85] have reached the opposite conclusion. While each of the latter state constitutions contains ripper clauses, the decisions in Colorado and Utah went beyond those clauses to rely generally on unconstitutional delegation doctrine. In California, the supreme court in a footnote in one case rather summarily dispensed with a constitutional attack raised by an amicus curiae to the constitutionality of a city-charter provision calling for binding interest arbitration,[86] but the vitality of that footnote is dampened somewhat by the reasoning of the same court in an opinion which holds that an arrangement by a general-law city for interest arbitration would constitute an impermissible delegation of wage-fixing authority under a state statute providing that "by resolution or ordinance the city council shall fix the compensation of all appointive officers."[87]

The delegation issue is the most formidable of the constitu-

N.W.2d 752 (1972).
   [78] City of Amsterdam v. Helsby, 37 N.Y.2d 19, 332 N.E.2d 290, 89 LRRM 2871 (1975); City of Buffalo v. New York State Employment Relations Board, 37 N.Y.2d 19, 332 N.E.2d 290, 89 LRRM 2871 (1975).
   [79] Town of Arlington v. Board of Conciliation and Arbitration, 352 N.E.2d 914 93 LRRM 2494 (1976).
   [80] City of Spokane v. Spokane Police Guild, 87 Wash.2d 457, 553 P.2d 1316, 93 LRRM 2373 (1976).
   [81] Dearborn Fire Fighters Local 412 v. City of Dearborn, 394 Mich. 229, 231 N.W.2d 226, 90 LRRM 2002 (1975).
   [82] City of Sioux Falls v. Sioux Falls Fire Fighters Local 814, 234 N.W.2d 535 (S. Dak. Sup. Ct. 1975).
   [83] Greeley Police Union v. City Council, 93 LRRM 2382 (1976); City of Aurora v. Aurora Fire Fighters Prot. Assn., 566 P.2d 1356, 96 LRRM 2252 (Colo. Sup. Ct. 1977).
   [84] Salt Lake City v. Int. Assn. of Fire Fighters, 563 P.2d 786, 95 LRRM 2383 (Utah Sup. Ct. 1977).
   [85] Maryland Classified Emp. Assn. v. Anderson, 93 LRRM 2997 (Md. Cir. Ct. 1976).
   [86] Fire Fighters Local 1186 v. City of Vallejo, 12 Cal. 3d 608, 526 P.2d 971, 87 LRRM 2453 (1974).
   [87] Bagley v. City of Manhattan Beach, 18 Cal.3d 22, 553 P.2d 1140, 93 LRRM 2435 (1976).

tional issues, and its various ramifications are best reflected in the diverse opinions that comprise the Michigan Supreme Court's decision in *Dearborn Fire Fighters Union* v. *City of Dearborn.* [88] The Michigan statute mandates interest arbitration for police and fire department labor disputes; like most interest-arbitration statutes, it provides for a tripartite arbitration panel comprised of one delegate named by each of the parties and a neutral member to be selected by those two. In the event they fail to agree upon selection, then the neutral is appointed by the chairman of the Michigan Employment Relations Commission (MERC). The City of Dearborn, at impasse in negotiations with both police and fire department employees, declined to designate a delegate to the arbitration panels, and so the MERC chairman appointed the neutral for each panel, and the two-person panels proceeded to consider and issue awards. The city refused to comply with the awards, and litigation ensued.

The four justices sitting on the case each wrote a separate opinion. Justice Levin, joined by Chief Justice Kavanagh, summarized their argument for the unconstitutionality of the statute as follows:

> The arbitrator/chairman of the panel is entrusted with the authority to decide major questions of public policy concerning the conditions of public employment, the levels and standards of public services and the allocation of public revenues. Those questions are legislative and political, not judicial or quasi-judicial. The act is structured to insulate the arbitrator/chairman's decision from review in the political process. It is not intended that he be, nor is he in fact, accountable within the political process for his decision. This is not consonant with the constitutional exercise of political power in a representative democracy.

Although the statute contained both standards to guide the exercise of the delegated power and procedural safeguards such as provisions for hearing, statement of findings and conclusions, and judicial review—characteristics generally considered adequate to validate the delegation of legislative authority—Justices Levin and Kavanagh considered the statute defective because it allocated such authority to private persons who did not have continuing responsibility for its exercise, ad hoc and "expend-

---

[88] *Supra* note 81.

able" arbitrators who were not accountable in any meaningful way. The fact that the neutral arbitrator in the Dearborn case happened to have been appointed by the MERC chairman did not make the arbitrator any more accountable in their view, since the statute called for the MERC chairman to appoint an "impartial" person rather than someone who would seek to render a decision "which will have the support of the electorate or of their elected representatives." The availability of judicial review of the award, while possibly assuring against the arbitrary exercise of discretionary power, could not in their opinion fulfill the constitutional need for "review and accountability through the political process":

> It is the unique method of appointment, requiring independent decision makers without accountability to a governmental appointing authority, and the unique dispersal of decision-making power among numerous *ad hoc* decision makers, only temporarily in office, precluding assessment of responsibility for the consequences of their decisions on the level of public resources and the cost of government, which renders invalid this particular delegation of legislative power.

The two remaining judges, whose combined opinions carried the day, agreed upon the conclusion in the particular case, but for quite different reasons. Justice Coleman adopted a pragmatic approach, reasoning that some system of interest arbitration was clearly called for if strikes were to be avoided and that the choice between ad hoc arbitrators and a permanent arbitration board involved a balancing process that should be left to the legislature. Justice Williams, in a lengthier and more analytical opinion, argued that whether a person to whom power is delegated should be characterized as "a private person, or better . . . a non-politically accountable person" should depend, not upon the label the person wears, but upon the "underlying reality"; and this reality, in the justice's opinion, should be viewed from the perspective of four criteria:

> First, how close by appointment is the person or agency to the elective process and political accountability? . . .
> Second, how clearly restricted is the operation of the person or agency by standards written into the law and the possibility of judicial review?
> Third, how much is the person or agency held to public accountability by the length of tenure on and the public exposure of the job?
> Fourth, . . . the importance and breadth of power granted.

Applying these criteria, Justice Williams found:

1. While selection of the arbitration panels is outside the ordinary political processes, appointment of the neutral by the MERC chairman "guarantees high public visibility and accountability."

2. While operators operate independently, the statute's specific and ample standards plus provision for judicial review assure a "high degree of legal accountability."

3. While tenure of arbitrators is brief, arbitrators are motivated both by professional dedication and concern for continuing acceptability; they operate in the focus of "intense public and media scrutiny"; and they are subject to legal standards, all evidencing a "considerable degree of personal accountability."

4. While the job is important, the areas of discretion are "suitably delimited."

Justice Williams concluded that while selection of the arbitrator by the parties would pose serious constitutional doubt, so long as the MERC chairman appointed the arbitrator, the statute was constitutional.

As Justice Levin observed in his opinion, the net result in Michigan may be that the statute is constitutional only to the extent it does not work as contemplated, that is, to the extent that the panel members designated by the parties fail to agree upon the election of a neutral arbitrator so that the MERC chairman is called upon to appoint him.

Determinations of Arbitrability

While in some states the scope of issues subject to arbitration appears to be narrower than the scope of issues over which bargaining is required, in most states the two scopes are congruent so that determining what issues are required to be arbitrated poses essentially the same task as determining the area of mandatory negotiation. Question has arisen, however, concerning the proper role of the court in passing upon disputed issues of arbitrability in advance of arbitration.

In *Fire Fighters Union* v. *City of Vallejo*,[89] the California Supreme Court was confronted with issues of arbitrability under a city charter provision calling for arbitration in disputes over "wages, hours and working conditions," but excluding "the merits, ne-

---

[89]*Supra* note 86.

cessity, or organization of any service or activity provided by law." The union sought to require arbitration of four issues labeled "Reduction of Personnel," "Vacancies and Promotions," "Schedule of Hours," and "Constant Manning Procedures." The scope of the actual disputes underlying certain of these labels, however, was somewhat obscure. With respect to "Constant Manning Procedures," for example, the union's initial proposal sought to add one engine company and to increase the personnel assigned to existing engine companies, but it subsequently modified its position to require only the maintenance of the existing manning schedule for the term of the agreement. The city contended that even the revised proposal fell within the exclusionary clause as a matter relating to "merits, necessity or organization." The court, applying federal precedent, decided that the manning schedule would be subject to arbitral determination insofar as it may be found to relate to questions of employee work load and safety, and that was a factual finding that should appropriately be made by the arbitrator in the first instance. However, the court declared,

> . . . the parties themselves, or the arbitrators, in the ongoing process of arbitration, might suggest alternative solutions for the manpower problem that might remove or transform the issue. Indeed, the union in the instant case has already abandoned one position and assumed another. There are the elements and considerations that argue against preliminary court rulings that would dam up the stream of arbitration by premature limitations upon the process, thwarting its potential destination of the resolution of the issues.

Similar reasoning with respect to the "Reduction of Personnel" and "Vacancies and Promotions" issues, and a finding that the "Schedule of Hours" issue was clearly arbitrable, led the court to order arbitration with respect to all the issues in dispute.

The court's opinion seems to call for deferral to the arbitrator where determination of arbitrability depends upon disputed factual questions or in any event where the identification of the issue is ambiguous and susceptible of change in the dynamic process of negotiation of which interest arbitration is viewed as an integral part. The result is a presumption of arbitrability somewhat analogous to that which exists in most states for grievance arbitration, but with this significant difference: whereas in the case of grievance arbitration the question of arbitrability depends upon the agreement of the parties and normally does not involve any question of public policy, in the case of interest

arbitration the question is one of statutory (or charter) interpretation and involves limitations presumably imposed by the
legislature or the electorate for policy reasons. The court
made clear that after arbitration, judicial review would be available to determine whether the arbitrators had exceeded
their powers.

Judicial Review

A considerable body of law is developing with respect to the
proper scope of judicial review once an interest award has been
rendered.[90] Some statutes purport to preclude review entirely,
or to limit review to the grounds available for setting aside an
award rendered pursuant to consensual agreement, such as par-
tiality, fraud, or acts in excess of the arbitrator's authority.[91]
Interest arbitration arguably requires a broader scope of review,
however, at least to the extent that the applicable statute specifies procedures or criteria for decision, since these presumably
reflect public-policy judgments that are binding upon the arbitrator.

In New York, the court of appeals held in a case involving
interest arbitration for hospitals in the private sector that the
legislature's attempt to limit review to the narrow grounds applicable in ordinary arbitration cases was unconstitutional, and
that due process requires review at least to the extent of determining whether the arbitrator acted in a manner that was "arbitrary or capricious."[92] The New York court has since applied
similar reasoning and the same standard to arbitration for fire
fighters and police under the Taylor Law, which contains no
provision for review.[93] In Pennsylvania, where the interest-arbitration statute provides that the tribunal's determination is to be
final and binding without appeal, the supreme court has held
that due process considerations require review on questions of
jurisdiction, the regularity of procedures, whether the arbitrator

---

[90]See, generally, Note, *Compulsory Arbitration: The Scope of Judicial Review,* 51 St. John's
L. Rev. 604 (1977).
[91]*Id.,* at 619 ff.
[92]*Mt. St. Mary's Hospital* v. *Catherwood,* 26 N.Y.2d 493, 260 N.E.2d 508, 74 LRRM 2897
(1970).
[93]*Caso* v. *Coffey,* 41 N.Y.2d 153, 359 N.E.2d 683, 93 LRRM 2133 (1976) (rejection
review based on "substantial evidence"). See Anderson, MacDonald, & O'Reilly, *Impasse
Resolution in Public Sector Collective Bargaining in New York,* 51 St. John's L. Rev. 453, 468
(1977).

exceeded his powers, and questions of constitutional dimension.[94]

Predictably, courts are reluctant to overturn arbitral judgments as to the propriety of particular wage or benefit adjustments. In New York, for example, the appellate division of the supreme court vacated an award granting salary increases to police in the City of Buffalo on the ground that the city was without means to fund the increase, but the court of appeals reversed this decision. The police association, the court noted, had introduced evidence showing that Buffalo police officers' wages and working conditions compared unfavorably with those of police in other areas and that cost-of-living increases had diminished their real wages. While the city pointed to a variety of fiscal problems, there were differences between the parties as to available revenues, and in any event the arbitration panel took fiscal problems into account, weighing them against the factors of entitlement relied upon by the police. That, the court said, was all the statute required when it called for consideration of ability to pay as well as other criteria:

> On this record, it cannot be said that the panel's award was irrational. It was within its province, under the applicable statute, not only to judge the facts but choose the priorities to which, in its judgment, some matters were entitled to over others. It had a right to balance this ability of the City to pay against the interests of the public and the PBA members. . . .

The statute, the court declared, "vests broad authority in the arbitration panel to determine municipal fiscal priorities within existing revenues."[95]

Courts have, however, overturned or modified awards which order a result found to be in substantive conflict with some constitutional or statutory provision, as for example where the award changed the retirement age in a pension plan without benefit of the actuarial study mandated by statute,[96] or imposed a contractual obligation beyond the one-year limit permitted by statute,[97] or awarded overtime pay for work in excess of 320 hours in an eight-week period without taking into account a statutory prohibition against requiring an officer to work more

---

[94] *City of Washington* v. *Police Dept.*, 436 Pa. 168, 259 A.2d 437, 72 LRRM 2847 (1969).
[95] *City of Buffalo* v. *Rinaldo*, 95 LRRM 2776 (N.Y.App. 1977).
[96] *In re Montgomery Township Police Dept.*, 91 LRRM 2815 (Pa. Comm. Ct. 1976).
[97] *City of East Providence* v. *Fire Fighters Local 850*, 94 LRRM 2571 (R.I. Sup. Ct. 1976).

than eight hours in a 24-hour period,[98] or established impermissible limitations upon the school district's authority to terminate probationary teachers.[99] In this respect, the nature of judicial review for interest awards is the same as for grievance
arbitration.

Concluding Observations

At the outset of the statutory era of public-sector labor relations, courts were almost uniformly receptive to grievance arbitration on the basis of principles analogous to those developed
in the private sector, but in recent years their enthusiasm appears to have waned. Recent decisions, in what might well be a
trend of judicial response, reflect a marked reticence toward
arbitral determination of certain issues, particularly where it is
unclear whether the parties contemplated arbitration of the
issue, where the issue calls for the exercise of discretion not
governed by explicit contractual criteria, or where the award is
seen as having potential impact upon the level or quality of
service or upon financial resources. This reticence is displayed
through rulings that limit the power of the parties to agree to
arbitrate certain matters, interpret narrowly the scope of matters that the parties have agreed to arbitrate, and subject the
arbitral award to a broader judicial review than is permitted
normally in labor arbitration cases.

Why this trend has developed is unclear. Perhaps courts are
responding to the tides of public opinion that appear at the
moment to be running against public-employee bargaining. Perhaps also the decisions reflect a belief that public entities, often
inexperienced in labor relations matters, require some degree
of insulation from their own errors of judgment in bargaining.[100] More fundamentally, perhaps the trend is indicative of a
reaction to an earlier premise of identity between public- and
private-sector labor relations that has proved difficult to maintain. Importation of private-sector labor relations principles to

---

[98]*Conley* v. *Joyce,* 94 LRRM 2114 (Pa. Comm. Ct. 1976).

[99]*Superintending Schools Committee* v. *Town of Winslow,* 93 LRRM 2398 (Me. Sup. Jud. Ct. 1976).

[100]Prior to its recent decision imposing strict standards in determining arbitration, the New York Court of Appeals often chided public entities concerning their obligation to protect their interest in bargaining. E.g., *City School Dist.* v. *Poughkeepsie Public School Teachers, supra* note 42.

the public sector is a little like the transplantation of American labor law to Japan after World War II. It is not that there was anything wrong with American labor law, but it was not immediately adaptable to the semifeudal system of labor relations upon which it was sought to be imposed. While the differences between the private and public sectors are not that great, differences do exist and may take some time to overcome. Indeed, in some respects the gap probably cannot be entirely closed.

But if courts are reacting to the realization that there are differences between the public and private sectors after all, their reaction in the case of grievance arbitration is excessive. While all of the premises stated in the trilogy cases for judicial deferral may not be present in the public sector,[101] certain crucial premises are: that effective labor relations requires a dynamic view of the collective bargaining agreement as establishing a process for resolution of a wide range of disputes, and that arbitration can be an effective method for resolving disputes quickly, peacefully, and in a manner most likely to be in accord with the ongoing relationship of the parties. The presumption-of-arbitrability and the finality-of-awards principles for grievance arbitration would appear to be principles as justifiable for grievance arbitration in the public sector as they are in the private.

Interest arbitration poses more difficult policy questions, the full extent of which have just recently begun to be recognized by the courts. As opinions in the Michigan case suggest, and as the recent New York case involving the City of Buffalo demonstrates, the interest arbitrator may be called upon to make decisions that go far beyond the scope of expertise which we normally attribute to a labor arbitrator, and which may intrude heavily upon areas of public policy normally considered appropriate for resolution by persons or tribunals more directly accountable to the political process. While courts early in the process tended to validate interest-arbitration statutes rather mechanically or formalistically, without significant analysis, more recent opinions reflect concern, sometimes resulting in a negative constitutional response.

The concern expressed by the courts is justified, but on the whole their analysis seems to miss the mark. To complain that

---

[101]Some of the premises states in the trilogy cases (e.g., presumed special competence of the arbitrator) are subject to question even in the private sector. See Feller, *Arbitration: The Days of Its Glory Are Numbered*, 2 Ind. Rel. L.J. 97, 98 (1977).

the arbitrator's award is lacking in the support of the electorate or their elected representatives overlooks the fact that it is precisely because the interests of the voters as expressed by their elected officials clashes in certain respects with the interests of the employees as expressed by their union that there exists a dispute which arbitration is intended to resolve.

The hypothesis underlying interest arbitration is that public employees, or at least certain public employees, ought not to be permitted to strike and that arbitration is necessary to protect their interests against the unilateral imposition of terms by the governing body.

Clearly, therefore, one would not expect the arbitrator to be politically responsive to the local electorate which, ultimately, constitutes the employer. Moreover, at least under the systems of interest arbitration so far utilized in this country, the arbitrator's role is not primarily to implement some neutral state policy as to what the wages and working conditions of local employees ought to be, but rather to function as an extension of the negotiating process in such a manner as to accommodate the interests of the public employer with the interests of the employees involved in the dispute. For this reason, the suggestion of Justice Williams in the Michigan case that the problem of delegation is solved so long as the neutral is appointed by a state official seems artificial. It is likely that the MERC chairman, recognizing the accommodative function of arbitration, would appoint arbitrators from the same list the parties would use in selecting them, and would consult with the parties in the process of doing so.

Similarly, Justice Levin's proposal that the problem can be solved by the establishment of a permanent state panel of arbitrators is at tension with the underlying premise that arbitrators are not expected necessarily to produce decisions acceptable to the appointing authority or to administer some overriding public policy with respect to the content of agreements; their political independence is an essential ingredient of the interest-arbitration process as presently conceived. In these respects, interest arbitration is *sui generis,* and not amenable to the sort of constitutional analysis normally brought to bear upon the delegation of power to administrative agencies.

Perhaps a better analysis would be as follows: Interest arbitration, for the reasons already mentioned, does pose problems in terms of democratic-process values. It appears, however, to be the only workable and just alternative to the strike as a means of accommodating the interests of public employers and their employees. Whether on balance it is preferable to a policy of permitting public employees to strike is debatable. That debate, however, is one that should be carried on in the legislature rather than in the courts.

If the legislature opts for interest arbitration, its option is not irrevocable; process values are ultimately preserved by the ability of the legislature to change its mind. Meanwhile, an acceptable degree of protection against arbitrary or unjust results can be secured through clear description of the issues subject to arbitration, and through standards and safeguards subject to judicial review.

Interest arbitration is still at an experimental stage in this country, and courts should not terminate the experiment before the results can be determined.

CHAPTER 8

PUBLIC-SECTOR LABOR RELATIONS IN CANADA

SHIRLEY B. GOLDENBERG*

In contrast to the private sector where labor relations have in large measure reflected patterns established in the United States, the public sector is an area in which Canada has broken new ground. Collective bargaining in the public sector, broadly defined, is currently more varied and more extensive in Canada than in the United States. It also has a considerably longer history. Given the unique relationship between private-sector labor relations in these two countries and their generally similar philosophy of collective bargaining, lessons learned from Canadian policy initiatives and bargaining experience may be equally relevant in the United States. In both countries, the problem of reconciling the rights that have so long been available to workers in the private sector with the particular characteristics and constraints of public employment is now recognized as one of the most serious issues on the labor relations scene.

Evolution and Present Status of Collective Bargaining in the Public Sector

In contrast with the United States, where some of the most bitter recognition disputes have involved employees of municipal governments, municipal workers in Canada apart from police and fire fighters[1] have, from the outset, enjoyed the same

---

*McGill University.
  [1]Police and fire fighters acquired the right to strike under the British Columbia Labour Code (1973), with voluntary arbitration as an alternative at the discretion of the bargaining agent. However, this right has been seriously limited by the Essential Services Act (1977) which now gives Cabinet discretion to stop a strike involving police or fire fighters. Police and fire fighters are prohibited from striking in all other provinces but Saskatchewan and Nova Scotia. Municipal police in Halifax and Sydney, Nova Scotia, exercised their legal right to strike in 1972. Montreal police and firemen have struck on a number of occasions, although they are prohibited from doing so by the Labour Code of Quebec. Each time they were forced back to work by emergency legislation.

rights under general provincial labor legislation as employees in the private sector. This has meant, among other things, a virtually blanket right to strike over impasses in contract negotiations. Recognition strikes by municipal employees are prohibited by law, as they are in the private sector, as a quid pro quo for formal certification procedures. Municipal workers in Canada have been exercising their bargaining rights for several decades. At the present time, almost all municipal corporations with a total of 50 or more employees and a population in excess of 10,000 have a collective bargaining relationship with at least one unit of their employees.

Collective bargaining is also practiced on a very wide scale by workers in the health and education sectors. While some provinces deny or otherwise restrict the right to strike in the case of teachers and/or hospital workers, others allow these occupational groups, like municipal employees, to bargain under general labor legislation without any particular restriction.[2] Workers performing a broad range of other public services, whether

[2]Teachers are specifically excluded from the coverage of labor legislation and consequently from the right to strike in Prince Edward Island, British Columbia, and Manitoba. The School Act of Prince Edward Island and the Public Schools Acts of British Columbia and Manitoba provide for collective bargaining with binding arbitration of unresolved disputes. Although teachers in Saskatchewan are not excluded from the Trade Union Act, they bargain under different legislation, the Teacher Salary Agreement Act which, as amended in 1971, gives the Minister discretion to impose arbitration if conciliation efforts fail to produce a negotiated agreement. Teachers in Quebec have the right to strike under the Labour Code, but Section 99 qualifies this right by prohibiting a strike without eight days' prior written notice, and also by giving the government discretionary power to delay a strike for up to 80 days by appointing a board of inquiry into the dispute and taking an injunction to prevent or terminate a strike. Ontario teachers, who previously lacked the right to strike because of their exclusion from labor legislation, recently acquired this right by virtue of a separate statute, the Education Relations Act (1975). However, the government has power to terminate a strike if advised by the Educational Relations Commission, appointed under the act to supervise negotiations, that the school year of a group of students is in jeopardy.

Hospital workers other than doctors are generally included in labor legislation, but are subject to particular restrictions in some of the provinces. Section 163 of the Alberta Labour Act (1973) gives the government discretion to forbid a strike or lockout in the hospital sector. Section 44 of the Labour Relations Act of Prince Edward Island substitutes binding arbitration for the right to strike in disputes involving hospital workers. While Ontario and Newfoundland do not exclude hospital employees from their general labor legislation, the Hospital Labour Disputes Arbitration Act (1965) in Ontario and the Hospital Employees Employment Act (1966–1967) in Newfoundland both prohibit strikes and lockouts in the hospital sector and provide for arbitration as a substitute. Section 99 of the Quebec Labour Code applies to the hospital sector as well as to other public services. As in the case of the teachers, this section may delay the exercise of the strike by hospital workers, but does not prohibit it indefinitely. The British Columbia Labour Code permits a hospital union, like the police and fire fighters' unions, to elect for arbitration at the point of impasse in negotiations as an alternative to exercising their right to strike. However, the Essential Services Disputes Act now qualifies the right to strike by hospital employees, as it does in the case of police and fire fighters.

under private or public ownership, as well as employees of many
government agencies and boards, federal and provincial, have
also enjoyed full collective bargaining rights under general
labor legislation in Canada as long as such legislation has existed. Thus workers in sectors such as railways, airlines, long-
shoring, and broadcasting, among others, at the federal level
and those employed by hydroelectric commissions, liquor
boards, etc., at the provincial level enjoy, and use, the bargaining rights that are available to employees in the private sector,
including the right to strike.

Although the right to bargain collectively, including the right
to strike, has long been taken for granted in Canada for employees of municipal governments, as well as for workers in
other areas of public-service employment, the federal government and all but one of the provinces were still resisting the
extension of this right to their own employees little more than
a decade ago. The exception was the province of Saskatchewan,
where a socialist government included its own employees in the
coverage of its original labor legislation, the Trade Union Act,
as far back as 1944.

The historical resistance to collective bargaining for federal
and provincial civil servants was based largely on the principle
of the sovereignty of the state. As in the United States, collective
bargaining and its corollary, the strike, were considered incompatible with this principle, with the obligation of public service
inherent in government employment and with the essential and
monopoly nature of many of the services involved. Moreover,
with the relative security of civil service employment to compensate for lagging wage levels, and a tradition of patronage appointments in certain areas of public employment, civil servants
themselves were not inclined to assert the rights that workers
were demanding, and achieving, in other sectors of the economy. The practice of unilateral decision-making by the government as an employer, except in the case of municipal governments, was not seriously challenged before the early 1960s.
Since that time, however, civil servants have discarded their
traditional docility in favor of collective action.

Spurred on by successfully negotiated settlements in the private sector and in certain areas of public employment, civil
servants in a number of jurisdictions began to challenge the
government as employer to grant them the right to bargain
collectively that the law guaranteed to other workers and im-

posed on other employers. In 1965 the government of Quebec took the lead over the other provinces and the federal government by granting broad collective bargaining rights, including the right to strike, to employees in the civil service.[3] The federal government followed suit in 1967,[4] New Brunswick in 1968,[5] and British Columbia in 1973.[6] Public-service bargaining legislation enacted in Newfoundland in 1970 ostensibly included the right to strike, but as will be seen later, it imposes greater constraints on the exercise of this right than is the case in other jurisdictions.[7] The remaining provinces, beginning with Ontario as early as 1962, have also granted their employees bargaining rights but deny them the legal right to strike.[8]

While collective bargaining came latest to employees at the senior levels of government, it is at this level that its coverage now is most complete. Virtually all federal and provincial government employees eligible to bargain are covered by collective agreements. The replacement in all jurisdictions of informal consultative relationships by genuine bilateral negotiations between associations of public servants and the governments that employ them, and the affiliation of the majority of these associations with the mainstream labor movement has in fact been one of the most interesting developments in labor relations in Canada in recent years. Among other things, it has had an important impact on the rate of unionization and on the composition of the organized labor movement.

Public-Sector Unions

The upsurge in union membership in Canada in the past decade, following a period of relative stagnation if not actual

[3]Civil Service Act, S.Q. 1965, c. 14.
[4]Public Services Staff Relations Act, S.C. 1967, c. 72.
[5]Public Service Labour Relations Act, S.N.B. 1968, c. 88.
[6]Public Service Labour Relations Act, S.B.C. 1973, c. 144.
[7]Public Service (Collective Bargaining) Act, S. Nfld. 1970, c. 85, as amended 1973.
[8]The original Public Service Act of Ontario (1962) has been replaced by the Crown Employees Collective Bargaining Act, S. Ont. 1972, c. 67, but prohibition on the strike has remained unchanged. The Alberta Public Service Act was amended in 1971 (S.A. 1971, c. 89) to provide for arbitration of unresolved disputes which were previously settled unilaterally by the employer. Recent amendments to the Alberta act (1977) have made no change in this respect. Arbitration was introduced in Manitoba in 1969 (S.M. 1969, c. 3) and in Prince Edward Island in 1972, the latter case being by special *regulations* (O.C. No. 958/72) under the existing Civil Service Act (S.P.E.I. 1962, c. 5) rather than by new legislation. Nova Scotia government employees are governed by the Joint Council Act (R.S.N.S. 1967, c. 35) which is presently under review.

decline, may be attributed almost entirely to the adoption of collective bargaining by government employees at the federal and provincial levels, as well as to the considerable increase in collective bargaining in the health and education sectors, particularly by nurses and teachers.[9] With the vast majority of workers in these burgeoning areas of collective bargaining being organized in exclusively Canadian unions, as was already the case for municipal employees, the numerical dominance of American-based unions in the Canadian labor movement has been substantially reduced.[10]

Apart from a few rather interesting exceptions in the province of Quebec,[11] Canadian teachers and nurses have resisted joining the mainstream labor movement. Some bargain through independent associations of employee members, organizationally separate from, but with close links to, their respective professional associations. In a number of provinces, particularly where negotiations are conducted on a centralized basis, the professional association itself may be the certified bargaining agent.

In contrast to the case of nurses and teachers, and to police and fire fighters, whose right to union affiliation is generally restricted by law, most municipal employees who bargain collectively are in unions affiliated with the mainstream labor movement. The majority are members of the Canadian Union of Public Employees (CUPE) which is affiliated with the Canadian Labour Congress (CLC), the main exception being some municipal workers in the province of Quebec who have been organized by a provincially based labor federation.[12] CUPE is the largest union in Canada, a distinction held until recently by the United Steelworkers of America. Its membership, apart from municipal employees, is drawn largely, though not exclusively, from nonprofessional hospital workers and employees of public

---

[9]Union membership as a percentage of total nonagricultural paid workers rose from 30.7 in 1966 to 38.2 in 1977. Labour Canada, Labour Organizations in Canada (Ottawa: 1977).

[10]Unions with headquarters in the United States accounted for 49 percent of total Canadian union membership in 1977 compared with 70.8 percent in 1966. Labour Organizations in Canada, *supra* note 9, for 1966 and 1977.

[11]The largest group of teachers in Quebec, the Centrale des enseignants du Quebec (CEQ) considers itself an integral part of the trade-union movement and has formed a Common Front with other unions in public-sector negotiations. One group of nurses was originally affiliated with the Confederation of National Trade Unions (CNTU), a militant Quebec-based labor federation, although it has recently become independent.

[12]Confederation of National Trade Unions.

utilities. It is also the certified bargaining agent for one unit of provincial government employees in the province of New Brunswick and for a police unit in Nova Scotia.

Unions of government employees in most provinces have evolved from associations of civil servants that were in existence prior to the bargaining legislation. The fact that a number of these associations, almost all of which had previously been unaffiliated, applied for and received local charters from the CLC in the past few years reflects a growing feeling of affinity by government employees with the mainstream labor movement. The National Union of Provincial Government Employees (NUPGE) was formed in 1976 to group provincial government employee unions affiliated with the CLC. This new union was originally made up of the government employee organizations of British Columbia, Alberta, Saskatchewan, Manitoba, Prince Edward Island, and Newfoundland. The Newfoundland association has since disaffiliated. The civil service associations of Nova Scotia and Ontario refused from the outset to become part of the new union, thereby forfeiting their CLC affiliation. The formation of a national organization had been a condition laid down by the CLC when it granted local charters to the provincial associations. For the moment, NUPGE seems to provide little more than a loose association between its constituent elements, each of which retains its own identity and executive and full autonomy with respect to collective bargaining and contract administration. However, NUPGE has not been in existence long enough to judge its potential effectiveness. Finally it should be noted that the fact that government employees in the province of Quebec have had no affiliation with the CLC has not isolated them from the mainstream labor movement. Government employee associations in Quebec affiliated with the provincially based Confederation of National Trade Unions in 1965, which was as soon as the law permitted. They broke ties with this central labor organization in 1972 as a result of ideological differences.[13]

The majority of federal government employees belong to the Public Service Alliance of Canada (PSAC) which was formed in 1968 by the merger of two existing associations of federal civil servants. PSAC is composed of 17 components representing

---

[13]The break came following a general strike of public and parapublic employees with which the civil servants were not in accord.

various occupational groups in the federal public service. Like the provincial associations mentioned above, its membership is confined to public employees, most of whom are employed directly by the federal government. Like CUPE and NUPGE, it is affiliated with the CLC. The Alliance is now the third largest union in Canada.

There are 15 bargaining agents in the federal public service, although none of the others is nearly as large as the Alliance.[14] The next largest is the Canadian Union of Postal Employees, one of the most militant elements in the service and which, along with the Letter Carriers' Union, was active long before statutory bargaining rights existed. While the postal unions, like the PSAC, are affiliated with the CLC, some bargaining agents in the federal service are independent. The largest of the independent bargaining agents is the Professional Institute of the Public Service of Canada (PIPS) which represents a majority of the workers with professional training. Of all the unions bargaining in the federal public service, only one, the International Brotherhood of Electrical Workers (IBEW), has its headquarters in the United States. The IBEW represents one bargaining unit, with a membership of 2,700 out of approximately 250,000 unionized employees in the federal service.

It is clear from the above that the vast majority of workers in government employment and other areas of public service such as health and education, with which this chapter will be concerned, have been organized by all-Canadian unions operating virtually exclusively in the public sector. On the other hand, in the case of railways, airlines, broadcasting, and even some municipal transportation commissions, a variety of national and international unions may be found. These sectors have long-established bargaining relationships in Canada, as in the United States, and while they might be included under a very broad definition of public service, they are beyond the scope of this study.

----

[14]Public Service Alliance of Canada, 165,000; Professional Institute of the Public Service, 17,000; Economists, Sociologists and Statisticians Association, 2,300; Research Council Employees' Association, 2,200; Syndicat Général du cinéma et de la télévision, 400; Letter Carriers' Union of Canada, 16,500; Canadian Union of Postal Workers, 23,000; Council of Graphics Arts Unions of the Public Service of Canada, 1,250; Canadian Air Traffic Control Association, 2,150; Professional Association of Foreign Service Officers, 1,000; Association of Postal Officials of Canada, 3,600; Federal Government Dockyards Trades and Labour Council, 2,600; Canadian Postmasters' Association, 8,200; Canadian Merchant Service Guild, 1,000; Local 2228, International Brotherhood of Electrical Workers, 2,700. *Total,* 248,900.

Management Organization in the Public Sector

Given the space limitations, this section will deal only with those aspects of management organization in the public sector that are relevant to the bargaining function and the administration of collective agreements. The problems of management organization with respect to collective bargaining vary between levels of government and are becoming particularly complex in the health and education sectors.

The Municipal Sector

Even at the municipal level where collective bargaining, on the whole, is a long-established practice, the question of who will represent the municipal corporation as an employer in the conduct of negotiations still remains a problem. A variety of practices may be found.[15]

Negotiations in smaller municipalities are frequently conducted by a committee of the municipal council, assisted by a senior staff official such as the municipal clerk or treasurer. While this practice may reflect the reluctance of some small municipal councils to delegate authority, sometimes they simply do not have a senior officer with sufficient skills in negotiation to assume the bargaining function as such. Two factors, separately or in combination—the fact that the members of municipal councils, more often than not, are lacking in negotiating skills, and the lack of continuity on the management team produced by the uncertainties associated with elective office—have not enhanced the effectiveness of negotiations on the employer side. While medium to large municipalities usually have a personnel department and frequently assign the responsibility for negotiations to the personnel director, the effectiveness of this practice depends, as it does at other levels of government, on the mandate that is given to the negotiator. When a union has reason to believe that the employer spokesman lacks authority to make a final decision, particularly on monetary matters, it is likely to pressure the elected officials to conclude an agreement rather than to negotiate seriously at the bargaining table. The implications for good-faith bargaining are self-evident.

---

[15]For a detailed examination of municipal bargaining, see T. D. Plunkett, *Municipal Collective Bargaining,* in Collective Bargaining in the Public Service (Toronto: Institute of Public Administration of Canada, 1973), 1–10.

Where municipalities have more elaborate administrative structures involving a chief executive officer or agency, e.g., city manager, city administrator, or board of commissioners, such officers usually have responsibility for the negotiations, even though the actual conduct of negotiations may be delegated to a personnel director or labor relations officer. The negotiator in such cases usually has a fairly clear mandate from the chief executive officer who himself will have obtained a mandate from the municipal council as to the limits within which he can negotiate.

There has been some talk, but little action, about establishing machinery to coordinate bargaining efforts of municipal managements in large metropolitan areas to avoid whipsawing tactics by unions. The Vancouver Municipal Labour Relations Bureau provides an interesting exception to the general practice of bargaining on a single-city basis. The bureau conducts negotiations for the city of Vancouver and several surrounding municipalities which finance it and give it a mandate to bargain on their behalf.

While there is no single pattern of employer organization for collective bargaining at the municipal level, at least one common management problem may be identified. As creatures of their respective provincial legislatures, municipalities in Canada, large or small, operate on a limited tax base, although the services they are required to provide are steadily increasing. When negotiations reach a point where a choice must be made between a wage increase that a municipality feels unable to pay and a work stoppage that would have adverse effects on the public, the locus of decision-making frequently shifts to the provincial government which will ultimately finance the whole or part of the settlement.

Hospitals and Schools

Local hospital managements and boards of school trustees in most jurisdictions are still legally autonomous units for the purpose of labor negotiations. In practice, however, there is a noticeable trend toward centralization of bargaining structures. Hospital and school boards, more often than not, delegate responsibility for negotiations to their respective regional or provincial associations. Responsibility for administration of the resulting agreements is retained in such cases by the individual hospitals and school boards, most of which have personnel or industrial relations divisions for this purpose.

Whatever the level of bargaining—local, regional, or provincial—the central role of government in distributing funds to hospitals and schools has seriously undermined their autonomy as employers. Thus, while local hospitals and school boards by and large have retained their positions of legal employers, provincial government is increasingly becoming the effective employer where financial matters are concerned. In most provinces, government influence over the results of negotiations is still exercised indirectly, by virtue of the financial constraints they place on hospital and school administrations. However, four provinces, New Brunswick, Quebec, Prince Edward Island, and Newfoundland, have put an end to the fiction of employer autonomy in labor negotiations in the health and education sectors by including, by statute, government representatives on the management side of the bargaining table at which a province-wide agreement must be negotiated, at least on the major financial issues. The role of the government representatives in these negotiations is best described by the maxim, "He who pays the piper calls the tune," but contract administration remains the responsibility of local hospital and school boards.

The Senior Levels of Government

A major problem in management organization at senior levels of government, federal and provincial, has been the need to accommodate the functions of long-established administrative structures to the new demands of a collective bargaining regime which, it should be noted, has not replaced the traditional "merit system" as a basis for selection, promotion, etc., in government employment but co-exists rather uneasily with it. Civil service commissions, the centralized personnel agencies originally established to enforce the merit system, have therefore continued to exist in all jurisdictions. In some provinces the adoption of collective bargaining has actually resulted in an accretion of the functions of the commissions by the addition of the responsibility for negotiations to their previous personnel functions. However, with decisions that were previously made unilaterally now subject to the provisions of negotiated agreements, civil service commissions find their functions considera-

bly reduced in jurisdictions that have assigned the bargaining
function to another agency of government—a separate civil service department, a management committee of the Cabinet, or a
staff division of the Treasury Board.[16]

Some provincial governments—in fact the majority—still
seem to consider it most appropriate for the agency formally
responsible for the staffing function, i.e., the Civil Service Commission, to be the employer spokesman in negotiations. Others,
including the federal government, see more logic in entrusting
the negotiating function to an agency like the Treasury Board
which is responsible for overall budgetary decisions, including
those related to personnel policy. Experience has shown, however, that effective bargaining depends more on the mandate
that is given to the government negotiators than on the agency
to which the negotiations have been entrusted. The most successful bargaining experience has been in jurisdictions in which
governments have delegated to experienced negotiators sufficient authority, within previously defined limits, not only to
make a deal, but equally important, to inspire confidence in the
union negotiators that they have the authority to do so. Where,
on the other hand, government negotiating committees lack a
precise mandate to effect a settlement, particularly on monetary
issues, they may require constant recourse to the political authority for which they are simply the spokesmen. In such cases
when it comes to the "crunch," decisions are made at the Cabinet level rather than at the bargaining table. This has been a
particular problem where governments have established a bargaining relationship with their own employees before defining
a clear-cut policy on the issues that are likely to arise. It is a
problem, therefore, that is amenable to solution through experience.

Finally, with respect to management organization, the fact

---

[16]The collective bargaining function is vested in the Civil Service Commission or its
chairman in British Columbia, Alberta, Saskatchewan, and Nova Scotia. In Prince Edward Island, representatives of Treasury Board and line departments sit with representatives of the Civil Service Commission on the government negotiating team. As in
the federal jurisdiction, New Brunswick and Newfoundland designate the Treasury
Board as employer for the purpose of collective bargaining; a management committee
of Cabinet is responsible for negotiations in Ontario and Manitoba, as is the Department
of the Civil Service (separate from the Civil Service Commission) in Quebec. For a
detailed discussion of the evolution of the personnel function in the provincial public
service, see J. E. Hodgetts and O. P. Dwivedi, Provincial Governments as Employers
(Montreal: McGill-Queen's University Press, 1974).

that the negotiating function, like the staffing function, is formally assigned in all jurisdictions to a central agency of government has not precluded departmental input into the negotiating process. In some cases this may take the form of departmental representation and active participation on the negotiating team, as in the post office and federal Agriculture Department where departmental boundaries virtually coincide with major occupational bargaining units. There is also considerable departmental influence in most jurisdictions over the hiring of personnel, subject to the monitoring authority of civil service commissions. There is full departmental autonomy in the administration of collective agreements, including the handling of grievance procedure.

Wage and Benefit Determination Through Collective Bargaining

There was a noticeable tendency, prior to the adoption of collective bargaining, for paternalistic governments and other public employers to establish salaries more with an eye to budgetary considerations than to the principle, to which some at least gave lip-service, of fair and equitable comparison with the private sector. With the adoption of collective bargaining, the determination of what was fair and equitable became a matter for negotiation.

It is difficult, if not impossible, to separate the impact of collective bargaining as such from other variables in the wage-determination process. However, there is evidence to suggest that it has been important in raising wages, particularly in the initial stages when catch-up with the unionized sector has been a factor. This compares with the experience in the private sector when collective bargaining was first adopted. A recent study shows that wage increases in first collective agreements in the public sector have been approximately 4-percent higher than corresponding increases in renewed agreements in all years since 1968, and also that the largest negotiated increases have been effected in the lower wage categories.[17] Since the distribution of workers on the basis of wages tends to be pyramidal, the

----

[17]Jean-Michel Cousineau and Robert Lacroix, Wage Determination in Major Collective Agreements in the Private and Public Sectors (Ottawa: Economic Council of Canada, 1977).

lower wage category is the class in which the majority of newly
unionized workers would belong. The union argument that the
public employer should set an example in compensation has
probably been most convincing at this level where the potential
for exploitation has been greatest.

That a combination of factors must affect the wage-determination process is illustrated by the fact that the increase in basic
rates from 1968 to 1975, when wage controls were adopted,
differed between and within subsectors, the average federal increase in this period (113 percent) being substantially lower
than increases in the provincial (129 percent) and municipal
(132 percent) sectors in both of which there has been a virtual
explosion in demand for services. The federal increase in base
rates in this period, contrary to popular opinion, was even less
than in the private sector (120 percent).[18]

The fact that the effect on the public of a work stoppage would
be less in most of the federal services than in many provincial
or municipal services might well have made it easier for the
federal government to hold the line. However, caution must be
exercised in interpreting the developments in base wage rates
on which most of the available comparative data have been
calculated. For one thing, they fail to take account of the phenomenon of "classification creep" which has been an important
factor, particularly in the larger public jurisdictions, in increasing individual incomes at the lower levels, and consequently the
total wage bill of the employer, without a corresponding increase in wage rates as such. They also fail to take account of
exceptional increases that have been negotiated in other categories, professional and supervisory, for example. Yet the federal
government's recent—and very unusual—proposal to place a
statutory ceiling on bargaining-unit salaries flows directly from
wage developments in these two categories.[19]

Given the problem of securing suitable disaggregated data on
wage developments in the wide range of public and parapublic
services in which collective bargaining now takes place, and in
view of the differences within and between these services in the
length of their bargaining history, the nature of their bargaining

---

18Unpublished Labour Canada statistics.
19A bill (c. 28) to amend the Public Service Staff Relations Act, recently introduced
in the Parliament of Canada, proposes to remove from the bargaining unit all employees
receiving an annual salary of $33,500 or more.

experience, and the environmental and institutional variables that affect their bargaining strength, a detailed examination of the impact of bargaining on wages and other benefits would, of necessity, require study on a case-by-case basis. As this is clearly beyond the scope of this chapter, a more general problem will now be considered—the difficulty of agreeing on the appropriate criteria for determining wages and salaries.

There has been no disagreement on the general principle that wages and salaries in the public service should be fair in comparison with the private sector where they have been determined largely through economic bargaining power. The principle of comparability, or at least lip-service to it, was an important element of compensation policy in the Canadian federal government service long before the present collective bargaining regime was established. With the adoption of the Public Service Staff Relations Act (PSSRA) in 1967, fair comparison with the private sector as well as between the various parts of the public service was, by implication at least, written into law. Section 68 of the Public Service Staff Relations Act specifies the following criteria to guide arbitrators of interest disputes:

> (a) the needs of the Public Service for qualified employees; (b) the conditions of employment in similar occupations outside the Public Service, including such geographic, industrial, or other variations as the Arbitration Tribunal may consider relevant; (c) the need to maintain appropriate relationships in the conditions of employment as between different grade levels within an occupation and as between occupations in the Public Service; (d) the need to establish terms and conditions of employment that are fair and reasonable in relation to the qualifications required, the work performed, the responsibility assumed and the nature of the services rendered; and (e) any other factor that to it appears to be relevant to the matter in dispute.

Similar provisions appear in the public-service bargaining statutes of a number of provinces. It is reasonable to assume that the governments concerned would be guided by the same criteria in the conduct of negotiations as they expect to be applied in arbitration.

While the general principle of fair comparison is endorsed by unions and employers alike, no consensus has yet emerged in Canada on its interpretation and application. The unions maintain that a public employer should be the best employer, that its wage policy should be based on the highest rates being paid for comparable work in the private sector. Some even argue that governments should assume the lead, that they should pay higher rates than the best employers in the private sector because of the essential nature of many public services, the restrictions on the use of the strike as a bargaining weapon in the public sector, and the desirability of raising basic standards by setting an example. Most governments, on the other hand, have favored a comparison with the "average" outside employer, or even with those who pay slightly above the average. The federal government in particular has maintained that anything more would be inflationary, thus incompatible with its overriding responsibility for the economy as a whole.

Apart from the philosophical differences between the parties as to the appropriate level at which comparisons should be made, there have also been serious practical problems in applying the comparability principle, particularly where public services are monopoly services, thus lacking in private-sector comparisons. The air-traffic controllers are a classic example. For while acceptable substitutes for direct comparisons may be worked out on the basis of the skills they require and time it takes to acquire them, it has been more difficult to agree on the weight to assign to the particular responsibility involved in the job and the psychological tensions flowing from it.

Some public-service wage demands in Canada are based on comparisons with the same or similar occupational groups in different parts of the country. It is common to hear demands by police, fire fighters, employees of municipal transportation commissions, teachers, and nurses, among others, for parity with their counterparts in cities and provinces where prevailing rates are higher. The employers, on the other hand, plead differences in ability to pay.

The one area in which regional disparities have been ignored, by and large, is the federal public service, but this too has raised problems. While regional rates based on various systems of pay zones are negotiated for a few federal bargaining units, most federal government employees are paid on the basis of a national wage, regardless of the location of their employment. As a result, wages in a federal bargaining unit may compare favorably with external rates in some parts of the country while placing employees at a relative disadvantage in others. The question of recognizing regional differences in national bargaining units still produces more controversy than consensus.

The difficulty of applying the comparability principle is self-evident where public-service occupations, by virtue of their monopoly character, are lacking in private-sector counterparts. But even where external comparisons exist, and putting regional differences aside, other problems have arisen, as in the case of construction. While the unions argue on the basis of equal pay for equal work, public employers who give year-round employment have been reluctant to be bound by wage rates that have been negotiated in the private sector to compensate for the seasonal nature of the industry. The construction case illustrates the distortions that can result if comparisons are limited to wages and salaries, and fail to take account of factors such as job security as well as benefits outside the collective agreement, superannuation plans, for example, that may be superior to those negotiated in the private sector.

The Canadian experience with public-sector bargaining has shown that if comparison with the private sector is to be realistic as a guide to pay determination, it must include, at the very least, all the elements in the compensation package that involve a measurable monetary value. This fact has been recognized in recently proposed amendments to the federal legislation, the Public Service Staff Relations Act. These amendments, if enacted, would add to the existing criteria on which arbitrators must base their awards the concept of total compensation comparability.[20] The proposal has provoked unanimous opposition from the labor movement, which views it as an affront to the principle of free collective bargaining. Others have criticized it on less emotional grounds, noting in particular the practical difficulty of comparing total compensation.

According to a recent study by the Pay Research Bureau, which collects and analyzes comparative data for the benefit of negotiators and arbitrators in the federal service, the difficulty of securing information, particularly consistent information, on the cost of fringe benefits to private employers, still presents a major impediment to the comparison of total compensation.[21] At least part of the problem flows from the difficulty of computing the cost of benefits, some of which, such as holidays, vacations, and sick leave, must be evaluated in conjunction with age,

---

[20] *Ibid.*
[21] Canada Pay Research Bureau, Public Service Staff Relations Board, Total Compensation: An Exploration Study (Ottawa: 1975).

seniority, and other relevant factors; others, like overtime, are difficult to measure in advance. The Pay Research Bureau is currently trying to evolve a more reliable measurement of total compensation. The task, though difficult, may be facilitated by an unexpected by-product of the recent Anti-Inflation Program under which employers have been required, for the past three years, to submit detailed reports on their total compensation costs. This requirement may have made available better and more consistent figures on private-sector compensation for purposes of comparison.

Public-Sector Legislation

Although virtually all public employees in Canada now enjoy the right to bargain collectively, the extent of their bargaining rights and the conditions under which these are exercised vary considerably between jurisdictions. It goes almost without saying that the legal framework within which negotiations take place can have an important bearing on their outcome.

As has already been noted, workers in municipal employment and in the parapublic sector are covered, by and large, by the provisions of the general labor legislation that applies in the private sector, with occasional restrictions on the right to strike. Collective bargaining by employees of senior levels of government, on the other hand, has been subject, from the outset, to special legislation in all jurisdictions but Saskatchewan.

Most provinces include the employees of at least some government agencies, such as provincially operated vocational schools and mental hospitals, in addition to the employees of government departments, under their civil service bargaining legislation. The federal Public Service Staff Relations Act (1967), like some of the provincial statutes, covers labor relations in a considerable number of government agencies and boards in addition to the civil service. These are listed in the act as "separate employers" for the purpose of collective bargaining.[22] Manitoba and Nova Scotia are the only jurisdictions apart from Saskatchewan that allow employees of all government

---

[22]The "separate employers" include the Atomic Energy Control Board, Economic Council of Canada, National Film Board, National Research Council, among others. They are subject to all the provisions of the PSSRA, but negotiate independently in contrast with government departments and other portions of the public service of Canada for which the Treasury Board is designated as employer.

agencies and boards to bargain under general labor legislation. Employees of Crown Corporations, on the other hand, enjoy full collective bargaining rights under labor legislation in all jurisdictions but Newfoundland. In that province, any Crown Corporation may be placed under the Public Service Collective Bargaining Act (1973) at the discretion of the Cabinet.

New Brunswick, Quebec, Newfoundland, and Prince Edward Island are the only provinces in which the government is directly involved in collective bargaining in the entire health and education sectors. By providing for government participation in collective bargaining in hospitals, schools, and community colleges as well as in the civil service and certain government agencies and boards, these provinces have, to a large extent, eliminated the demarcation line between the public service as traditionally defined and the so-called parapublic services where labor relations are concerned. While the statutes governing labor relations in the health and education sectors are different in each of the above-named provinces, the fact that the government is a party to the bargaining relationship in all cases and that negotiations are carried out on a province-wide basis has introduced an element of consistency, within each province, in the treatment of workers in these sectors.

The Bargaining Agent

When public-service bargaining legislation was introduced at the federal level and in the provinces of New Brunswick, Newfoundland, and British Columbia, government employees in these jurisdictions acquired the right to associate in unions of their choice, subject to regular certification procedures, as was already the case in Saskatchewan. (Certification is handled by separate boards at the federal level and in New Brunswick and by the Labour Relations Boards of the other provinces). But when the governments of Alberta, Manitoba, Ontario, Prince Edward Island, and Nova Scotia gave bargaining rights to their employees, they gave statutory recognition to the associations of civil servants with which they already had informal consultative relationships. Quebec gave statutory recognition to one group of civil servants by designating an existing association as bargaining agent for clerical and blue-collar employees but left others, notably the professionals, relatively free to organize in unions of their choice.

Recent amendments to the law in Manitoba, Ontario, Prince Edward Island, and Alberta allow another bargaining agent to replace the Civil Service Association originally recognized by statute should it (the association) cease to represent the majority in the bargaining unit. The practical implications of these amendments are virtually nil, however, in view of a continuing provision in the laws of these provinces for service-wide bargaining units. The difficulty of displacing the bargaining agent of a service-wide bargaining unit should be self-evident.

The Bargaining Unit

The criteria for determining appropriate bargaining units and the mechanisms by which they are established vary between jurisdictions as do the means and criteria for the selection of bargaining agents.

Although workers employed in a managerial or confidential capacity tend to be excluded, by definition, from collective bargaining, as in the private sector, the line for managerial exclusions in public employment has generally been drawn at a higher level than in private industry, with the result that employees performing a variety of supervisory functions are frequently included in civil service bargaining units. The decisions on managerial exclusions are made by the Labour Relations Board in some jurisdictions and by arbitration, or even by negotiation between the parties, in others.

The federal and New Brunswick statutes are the only ones with specific provisions for supervisory employees to be included in civil service bargaining units, either with other workers in their occupational group or in separate units of their own. Amendments to the Public Service Staff Relations Act currently before the Canadian Parliament indicate that the federal government at least is rethinking this provision because many middle managers, mainly in the professional category, have succeeded in negotiating salaries higher than those received by occupants of more senior positions whose pay levels are set unilaterally. The proposed amendment would exclude from the definition of employee under the act, and therefore from bargaining rights, all personnel receiving an annual rate of pay higher than a specified statutory ceiling.[23] This would have the

----

[23]*Supra,* note 19.

effect of adding approximately 6,500 middle- and lower-level managers to the 15,000 who are presently excluded.

There are more policy differences between jurisdictions with respect to the appropriate occupational composition of bargaining units than over the criteria for managerial exclusions. Saskatchewan alone has no statutory restrictions on the formation of bargaining units in the public service. At the federal level and in some of the provinces, the law requires bargaining units to be certified according to predetermined occupational classifications. A number of alternatives exist. For example, the Quebec Civil Service Act requires separate bargaining units only for professional and nonprofessional employees, whereas both the New Brunswick and federal statutes establish five occupational classifications—scientific and professional, technical, administrative, administrative support, and operational (and separate groups within each classification)—for certification purposes.[24] The British Columbia Act requires three bargaining units in the civil service, one for licensed professionals, one for registered nurses, and one for all the others combined. However, British Columbia also has introduced an innovative system of two-tier bargaining within each of these broad classifications. The act provides for every collective agreement to consist of two or more parts: a master part covering the terms and conditions of employment that are common to all employees in the bargaining unit, and a subsidiary part for each occupational group within the unit covering the terms and conditions that apply only to employees in the specific occupational group.

Where governments have granted bargaining rights to their own employees by formalizing a de facto negotiating arrangement with an existing association of civil servants, in other words by statutory recognition, the practice has usually been to entrench all-inclusive bargaining units covering the entire civil service in the provisions of the law. Although negotiating structures have generally been established, in practice, to accommodate the interests of different occupational groups in the context of these service-wide units, some groups, notably the professionals, have objected to being included in a unit against their will. In one province, Alberta, the legislation recognizes this objection by allowing the professionals in the public service to

---

[24]At the federal level, this has resulted in 81 occupational bargaining units for which the Treasury Board is the employer. These are certified on a nationwide basis.

opt out of the general bargaining unit if a majority so desires; if they do so, however, they forfeit their bargaining rights, which is what has happened in practice. Two provinces exclude the members of certain professions from any bargaining rights. All licensed professionals in Ontario are excluded from the coverage of public legislation, and members of the legal profession are excluded in British Columbia.

Limitations on the Scope of Bargaining

The range of negotiable issues in Canada is generally narrower in government service than it is in the private sector. Full collective bargaining on the private-sector pattern is denied to government employees in all jurisdictions by the considerable list of management rights that continue to be exercised by civil service commissions. These include the personnel functions of recruitment, classification and promotion, and sometimes suspension and dismissal. Also generally excluded from collective bargaining are items such as superannuation plans which are governed by separate legislation. Some statutes, like the PSSRA, specifically prohibit collective agreements from altering, eliminating, or introducing terms or conditions of employment which "would require or have the effect of requiring the enactment or amendment of any legislation . . . except for the purpose of appropriating moneys required for its implementation. . . ."

When the legislation specifies a limited list of negotiable items such as wages, working conditions, and holidays, all other issues are taboo, by implication at least. In practice, however, some of the excluded issues have found their way to the bargaining table when unions have been strong enough to insist. In Quebec, for example, some issues such as job security which were "nonnegotiable" under the original Civil Service Act (1965) were not only discussed at the bargaining table, but appeared as clauses in the first negotiated agreements. When the act was amended in 1969, it broadened the scope of negotiable issues for the purpose of future bargaining. In addition, the new legislation validated all items in collective agreements that had already been negotiated. This was particularly significant, as many of the provisions in these collective agreements went beyond the legally negotiable issues under the original Civil Service Act.

In some cases, "nonnegotiable" items have been handled separately, with an agreement taking the form of a "letter of understanding" between the parties rather than forming part of the collective agreement itself. This was the case in the matter of job security, a nonnegotiable item under the PSSRA, arising out of technological change in the post office. A letter of understanding was eventually signed between representatives of the government and the postal unions, but only after prolonged mediation sessions outside the normal bargaining period and several bitter illegal strikes. In an extensive review of the federal legislation,[25] Jacob Finkelman, first chairman of the Public Service Staff Relations Board (PSSRB), recommended that a formal technological-change provision be added to the act in the light of the experience in the post office. This would permit negotiation over the impact of technological change, rather than over the change itself, with arbitration in case of impasse. Finkelman recommended that other items, such as classification standards, which are currently nonnegotiable, eventually be subject to negotiation, but outside the normal bargaining period and without the right to strike. These recommendations were endorsed, with minor modifications, by the Joint Parliamentary Committee that was subsequently appointed to consider the Finkelman Report.[26] However, no legislative action has yet been taken to broaden the scope of bargaining on the basis of these recommendations.

A serious problem flowing from the limitation on bargainable issues is the fact that items not covered by a collective agreement are usually not subject to a grievance procedure. The fact that appeals on classification, and even on suspension and dismissal, are decided in many jurisdictions by a civil service commission which may have been responsible for the original decision does little to inspire employee confidence in the objectivity of the system. The federal government and New Brunswick innovated in their legislation by providing adjudication machinery to hear complaints under the act, even by employees outside the bargaining unit, as well as grievances flowing from a collective agreement, but few other jurisdictions have followed suit.

The federal act and some provincial statutes have retained the

---

[25]Jacob Finkelman, Employer-Employee Relations in the Public Service of Canada (Ottawa: Information Canada, 1974), Supplementary Observations and Recommendations, 1975.

[26]Government of Canada, Report to Parliament of The Special Joint Committee on Employer-Employee Relations in the Public Service of Canada (Ottawa: Information Canada, 1976).

mechanism for consultation through joint councils[27] that
preceded the adoption of formal collective bargaining as a
means of dealing with nonnegotiable items. While most unions
do not consider this an acceptable substitute for the right to
bargain over the excluded issues with a view to including them
in collective agreements, the mechanism has been useful for
dealing with issues of service-wide interest that transcend individual bargaining units. Should some of the presently excluded
issues of service-wide interest eventually become subject to negotiation, as is currently being suggested, statutory provision
for coalition bargaining by the unions concerned on these issues
would clearly be required, as recommended in the Finkelman
Report. Negotiations over other issues would be carried on in
separate units as is presently the case.

Provisions for Dispute Resolution

The most contentious issue facing the policy-makers is the
procedure to be followed when negotiations break down. This
is the aspect of public-service labor relations in which the most
significant differences still occur and in which considerable experimentation undoubtedly must take place before an acceptable formula is found. The subject still provokes more controversy than consensus.

Half the provinces in Canada (Nova Scotia, Prince Edward
Island, Ontario, Manitoba, and Alberta) deny the right to strike
to government employees. The others (Saskatchewan, Quebec,
New Brunswick, Newfoundland, and British Columbia), as well
as the federal government, allow them to strike after observing
prescribed conciliation procedures and occasionally other
delays. British Columbia is the only jurisdiction that grants a
government employer the right to lockout as a counterpart to
the unions' right to strike. This right has not been exercised in
practice. The Finkelman Report recommended the addition of
a lockout provision to the PSSRA. No action has yet been taken
on that recommendation, which was also supported by the Joint
Parliamentary Committee. While the question of a lockout by a
government employer was virtually unthinkable when the early
public-service legislation was being drafted, experience sug-

---

[27]Joint councils are consultative bodies made up of equal numbers of employer and
employee representatives.

gests that the right to lockout, judiciously exercised, might expedite the settlement of certain disputes. The Finkelman recommendation was undoubtedly influenced by the experience of rotating strikes in the post office. These caused disruption of service to the public comparable with the effects of a general strike at minimal financial loss to the membership.

The jurisdictions that grant the right to strike allow voluntary arbitration as an alternative, with the notable exception of Quebec, where the government refuses to permit a third-party decision on matters affecting the provincial budget. The federal situation is unique in that the employee bargaining agent must decide on the ultimate method of dispute resolution before serving notice to bargain. Two options are available: referral of a dispute to a conciliation board with the ultimate right to strike, or binding arbitration. Whichever option is chosen, conciliation officers may be named to assist the parties to reach agreement prior to the ultimate step in the process. The bargaining agent may change its choice of method of dispute resolution prior to the commencement of negotiations for another collective agreement. It is interesting to note that the bargaining agent has the sole right of choice of method. This cannot be vetoed by the employer.

Procedural Delays

Most provinces that grant government employees the right to strike require specific conciliation procedures before a legal strike may take place, these procedures as a rule being virtually the same as those required in the private sector. Employees who choose the conciliation-strike option at the federal level acquire the right to strike only after an ad hoc conciliation board appointed by the chairman of the PSSRB has tried and failed to effect a settlement. The New Brunswick statute, on the other hand, sets out a specific timetable for negotiation, conciliation, and other procedures before the right to strike may be exercised. Given the innovative nature of these procedures, it may be of interest to examine them in some detail.

There is a 45-day statutory limit on public-sector negotiations in New Brunswick unless the parties agree otherwise. The chairman of the Public Service Labour Relations Board (PSLRB) *may* appoint a conciliator to assist in the negotiations if asked to do so by either of the parties. However, if it appears to him that the parties are not likely to reach agreement, he must appoint a conciliation board within 15 days of the statutory or agreed-upon time limit on the bargaining. A conciliation board consists of a member selected by each of the parties who in turn select a chairman, as is the case at the federal level.

A conciliation board must submit a report to the chairman of the PSLRB if it fails to effect a settlement, but if the parties do not settle following the report, they are still not free to strike. At this stage, either party may request the chairman of the PSLRB to declare that a "deadlock" exists. If he is satisfied that the required conciliation procedures have been observed, the chairman declares a deadlock and asks the parties if they are prepared to submit the dispute to arbitration. The act provides for an arbitration tribunal consisting of a chairman appointed by the government and two other members, representative of the interests of the parties. The latter are selected by the chairman of the PSLRB from two permanent panels of arbitrators, originally named by the board. (The method of appointing the arbitration tribunal followed the pattern established at the federal level.) The award of the tribunal is binding, should the parties accept the "arbitration route." If either party rejects arbitration, the union is free to conduct a vote among its members "to determine whether they desire to take strike action." A majority vote in the affirmative gives the union the legal right to strike. Should a majority vote against a strike, the chairman of the PSLRB orders the parties to resume negotiations for a period of 21 days after which if agreement has not been reached, either party may again request the chairman to declare that deadlock exists. The process continues to repeat itself until the parties either reach a negotiated settlement, agree to submit to arbitration, or the bargaining agent secures a majority strike vote after which a legal work-stoppage may take place.

The New Brunswick statute made an interesting modification to the federal act on which it was patterned. For while the federal act requires the bargaining agent to choose between conciliation with the ultimate right to strike and binding arbitration prior to commencing negotiations, this decision may be taken at any time in New Brunswick and may actually be changed as negotiations proceed. There have been some occasions, in practice, where after the completion of conciliation procedures, the union has indicated a willingness to accept binding arbitration.

It should be noted that New Brunswick differs from the other jurisdictions in which a strike is permitted by requiring a strike vote after all other legal delays have been exhausted. A noted Canadian expert on labor relations made the following comment on this particular feature of the New Brunswick legislation:

> The compulsory strike-authorization vote in New Brunswick introduces an element of realism in that province's procedure. It is the membership of the unit of employees, acting after an impasse has been reached and at least one party has rejected arbitration, who really make the strike decision. On balance, the option of voting for a strike or for further negotiations can probably be expected to have a conservative effect since the voter will be concerned with an imminent strike situation, whereas in the federal procedure the decision has been taken when those who take it are protected by a very considerable period of time from the strike itself. Also in New Brunswick a vote against a strike does not carry with it a repudiation of the strike procedure, but only an instruction from the membership to their bargaining agent to have another try. If this leads to failure the membership may revise their vote after a relatively short period of time.[28]

Protection of Essential Services

Although the federal government and half the provinces have now accepted the strike as a legitimate element of the bargaining process, all of them except Saskatchewan have special provisions in their statutes for the protection of essential services. At the federal level and in New Brunswick, for example, before the conciliation procedures can be invoked, agreement must be reached on a list of "designated employees" to remain on the job in the event of a legal strike. In Quebec, on the other hand, agreement on the essential services and the means of maintaining them is left until after the regular conciliation procedures have been exhausted. At the federal level and in New Brunswick, the public-service boards make the final decision on designated employees in the absence of agreement by the parties; this decision is made by the Labour Court in Quebec.[29] Newfoundland has a special provision which is absent in other jurisdictions, whereby the right to strike is removed from an entire bargaining

[28]H. D. Woods, Labour Policy in Canada, 2d ed. (Toronto: Macmillan of Canada, 1973), 315.

[29]Amendments to the Quebec Labour Code in 1969 established decentralized machinery for certification procedures which were previously vested in a Labour Relations Board. The Labour Court is the court of last resort in appeals arising out of the earlier stages of the certification procedure. Among its other functions, it also acts as the court of first instance in penal procedures under the code.

unit if 50 percent or more of its members are designated as performing essential services. This provision might well be a serious practical constraint on the exercise of the right to strike. While there is no provision in the public-service statute of British Columbia with respect to essential services, recent legislation in that province, the Essential Services Disputes Act (1977), provides for government intervention in specified public services, some of which could include government employees, when in the opinion of the Cabinet the interruption of these services or part of them would be a threat to life, health, and safety of the economy and welfare of the public.[30]

There is a "Taft-Hartley" provision in Quebec which applies to the civil service as well as to a list of other public services[31] defined in the Labour Code. In addition to the regular conciliation procedures and consequent delays on strike action that apply to all workers under the Labour Code, Article 99 requires public-service employees to give the Minister of Labour a minimum of eight days' notice of intention to strike and provides for an 80-day suspension of the right to strike when, in the opinion of the Cabinet, "a threatened or actual strike in a public service endangers public health or safety" or "interferes with the education of a group of students." This delay is achieved by the appointment of a board of inquiry which is given 60 days in which to ascertain the facts and make a report of its findings. The board has no power to make recommendations. Upon the establishment of a board of inquiry, the attorney general may then petition a superior court judge for an injunction to prevent or terminate a strike if he (the judge) finds that it imperils public health or safety or the education of a group of students. The injunction may continue for 20 days after the 60-day period in which the board of inquiry is required to report. The union then

---

[30]Services specified in the Essential Services Disputes Act are those performed by members of fire fighters', policemen's, and health-care unions. The act provides for a choice of procedures: the government could direct the Labour Relations Board to designate the services that must be maintained for the protection of life, health, safety, etc.; it could order a suspension of the strike or lockout for a nonrenewable period not exceeding 90 days; or it could appoint a special mediator or mediators to assist the parties in reaching a settlement.

[31]The following categories of employers are listed as "public services" in the Quebec Labour Code: municipal and school corporations; hospitals, sanitoriums, and institutions for the mentally ill; orphanages; universities and colleges; telephone and telegraph companies and companies providing boat, tramway, bus, or railway transportation; enterprises for the production, transportation, distribution, or sale of gas, water, or electricity; garbage-removal undertakings; and the services of the government of the province and all other agencies of the government except the Quebec Liquor Board.

acquires the legal right to strike; no further injunction is permitted. This formula for the suspension of the strike is intended to permit the government to act without delay in a situation it judges to be urgent. Its effectiveness depends on its enforceability, as is the general case of proscriptions on the use of the strike. This problem will be considered in a later section.

Administration of the Procedures

In addition to differences between jurisdictions on the contentious issue of the right to strike and the measures to protect essential services, significant differences may also be noted in the administration of conciliation and arbitration procedures. In some provinces, the Minister of Labour still appoints the conciliation officer or board in public-service labor disputes, as he does in the private sector. Public-service unions have complained of the conflict of interest inherent in a system in which a minister administers the conciliation machinery when the government of which he is a member is a party to the dispute. However, while all unions have recognized this problem, they have reacted differently to it in different jurisdictions. Much depends on the general climate of labor relations. For example, while the unions in Saskatchewan have drawn attention to the problem, they have never made a serious issue of it. Conciliation procedures have seldom been required in that province as public-service labor relations have been remarkably peaceful, a brief strike in 1976 being the first since bargaining began. In the few cases where conciliation has taken place, the government has implemented the recommendation of the board. The experience has been different in Quebec, however, where a climate of confidence has been lacking. Some public-service unions in Quebec have refused to use the conciliation machinery provided in the law on the grounds that the minister, being a party to the dispute, could not be trusted in the appointment of a conciliator. The federal and New Brunswick statutes have removed the decision on the conciliation procedure from all political influence by entrusting this function to the chairmen of independent boards (the Public Service Staff Relations Board at the federal level and the Public Service Labour Relations Board in New Brunswick) that also handle certification procedures and administer the machinery for arbitration and adjudication of grievances. While British Columbia has not set up a separate board, the Labour Relations Board of that province performs the same functions.

In the case of arbitration, whether voluntary or compulsory, confidence in the impartiality of the system is of particular importance. This was recognized in the federal statute which was the first to provide for a permanent tribunal for interest arbitration.[32] The pattern has since been followed in other jurisdictions in some of which, like New Brunswick, arbitration is voluntary and in others, like Ontario and Alberta, where it is compulsory.

The Dynamics of Dispute Resolution

The experience in Canada, as in the United States, provides conclusive evidence that laws alone will not determine the course that events will take, particularly when negotiations break down. The variety of experience in jurisdictions that grant the right to strike and the cases of defiance of the law where strikes are prohibited show that the socioeconomic and political environment and the historical context of the bargaining relationship have at least as important an impact on the dynamics of dispute resolution as the procedures for dealing with an impasse provided in the law.

Provincial Impasse Procedures in Practice

In Saskatchewan, for example, there has been only one brief strike by government employees, and that after more than 30 years of peaceful negotiations. In New Brunswick, too, the experience has been peaceful under a decade of permissive legislation. In Quebec, on the other hand, the rash of public-sector strikes that followed the granting of the right to strike has con-

---

[32]The PSSRA provided for the establishment of a permanent arbitration tribunal consisting of a neutral chairman, appointed by the government for a five-year term, and two panels of "partisan" members appointed by the PSSRB to represent the interests of the parties. The act provided for the chairman of the PSSRB to select one member from each panel to sit on the arbitration tribunal when a dispute has been referred to arbitration. The arbitration tribunal has since been absorbed into the structure of the PSSRB by amendments to the PSSRA (S.C. 1974–1975, c. 675. 12). In respect of each dispute referred to arbitration, an arbitration board now consists of a member of the PSSRB, acting as chairman, and two other persons selected from the panels representative of the interests of the parties. As a result of this amendment, there is now a pool of alternate chairmen, and several arbitration boards may sit concurrently. The amendment was recommended in the Finkelman Report as a means of expediting the arbitration procedure which had become seriously bogged down by delays.

tinued virtually unabated. It is generally agreed that the unstable climate of labor relations in Quebec, in both the private and public sectors, particularly in recent years, has had more to do with social and political factors than with the statutory right to strike. When a "Common Front" of public-sector unions entered negotiations in 1972 with the slogan of "Cassez le systeme" (Down with the system), they surely would not have felt inhibited by a prohibition on the strike, any more than they felt obliged to comply with a court injunction to maintain essential services when their leaders decided, for political reasons, that the injunction should be defied. When negotiations are politicized to the point that the legitimacy of the system itself is being questioned, it can hardly be expected that the law would be observed.

There have been brief work stoppages on a few occasions, but no major strikes, by government employees in provinces where the strike is prohibited. There are signs, however, that civil servants in some of these provinces are becoming increasingly militant, both in the demands they are making for changes in the law and in occasional threats to defy it. In one province at least, an eleventh-hour settlement on the eve of a strike deadline, at a figure far higher than the government was originally prepared to consider, indicates that the threat of a strike that would have been illegal was nevertheless taken seriously.

The Federal Experience

The experience under the Public Service Staff Relations Act has not borne out the forebodings of the early prophets of doom. Although the federal service has not been entirely free of strikes since the right to strike was granted, neither was it before. Legal strikes have been few and far between and have, more often than not, involved groups that previously struck illegally. Of the 11 legal strikes of public employees since the PSSRA has been in force, half were by postal workers and air-traffic controllers. Both these groups struck in Canada when the law did not allow it, as they did in the United States.

While legal strikes have been relatively rare under the PSSRA, unlawful strikes have been more common. Some, by postal workers in particular, have occurred during the term of collective agreements, the so-called "closed period" in which strikes are prohibited as a general rule in Canada. Others have involved refusal to work by "designated employees"—those required to maintain previously defined "essential services." The refusal to work by designated employees has given some public-service strikes a greater impact than they otherwise might have had. This was the case when the General Labour and Trades Group struck and the employees designated to keep the airport runways clear decided to defy the law. Concern over unlawful strikes is reflected in recent recommendations to enforce the law more strictly and to increase the penalties for noncompliance. These recommendations will be discussed below in the section on Labor Relations and the Courts.

The Choice of Procedures

The Public Service Staff Relations Act has undoubtedly been the most innovative piece of public-sector labor legislation in Canada. It broke new ground in a number of respects, one of the most important being the establishment of an independent board to administer it. Its most original contribution, however, was its built-in choice of procedures for dispute resolution, including the unique requirement that the choice be made by the bargaining agent prior to the commencement of negotiations.

There have now been four rounds of bargaining under the PSSRA; in other words, each bargaining unit has already negotiated four collective agreements. As expected and hoped by the policy-makers, the initial choices of impasse procedure leaned heavily in favor of the arbitration option, indicating confidence in the arbitration mechanism provided under the act. But a significant number of bargaining units have since switched their original option, with the result that the majority of public employees are now in units committed to the conciliation-board route, with the possibility of a strike at the end of the road. The experience generated by four rounds of bargaining under the PSSRA raises some interesting questions with respect to the acceptability of arbitration, in its present form, as an alternative to the possiblity of a strike. It also provides a unique opportunity to compare the impact on the bargaining process of alternative impasse procedures.

Most of the groups that chose the arbitration route in the first round of bargaining managed to conclude a negotiated agreement before the arbitration stage was reached. However, there was a marked decline in the percentage of negotiated settlements under this option in subsequent rounds and a corresponding increase in resort to arbitration. A recent study of bargaining experience in federal units of 500 or more in which the Treasury Board is the employer, and representing all occupational groups in the service,[33] found that agreements negotiated by the parties without resort to impasse procedure dropped from 83 percent of total settlements under the arbitration option in the first round of bargaining to 47, 56, and 23 percent in the subsequent rounds. A relatively small percentage of settlements in each of the four rounds of bargaining under the arbitration option was reached with the assistance of conciliators after negotiations between the parties had broken down. The rest (5, 33, 34, and 54 percent) went all the way to arbitration. While half of the agreements under the strike option were concluded by the parties themselves in the first round of bargaining, not one settled without third-party intervention in the third. The figures for the second and fourth rounds were 22 and 17 percent, respectively. It is not surprising that the groups that chose the more militant option would be the ones less likely to settle easily. The fact that the percentage of total settlements reached in the intermediate stages of conciliation and mediation was significantly higher in each round of bargaining for the groups where a strike might be the end of the road (39, 67, 70, 67 percent) than for those that had opted for arbitration (12, 20, 10, 23 percent) is also not surprising. The costs of disagreement associated with a strike undoubtedly provide greater pressure to settle than the costs of going to arbitration.

But while the groups that opt for the arbitration route have been more inclined, in each round of bargaining, to go to the terminal stage of the procedure, thereby appearing to confirm the conventional wisdom that arbitration undermines the bargaining process, the percent committed to the procedure as such has shown a dramatic decline, particularly between the third and fourth rounds. The following data on dispute-settlement specifications were compiled in a recent study of interest arbitration in the federal service.[34] They are for all bargaining units certified under the PSSRA, including the units of employees of the "separate employers."

[33]John C. Anderson and Thomas A. Kochan, *Impasse Procedures in the Canadian Federal Service: Effects on the Bargaining Process*, 30 Ind. & Labor Rels. Rev. 283 (April 1977).
[34]L.W.C.S. Barnes and L. A. Kelly, Interest Arbitration in the Federal Public Service (Kingston, Ont.: Queen's University Industrial Relations Centre, 1975).

In March 1970, by which time the certification of bargaining units had been virtually completed, 100 units (representing 81 percent of the employees involved in bargaining) had specified arbitration as the dispute-resolution process; only 14 had opted for conciliation with the ultimate right to strike. While six bargaining units covering 3,500 employees switched from conciliation to arbitration between March 1970 and March 1974, 12 units covering 42,000 employees, including the 22,000 in the General Labour and Trades Groups, changed from arbitration to conciliation in the same period. The pace of change accelerated in the following year. There were 14 switches between April 1974 and October 1975, all of them from arbitration to conciliation. Among those changing were the Clerical and Regulatory Group, with 48,000 members (the largest bargaining unit in the federal public service) and the 22,000 Programme Administration Group. As a result of these changes, 70 percent of the employees covered by collective bargaining in the federal public service are now in units which have chosen the conciliation-board procedure with the ultimate right to strike, compared with 19 percent in 1970.

As would be expected, the groups that originally chose the strike route were the ones that could bring the greatest pressure by threatening to withdraw their services: postal workers, air-traffic controllers, the electronics unit, the heating and power plants unit, the ship crews and ship repair units. The fact that groups that had voluntarily relinquished their right to strike and had been generally satisfied with the arbitration option, particularly in the earlier rounds when large catch-up increases were being awarded, would choose to switch their option in such significant numbers raises some serious questions. The authors of the study on interest arbitration contend that the shift away from the arbitration process reflects serious deficiencies in the system.[35] They cite union complaints on a number of issues, among others the failure of arbitrators to explain their awards and the lengthy delays inherent in the procedure. But the most serious criticism has to do with the limitation on arbitrable issues.

The PSSRA is very specific on the subject matter of arbitral awards, and also on the matters which may not be included. The

----

[35] *Ibid.*

act specifies rates of pay, hours of work, leave entitlements, standards of discipline, and other terms and conditions of employment directly related thereto as permissible subject matter of arbitral awards. No arbitral award may deal with the standards, procedures, or processes governing the appointment, appraisal, promotion, demotion, transfer, layoff, or release of employees or with any term or condition of employment that was not a subject of negotiation between the parties before arbitration was requested. Although there are some limitations on the subject matter of conciliation-board recommendations, strong unions, in practice, have argued before conciliation boards on issues technically not subject to negotiation and have occasionally worked out informal arrangements on them. This would be impossible under arbitration. Union leaders and some independent observers have been suggesting that the scope of arbitral issues be broadened to make the arbitration option more palatable. However, neither of the major inquiries into the operation of the PSSRA recommended changes in this respect.

According to the most recent reports, the wholesale movement of the past three years away from the arbitration option now appears to have been halted, or even marginally reversed.[36] This may vindicate the decision by Finkelman and the Joint Committee to leave the scope of arbitration unchanged. It may also reflect certain improvements in the procedure that have been introduced by the arbitrators themselves. There have been noticeable efforts to reduce the delays and a growing willingness by arbitration tribunals to give the rationale for their awards. However, the most recent developments may also reflect factors of a temporary nature which are external to the system itself. It has been suggested that the combined effects of the anti-inflation program, the general unemployment situation, and the overall state of the economy have made the strike threat less attractive to the unions. It may also be that the bargaining units that had remained with the arbitration option by the end of 1976 were those which, for one reason or another, find the strike threat completely unacceptable. There may just be no more switches to be made.

---

[36]L.W.C.S. Barnes, *Dispute Resolution in the Federal Public Service,* 2 IR Research Reports (Kingston, Ont.: IR Research Services, January 1978).

Public-Service Labor Relations and the Courts

Resort to the courts in public-sector labor relations has taken three principal forms: injunctions to prevent or terminate a strike, prosecutions for failure to observe such injunctions, and prosecutions for calling or engaging in strikes specifically prohibited by law, as in the case of police and fire fighters in some of the provinces and designated employees at the federal level.

Resort to the courts has generally not been required to enforce the law in provinces where strikes are still prohibited. Of the provinces that grant the right to strike to government employees, only Quebec uses the courts to limit it. Article 99 of the Quebec Labour Code envisages an important role for the courts in disputes involving a wide range of public services including government employment. This is the Canadian "Taft-Hartley" provision described above under which the government may seek a nonrenewable court injunction for 80 days in the case of strikes which it considers a threat to "public health, safety or the education of a group of students." Injunctions issued under this clause have been obeyed in certain cases. But in other cases they have been defied, leading to the next step in legal procedure— prosecution for contempt of court, i.e., for failure to comply with the injunction. The most dramatic example of defiance of an injunction occurred in 1972, because of both the magnitude and nature of the strike and the prominent labor leaders who were involved. When the Common Front of public-service employees declared a general strike, hospital workers ignored an injunction to maintain essential services, on the advice of the top union leadership. Prosecutions of the union leaders resulted in heavy prison sentences. But the political ramifications of putting the union leaders in jail were such as to ensure that the procedure will not be repeated.

The tendency toward resort to the courts in labor disputes, particularly in the public sector, has come under considerable criticism in Quebec. In an interesting decision in 1974 the chief justice of the Superior Court of Quebec refused to maintain a charge of contempt of court against a municipal transportation union for failure to comply with an injunction. While the technical legal reason was that the court lacked jurisdiction in the particular case, the judge took serious issue with the use of injunctive procedures by means of which, in his view, the public authority was shifting responsibility to the courts for matters that should be handled at the political level. He noted that labor problems that affect the public are the proper responsibility of government. A recent committee of inquiry into public-service labor relations in Quebec has recommended that the Cabinet be empowered to act on its own initiative, i.e., without resort to courts, to postpone (not prohibit) a strike in cases where it judges the public interest to be at stake.[37] The same committee recommended that the penalties for illegal actions be reduced, the rationale being that fines imposed in the past have been unreasonably high, and consequently virtually impossible to enforce. As for imposing prison sentences on union leaders, these have been self-defeating, not unlike the experience in the United States.

While the Joint Parliamentary Committee at the federal level has recommended that the penalties for illegal activities be substantially increased in cases involving designated employees, its general aim was to limit legal proceedings to the most serious infractions of the law. The joint committee would increase the powers of the PSSRB by adding to its present power to declare a strike illegal the power to issue a "cease and desist" order that would have the effect of a court order and be enforceable as such. No action has yet been taken on these recommendations.

The Future of Collective Bargaining in the Public Sector

The inconsistencies in policy and practice between jurisdictions and the reevaluations that are currently taking place reinforce the conclusion that labor relations in the public sector are still in a fluid and experimental stage in Canada. The only prediction that can be made with certainty is that public-service bargaining, in one form or another, is definitely here to stay. But it will be a long time, if ever, before a consensus can be reached on the most appropriate mechanism, at each stage of the bargaining relationship, by which to accommodate the rights that are available to workers in the private sector to the particular characteristics and responsibilities of public-service employment.

Of all the issues that plague the policy-makers and the parties,

---

[37]Rapport de la commission d'étude et de consultation sur la révision du régime de négociations collectives dans les services publics et para-publics (Québec: 15 fevrier, 1978).

the question of dispute settlement remains paramount, and the one most difficult to resolve. For if there is one lesson to be learned from the Canadian experience, it is that laws alone will not determine the form that labor relations will take. This has been demonstrated by the variety of experience in jurisdictions that have granted the right to strike, and also by cases of defiance of the law where the right to strike is prohibited.

Some jurisdictions seem unlikely to abandon their prohibition on the strike, at least in the foreseeable future. Most of these, however, have recognized the importance of providing impartial mechanisms, in the form of independent boards, to administer the dispute-settlement machinery. There is a growing realization that unions must at least be assured of the impartiality of the available impasse procedures if a prohibition on the strike is to be respected.

For those jurisdictions that have accepted the strike as a legitimate element of the bargaining process, the crucial problem is the definition of "essential services" and the guarantee that these will be maintained. Where a private right, the right to strike, becomes a public wrong by jeopardizing the health or safety of a community, it is clear that the public interest must prevail. Although provisions already exist in a number of jurisdictions to ensure that essential services will be maintained in the event of a legal strike, the defiance of these provisions on a number of occasions has shown that present statutory penalties for noncompliance are not a deterrent if workers are sufficiently determined to defy them. While recent inquiry commissions have addressed themselves to the problem of defining essential services and ensuring that they be maintained, the problem of enforceability remains crucial. Unless this problem is satisfactorily resolved, and it is unlikely that it can be entirely, ad hoc legislative measures, appropriate to particular circumstances, remain the last resort. The elected representatives of the people have the ultimate power, and responsibility, to respond to a threat to the public welfare. This presumes, of course, that the federal Parliament or provincial legislature, as the case may be, is in session or available for recall when an emergency arises. An amendment to the PSSRA, similar to an existing provision in the Canada Labour Code, has been introduced in the federal Parliament to empower the Cabinet to suspend the right to strike during the election period following the dissolution of Parliament where, in its opinion, a strike would be against the public interest. The measure has not yet been enacted but, in anticipation of an early dissolution, a special law to the same effect was enacted in April 1978 to avert a threatened postal strike during the election period.

CHAPTER 9

FUTURE OF COLLECTIVE BARGAINING IN THE PUBLIC SECTOR

Benjamin Aaron*

Exercises in "futurology," as I have noted elsewhere,[1] are apt to be unrewarding in areas outside the physical sciences and related fields. The foregoing essays in this volume provide ample evidence that our vision of the future of specific aspects of collective bargaining in the public sector[2] must necessarily be as through a glass, darkly.

Extent of Bargaining

This point is made perhaps most emphatically in John Burton's essay (Chapter 1) on the extent of bargaining in the public sector. After extensive review and analysis of the relevant data, Burton concludes that the mushroomlike growth of bargaining-organization[3] membership in government employment in the 1960s was largely unanticipated before the fact and is not fully explainable after the fact. Even more surprising is his judgment that public-policy changes were a relatively unimportant factor in the surge of membership in bargaining organizations. If Burton's conclusions are correct, there seems little reason to suppose that we can confidently forecast the future of the extent of collective bargaining in the public sector.

In the short term, however, there is at least the possibility of

*School of Law, University of California, Los Angeles.
[1]Benjamin Aaron, *Legal Framework of Industrial Relations,* in The Next Twenty-Five Years of Industrial Relations (Madison, Wis.: Industrial Relations Research Association, 1973), 101.
[2]By "public sector," I mean only government employment, whether at the federal, state, or local level.
[3]Employees in the public sector are represented in some cases by unions and in others by associations. Although the differences between the two types of organizations, in respect of collective bargaining attitudes and tactics, are gradually disappearing, some associations still object to being called unions. The term "bargaining organizations" employed in this chapter is designed to overcome this difficulty.

a rather anomalous development: continuing, steady, if not spectacular growth in the total membership of all public-sector bargaining organizations, accompanied by a diminution in the membership of some, together with an overall decline in bargaining effectiveness in the context of an unfavorable economic and political environment. For example, the American Federation of State, County, and Municipal Employees (AFSCME), having absorbed the 262,000-member Civil Service Employees Association of New York, has become the largest union affiliated with the AFL-CIO, paying a per capita dues for a membership of more than one million. At the same time, AFSCME's District 37 in New York is struggling to retain its 105,000 members in the face of New York City's work force reductions and hard-bargaining stance—part of the price of continued willingness by the federal government to rescue the city from its chronically desperate financial plight. Similarly, in California, the sharp reduction in local property taxes as a result of the adoption of Proposition 13 is already causing cut-backs in government employment; moreover, politically sensitive public employers will almost certainly stiffen their resistance to the bargaining demands of their employees. There is a substantial likelihood that these conditions will recur in an increasing number of other cities and states.

The question is, how will such developments affect the extent of bargaining in the public sector? Burton's study suggests the possibility of two quite different, and countervailing results. On the one hand, bargaining organizations of public employees may pull themselves up by their own bootstraps by lobbying successfully to strengthen collective bargaining laws in states that already have them and to obtain enactment of such laws in states that do not presently have them; success in these efforts would, presumably, lead to increases in membership and further gains at the bargaining table. On the other hand, the legislative process is characteristically slow, and there is usually a considerable lag between enactment of new legislation and any tangible benefits to its intended beneficiaries; meanwhile, lack of immediate success in improving the lot of their members may lead to defections and consequent loss of membership by many public-sector bargaining organizations.

On balance, it appears that organization in the public sector will continue, but at a greatly reduced rate, for the foreseeable

future. Much depends upon factors over which public employees have little or no control, including the general state of
the economy, the rate of growth in public employment, and
shifts in political power at both federal and state levels. A factor
of particular significance is the current and rather pervasive
rebellion against higher taxes, growing government employment, and greater centralization of power in the hands of the
federal government. This rebellion is not new, but its present
manifestation has been exploited more skillfully and seems better and more purposefully organized than at any previous time
in the past 40 years. The term "government employee" has now
joined "politician" and "bureaucrat" in the lexicon of oppro-
brium of many members of the general public who urge sharp
reductions in government services and greater reliance upon
the private sector to provide them. It is still too early to discern
whether this new mood signals a major change in our society,
or merely a temporary uprising, or, perhaps, something in between—a permanent, though more subdued than at present,
countervailing pressure against the growth of government and
expansion in the number, size, and power of employee bargaining organizations in the public sector.

Unionism in the Public Sector

Prospects for Growth

Despite the spectacular growth of AFSCME, the outlook in
the next decade for public-employee bargaining organizations
is not particularly sanguine, although, in the judgment of James
Stern (Chapter 2), total membership growth of such organizations, while tapering off, will probably not go into an absolute
decline, as has the AFL-CIO in the past few years.[4]

Faced with the prospect of a declining growth rate at best,
public-sector bargaining organizations may be expected to un-
dergo certain changes in structure and in ideology. Once again,
however, the anticipated changes are likely to offset each other.
One may reasonably anticipate continuing mergers and consoli-
dations among bargaining organizations, but, as Stern points
out, there is a stronger emphasis on local decision-making in the

---

[4]The latest (1977) membership figures available for the AFL-CIO reveal that since
1975 its membership has declined by about 500,000, and is now about 13.5 million.
AFL-CIO Executive Committee Report, BNA Daily Labor Report, No. 235, December
6, 1977, E13–15.

public-sector bargaining organizations than in those in the private sector. This is to be expected because the wide variety of state laws and local ordinances applicable to members of a national organization makes it impossible for such an organization to formulate a single national bargaining policy that will be applicable to all affiliates. Thus, the added economic power and administrative efficiency normally resulting from a merger may be offset by the demand for autonomy in general policy-making by the constituent units of the new organization.

The Federal Executive Branch

Stern's essay indicates that the outlook for the principal bargaining organizations of employees in the federal executive branch is mixed, but generally not very promising. The substantive limitations (particularly the prohibition against compulsory payment of union dues) of the various executive orders governing labor-management relations between the executive departments and their employees, combined with administrative interference with arbitral decisions in rights disputes by the office of the Comptroller General,[5] have hampered effective collective bargaining and have resulted in a large percentage of "free riders" in some of the organizations.

The present situation was dramatically summed up by former Secretary of Labor W. L. Usery, during his tenure as Director of the Federal Mediation and Conciliation Service:

> The truth is that there is precious little real collective bargaining in the federal sector—and far too much collective begging. . . .
> The reason there is so little true collective bargaining . . . is because there is so little that can be bargained for.
> Congress preempts the economic issues. . . .
> Many of the primary noneconomic issues—seniority, job transfers, discipline, promotion, the agency shop, and the union shop, are nonnegotiable—because of a combination of law, regulation, management rights, and thousands of pages in the Federal Personnel Manual.
> The result, all too frequently, is a contract that simply restates what management says management will do—providing only the protection to grieve should management violate its own rules.[6]

---

[5]See John Kagel, *Grievance Arbitration in the Federal Service: How Final and Binding?*, 51 Ore. L. Rev. 134 (1971).
[6]W. J. Usery, Jr., at the Collective Bargaining Symposium for Labor Relations Executives, Warrenton, Va., July 8, 1974.

Usery predicted that the executive orders "will one day be replaced by legislation,"[7] presumably transferring many substantive issues from management's exclusive domain into the arena of collective bargaining. That day seems at the moment, however, to be far removed—too far, indeed, to permit any reliable prediction as to when, or even if, it will come. The Carter Administration has pushed for a comprehensive reorganization of the federal Civil Service and improved collective bargaining mechanisms, but the mood of the Congress sitting in 1978 is typified by the heightened concern over the question of whether the armed services will become organized—a largely irrelevant issue.

The Postal Service

The system of collective bargaining in the federal service that most nearly approximates that in the private sector is, of course, the one established in the quasi-governmental Postal Service by the Postal Reorganization Act of 1970. The results so far have been mixed. Three national agreements between the Postal Service and the principal labor organizations have been negotiated, and the principle of joint decision-making has been established. Contrary to the general situation in government employment, Postal Service management is far more skilled and much better organized than the representatives of the several labor organizations with which it deals—at least in respect of the day-to-day administration of the national agreement. Indeed, the failure thus far of the postal unions to eliminate grievances that are obviously without merit and to present effectively those which appear to have some foundation has put great strains on the grievance-arbitration system established by the national agreement.

Under the Postal Reorganization Act, the employees are forbidden to strike; the ultimate means of resolving interest disputes is arbitration. As of September 1978, new contract negotiations had reached an impasse, the tentative agreement accepted by union officers had been rejected by their memberships, and the final process of mediation-arbitration had begun. Despite official denials, it seems clear that the federal govern-

[7] *Ibid.*

ment interfered actively in the negotiations in order to ensure that the Postal Service's wage proposal would not exceed a predetermined percentage compatible with the Administration's anti-inflationary policies. This government intervention caused considerable resentment on the part of the rank-and-file Postal Service employees and was a major factor leading to both rejection of the tentative agreement and sporadic wildcat strikes across the country.

The apparent inability of the leadership of the larger postal unions to control their members, the superior organization on the management side, and the unwillingness of the federal government to remain aloof from new contract negotiations suggest that labor-management relations in this sector will be somewhat unstable in the years immediately ahead.

Education

Among the larger specialized groups of government employees, the outlook for bargaining organizations of teachers seems the brightest. As Stern has observed, one of the major developments in public-sector labor relations has been the shift of teachers from a passive role to that of militant unionists. Continued rivalry between the American Federation of Teachers (AFT) and the National Education Association (NEA), and between their respective affiliates, has tended to increase organizational successes rather than to diminish them. In most communities, the economic welfare of teachers in the elementary and secondary grades, up through the first two years of college, is almost entirely dependent upon property taxes, which are currently under sustained attack, not only in California, but also in other parts of the country.

Here again, we may expect continued organizational gains by the AFT and the NEA, even while they may be suffering from reductions in jobs and little or no successes in negotiations over economic issues. In situations of this kind, the law of inertia seems to apply: once a certain degree of militancy has been achieved, it tends to continue in spite of various obstacles, unless it meets one that can be neither surmounted nor sidestepped. On the other hand, the tendency among unorganized teachers to remain apathetic toward organizational initiatives may well be broken by the shock of the latest assault on their jobs and their working conditions.

The same cannot be said, however, for faculty members of state colleges and universities above the junior-college level. The great organizing drives of the 1960s among teachers at the lower levels left the situation in higher education virtually unchanged. They did, however, have the belated effect of compelling the American Association of University Professors, as well as independent associations of faculty members in a number of four-year colleges and universities, to focus on the issue of collective bargaining for faculty members, and in some cases to enter the lists against affiliates of the AFT and the NEA for the right to represent units of faculty members. For the most part, however, college and university professors, especially those with tenure, have remained cool to the idea of collective bargaining, either because they are reasonably satisfied with things as they are, because they distrust the motives, the philosophy, or the competence of the organizations seeking their support, or because, although dissatisfied with their present lot, they prefer to seek to improve it in other, more traditional ways.

Yet there is at least the possibility that this mood may change to a more aggressive one. By way of illustration, faculty salaries at the University of California—the largest and most prestigious state university in the nation—have declined steadily in terms of real earnings and comparability with both private and public universities of similar rank during the past decade. A recent survey of faculty opinion indicated that a majority favored some form of "collective bargaining"; but the answers to more specific questions suggested that relatively few understood what the term implied, and that their endorsement of collective bargaining was, in varying degrees, offset by their preference for qualifications incompatible with it. The point is, however, that if the prospects for tenure of junior faculty, the economic status of the entire faculty, and the opportunities for recruiting new faculty continue to deteriorate, those who favor collective bargaining may eventually gain the upper hand.

Management Organization for Collective Bargaining in the Public Sector

Management Attitudes

In order for collective bargaining to endure in the public sector, government managers must establish their credibility as an effective countervailing force against the political and economic power of the employee bargaining organizations. This formidable task was at first made still more difficult by the attitude of managers at all levels of government; collectively, and with all too few exceptions, they presented in their behavior complete confirmation of the aphorism that those who pay no attention to the mistakes of the past are condemned to repeat them in the future.

Long after the portents of the approaching collective bargaining revolution in the public sector had become unmistakably clear, most government managers persisted either in pretending that the problem did not exist or in magisterially ordering the tidal wave about to engulf them to recede. When, finally, they were forced to confront reality, some of them acted as if the ship of state had been captured by pirates and that unconditional surrender was the price of survival; a somewhat greater number, however, still unwilling to abandon their fantasies and continuing to act as if nothing had happened, violated both the letter and the spirit of the new laws governing their relations with their employees, while neglecting to prepare for the day when those laws would be enforced against them.

This strange initial failure of government managers to adjust to the changing attitudes and patterns of behavior of their employees can, in retrospect, be attributed to two major factors. The first was their unshakable conviction that the differences between the public and private sectors were so great that no useful purpose would be served by studying the development of collective bargaining in the latter. The second was their belief, often proved to be correct, that even under the new dispensations they could successfully frustrate efforts by their employees to engage in genuine collective bargaining by drastically limiting the scope of bargaining and maintaining a broad area of undisturbed management rights.

The second factor, bolstered by some state statutes and local ordinances, as well as by the executive order governing federal employees, remains a major barrier to genuine collective bargaining in the public sector. The myth of the complete uniqueness of government employment is slowly eroding, however, although it is generally conceded that there are some genuine and important differences between employment in the public and private sectors. Thus, an increasing number of government managers are becoming aware of both the need to learn more about labor-management relations in the private sector and the benefits that can be derived from that knowledge.

Outside Pressures

The problems of developing an effective management organization that meets the responsibilities of a system of shared decision-making, while at the same time preserving management's right to ensure that the mission of a given agency will be carried out, are analyzed in detail by Milton Derber (Chapter 3). Of growing significance is the role of various citizen groups, which, under the banner of participatory democracy, seek ways in which to advance their special interests. The pressures that these groups exert are directed primarily at management; employee organizations usually feel it indirectly. Thus, most state "sunshine laws" have been construed to require only that meetings of legislative bodies be held in public. It is doubtful that laws requiring active participation of outside groups in the collective bargaining process will prove feasible.

That the pressures upon public managers by special-interest groups have already, and will continue to be, effective in some situations seems clear. In relatively small communities, one may assume that the requirement that all negotiated collective bargaining agreements or "memoranda of understanding" be ratified by the voters in a special election[8] will continue to gain in popularity, at least during the period of widespread public revolt against any increase in the cost of government. I think it doubtful, however, that such a procedure will ever be adopted by many of the larger towns and cities; and it seems to me much more likely that as both public managers and the bargaining organizations become more skilled and sophisticated in bargaining techniques, both sides will take steps to neutralize what they regard as undue interference by outside pressure groups. The latter will thus have to confine themselves to the traditional practice of lobbying the appropriate legislative bodies rather than the bargaining parties.

---

[8]See, e.g., statements by David H. Rodgers, Mayor of Spokane, Wash., and A. Herbert Abshire, President, National Public Employer Labor Relations Assn., in 8 LMRS Newsletter 2 (September 1977), and 8 LMRS Newsletter 3 (October 1977), respectively.

Supervisors

The rapid sophistication of government managers in bargaining philosophy and techniques is a consummation devoutly to be wished. Despite a slow start, for the reasons previously mentioned, this process is now going forward at all levels of government, although not at a uniform pace and with many exceptions. Most government bodies are now aware of the need for a strong management team to represent them in contract negotiations. Derber notes that the majority of states with specific laws dealing with public-sector collective bargaining, as well as the federal executive branch, have opted to treat supervisors as they are treated under the National Labor Relations Act. This means that supervisors can be made key members of the management team. A number of states, however, permit supervisors to bargain collectively in units of their own. Thus, the pattern of future relationships of supervisors to higher management and to the employees they supervise is still unclear. For the short term, it appears that the present diversity of practice will continue. I think it likely, however, that in the relatively near future serious efforts will be made in states and communities now permitting supervisors to bargain separately, or as part of the bargaining unit they supervise, to remove the bargaining rights of supervisors and to incorporate them in the management group.

It should be borne in mind, however, that many, if not most, associations of government employees have traditionally accepted into membership not only supervisory employees, but also top managerial employees. This policy had much to do with the resistance within such organizations to the idea that they should switch their principal activities from lobbying to collective bargaining. Even now, after most of them have apparently accepted the inevitability of the latter development, supervisor-members continue to exercise considerable influence, of a relatively conservative character, on their policies.

In a few governmental services—notably those performed by the police, fire fighters, educators, and social workers—the rank-and-file employees seem to prefer to retain their traditionally close relationship with first-line supervisors and to include the latter in their bargaining units. In most areas of public employment, however, particularly those in which unions have taken over employee associations, the apparent dominant feeling is that supervisors should be excluded from the bargaining unit of employees whom they supervise, although this contention is usually accompanied by the argument that supervisors should be allowed to comprise a bargaining unit of their own.

The status of supervisors under applicable legislation in California, for example, has been among the most controversial issues raised every time proposals are made for new legislation covering labor-management relations in government employment. At least some of the bargaining organizations insisting upon bargaining rights for supervisors, however, have indicated a willingness to amend their constitutions to exclude supervisors from membership in return for a statutory provision for a compulsory agency shop. The rationale of that position is that the loss of dues paid by supervisory members would be considerable and would have to be offset by the payment of a compulsory "service fee" by all employees in the bargaining unit. The expulsion of supervisors, as Stern points out, could be expected to result in a more militant stance being taken by the bargaining organization in its dealings with the government employer. At the same time, this move might also lead to inclusion of the supervisors in the employer's management team and increase its effective resistance to the organization's demands.

Ultimately, the status of supervisors who are members of bargaining organizations in collective bargaining rests with legislative bodies or administrative agencies. My best guess, however, is that future attempts to organize groups of government employees not previously organized will probably not include supervisors.

Multi-Employer Bargaining Units

Derber has observed that there has been surprisingly little interest among local management groups in establishing multi-employer bargaining units with corresponding coordinating organizations. Such an alignment seems to me, however, to be virtually inevitable, if only in order to match similar developments among employee bargaining organizations. It is also required as an effective counter to strikes by particular groups of government employees, and as a means of reducing the number of what the late Arthur Ross termed "orbits of coercive comparison."[9]

---

[9]Arthur M. Ross, Trade Union Wage Policy (Berkeley: University of California Press, 1956), 53–64.

Management Training

Experience has shown that properly conceived and executed training programs in collective negotiations and contract administration produce excellent results. Generally, managers have access to greater amounts of money for such training than do the employee bargaining organizations, but Derber has found that government managers have scarcely begun to take advantage of this opportunity. This situation, too, is likely to change rather rapidly. Once government management comes to understand that its relationship with employee bargaining organizations is a dynamic one, subject to constant pressures for change, it will also learn to appreciate the need for the continuous training of its supervisors and executives to keep pace with new developments and techniques.

I look for no major changes in the attitudes or practices of managers in the federal executive branch in the absence of more liberal legislation to replace the present executive order. Managers do only what they consider necessary, and the lack of a need to show a profit in dollars and cents makes those in government more indifferent than they might otherwise be to such aspects of employment as morale and productivity. Many state and local government managers are now required by law, however, to engage in some form of collective negotiations with representatives of their employees. They have been forced, therefore—often against their wishes—to come to grips with problems of labor-management relations that were previously ignored. A large number of government managers have already developed an awareness of their problems and acquired the skills to deal with them rather rapidly, and I expect this trend to continue at an accelerating rate. I do not mean to suggest, however, that the path of collective bargaining in state and local governments will therefore run smoothly. The constitutional, political, and bureaucratic considerations discussed in Derber's essay point up the magnitude and complexity of management's task in the public sector.

The Impact of Collective Bargaining on Compensation in the Public Sector

The same controversy over the impact of collective bargaining on wage rates that has continued for so long in the private sector exists also in the public sector. Daniel Mitchell deals with these and related questions in his essay (Chapter 4) and further comment on his major findings and conclusions is beyond both the scope of this chapter and my own professional competence. There are several points, however, that have particular significance for the future of collective bargaining in the public sector.

Public-Employee Bargaining and Urban Financial Problems

Mitchell notes that public-employee bargaining organizations have been widely blamed for the financial plight of the big cities. His analysis of the "New York City Syndrome" leads him to conclude that the New York City problem was the result of an unfortunate compounding of several factors, including erosion of an industrial base, a growing level of dependency on city services, and shortsighted budgeting, and that although collective bargaining may have speeded up the city's slide into bankruptcy, it was not the sole cause, and probably not the principal cause. Indeed, he finds that the chief source of pressure for more revenue for labor costs comes from the employment side rather than from the wage side.

These findings suggest that the financial plight of our big cities is likely to continue, regardless of the rise or decline of collective bargaining in the public sector. On the other hand, they also suggest that if the general public can be persuaded to demand fewer government services, thereby slowing down appreciably the rapid growth in government employment (largely at state and municipal levels), the main cause of increased labor costs will be eliminated; for, as Mitchell points out, pressure for expansion of government activities and programs has stemmed from forces exogenous to collective bargaining.

Counterpressures Against Increased Labor Costs

Additional factors noted by Mitchell will exert greater counterpressure against increased labor costs in government employment in the future. The prevailing-wage provision in many city and county charters is under heavy attack and will, doubtless, be repealed in a number of instances. Moreover, unlike the employee bargaining organizations, government managers are not free to disregard budgetary information, but must use it as the principal basis for formulating their bargaining positions. As managers become more skilled in bargaining, they will be better able to convince the employee organizations that resistance to their demands has a factual, rather than a purely ideological, basis. In this regard, they will be able, at least in the short term, to exploit the prevailing mood of the country against any expansion of government services and in favor of cutting out "government waste"—a term that is varyingly defined, depending upon the points of view of the numerous, competing interest groups in any given community.

One hopes, however, that government managers will not misread this mood as favoring an all-out assault against the principle of collective bargaining in the public sector. As I shall explain at the conclusion of this chapter, it is either too early or too late for such an attempt.

Dispute Resolution in the Public Sector

It is unfortunate, but true, that popular attitudes toward collective bargaining in the public sector seem to be unduly influenced by the incidence of strikes by government employees, to which the great majority of the general public is opposed. But strikes, as Thomas Kochan reminds us in his essay (Chapter 5), occur because of the absence or the failure of alternative methods for resolving collective bargaining impasses. In respect of this aspect of public-sector collective bargaining, therefore, the emphasis now and for the foreseeable future should be (1) on how to prevent impasses from arising and (2) on weighing the advantages and disadvantages of a number of methods, including the strike, for resolving those impasses which will inevitably occur.

Advantages of Pluralistic Approaches to Strike Legislation

The country is fortunate, I think, in not having a single, uniform law governing the procedure of impasse resolution. In the absence of such a law, the individual states have engaged in a number of interesting experiments for resolving impasses, thereby adding substantially to the general knowledge about that problem. Kochan's conclusion, reached after an exhaustive review of the available evidence, deserves the same credence now generally accorded the economist's aphorism that there is no such thing as a free lunch; for it is equally true, as he says, that there is no "best way" for resolving all types of disputes. Perhaps, if that idea gains common acceptance, we may be spared, so far as the public sector is concerned, from the futility of the seemingly endless search by legislators and labor-law scholars for a single formula for dealing with "emergency disputes."

Some aspects of strikes by government employees are well known by now: the total number is increasing annually; the existence of laws making strikes illegal has not been a significant deterrent; and punishment of strikers, more often than not, is inconsistent, unequal, and arbitrary. That many strikes have occurred only because of an absence of any credible alternative cannot be doubted. The task ahead, therefore, is not only to improve the quality of public-sector collective bargaining and continue to evaluate the experience under existing laws, but also to keep experimenting with new methods of impasse resolution for dealing with specialized types of disputes.

Choices of Impasse-Resolution Techniques

The choice of an appropriate impasse-resolution mechanism obviously depends upon the nature of the dispute involved. It is important to keep an open mind concerning the advantages, as well as the disadvantages, that conventional wisdom has assigned to strikes and compulsory arbitration, as well as to the various procedures falling somewhere in between those polarities. A society that deplores strikes by government employees cannot afford to ignore the alternative of compulsory arbitration, despite the undesirable features of that procedure. Just as there is no best method for settling impasses, so is there no method that is without any undesirable aspect.

As of mid-1978, the ratio of states that have opted for compulsory arbitration of public-sector impasses to those that grant a limited right to strike is a little more than two to one. There does not seem much likelihood either that this ratio will change significantly in the near future, or that compulsory arbitration will be abandoned in favor of combinations of mediation and fact-finding that do not necessarily result in some resolution of the dispute. Indeed, states that have thus far authorized the use only of inconclusive procedures, and have experienced a larger number of strikes than is acceptable, may eventually conclude that the best way to control strikes, without resorting to compulsory arbitration, is to authorize the use of the strike within carefully defined limits.

Lockouts

I have predicted, on several previous occasions, that the use of the lockout by government managers is a potent weapon in collective bargaining and one that will very likely be used more frequently in the future. Not so many years ago, the possibility of strikes by government employees was viewed by most persons as simply unthinkable. When the unthinkable became a reality, the modified version of the former view was that strikes by employees in "essential services," such as police and fire fighters, were unthinkable. A number of strikes by these groups of employees have demonstrated that although they may result in temporary and severe hardship, government has not been paralyzed and the world has continued to turn. The knowledge that most government services can be temporarily discontinued without undue hardship to the citizen-consumers will, I believe, persuade government managers increasingly to attempt to re-solve collective bargaining impasses on favorable terms by lock-ing out their employees.

Essential Considerations

The one proposed solution that I feel sure will not work is that embodied recently in a proposed initiative to amend the Califor-nia constitution by prohibiting both strikes by government em-ployees *and* arbitration of interest disputes, even when agreed to by the government employer. Fortunately, this ill-conceived plan did not receive enough signatures to qualify it for a place on the ballot. The problem of eliminating strikes in such dis-putes can be solved only by providing one or more credible and workable options; it will merely be further complicated by out-lawing not only strikes but also effective alternatives acceptable to the parties to a given dispute.

Public-Sector Labor Legislation

In her "evolutionary analysis" of public-sector labor legisla-tion (Chapter 6), Betty Schneider traces the gradual disappear-ance of statutory and judicial barriers to collective bargaining by

PUBLIC-SECTOR BARGAINING

308

government employees in the key areas of right to bargain, impasse resolution and the strike, scope of bargaining, and union security. She concludes that despite these developments, there remain tensions between the concept of government sovereignty and that of bilateral, or shared, decision-making authority.

Schneider also recognizes the strong, perhaps controlling, influences that the prevailing economic and political environmentalists have upon the continued development of public-sector collective bargaining. She believes that the reluctance of Congress to enact a federal statute covering the collective bargaining rights of all government employees, in the same way that the amended National Labor Relations and Labor Management Relations Acts cover those of employees in the private sector, is due more to the general feeling that government employees are now about as "equal" as they ought to be, rather than to doubts about the constitutionality of such legislation.

Federal Minimum Standards Versus a Federal Preemptive Law

I think Schneider is right. *National League of Cities* v. *Usery*[10] was a bad decision and should be overruled. That it will be is very doubtful, but the Supreme Court has other ways of dealing with unsound precedents, the principal one being to "distinguish" it from subsequent cases on the basis of its particular facts. Even assuming, however, that the *National League of Cities* case does not negate the possibility of a preemptive federal law governing labor-management relations in the public sector, the question remains whether the enactment of such a policy would be in the best interests of the country.

In my view, the nation has benefited immeasurably from the experimentation with public-sector collective bargaining laws within what Justice Holmes called "the insulated chambers of the several states."[11] A substantial body of descriptive and analytical research provides ample evidence that the extreme variety of labor-management problems to be found in the different states is the result of the particular economic, political, and social climates in those states. To adopt a law for all government

[10]426 U.S. 833, 96 S.Ct. 2465, 22 W.H. Cases 1064 (1976).
[11]*Truax* v. *Corrigan*, 257 U.S. 312, 344 (1921) (dissenting opinion).

employees similar to those governing labor relations in the private sector, and administered by the National Labor Relations Board or some other agency in Washington, would be, in my judgment, the height of folly. What I[12] and others[13] have suggested as an alternative is a different kind of law designed merely to establish a minimum standard for all federal, state, and municipal employees. According to my proposal, the federal law would establish the following: (1) the absolute right of all government employees at state and local levels to organize and to engage in collective bargaining over wages, hours, and working conditions; (2) the right to an orderly procedure for dealing with all questions concerning representation, including determination of appropriate units, conduct of elections, and related matters; (3) the right to negotiate, but not to compel, a provision for the final and binding arbitration of grievances by a neutral third party; (4) the right, in the absence of the legal right to strike, to an impasse procedure leading to specific settlements of interest disputes; (5) the right of access to an independent agency with the power and the means to administer adequately all provisions of the statute; and (6) the right of judicial review of any final orders of that agency. Finally, recognizing that the federal law would probably contain a statutory proscription against strikes by any government employees, I recommend a provision that would permit individual states to grant the right to strike to their own employees.

At least for the foreseeable future, this seems to me to be the only type of law that has much of a chance of enactment by the Congress, and that chance is a slim one. In any event, it would be better to have no federal legislation of any kind in this area than to subject the states to a single, preemptive statute that would put an end to the valuable experimentation now taking place.

---

[12]See Benjamin Aaron, *Federal Bills Analyzed and Appraised,* 5 LMRS Newsletter 4 (November 1974).

[13]See, e.g., statement of Arvid Anderson, Chairman, New York City Office of Collective Bargaining, at Hearings on H.R. 12532, H.R. 7684, & H.R. 9324 Before the Special Subcommittee on Labor of the House Committee on Education and Labor, April 18, 1972.

Judicial Response to Public-Sector Arbitration

In the early stages of development of collective bargaining in the public sector, management's preoccupation with the concept of government sovereignty, and its paranoid fear of making the slightest concession to bilateral decision-making, resulted in widespread resistance to the idea of grievance arbitration, which is, of course, one of the key principles underlying our national labor policy for the private sector. The more daring managers were willing to experiment with "advisory arbitration," a meaningless and misleading term to describe what is no more than fact-finding with nonbinding recommendations. Genuine arbitration—a decision by a third party or parties that is final and binding on both disputants—was eschewed primarily on the ground that it constituted an impermissible limitation on government sovereignty.

Government management's opposition to interest arbitration had a firmer foundation than the sovereignty concept; its most persuasive argument was, and is, that the submission of disputes over new terms and conditions of employment to an independent third party constitutes an unlawful delegation of legislative power.

The development of judicial doctrine in this area of public-sector collective bargaining is traced by Joseph Grodin (Chapter 7). He finds that the courts have generally accepted the constitutional legitimacy of grievance arbitration in the public sector, but have been reluctant to defer to arbitration awards to the extent decreed by the Supreme Court in the private sector.[14] He also notes that in respect of the legality of interest arbitration, the courts are divided.

The first reaction of the courts to arbitration, in both the public and the private sector, has always been essentially hostile; the very existence of a procedure for the final settlement of disputes formerly within the exclusive jurisdiction of the courts has been perceived by judges as a threat to judicial supremacy. In the private sector, Section 301 of the Taft-Hartley Act, and the Supreme Court decisions in *Lincoln Mills*,[15] the *Steelworkers'*

---

[14]See *United Steelworkers* v. *Enterprise Wheel & Car Corp.*, 363 U.S. 593, 46 LRRM 2423 (1960); *United Steelworkers* v. *Warrior & Gulf Navigation Co.*, 363 U.S. 574, 46 LRRM 2416 (1960); *United Steelworkers* v. *American Mfg. Co.*, 363 U.S. 564, 46 LRRM 2414 (1960).
[15]353 U.S. 448, 40 LRRM 2113 (1957).

trilogy,[16] and their progeny, virtually removed grievance arbitration from the initial restraints and the power of substantive judicial review formerly exercised by the courts. In the public sector, however, the battle has been fought all over again, and grievance arbitration has not won the conclusive victory it gained in the private sector. Indeed, Grodin characterizes as a "trend" recent judicial decisions which have ruled against the arbitrability of issues as to which it is not clear that the parties contemplated arbitration, or which call for the exercise of discretion not governed by explicit contractual criteria. Similarly, the courts have shown an increasing reluctance to enforce arbitral awards that have potential impact upon the level or quality of government services or upon financial resources.

It would be a mistake, I think, to attribute the current judicial attitude merely to jealousy of a rival authority and to assume that the precedents from the private sector will be gradually absorbed and will eventually control the issues of arbitrability of grievances and judicial review of arbitral awards in the public sector. There are, of course, important differences between the public and private sectors, and Grodin believes that the courts, influenced perhaps by the current public hostility toward government employees and collective bargaining, have seized upon those differences as the justification for not following private-sector precedents.

Presumption of Arbitrability

Like Grodin, I believe that the courts' preoccupation with certain differences between the public and private sectors is, in the case of grievance arbitration, excessive, and that the presumption of arbitrability and deference to the substance of arbitration awards are as justifiable in the public sector as they are in the private sector. Whether the courts will eventually come to that point of view, however, is problematical. The chances for that result seem to me somewhat better for the presumption of arbitrability than they are in respect of judicial deference to arbitral awards. Arbitrability usually invokes the "scope clause" of public-sector bargaining agreements, and restrictions on the scope of bargaining are frequently incorporated in state laws.

---

[16] *Supra* note 14.

Courts are more likely to uphold the arbitrability of issues not specifically precluded by statutory language than that of issues not specifically proscribed by collective agreements; for, as Grodin points out, the absence of midterm strikes in public employment renders irrelevant the Supreme Court's dicta that in the private sector, the agreement to arbitrate is a quid pro quo for the agreement not to strike.

Judicial Review

In the area of judicial review, however, I think the courts will continue to resist the private-sector precedents requiring virtually total deference to arbitral awards. Not only are they reluctant to give rubber-stamp approval to awards which they believe are wrong and perhaps mischievous,[17] but they have some reason to challenge the rationale of the *Steelworkers'* trilogy. In the case of public employment, much of which is governed by statute and was, at least formerly, administered by civil service commissions or personnel boards, it is by no means clear that the parties to a collective agreement had in mind that it be administered according to the "law of the shop," or that arbitrators are more qualified than "even the ablest judge"[18] to construe and apply collective agreements. If this prediction proves correct, then it is not beyond the realm of possibility that some federal judges will become emboldened by the example set by the state courts in public-sector cases to begin whittling away at the doctrine of deference to arbitral awards in the private sector.

Interest Arbitration

So far as the legality of interest arbitration in the public sector is concerned, I think the state legislatures rather than the courts will have the ultimate power of decision. The argument that interest arbitration is an unconstitutional delegation of legislative power can be almost completely undermined by a statutory delegation that is accompanied by a reasonably specific set of standards to which arbitrators must adhere. Therefore, it seems to me that the real battles ahead will be over the desirability of

---

[17]See Paul R. Hays, Labor Arbitration: A Dissenting View (New Haven, Conn.: Yale University Press, 1966), Ch. 2.
[18]See *United Steelworkers* v. *Warrior & Gulf Nav, Co.*, 363 U.S. 574, 582 (1960) (opinion of Douglas, J.).

adopting a policy of voluntary or compulsory arbitration of interest disputes in the public sector, rather than over the constitutionality of a carefully drawn statute.

Foreign Influences

The indifference of American lawmakers, whether legislators or judges, to foreign laws and practices in both public- and private-sector labor law is well known. Because of the uniqueness of our society—the product of peculiar geographical, historical, economic, political, and social factors—they seem to have automatically assumed that the experience of other highly industrialized countries with roughly similar political and economic orientations is completely irrelevant to our concerns. That the labor laws in the Western European democracies for the private and public sectors are tending to merge into a single body of law applicable to both either is unknown or, if known, is regarded with disapproval or alarm.

Hence, the increasing interest in this country in the various laws governing labor-management relations in the public sector enacted by the federal and provincial governments of our more advanced neighbor to the north is a welcome surprise. In her essay on the Canadian experience (Chapter 8), Shirley Goldenberg traces developments in her country that deserve careful study by federal and state governments in the United States. A few of these are of particular interest. First, the federal government of Canada has been a leader in accepting collective bargaining as the basis of its relations with its own employees, in permitting employees to strike in some circumstances, and in introducing a choice of alternatives—either arbitration or compulsory conciliation followed by the right to strike, if necessary —as the means of resolving impasses in interest disputes. Second, in addition to the federal government, approximately one half of the provinces have granted government employees the right to strike, subject to the requirement that essential services be maintained; and although these arrangements have not been uniformly successful, none has seriously interfered with the functions of government. Third, some of the provincial courts have resisted the use of injunctions against illegal strikes, on the ground that the appropriate legislative bodies should not ask relief from the courts in dealing with what is primarily a political question. This has led to suggestions at the federal level that the

Cabinet be empowered by legislation to postpone (not prohibit) a strike in cases in which it deems the public interest to be at stake. Finally, the Canadian experience reaffirms evidence in this country that, in Goldenberg's words, "the socioeconomic and political environment and the historical context of the bargaining relationship have at least as important an impact on the dynamics of dispute resolution as the procedures for dealing with an impasse provided in the law."

It seems to me both likely and desirable that state legislatures —aided and perhaps prodded by scholars—will turn increasingly to foreign experience in their search for improved policies and procedures applicable to collective bargaining in the public sector. I do not mean to suggest that foreign ways can be adopted wholesale, without change, in our different economic, political, and social climate; but a study of how different countries deal with problems similar to those we face is likely to cause us to view our own system from a different perspective which may, in turn, lead to new and better approaches.

Conclusion

In relative terms, collective bargaining in the public sector is in its infancy; moreover, it is still developing. It is, therefore, much too soon to pronounce it a success or a failure. On the other hand, collective bargaining in one form or another now affects probably a majority of state, county, and municipal government employees. It is, therefore, too late to reject it as a workable system for determining wages, hours, and working conditions for government employees. Indeed, the organization of the public sector and the spread of collective bargaining seems to many, including myself, to be an irreversible process.

It is possible, of course, that changing policies and practices may, in the still unforeseeable future, lead to the substitution of some other system of labor-management relations for collective bargaining. In my opinion, however, such a possibility is extremely remote, and should it be realized, it would affect both the private and public sectors.

In the meantime, some of the more interesting developments will involve the relationships between policies and practices in the public sector and those in the private sector. Thus far, the former has borrowed much from the latter, but as I suggested earlier in this essay, we may soon witness some significant reversals in that trend. In addition to principles of judicial review previously mentioned, I think the treatment by the courts of individual rights in the public-sector cases may have an increasing influence in similar cases in the private sector.[19]

Certainly, the underlying conditions that gave impetus to the great organizational wave in the public sector in the 1960s have not gone away; in many instances they have become aggravated. The current admonition to "lower our expectations in an era of limits," so beloved by politicians, is completely irrelevant to the natural and unquenchable demand by those who work for their living—whether in the public or the private sector—to have some voice in determining the terms and conditions under which that work shall be done. The sooner government managers stop resisting the idea of collective bargaining by their employees, the sooner the employee bargaining organizations will recognize their own responsibilities to the general public. Notwithstanding the very real differences between government and private employment, the collective bargaining *process* in both sectors is fundamentally the same: a cooperative sharing of decision-making responsibility within a carefully defined framework, with restrictions and exceptions specifically tailored to the functions and requirements of the activity involved.

---

[19]See Benjamin Aaron, *The Impact of Public Employment Grievance Settlement on the Labor Arbitration Process*, in The Future of Labor Arbitration in America (New York: American Arbitration Assn., 1976), 1, 30–44.

TOPICAL INDEX

A

Aaron, Benjamin 292-315
AAUP (*See* American Association of University Professors)
ABA (*See* American Bar Association)
Abood v. *Detroit Board of Education*
 agency shop as not violating freedom of association 28, 219-220
Administrators, exclusion from bargaining unit (*See* Management, organization for collective bargaining)
AFGE (*See* American Federation of Government Employees)
AFL-CIO
 civil service reform, approval of 21
 membership decline 294
 public-sector organization, emphasis on 12
AFSCME (*See* American Federation of State, County, and Municipal Employees)
AFT (*See* American Federation of Teachers)
AGE (*See* Assembly of Governmental Employees)
Agency shop
 Abood effect on 28, 219-220
 Hanson effect on 218, 220
 IAM v. *Street* effect on 220
 states permitting 217
Alabama, bargaining in 196
Alaska
 bargaining in 196
 strike right in 154, 203*n*
 union shop 217*n*
Amalgamated Transit Union (ATU) 73
American Bar Association (ABA)
 bargaining scope, report on 210
 example of nonbargaining organization 4
American Association of University Professors (AAUP)
 AFT and NEA, competition with 69-70
 as bargaining association 30
 bargaining, attitude toward 34-35, 68-69, 298
 history and policies 68-70

membership 63, 69
 table 29
American Federation of Government Employees (AFGE) 74, 79
 AFT, agreement with 58
 bargaining units, management exclusion from 78
 civil service reform, approval of 21
 history and policies 56-59
 membership 54, 56
 NFFE, possible merger with 60-61
 strike fund establishment 58
 women, role of 58
American Federation of Labor (*See* AFL-CIO)
American Federation of State, County, and Municipal Employees (AFSCME) 78, 79, 164, 167
 CAPE, membership in 32, 75
 conflicts with other unions 70, 71
 CSEA, affiliation 26, 73, 293
 history and policies 9, 74-76
 jurisdiction, overlap with AFT 32
 labor-management training program 111
 membership 74
  effect of *Abood* 28
  table 72
 NEA, cooperation with 32, 75
 PED, suspension from 75
 problems, New York 293
 strike right, insistence on 199
American Federation of Teachers (AFT)
 AAUP, rivalry with 69-70
 AFGE agreement, overseas organization of federal employees 58
 AFSCME, conflict with 70
 future prospects 297
 higher education, dominant bargaining organization in 34
 history and policies 30-31, 65-68
 jurisdiction, overlap with AFSCME 32
 membership 62, 66
  declines in 30,·32, 35
  table 29
 NEA, competition with 63-64, 67-68
 NEA merger, failure of 31-32
 paraprofessionals, inclusion in 66-67
 PED, membership in 75

AFT—contd.
　UAW, support from 12
American Nurses Association (ANA)
　membership, table 72
　policies 70-71
American Postal Workers Union (APWU)
　membership 49
　　minorities percentage 52
　NALC merger possibility 53
　problems 50-52
　　bargaining v. political action 52
　　integration of minorities into leader-
　　　ship 52
　　reform of union structure 50-52
　unions comprising 45, 48
Andrews, Emmet 51, 52
APWU (*See* American Postal Workers
　Union)
Arbitration (*See also* Compulsory arbitra-
　tion; Final-offer arbitration; Griev-
　ance arbitration; Interest arbitra-
　tion)
　awards (*See* Awards)
　Canada 277-279, 281-282, 284-287
　fact-finding, relation to 184-185
　judicial review of 224-225, 250-253
　med-arb process 182, 185
　mediation under, success of 180
　New York City experience 185-186
　reliance on, fact-finding compared
　　171-177
　tripartite 185, 188
Arbitrators
　med-arb process, use of 182
　role 226
Assembly of Government Employees
　(AGE)
　membership, table 72
　policies 70, 72-73
Assistant Secretary of Labor for Labor-
　Management Relations 113-115
Association, freedom of, public employ-
　ees, effect of *Abood* on 28,
　219-220
Association of Government Employees 26
Atlanta, Georgia, strike experience 167
Awards
　Canada 286-287
　design criteria for 186-187
　external statutes, conflict with 236-238,
　　248-250
　judicial review of 312

B

Bakke, E. Wight 76, 77
Bargaining association, definition 2, 4-5

Bargaining organization, definition 5
Bargaining rights (*See* Collective bargain-
　ing)
BCDL (*See* Bureau of the Census)
Benefits (*See* Compensation)
Blaylock, Kenneth 57-59
BLS (*See* Bureau of Labor Statistics)
Bornstein, Tim L. 88
Boston, union shop in 217
Brookings Institution 90
Buffalo, New York, teacher strike experi-
　ence 167
Bureau of Labor Statistics (BLS)
　survey, grievance and arbitration proce-
　　dures 224
　union membership data, analyzed 16,
　　19, 23, 25, 35-36, 38
Bureau of the Census (BCDL)
　union membership data, analyzed 23,
　　25, 36, 38
Burton, John F., Jr. 1-43, 90, 143, 292,
　293
Bus drivers, representation of 73

C

California
　agency shop permitted 217*n*
　bargaining in 196, 211, 216
　compulsory arbitration in 207
　grievance arbitration, delegation of au-
　　thority issue 232
　interest arbitration
　　arbitrability, judicial determination of
　　　246-248
　　constitutionality issue 243
　　proposed ban on　307
　junior colleges, organization in 35
　management organization for collective
　　bargaining 302
　Proposition 13, effects on government
　　employment 293
　strikes
　　proposed ban on 307
　　resolution of 168
　sunshine laws 214, 215
California, University of, faculty salaries,
　decline of 298
Canada 254-291, 313-314
　arbitration 187, 284-287
　awards, arbitral subject matter of 286-
　　287
　collective bargaining
　　bargaining agent 271-272
　　bargaining unit 272-274
　　evolution and present status 254-257
　　legislation 270-271